UNION INTERNATIONALE DES SCIENCES PRÉHISTORIQUES ET PROTOHISTORIQUES
INTERNATIONAL UNION FOR PREHISTORIC AND PROTOHISTORIC SCIENCES

PROCEEDINGS OF THE XV WORLD CONGRESS (LISBON, 4-9 SEPTEMBER 2006)
ACTES DU XV CONGRÈS MONDIAL (LISBONNE, 4-9 SEPTEMBRE 2006)

Series Editor: Luiz Oosterbeek

VOL. 7

Session C68 (Part I)

Monumental Questions: Prehistoric Megaliths, Mounds, and Enclosures

Edited by

David Calado
Maxiliam Baldia
Matthew Boulanger

BAR International Series 2122
2010

Published in 2016 by
BAR Publishing, Oxford

BAR International Series 2122

Proceedings of the XV World Congress of the International Union for Prehistoric and Protohistoric Sciences/Actes du XV Congrès Mondial de l'Union Internationale des Sciences Préhistoriques et Protohistoriques
Session C68 (Part I): Monumental Questions: Prehistoric Megaliths, Mounds and Enclosures

ISBN 978 1 4073 0663 6

Outgoing President: Vítor Oliveira Jorge
Outgoing Secretary General: Jean Bourgeois
Congress Secretary General: Luiz Oosterbeek (Series Editor)
Incoming President: Pedro Ignacio Shmitz
Incoming Secretary General: Luiz Oosterbeek
Volume Editors: David Calado, Maxiliam Baldia, Matthew Boulanger
Signed papers are the responsibility of their authors alone.
Les texts signés sont de la seule responsabilité de ses auteurs.
Contacts :
Secretary of U.I.S.P.P. – International Union for Prehistoric and Protohistoric Sciences
Instituto Politécnico de Tomar, Av. Dr. Cândido Madureira 13, 2300 TOMAR
Email: uispp@ipt.pt www.uispp.ipt.pt

BAR Publishing is the trading name of British Archaeological Reports (Oxford) Ltd. British Archaeological Reports was first incorporated in 1974 to publish the BAR Series, International and British. In 1992 Hadrian Books Ltd became part of the BAR group. This volume was originally published by Archaeopress in conjunction with British Archaeological Reports (Oxford) Ltd / Hadrian Books Ltd, the Series principal publisher, in 2010. This present volume is published by BAR Publishing, 2016.

Printed in England

BAR
PUBLISHING

BAR titles are available from:

BAR Publishing
122 Banbury Rd, Oxford, OX2 7BP, UK
EMAIL info@barpublishing.com
PHONE +44 (0)1865 310431
FAX +44 (0)1865 316916
www.barpublishing.com

TABLE OF CONTENTS

Volume 7 – PART I

Megalithisme et sédentarisation en Europe occidentale 3
Jean-Pierre Mohen

Some stones can speak! The social structure, identity and territoriality of SW Atlantic Europe complex appropriator communities reflected in their standing stones 7
David Calado, Francisco Nocete, Maria Dolores Càmalich, Dimas Martín-Socas, José Miguel Nieto, António Delgado, Amelia Rodriguez, Moisés Bayon, Esther Alex, Nuno Inácio

Time and signs: Southern Portuguese megalithic art diachrony 17
Mário Varela Gomes

Megaliths as rock art in Alentejo, Southern Portugal 25
Manuel Calado & Leonor Rocha

"The-teeth-under-the-sky": mountain steles and green stone workings in the Kuznetskii Alatau, Southern Siberia (Khakassia, Russia) 33
S. Cassen, W.M. Torgunakov, P. Pétrequin, B. Lasnier

Neolithic rock art at the Avebury stone circles in Southern England 43
Terence Meaden, Kate Prendergast, Di Pattison

Ciertos aspectos funerarios en la necropolis del III milenio de Valencina-Castilleja (Sevilla) 51
Rosario Cruz-Auñon, Francisco Nocete, Juan Carlos Mejias

Estudio geoarqueológico del conjunto de los dólmenes de Antequera (Málaga, España) 57
Francisco Carrión Méndez, José Antonio Lozano Rodríguez, David García González, Teresa Muñiz López, Paulo Félix, Carmen Fátima López Rodríguez, José Antonio Esquivel Guerrero & Israel Mellado García

More than big stones! Peripheral and confined or resistant lineage societies in the pristine class-society territorial framework of the South-Western Iberian Peninsula (2900-2000 Bc) 71
Francisco Nocete & Ana Peramo

Moon, spring and large stones – landscape and ritual calendar perception and symbolization 83
Catarina Oliveira & C. Marciano Da Silva

Megaliths, memory and the power of stones 91
Chris Scarre

Landscape, architectural and ritual aspects of the Chalcolithic (Calcolithic) sanctuaries in the Lombardy Alps (Italy) 97
Raffaella Poggiani Keller

Anonymous ancestors? The Tilley/Shanks hypothesis revisited 111
Karl-Göran Sjögren

Two Neolithic enclosures at Sormás-Török-Földek (Southwest-Transdanubia, Hungary) and their possible geometrical and astronomical role: a case study 119
Judit P. Barna & Emília Pásztor

Houses of living and houses of dead in the Neolithic and Copper Age of Central Europe 127
Jan Turek

La region de Tagrera (Tassili-wan-Ahaggar, Ahaggar, Algerie) – representations rupestres et monuments funeraires protohistoriques 139
Iddir Amara, Abdelkader Heddouche & Smaïl Iddir

Structured deposition and ditched enclosures in the Late Prehistory of Southern Iberia (IV-III millennia B.C.) 145
Víctor Jiménez Jáimez & José Enrique Márquez Romero

Volume 8 – PART II

Notes sur quelques structures funéraires de la région de Tindouf (Sud-sud-ouest, Algérie) 155
I. Amara, C. Yass

Conceptual framework and archaeological data of the initial classist society in the Atlantic Band of Cadiz (SW Spain) in 3rd and 2nd millennia BC 161
José Ramos, Salvador Domínguez-Bella & Manuela Pérez

Archaeometric analyses of pottery from TRB barrows and hilltop enclosures 169
Matthew T. Boulanger & Michael D. Glascock

Megaliths of the Vera Island in the Southern Urals 179
Stanislav A. Grigoriev & Julia V. Vasina

Memories of a megalithic landscape: mortuary practices and gallery graves in western Sweden during the Late Neolithic 187
Eva Stensköld

Monumental questions: prehistoric megaliths, mounds and enclosures of Central and Northern Europe 195
Maximilian O. Baldia

Approaching the dead – social and architectural interaction reflected in a megalithic tomb 213
Lars Larsson

Earthen architecture in Classic period Central Veracruz, Mexico: development and function 223
Annick Daneels

Monumentality and complex hunter-gatherers in southeast coastal Brazil 231
Suzanne K. Fish & Paul R. Fish

From Moundville to Angel: a comparison of the organization of monumental architecture and central places at three points in space and time in the Mississippian world 237
Christopher S. Peebles & Staffan Peterson

Sambaquieiros of the Southeastern coast of Brazil: the beginning of settlement, functioning and collapse 243
Maria Dulce Gaspar, Márcia Barbosa

New perspectives on moundbuilding societies – from coastal southern Brazil natural dynamics and regional archaeology 251
Paulo DeBlasis

Shellmidden formation at the Beagle Channel (Tierra del Fuego, Argentine) 263
Ernesto Luis Piana & Luis Abel Orquera

Homogeneity ideology versus status distinction: changes in burial system in the southwestern Korean Bronze Age 273
Jangsuk Kim & Jaehoon Hwang

Megalithic tombs, power, and social relations in West Sumba, Indonesia 279
Ron L. Adams

Gurdadaguji stone arrangements: late Holocene aggregation locals? 285
Fiona Hook & Adrian Di Lello

Small things in big places – coloration and fabric structure of selected polychrome textiles from the Seip Mound Group in Eastern North America 299
Christel M. Baldia, Kathryn A. Jakes & Maximilian O. Baldia

LIST OF FIGURES

Volume 7 – PART I

Fig. 2.1. Buried deposit underneath the erected stone 9
Fig. 2.2. Distribution of early menhirs in the Algarve 10
Fig. 2.3. Mama symbol 11
Fig. 2.4. Vulva B symbol 11
Fig. 2.5. Vulva A symbol 12
Fig. 2.6. Onda symbol 12

Fig. 3.1. Menhirs 2 (A), 1 (B) and 3 (C) from Pontais (Silves, Algarve) 18
Fig. 3.2. Menhir-*stelae* from Herdade do Barrocal (A) and Monte da Ribeira (B) (Reguengos de Monsaraz, Évora) 19
Fig. 3.3. Vele-de-Rodrigo (Évora). Barrow and menhir-stele (faces A and B) 20
Fig. 3.4. Menhir 83 (A), 89 (B) and 58 (C) of the Almendres cromlech 21
Fig. 3.5. Menhirs transformed into menhir-statues from Almendres (A) and Portela de Mogos (B) 23

Fig. 4.1. Distribution of menhirs and rock art in Alentejo 26
Fig. 4.2. Painted anthropomorphic motif in the rock shelter of Gaivões (Arronches) 27
Fig. 4.3. Carved anthropomorphic motifs of the Alqueva Rock art complex 27
Fig. 4.4. The single standing stone of Monte da Ribeira (Reguengos de Monsaraz) 28
Fig. 4.5. Plan of the Mesolithic shell-midden of Romeiras in the Sado Valley, showing the horse-shoe shaped stone setting, similar to the Alentejan megalithic enclosures 29
Fig. 4.6. Bas-relief motifs carved on a menhir from the enclosure of Vale Maria do Meio (Évora) 30

Fig. 5.1. Situation of Taskyl montain, south of Kuznetskii Alatau plan and elevation of stele 3, with simulation of erected position 35
Fig. 5.2. Stele 3 with indication of a basin of erosion in the granite, in a non functional position two specimen of axe rough-out in vaugnerite picture of a workshop on the top of Taskyl, directly on the vaugnerite source comparisons with steles from Khakassia and Altaï 37

Fig. 6.1. Stone 26A from the East 46

Fig. 6.2. Stone 206 from the SW (above) features as carved, horned, human head (boxer) senn in close-up bellow ... 48

Fig. 8.1. Ubicación de los monumentos ... 58
Fig. 8.2. Litologias ... 61
Fig. 8.3. Ubicación de los dólmenes conm respecto al Cerro de la Cruz ... 63
Fig. 8.4. Estudio litológico de detalle. Dolmen de Menga ... 64
Fig. 8.5. Estudio litológico de detalle. Dolmen de Viera ... 66
Fig. 8.6. Estudio litológico de detalle. Tholos de Romeral ... 67

Fig. 9.1. Ordenación del territorio en el Andévalo Central ... 72
Fig. 9.2. Tumbas centrales de las necrópolis megalíticas de El Labradillo, Las Palomas, La Venta, Los Gabrieles y El Pozuelo ... 74
Fig. 9.3. Necrópolis de El Pozuelo. Programa de limpieza y delimitación 1988 ... 75
Fig. 9.4. Necrópolis de El Pozuelo. Programa de documentación arqueológica 1988 ... 76
Fig. 9.5. Necrópolis de El Pozuelo. Programa de restauración y puesta en valor 1999 ... 77
Fig. 9.6. Contextos internos. Necrópolis de El Villar. Tumba de Las Palomas. Excavación microespacial y productos ... 79
Fig. 9.7. Contextos externos de menhires en tumbas centrales. Necrópolis del Villar (1,2,3 Tumba de la Venta). Necrópolis de El Pozuelo (4 Tumba Pozuelo 2, 5 Tumba Pozuelo 6) ... 80

Fig. 10.1. Full Moon directly on the symmetry axis of the horseshoe enclosure at Vale d'elRei (Pavia) ... 85
Fig. 10.2. Ondulations on the horizon, relevant to the observation of the "Spring Full Moon" rise (Outeiro, Monsaraz) ... 86

Fig. 12.1. Lombardy map with megalithic sanctuaries (triangle), calcolithics monoliths isolated (point) and coevals settlements (square). The full symbol: original sites excavated; the empty symbol: the sites non investigated ... 98
Fig. 12.2. Ossimo area: four sanctuaries of Pat, Anvoia, Passagròp and Ceresolo-Bagnolo ... 100
Fig. 12.3. The Teglio hills: the sanctuaries (Caven and Somasassa) are sited on hillside terraces overlooking the valley ... 101
Fig. 12.4. Teglio-Caven. The development and architecture of this cult site ... 102
Fig. 12.5. Ossimo-Pat. The Copper Age platforms ... 103
Fig. 12.6. Ossimo-Pat. Alignment N-S of boulder-menhirs and engraved steles, Early Bronze Age level ... 104
Fig. 12.7. Ossimo, Pat-excavation 2003. The votive fires in front of the monument "Pat 2" ... 104
Fig. 12.8. Ossimo, Pat. The circular enclosures north ... 105
Fig. 12.9. Stratigraphy around the "Pat 2" with the fires (US 15, 7, 151, 154 e 156) ... 105
Fig. 12.10. The Massi di Cemmo National Archaeological Park-excavation 2005. Boundary wall before the Massi "Cemmo 1 e 2" ... 106
Fig. 12.11. Cemmo. The sanctuary during the Roman period ... 107

Fig. 13.1. Map of Swedish dolmens and passage graves ... 113
Fig. 13.2. Plan of the chamber with density of bones ... 114
Fig. 13.3. Individual B, a 40-50 year old female ... 115

Fig. 13.4. ^{14}C and stratigraphy of individuals 116

Fig. 14. 1. The double roundel system at Sormas-Török-földek, Hungary 120

Fig. 15.1. The plan of the Linear Pottery Culture longhouse at Olszanica, Poland, compared with that of Kilham long barrow, England 128

Fig. 15.2. A Bell Beaker female burial from Tišice District Mělník in Central Bohemia. Along the wall are visible traces of wooden lining 130

Fig. 15.3. Box-and-whisker plot of Corded Ware and Bell Beaker ditch diameters 200 (max. dimensions). Corded Ware Bell Beaker Median 25%, -75% Outlier Extreme 131

Fig. 15.4. An early reconstruction of the Bell Beaker tomb at Smolín (District Břeclav, south Moravia) 133

Fig. 15.5. A Bell Beaker grave with a ring ditch from Dolní Věstonice III. Traces of palisade made of halved tree trunks 134

Fig. 15.6. Comparison of similar funerary features (left) Early Bronze Age funerary structure called Seahenge, Holm-next-the-Sea, Norfolk, England and (right) a multiple cremation burial 2/91 encircled by a ring ditch and pottery found inside the ditch. There were visible traces of 'zick-zack' small postholes in the bottom of the ditch 135

Fig. 16.1. Les principaux sites du Tassili Wan Ahaggar 141

Fig. Volume 8 – PART II

Fig. 18.1. Affleurements et bassins carbonifères dans le nord ouest de l'Afrique 156

Fig. 18.2. Couvert végétal 157

Fig. 18.3. Figure animal de style Tazina 158

Fig. 18.4. Monuments funéraire de type tumulus simple 159

Fig. 18.5. Monuments funéraire de type bazina 159

Fig. 18.6. Monument funéraire de type bazina évolué 159

Fig. 19.1. Sites distribution in the Low Guadalquivir valley 162

Fig. 19.2. Regional geology 164

Fig. 20.1. Map of eastern Czech Republic showing the locations of (1) Rmíz u Laškova hillfort and (2) Náměšť na Hané-Džbán mound group. Major rivers and modern political boundaries are shown 171

Fig. 20.2. Planviews of (1) Rmíz u Laškova hillfort and (2) Náměšť na Hané-Džbán mound group after Šmíd. Shaded areas are locations of CARPro excavations. Thick lines in 1 depict walls. Dotted lines in 2 are margins of burial mounds 172

Fig. 20.3. Bivariate plot of lutetium and ytterbium concentrations of ceramic samples analyzed as part of this study. Ellipse represent 90% confidence interval of group membership within the *Northern Morava Macrogroup.* Dashed line represents possible division of samples 176

Fig. 20.4. Bivariate plot of lutetium and chromium values of ceramic samples from Moravia. Data from the current project are projected against data produced by Rehman *et al.* (1992). Solid ellipse represents 90% confidence interval of group membership. Dashed lines represent possible groupings or divisions in these data 176

Fig. 21.1. Megalith 3 180

Fig. 21.2. Megalith 2 180

Fig. 21.3. Megalith 1 plan ... 181
Fig. 21.4. Megalith 1 drywall construction ... 181

Fig. 22.1. Chronology of the Late Neolithic of Southern Scandinavia in relation to western and central Europe ... 188
Fig. 22.2. Distribution of gallery graves in western Sweeden ... 188
Fig. 22.3. Province of Västergötland ... 189
Fig. 22.4. The mountain of Alleberg seen from Mösseberg ... 189
Fig. 22.5. Gallery graves in Falbygden ad Torbjörntorp ... 190
Fig. 22.6. Sketch of gallery graves by Hilding Svensson, in 1927 ... 191

Fig. 23.1. Research Area and the TRB Interaction Sphere ... 196
Fig. 23.2. Radiocarbon Curve and Monumental Architecture ... 197
Fig. 23.3. Chamber Typology ... 203

Fig. 24.1. The investigation area – Vale de Rodrigo – and its surroundings. Legend: 1: megalithic tomb and 2: menhir ... 214
Fig. 24.2. Topographic conditions of Vale de Rodrigo, monument 2 and the position of the excavated areas ... 215
Fig. 24.3. A part of the outside of the megalithic chamber after its excavation with almost four metres high orthostats ... 216
Fig. 24.4. The chamber of the tomb with two large slabs fixed between the orthostats, which divide the chamber into two cells of roughly equal size. Parts of a grave pit, cut through the original floor, are visible in the centre ... 216
Fig. 24.5. A limited section where the ring of bordering stones around the mound was intact ... 217
Fig. 24.6. The passage and part of the forecourt of monument 2. In the centre, the stone slabs, three in total, which sealed the entrance to the passage. Two rows of stones mark the edges of a rampart. The paved area runs along the northern side of the forecourt ... 217
Fig. 24.7. Distribition of artefacts in the area outside the passage. 1–2: slate objects, 3–4: fragments of slate objects, 5: cores of rock-crystal, 6: rock-crystal, 7: stone axe, 8: flint blade, 9: arrow-head, 10: flint waste, 11: bead, 12: vessel, 13: bone fragment, 14: dental enamel and 15: pit with charcoal ... 218
Fig. 24.8. Artefacts found during the excavation of Vale de Rodrigo, monument 2. 1–2 decorated slate plaques, 3–4: fragments of an axe symbol in state, 5–6: microliths and 7–8: arrowheads ... 219
Fig. 24.9. The engravings on a stone found in the centre of the chamber ... 220
Fig. 24.10. Different stages of activities before, during and after the building of the megalithic tomb Vale de Rodrigo, monument 2. The arrows mark access, and the lines mark screening or delimitation of the tomb. Legends: 1: burial, 2: grave good deposition, 3: sacrificial deposition ... 220

Fig. 25.1. Location of site within study area in Central Veracruz, Mexico. Emplacement du site dans l'aire de recherche du Centre du Véracruz, Mexique ... 224
Fig. 25.2. Central part of site according to 1937 map, with surviving areas shown in solid black. Zone centrale du site d'après le croquis de 1937; les aires conservées sont montrées en noir ... 225
Fig. 25.3. North Platform, second building stage (AD 100-350): five functionally distinct buildings. Deuxième étape de construction de la Plateforme Nord (AD 100-350): cinq bâtiments de fonctions différentes ... 226

Fig. 25.4. East Platform, third building stage sequence (AD 200-570): left, partial view of first residence (dashed lined unexcavated), center: partial view of later residence, right: extended rectangular stepped platform with a flat featureless top. Plateforme Est, troisième étape de construction (AD 200-570): à gauche: vue partielle de la première résidence (ligne en pointillé indique la zone non fouillée), au centre: vue partielle de la résidence postérieure, à droite: plateforme à trois corps superposés, cîme plate 227

Fig. 25.5. East Platform, fourth building stage (ca. AD 700): termination offering with cross-legged burials (sacrificial victims?). Plateforme Est, quatrième étape de construction (ca. AD 700): offrande de terminaison avec des enterrements assis en tailleur (victimes sacrifiées?) 228

Fig. 25.6. East Platform, fourth building stage (ca. AD 700): figurines, serving dishes and broken jars part of the termination offering. Plateforme Est, quatrième étape de construction (ca. AD 700): figures, coupes et jarres fragmentées qui font partie de l'offrande de terminaison 228

Fig. 26.1. The relationships and densities of occupation surfaces, burials, postholes, and hearths are revealed in a segment of one long profile at Jabuticabeira II 233

Fig. 27.1. Topographic map of the site 241

Fig. 28.1. Shell-middens and settlements distribution in the coast of the State of Rio de Janeiro 246

Fig. 29.1. The research area at the southern coast of Santa Catarina, Brasil 252

Fig. 29.2. The double-mounded sambaqui from Encantada, Jaguaruna 253

Fig. 29.3. Chronological chart for the sambaquis of the research área. Note the approximate relative sea level indications (NRM) along the period. Dashed lines refer to estimated time of occupation for some sambaquis, based on available dates location on stratigraphical sequences 254

Fig. 29.4. Natural evolution of the paleolagoon of Santa Marta and concomitant sambaqui occupation between 4,2 to 2 kyBP 256

Fig. 30.1. a) Beagle Channel Region; b) dome-like shellmidden; c) ring-shaped shellmidden; d) ring-shaped shellmidden profile, depression to the right; e) ring-shaped shellmidden profile, note that the soil was not dug to form a pit-house; f) dome-like hut (taken from De Agostini, 1933); g) huts and adjacent shellmidden (picutre taken from Mission Scientifique du Cap Horn in 1882-1883); h) camps, normally clustering but a of few huts 264

Fig. 30.2. a) experimental juts; b) experimental shellmidden by a hut; c) grass cover after seven months form shell's dropping; d) loggers hut built in 1965, pictured in 2003; e) selk'nam hut built in 1903/4, pictured in the 1970's; f) tourists fireplace within a ring-shaped shellmidden; g) Roca Lake rockshelter 267

Fig. 30.3. A branch frame long enough as to allow the formation of a first and low ring-shaped sehellmidden (a-c). After the branch frame decayed, the same spot was used to build a new hut due to the existence of the previous shellmiden ring, but later occupations enlarged its basal diameter turning it useless for occupation (b-d). A new just as raised by the already useless one (e), until this new ring-shaped shellmiden also became useless (f). The process went on and on (g), up to form a large ring-shaped cluster of shellmiddens (h) 269

Fig. 31.1. Dolmen 274
Fig. 31.2. Lower structure cist type dolmenic burial 274
Fig. 31.3. Elite burial in cist 275
Fig. 31.4. Bronze daggers 275
Fig. 31.5. Elite pit tombs with and without piled stones 275
Fig. 31.6. Bronze burial goods 275
Fig. 31.7. Labour and burial goods investment through time 275
Fig. 31.8. Status cycles of emphasis on hoards or on grave goods 277

Fig. 32.1. Large stone tomb with *kado watu* upright stone in Anakalang, West Sumba 280
Fig. 32.2. Pulling a large capstone for a tomb in Anakalang, West Sumba 282

Fig. 33.1. Upland Pilbara 287
Fig. 33.2. Packsaddle Valley 287
Fig. 33.3. Gurdadaguji arrangements 288
Fig. 33.4. Stone Arrangement examples 288
Fig. 33.5. Upland Pilbara – location of stone arrangement sites 289
Fig. 33.6. Graph of Upland Pilbara stone arrangements designs 290

Fig. 34.1. Seip textiles in Case #4, yellow-brown coloration 301
Fig. 34.2. Seip textiles in Case #10, close-up displaying layers with different colors 303
Fig. 34.3. Yellow, green, red, brown rabbit hair, darkfield image 304
Fig. 34.4. Yellow, green, red, brown rabbit hair and the "other" bast, brightfield image 304
Fig. 34.5. Seip textile in Case #10, close-up displaying fringe 304
Fig. 34.6. Seip textiles in Case # 31, close-up displaying fringe 305
Fig. 34.7. Seip textile in Case #30, reverse side, close-up, composite 305
Fig. 34.8. Seip textile in Case # 32, close-up, composite 306

LIST OF TABLES

Volume 7 – PART I

Tab. 10.1. Compilation of observed relevant sites and events 87

Tab. 15.1. Table summarising the basic characteristics of the Bell Beaker burial rites within some regions of the Eastern Province 132

Volume 8 – PART II

Tab. 20.1. Contextual information for sherds analyzed in this study 173

Tab. 20.2. Principal components analysis showing the first 10 components of the 34-sample pottery dataset from Rmíz and Džbán in the upper Morava Valley, Moravia, Czech Republic 175

Tab. 26.1. New World Mound Volumes. Study area sambaquis are highlighted 232

Tab. 26.2. Burial density comparison of Jabuticabiera, Cabecuda, and Forte Marechal Luz 234

Tab. 26.3. Total burial estimates for Jabuticabeira II based on burial/M3 indices from Jabuticabeira, Cabeçuda, and Forte Marechal Luz 234

Tab. 26.4. Estimated burial rates for Jabuticabeira II 234

Tab. 27.1. Relative efficiency and effectiveness of various exploratory methods 240

Tab. 28.1. Sites and radiocarbon datings from Região dos ~Lagos, RJ, Brazil 245

Tab. 33.1. 286

Tab. 34.1. Seip textiles selected for study 301

Tab. 34.2. Summary of results: textiles in case #4, #10, #31 302

Tab. 34.3. Summary of results: textiles in case # 30, #32 303

Session C68
Part I

MONUMENTAL QUESTIONS: PREHISTORIC MEGALITHS, MOUNDS, AND ENCLOSURES

MEGALITHISME ET SÉDENTARISATION EN EUROPE OCCIDENTALE

Jean-Pierre MOHEN

Abstract: *An overview of the most recent advances in megalithic research in Portugal, France, Great Britain, Ireland, Germany and Scandinavia. The paper stresses the role of megaliths in re-grouping dispersed communities on the basis of ceremonial centres.*
Key-words: *Megaliths – Sedentism – Cerimonial gatherings*

Résumé: *Une vision panoramique sur les plus récentes découvertes sur le mégalithisme au Portugal, en France, en Grand-Bretagne, en Iralnde, en Allemagne et en Scandinavie. L'article discute le role des mégalithes dans le regroupement de groupes humains dispersés, autour de centres cérimoniels.*
Mots-clé: *Mégalithes – Sédentarisation – Rassemblements cérimoniels*

La découverte au Portugal méridional (Algarve) et les études réalisées par nos collègues portugais sur un stade mégalithique précoce, prénéolithique donc antérieur aux premières traces de graines cultivées, nous révèlent une phase ancienne qui expliquerait des ensembles mégalithiques monumentaux précoces de la façade atlantique (Portugal, Centre-Ouest et Ouest de la France) et probablement des situations mixtes plus tardives du nord de l'Europe, dans lesquels des communautés rurales et pastorales séparées auraient vécu selon des rythmes saisonniers avec des rencontres à certains moments de l'année, dans des lieux cérémoniels dont la fonction serait liée aux monuments mégalithiques.

Une importante documentation concernant les mégalithes de l'Ouest européen est maintenant disponible. Elle a été renouvelée ces vingt dernières années, à la suite de travaux de terrain de grande valeur, d'une méthodologie plus attentive aux détails architecturaux, à l'origine des matériaux de construction et des offrandes, à l'identification des restes humains et animaux, à l'organisation complexe des espaces funéraires, aux phases souvent multiples de fréquentation, aux motifs gravés, bouchardés ou peints relevés de plus en plus fréquemment sur des piliers où ils étaient passés inaperçus, aux autres structures non mégalithiques pourtant liées à ces centres cérémoniels, etc... Parce que les archéologues sont plus spécialisés mais aussi parce que les monuments mégalithiques sont mieux compris comme des expressions multiples, d'une portée temporelle, sociale, technique, spaciale, paysagère, rituelle, iconographique, etc... il est devenu nécessaire d'approfondir des synthèses qui rendent compte de l'interaction de tous ces différents facteurs tout en reconnaissant la variété des identités locales et régionales. Cette perspective pluridisciplinaire bénéficie aujourd'hui de réflexions collectives et d'une vision faisant appel au delà de l'archéologie et de l'anthropologie biologique, à des disciplines comme la géologie, la géomorphologie, la géographie humaine, la topographie, la cartographie, la chronologie fine des évènements et des durées... L'objectif est de construire une paléo-histoire des territoires "mégalithiques", c'est à dire un essai de compréhension du phénomène évènementiel dans son contexte humain et environnemental. Il apparaît évident que la recherche des autres vestiges archéologiques autres que les mégalithes et les monuments, mais présents dans leur proximité, comme les différents types de lieu d'occupation (camps?) ou d'habitats regroupés ou isolés, des lieux comme les carrières de roches utilisées, les sources ou le réseau hydrographique ou encore la topographie du littoral à condition de restituer le bon niveau de la mer à une époque donnée, les points de vue paysager de tel ou tel site surtout quand il est cérémoniel , puisse éclairer le rôle des mégalithes qui ont répondu à des besoins immédiats des populations mais qui ont aussi créer sur la société des contraintes non négligeables qui se sont exercées pendant souvent, plusieurs millénaires.

Parmi les grand thèmes, nous en avons sélectionné 9 lors de nos investigations dans la nécropole mégalithique de Bougon (Deux-Sèvres-France) (Mohen et Scarre, 2003) que nous pouvons appliquer à quelques grands sites cérémoniels de l'Europe occidentale:

1. mégalithisme et chronologie: chronologies longues, relatives et absolues, durée
2. mégalithisme et monuments: phases d'aménagement, iconoclasme, réutilisation, structures de condamnation, variété
3. mégalithes et démographie: restes humains, nombre d'hommes nécessaires pour les travaux mégalithiques, pélerins
4. monuments et rites funéraires: ossuaire, manipulations, sélections, ajouts, trépanations, offrandes, autres formes funéraires
5. mégalithisme et imagerie: symbolisme et identités, imagerie et offrandes
6. mégalithisme et offrandes: matériaux locaux et lointains, référence à la faune sauvage terrestre et marine
7. mégalithisme et paysage: territoire et horizons lointains, évolutions des paysages surtout littoraux
8. mégalithisme et la mer: quel lien? double écologie terrestre et marine, le traumatisme de la formation du

channel, symbolisme des coquillages et des iconographies (?), communications nord-sud

9. centres cérémoniels, densité des monuments, pierre pérenne des mégalithes, offrandes prestigieuses en matériaux lointains, jadéïte, variscite, ambre...relations avec les habitats souvent dispersés:

La mise en évidence de grands centres cérémoniels particulièrement impressionnants dont le rayonnement dépasse sans nul doute le territoire de la vie quotidienne locale, nous amène à présenter quelques uns de ces grands sites de l'Ouest européen, de manière à engager une discussion sur leur double fonction sociale et religieuse qui répond à des besoins existants et propose des modèles pour un avenir évolutif qui marque une relative stabilité sociale pendant plusieurs siècles, voire millénaires.

LA PÉNINSULE IBÉRIQUE

La région occidentale de la péninsule ibérique présente une situation intéressante pour notre sujet du rôle de sites cérémoniels dans le processus de sédentarisation des groupes humains à partir de sociétés de chasseurs-pêcheurs mésolithique (site de Muge). La révélation de cette situation vient de l'étude dans l'Algarve occidental, de pierres dressées en grès ou calcaire, parfois ornées de lignes piquetées évoquant les symboles sexuels, masculin et féminin ainsi que des lignes ondulées. Ces pierres sont nombreuses et sur certains sites, elles sont très anciennes puisqu'elles dateraient entre le VIIè et le VIè millénaires. Vers 5000 avant notre ère, le contexte serait encore mésolithique (économie non productive) et ces sites seraient des lieux de réunions saisonnières.

Dans l'Alentejo central, les pierres dressées sont en granite et forment des cercles comme à Almendres, Portela de Mogos et Vale Maria do Meio; les motifs obtenus en bas relief sont surtout la crosse et plus rarement le croissant et le rectangle qui présentent des similitudes avec les ensembles de l'ouest français, selon Manuel Calado (2002-2006). Cet auteur signale aussi dans cette région, des exemples de bris de grands menhirs ornés dont les fragments étaient réutilisés dans la construction de dolmens à Granja de San Pedro, Sobreira, Alcalar, comme à Locmariaquer en Bretagne méridionale.

Victor S. Gonçalves a fouillé un ensemble mégalithique à Regengos de Monsaraz (Evora) où une chambre mégalithique à dalle de couverture et à long couloir de type ancien, a été complété par trois autres chambres annexées, de type à encorbellement, vers 3000 avant notre ère. De tels regroupements ont été aussi étudiés par Vitor Oliveira Jorge.

Le phénomène de la construction de monuments mégalithiques groupés apparaît au centre de la péninsule ibérique peu de temps avant 4000 avant notre ère. Les auteurs de ces découvertes, Delibes, Rodrigo de Balbin Behrmann, Primitiva Bueno Ramirez et R. Barroso constatent le décalage chronologique avec les constructions mégalithiques plus anciennes de l'ouest. Ils remarquent que plusieurs des tombes mégalithiques sont alors construites à l'emplacement de lieux d'habitation, ce qui semble nouveau et semble correspondre à l'apparition (ou la généralisation) de l'habitat permanent regroupé et fortifié (type de Los Millares). Apparaissent aussi dans le sud de la péninsule ibérique, les monuments d'Antequera qui représentent un travail collectif considérable et des constructions impressionnantes dont le prestige devait dépasser la simple fonction funéraire.

CENTRES CÉRÉMONIELS ET MÉGALITHIQUES DE FRANCE OCCIDENTALE

Quelques exemples étudiés récemment montrent le rôle de ces centres construits à l'écart des zones d'habitat, et sans doute au milieu d'un territoire dont ils étaient la référence essentielle.

La nécropole de Bougon (Deux-Sèvres), non loin de La Rochelle et peu éloignée du marais poitevin. Elle a été fréquenté pendant deux millénaires (4700 à 2500 BC). Evolution des architectures et des rites funéraires. Preuves de prélèvement néolithique d'ossements humains pour d'autres lieux. Trépanations; parmi les offrandes, matériaux lointains pour de petits objets en variscite, jadéïte; références pour les parures aux animaux sauvages; présence de zones d'habitat à 1 et 2 kilomètres; situation des différentes carrières jusqu'à 5 à 6 kilomètres; recherches des implications paysagères...

Carnac-Locmariaquer-Gavrinis (Morbihan); la plus grande concentration de monuments de typologies diverses sur environ 15 kilomètres sur une zone bordant le rivage; art mégalithique abondant nouvellement interprété par Serge Cassen; aucune trace d'habitats!

Saint-Just (Ille-et-Vilaine); éperon avec une grande concentration de monuments mégalithiques de types diversifiés, révélés par Jacques Briard qui évoque un centre de cérémonies interrégionales et de pélerinage.

CENTRES CÉRÉMONIELS ET MÉGALITHIQUES DE GRANDE BRETAGNE ET D'IRLANDE

Newgrange, Knowth et le complexe de la vallée de la Boyne; des fouilles ambitieuses; des architectures en liaison avec les orientations solsticiales; un art très original et quelques hypothèses d'interprétation. Ensemble grandiose et cérémoniel, à l'écart des habitats.

Les Orcades (Orkney), autre exemple d'une grande cohérence et de diversité architecturale; relation forte avec le paysage; plus qu'une simple série de tombes mégalithiques.

Avebury et Stonehenge dont l'étude est complètement modifié à la suite des prospections et études systématiques du plan de mise en valeur des grands monuments dont les "cursus". La concentration "cérémonielle" est impréssionnate.

CENTRES CÉRÉMONIELS ET MÉGALITHIQUES D'ALLEMAGNE DU NORD, DU DANEMARK ET DE SUÈDE

Les pratiques funéraires et rituelles mégalithiques sont nées dans le nord de l'Europe entre deux traditions, celles des sépultures essentiellement individuelles mais souvent regroupée des chasseurs mésolithiques et celles des sépultures également individuelles regroupées souvent en cimetières, des premiers agriculteurs d'Europe centrale.

Alors qu'à la suite de Gordon Childe, dans les années 1950, la notion de collectivisme néolithique s'était répandue, les observations faites pendant les fouilles récentes des cimetières des cultures danubiennes et post-danubiennes firent apparaître des hiérarchies sociales marquées par des objets de prestige (colliers, grandes herminettes perforées et polies, bracelets en spondyle de la mer Noire). Ces personnages puissants dominaient sans doute la société. Vers la fin du VIè millénaire, l'évolution de la culture de la céramique à décor rubané fait apparaître de grande nécropoles de plus de 100 tombes (Jeunesse, 1998) à Niedermerz (Westphalie), Elsloo (Pays-Bas), Aiterhofen (Bavière) et Ensisheim (Haute-Alsace) avec ces tombes riches d'adultes et d'enfants, ce qui suppose une vraie classe sociale. Ces cimetières sont en relation avec des concentrations villageoises. C'est alors que l'on constate des fosses communes révélant des massacres collectifs à Talheim (Bad-Wurtemberg), Schletz (Basse-Autriche), Herscheim (Palatinat). A Talheim, par exemple, près de Stuttgart, les fouilles menées en 1983-84, ont découvert 16 enfants, 9 hommes au moins et sept femmes; dis-huit crânes présentent des enfoncements à la hache de pierre. Ils représentent sans doute une unité d'habitation. Cette crise est peut-être le reflet de l'implantation rurale de cette société agricole dans des régions à la périphérie nordique et occidentale où les phénomènes furent différents de la "néolithisation danubienne". Les contacts à partir du début du Vè millénaire avec les chasseurs-cueilleurs ou éleveurs, provoquèrent des adaptations originales, réponses sociales à des acculturations parfois brutales, impliquant la montée des pouvoirs.

L'un des modèles concernant directement les mégalithes, est le système de Sarup au Danemark, étudié par Niels H. Andersen et son équipe (Andersen, 1997). Le site est un vaste éperon entouré de fossés, et aménagé entre 3400 et 2800 avant notre ère, pour des cérémonies funéraires destinées à préparer les squelettes des défunts, avant de répartir les reliques dans les chambres mégalithiques périphériques, construites près des parcelles pauvres en partie cultivées et attribuées à des familles dispersées dans la campagne. L'unité de cette population n'était pas d'être rassemblée dans un espace construit de type village par exemple, mais d'avoir la même légitimité venue des ancêtres.

Le dernier exemple que nous prenons est le monument mégalithique aux dalles historiées de Kivik en Suède; il date du milieu du IIè millénaire avant notre ère. Il est issu d'une vieille tradition de plusieurs millénaires; l'iconographie des parois raconte le cérémoniel mais ne dit plus ce qu'il vise. Il n'est pas certain, que ce caveau de dimensions réduites ne soit pas réservé pour une seule personne et dans ce cas aussi, malgré l'aspect mégalithique des dalles, le tumulus qui ressemble aux monuments mégalithiques antérieurs, n'a plus du tout la même fonction.

ELÉMENTS DE DISCUSSION EN GUISE DE CONCLUSION

Le mégalithisme n'a pas été seulement le résultat de la sédentarisation, plus complexe que le simple attachement à la terre nourricière. Il a favorisé les rassemblements cérémoniels de communautés assez dispersées, collecteurs, chasseurs, pêcheurs, éleveurs, premiers agriculteurs.

Le mégalithisme a sans doute joué aussi un rôle important dans la fixation des populations, et l'équilibre des forces sociales en proposant l'exemple de constructions et de cultes collectifs au bénéfice au début d'individus symboliques peu nombreux puis d'une population de plus en plus exhaustive.

References

ANDERSEN, N.H., 1997, *Sarup, vol. 1: The Sarup enclosures*. Moesgaard: Jysk Arkaeologisk Selskab.

JEUNESSE, C., 1998, *Pratiques Funéraires au Néolithique Ancien: sépultures et nécropoles danubiennes 5500-4000 av. J.C.* Paris: Errance.

MOHEN, Jean-Pierre & SCARRE, Chris, 2003, *Les tumulus de Bougon: complexe megalithique du Ve au IIIe millenaire*. Paris: Errance.

SOME STONES CAN SPEAK! THE SOCIAL STRUCTURE, IDENTITY AND TERRITORIALITY OF SW ATLANTIC EUROPE COMPLEX APPROPRIATOR COMMUNITIES REFLECTED IN THEIR STANDING STONES

David CALADO
The Portuguese State Ministry for Cultural Affairs; Email: calado.david@gmail.com

Francisco NOCETE
Huelva University; Email: nocete@uhu.es

Maria Dolores CÀMALICH, Dimas Martín-SOCAS, José Miguel NIETO, António DELGADO, Amelia RODRIGUEZ, Moisés BAYONA, Esther ALEX, Nuno INÁCIO

***Abstract**: In the extreme southwestern Atlantic Europe numerous permanent settlement sites with standing stones, decorated with recurring symbols, have been identified. Chronologically, these standing stones started to be erected before the first existing evidences of cereal agriculture in the area. Moreover, the dispersion of the settlement sites, standing stones and symbols, allows the interpretation of patterns of the social organization of the menhir-makers with evidence and detail not previously possible for a European prehistoric society.*
***Keywords**: Atlantic Europe, Appropriator Communities, Standing stones, Symbols, Ethnicity, Boundaries, Lineages*

Algunas piedras hablan! La estructura social, identidad y territorialidad, de las comunidades de apropiadores complejos, reflejada en sus menhires

***Resumo**: En el extremo suroeste peninsular se identificaran numerosos poblados permanentes con menhires decorados por símbolos recurrentes. Al nivel cronológico, esos menhires empiezan a ser erigidos previo a las primeras evidencias inequívocas, conocidas, de agricultura de cereales en la zona. La dispersión de estos poblados, menhires y símbolos, permite la inferencia de los padrones de organización social de estas comunidades con un nivel de evidencia y detalle anteriormente no posible en la comprensión de una sociedad prehistórica Europea.*
***Mots-clés**: Europe Atlantique; epipaleolitique; mésolithique chasseurs-cueilleurs; menhirs; symboles; ethnicité; lignages*

INTRODUCTION AND CHRONOLOGICAL SETTING

Following our investigations into pristine-state societies and the origins of social complexity in SW Europe, a systematic survey was carried out of a 50 km^2 sector in Lagos, Algarve, Portugal. During the survey 17 sites with standing stones were registered. Some of them were already known, but the vast majority had not previously been recorded. Surprisingly, all the groups of standing stones seemed to be linked to settlements with an artefact set dating before the middle of the 5th millennium BCE (D. Calado 2000, Nocete 2001). Other researchers identified a similar pattern among the standing stones of Algarve (Gomes & Cabrita 1997). Furthermore, the surface surveys document the absence or extreme rarity of prehistoric pottery in some standing stones settlement sites.

It was possible to assert the reliability of the inferred chronology of the western Algarve standing stones through optically stimulated luminescence, single aliquot regeneration (OSL-SAR) dating of the strata related to a still *in situ* menhir in the Quinta da Queimada settlement site, Odiáxere, Lagos. During the excavation two moments of occupation were observed. One related to what Fortea (Fortea 1973) described as the "Epipalaeolithic Microblade Tradition", corresponding to an approximate chronology between the 9th and 7th millennia BCE, and the other from late Bronze Age, typically dating to the late 2nd and early 1st millennia BCE. The OSL-SAR results from a soil sample collected inside the undisturbed and sealed menhir`s implantation pit yielded an age of 9095 ± 445 years BT (Shfd 02014), suggesting that, with 95.4% probability, the soil that filled the implantation pit was last exposed to light between 7983 and 6203 BCE, a period that ought to be related to the original erection of the standing stone. This result demonstrates that at least one of the Quinta da Queimada standing stones, with 95.4% probability, must be no younger than 6200 BCE (Bateman 2002, D. Calado, Nieto & Nocete 2004). The two other existing radiometric dates that are connected with a standing stone in Western Algarve also yield very old dates. At Padrão, a large settlement site with Algarve-type standing stones in Vila do Bispo, approximately 22 km west of Quinta da Queimada, Varela Gomes (unpublished report) obtained two consistent calibrated radiocarbon ages from the third quarter of the 6th millennium BCE (Icen 645: 6440 ± 60 BP; Icen 873: 6560 ± 70 BP) from a hearth apparently covering a fallen menhir-implantation pit.

The Central Portuguese Alentejo-type standing stones are substantially different from the Algarve ones and their chronology and function are difficult to establish. The Algarve and the Alentejo standing stone differences are related to the symbolic decoration as well as to the distribution pattern. The Algarve standing stones are decorated with feminine symbols in profoundly high relief, and they are located in permanent settlement sites. Incised "shepherd-staff" symbols and small pitted lines decorate the Alentejo standing stones and many of them are organized in cromlechs, probably defining ritual centres.

In opposition to the Algarve standing stone sites, that stand in large settlement sites with abundant artefacts, Alentejo's cromlechs are very parsimonious with archaeological elements other than the standing stones themselves. A direct relation between an Algarve standing stone and the Alentejo-type "shepherd-staff" symbol is known from the Gregórios menhir, near Silves. This menhir is a typical Algarve standing stone with an undulating decoration of strong relief and with "shepherd-staff" symbols that were incised superficially during later prehistoric times, when the old symbols were already partially eroded. Thus, the only available evidence suggests that the Alentejo "shepherd-staff" symbols seem to be a good deal younger than the western Algarve feminine symbols.

Based on several archaeological excavations, Manuel Calado (2002, 2005) suggests an "Early Neolithic" chronology for at least some of the Alentejo-type standing stones. Further, the only existing radiometric date related to an Alentejo menhir supports the inferences of Manuel Calado, because charcoal recovered from inside the Meada menhir`s implantation pit provided a calibrated ^{14}C age from the first quarter of the 5th millennia BCE (UtC 4452: 6022 ± 40 BP) (Oliveira 1996). Nevertheless, an Alentejo-type standing stone, in apparent association with artefacts from the late 4th or early 3rd millennium BCE, was excavated by João Luis Cardoso in the eastern Algarve mountain region. In a general sense what has been understood as Alentejo-type standing stones perhaps reflects chronologically and functionally different kinds of monuments? This may indeed be suggested by the wide time span, and the dissimilar types of structures, ranging from large cromlechs to isolated stones.

In conclusion, there exists growing and consistent evidence for the very early erection of standing stones in Southwest Atlantic Europe. In Western Algarve, standing stones were erected prior to the late 7th millennium BCE. The standing stones of Western Algarve are associated with permanent settlement sites (Gomes & Cabrita 1997, D. Calado 2000, Ramos 2000, Nocete 2001, CALADO, Nieto & Nocete 2003b, Martín-Socas *et al.* 2003), some of them seemingly belonging to an aceramic period.

STRUCTURE OF THE SETTLEMENT

Analysis of the spatial distribution of settlements with standing stones in a 50 km^2 sector of the Bensafrim–Odiáxere interfluve, using the Delaunay triangulation method, yielded a convex hull with an area of 24 km^2 and a perimeter of 21.7 km for a total of 17 settlement sites. Nearest neighbour analysis indicates that settlements are less than 900 m apart, with a standard deviation of 440 m (D. Calado 2000). Settlement sites with standing stones from the neighbouring Vila do Bispo region, as well as 7th and 6th millennium BCE settlement sites without menhirs from the Spanish provinces of Huelva (Nocete 2001) and Cádiz (Ramos 2000) exhibit similar distributional patterns. These results indicate a regular pattern of territorial occupation over the Mesozoic, Cenozoic, and Quaternary geological layers common to the whole of the extreme SW Atlantic Europe between Gibraltar and the western coast of the Algarve (Ramos 2000).

In the Bensafrim–Odiáxere interfluve, the extents of settlement sites with standing stones vary between six and 40 ha (D. Calado 2000). In the specific instance of Milrei–Padrão, in Vila do Bispo, the settlement extends for roughly 1500 m. In fact, the large settlement sites with standing stones seem to have been permanent settlements with dispersed house compounds, likely analogous to those of some modern farmer-herdsman societies (e.g., the Sidama of Ethiopia). This pattern is best described as one of *intra-site* occupation, which is particularly difficult to understand and interpret via archaeological excavation. It was possible to identify this pattern in the Algarve, because of the incorporation of the standing stones in the settlement sites.

Although the Sidama are a farmer-herdsman society, the earliest phases of Algarve settlements with standing stones appear to be older than the currently known earliest indications of domesticated cereals in Southwest Iberia. Excavations at the Murciélagos and Toro caves in Andalusia, Spain, (D. Calado *et al.* 2003b, Buxó 2004) identified evidence of domesticate cereals dating no earlier than to the middle 6th millennium BCE onwards. Further, pollen diagrams of Lagoa Travessa, in the Alentejo coast, show that the earliest cereal pollen appears, during the second half of the 6th millennium BCE (Mateus 1992, Calado *et al.* 2003a). This is quite similar to Murciélagos and Toro caves and suggests that the rise of complex sedentary societies preceded cereal agriculture in SW Atlantic Europe. Therefore, we infer that the generalist pattern of subsistence proposed by Melvin Aikens (1981) best fits this evidence and that it appears to be a common and widespread phenomenon (Chang 1981, Price & Brown 1985, D. Calado *et al.* 2003b, Okada 2003).

TERRITORY AND SOCIAL ORGANIZATION

Apart from the *intra-site* analysis, the standing stones of the extreme SW Atlantic Europe have been shown to be a powerful and singular instrument of *inter-site* territorial analysis. Their uniformity of manufacture and recurring symbolism enables the inference of elements of the 8th and 7th millennia BCE non-material culture of an Atlantic Europe society reproduced in symbolic artefacts—the

Fig. 2.1. Buried deposit underneath the erected stone

standing stones themselves—and defines a divisional cultural trait in the common material complex that typifies the entire region from Gibraltar to the south-western Atlantic coast of Iberia. We understand the distribution of the very particular type of Western Algarve menhir as being a reflection of some specific and uniform elements of a common superstructure shared by its builders, an *emic* manifestation of a *them/us* dichotomy that seems to fully correspond to the demands of self-perpetuation, unity, interaction and identification, postulated by Fredrik Barth (1966, 1969) for the determination of ethnic distinction. This spatial distribution replicates a concept of identity throughout a region of almost 1000 km^2 that seems to reflect a specific territory of a supra-local polity (Johnson & Earle 1987, Nocete 2001) organized through lineages (Dupre & Rey 1973, Meillassoux 1977, Nocete 1984, Plog 1990, Gailey & Patterson 1998) that we understand as being of a totemic kind (D. Calado *et al.* 2003a, 2003b). We define totemic lineages as those where the ego identity and his ancestors are totem related, whereas true or biological lineages are those by which ego is related by real or pretended biological ancestry.

Utilization of symbols in standing stones have been used to identify patterns of social organization. The work of Driscol (1998) in Scotland is of particular note. However, the society described by Driscol is very different in social organization and time than the one in Western Algarve. The Pictish symbols from Scotland's standing stones are interpreted as a coercive expression emanating from the local socio-political elite. The symbols are believed to articulate the relation between the force of production (serfs) with the means of production (the land) in space and time. As such, they are an expression of control over natural resources that reflect the ideology of an utterly hierarchical society. On the other hand, the 6000-year-older standing stones and symbols from southwest Algarve are not linked to a class-related appropriation inequality of the means of production and labour. Rather, they appear to be convening symbols within the villages, seemingly reflecting totemic lineages of different house compounds.

The standing stones of south-western Atlantic Europe, more precisely in Western Algarve, exhibit unique features. All of them are expressive sculptures of phalluses, with clear delineation of the gland and urethra being a general feature. The size and weight of the menhirs in a particular settlement may vary considerably. Stones of less than 1000 kg may stand alongside giants weighing more than ten times that weight. Symbols that decorate the stones are consistently from only four different types, expressing mostly feminine sexual attributes, i.e. female breasts (*Mama*), vulvas with one or more of the labia open (*Vulva B*), vulvas with the outer labia closed (*Vulva A*), and undulating patterns (*Onda*).

There seems to be no clear relationship between an explicit type of symbol and a particular settlement site. A settlement may contain a great number of standing stones, each with randomly distributed symbols, yet each menhir bears only one type of symbol. This suggests an internal division of the *intra-site* space through symbols that we understand as seemingly expressing a totemic ritual of solidarity where each basic cluster of people is identified through the symbols engraved on objects whose shape denotes an intrinsic value of an intensification rite (Calado, Nieto & Nocete 2003b). Moreover, the recurrence of the same four types of symbols in the numerous settlement sites seems to define four huge leaderless totemic lineages that spread throughout the territory of the menhir-makers (D. Calado, Nieto & Nocete 2003b), that we interpret as reflecting a section system of organization for the society as a whole.

At least one kind of symbol, the *Mama*, is very common in the westernmost area, yet it is rare in the very eastern part of the menhir-makers' territory. Further, settlement sites with standing stones become more scarce in the east, with the easternmost boundary being in the middle of the Algarve. The combination of the progressive disappearance of settlement sites with standing stones and the scarcity of the *Mama* symbol in the east, seems to reflect a phenomenon of multiple fission of the primordial social units that began to erect the standing stones in their large villages. The phenomenon of social fission has been understood as a way of resolution of conflict and demographic pressure among societies with a low level of social stratification and capacity for territorial expansion (Kent 1989). Because of the specific characteristics of Algarve's standing stones and high amount of evidence of territoriality, boundaries and ethnic incorporation projected into artefacts that ought to be integrated in the superstructure of a society, it seems to be the very first time that a social-fission phenomenon, that might have been a very common occurrence in pre-hierarchical societies, seems to be recorded in Atlantic Europe for such an early chronology.

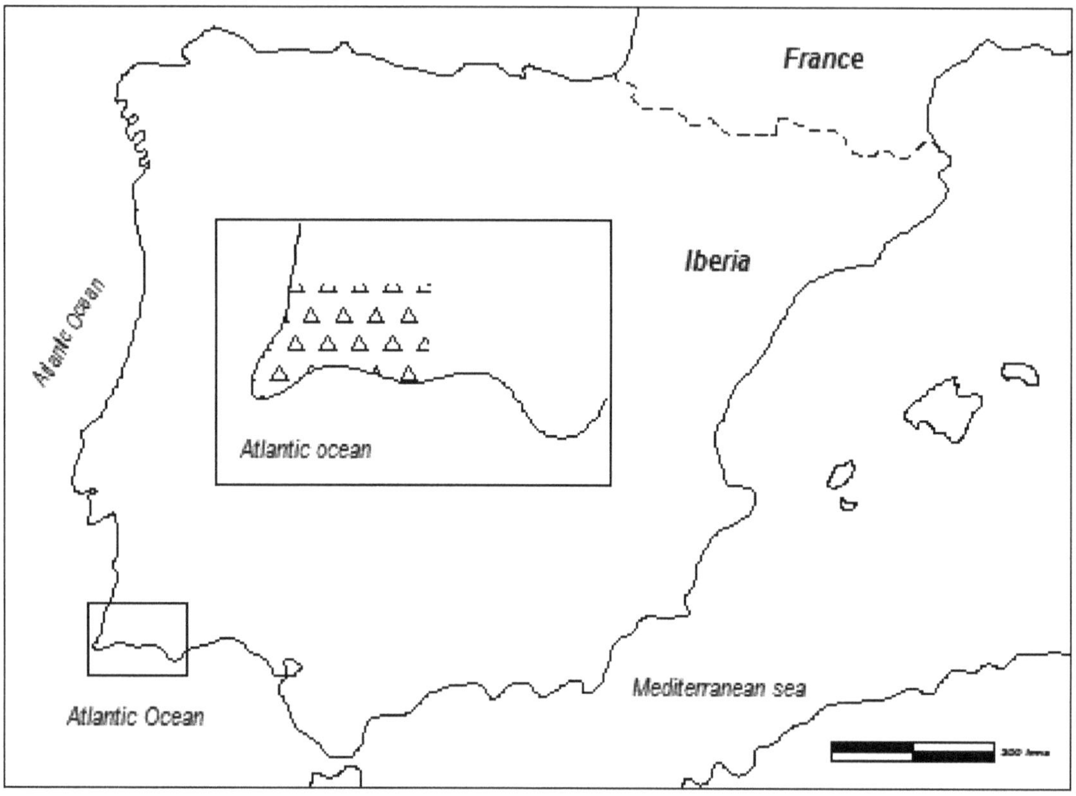

Fig. 2.2. Distribution of early menhirs in the Algarve

RAW MATERIALS AND NATURAL OUTCROPS

Analysis of the lithic items from the settlement site of Quinta da Queimada indicates that, apart from bracelets made from black shale (the nearest outcrops of which are located roughly 25 km away), all the artefacts found at the site are made from rocks collected close to the site. Standing stones at other settlements are made from rock types chosen for their hardness and splitting quality, usually oolitic, crinoidal, and micritic limestones, as long as these types of rocks exist nearby. In the few cases where such stone do not exist nearby, other types of rocks were used for the standing stones. Thus, it may be concluded that, with the possible exception of the black-shale bracelets, there is no indication of items or raw materials acquired from far-off places.

The variety of imported items introduced into intricate exchange circuits is a common feature of hierarchical and politically centralized societies (Brunfield & Earle 1987, Bayman 2002) and is amply demonstrated in the archaeological records of Eastern North America in the early part of our era (Binford 1983) and in SW Atlantic Europe from the 4th millennium BCE onwards (Nocete 2001). This phenomenon must not be confused with the model of dispersal through personal exchange of restricted sets of objects, as observed among the Yir Yoront of Australia (Sharp 1964) and demonstrated in Europe and elsewhere since the Palaeolithic (Lyons, Glascock & Mehinger 2003). Thus, the information at hand does not support a hypothesis of integration of the menhir-makers' society with a grouping of hierarchical or political centralized societies.

In the specific case of the Algarve, the existing evidence from Quinta da Queimada points towards a model of mainly local exploitation of raw materials for artefact production. The only recorded exogenous objects are the bracelets made from black shale, which could also be related to the 2nd millennium BCE (Bronze age) occupation of the site. The nearest black-shale outcrops are roughly a one-day journey from the site. Nevertheless, the origin of the black shale could be from much farther north or northeast, that is from the Palaeozoic strata of Alentejo or Andalusia, where outcrops of this type of rock are identified. If this last hypothesis is correct, than the data could be interpreted as evidence of egocentric-type long exchange lines of restricted sets of status objects (Fitzhugh 2003). However, as we stated before, for now we have no evidence to allow the integration of the black-shale bracelets in a specific chronological context.

SETTLEMENT STRUCTURE AND IMPACT UPON THE ENVIRONMENT

It has been largely understood that the first large-scale human-induced impact on the environment in the extreme southwest of Europe was related to the introduction of cereal agriculture. However, recent data questions this traditional view.

Fig. 2.3. Mama symbol

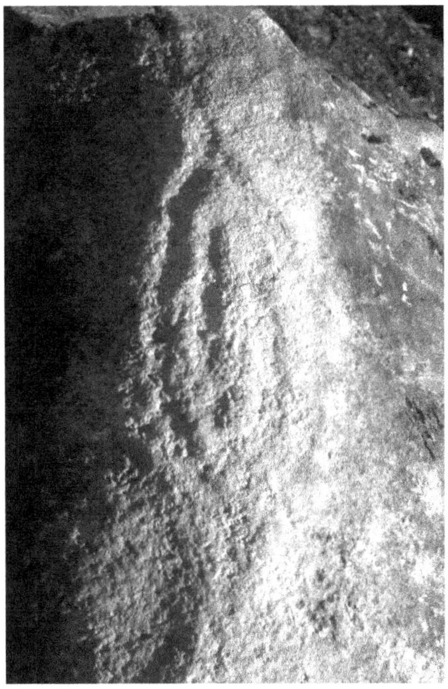

Fig. 2.4. Vulva B symbol

As noted, the earliest evidences of cereals (*T. durum, T. aestivum, T. monococcum, T. dicoccum, H. sativum)* in Western Iberia dates to the middle of the 6th millennium BCE and comes from the caves of Murciélagos and Toro, in inland Andalusia. In the Toro cave, legumes (*Vicia faba, Lens culinaris, Pisum sativum, Lathyrus sativus, Vicia ervilia*), edible indigenous fruits (*Quercus* sp., *Olea europea, Myrtus communis, Rubus* sp., *Pistacia lentiscus, Myrtus communis*), opium poppy (*Papaver somniferum*), and other indigenous plants (*Plantago lanceolata, Bromus* sp, *Lolium* sp., *Lolium termulentum, Sherardia arvensis, Trifolium* sp.) were found alongside cereals (Buxó 2004). At the 6th millennium BCE coastal settlement site of El Retamar, near Cádiz, the exploitation of domesticated (or able-to-be domesticated) specimens of possible native origin, such as pig (*Sus domesticus*), ox (*Bos taurus*), and horse (*Equus sp.*), together with the non-endemic species of goat (*Capra hircus*) and sheep (*Ovis aries*) was evidenced. However, at El Retamar, the wild species, red deer (*Cervus elaphus*), rabbit (*Oryctolagus cuniculus*), and hare (*Lepus capensis*), seem to have constituted a major portion of the diet (Cáceres 2002). Even among SW Iberia politically organized polities of the 3rd millennium BCE, hunting could have provided sources of dietary protein, since it is attested in the fortified villages of Junta de Los Rios and Cerro Juré (Nocete *et al.* 1997, 2005). The data from El Retamar, where a secondary exploitation of domesticated animal specimens in comparison to wild ones is documented, can be related to the pollen diagrams of Lagoa Travessa, in which the production of cereals in southwestern Atlantic Europe appears to have been marginal until approximately the middle 5th millennium BCE. Thus it is possible to extrapolate that the production economy based on cereals and domesticated animals is relatively marginal before approximately 4500 BCE and there is no evidence of it before about 5500 BCE though. Yet, the increasing level of evidence from river estuarine cores and pollen diagrams establish a much older and potent human impact upon the environment.

Sediment cores obtained from the Tinto (Leblanc *et al.* 2000) and Guadiana (González-Vila *et al.* 2003) rivers attest to a strong soil erosion incident starting approximately in the 7th millennium BCE. This phenomenon is well expressed in the standing-stone settlement sites, where an almost complete destruction of ancient soils related in time to the use of the sites is identified (D. Calado 2000, D. Calado *et al.* 2003b). Likewise, the pollen cores from Lagoa Travessa evidence an episode of heavy deforestation since middle of the 7th millennium BCE. These happenings are linked with a dense network of settlement sites, and we understand it as reflecting an intense human impact upon the environment (Nocete 2001, D. Calado *et al.* 2003b). The pristine pinewood forest documented in the SU81-18 maritime pollen core as having existed since approximately 21,000 BCE (Turon *et al.* 2003) was devastated during the 8th and 7th millennia BCE, an event in which, maybe with the help of natural causes, man must have been a principal actor (D. Calado *et al.* 2003a).

However, the pollen charts also suggest that this very old process of man-related deforestation was not chaotic, but selective. Concurrent with the disappearance of the pine forest documented in the Lagoa Travessa cores, fruit trees, oak (*Quercus*), and olive (*Olea*) seem to have been spared, suggesting some form of primitive forest management. This inference is substantiated by the recent finds from Los Baruecos in central Iberia, where acorn phytoliths have been identified in a hand-mill from a late 6th millennium BCE context (Cerrillo *et al.* in press). In the soil analysis from Quinta da Queimada, large quantities of dwarf palm (*Chamaerops humilis*) phytoliths are registered. The very large quantity of dwarf palm phytoliths seems to reflect an economic

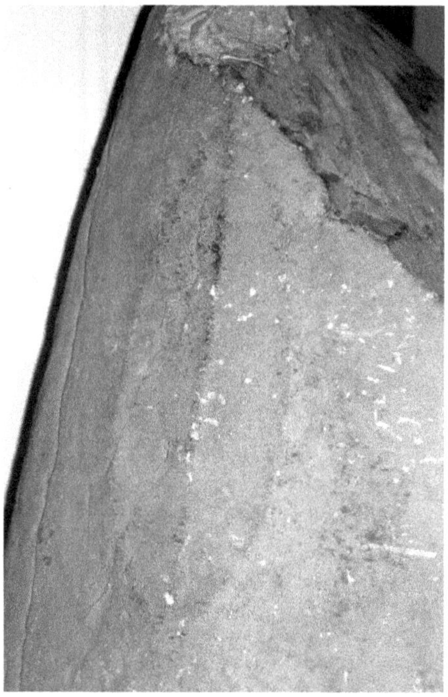

Fig. 2.5. Vulva A symbol

Fig. 2.6. Onda symbol

option of the SW Atlantic Europe prehistoric communities through the management of wild plants. Economically, the dwarf palm has been an important plant in the Mediterranean basin, not just for the production of ropes, mats and brooms, but the stem of the plant is edible and very appreciated by the North African peasants.

Despite the large amount of information from all over the world about complex appropriators communities, including the Ohallo II finds (Nadel & Werker 1999), where use of a broad spectrum of edible plants by Old World Palaeolithic communities and how such an economy could support semi-permanent or permanent settlements has been documented, traditional research of the origins of the Neolithic in Spain and Portugal has been too focused on non-endemic plant and animal species. Further, this research has consistently downplayed the possibility of an important economic role of native flora and fauna (D. Calado *et al.* 2003b). Yet the existing data suggests that the relative high level of social complexity reflected in the settlement sites with menhirs should not have its origins in cereal farming and stock-rearing, activities that seems to be relatively marginal before approximately 4500 BCE, and whose earliest undisputed evidence in SW Europe dates from the middle of the 6th millennium BCE – at least 700 years *after* the erection of one of the Quinta da Queimada settlement site's standing stones.

The reality of pre-cereal producers developing patterns of social organization with relatively high levels of social complexity and a sedentary way of life seems to be a common occurrence in mankind's history. However, further research is necessary in order to understand if such societies ought to be characterized just as complex hunter-gatherers or, as we believe in face of the enormous impact that these polities seem to have had upon the environment, as societies with a broad-spectrum economy and a high level of management of natural resources that, like cereal agriculture, must be understood as a model of social behaviour for production intensification.

The powerful social classification that menhirs and symbols convey may reflect a pattern of critical resource shortage (Saxe & Gall 1977, Wobst 1977) that could strengthen a dialectic model of symbolic recognition as a result of frictions between dissimilar ethnic entities but also, as a result, would intensify inner inconsistencies (Scott 1985, Wolf 1990). In other words, menhirs would identify the society of the standing-stone makers against foreign societies, delimiting a factual territory where access to natural resources would be severely restricted. On the other hand, the implementation of totemic-lineage identification through symbols inscribed on the menhirs would break the internal social cohesion along lines of mythic descent.

The evidence that exists so far from the archaeological record indicates that many standing-stone settlements were abandoned before the middle of the 5th millennium BCE. The Quinta da Queimada settlement site seems to have been abandoned before the use of pottery, to be reoccupied several millennia later at the end of the 2nd millennium BCE. Thus, the erection of Western Algarve standing stones seems to reflect the final stages of a society before its utter disarticulation (D. Calado *et al.* 2003b).

CONCLUSION

In the extreme southwest of Atlantic Europe, a dense network of large permanent settlement sites with standing stones decorated with recurrent symbols has been identified. Chronologically, these settlements date, at least, from the 7th millennium BCE and are substantially older than the first evidence of cereals and domesticated animals in SW Iberia.

The dispersion of settlement sites, menhirs and symbols, allowed the first convincingly recorded indication about the existence of a tangible territory, boundaries, ethnicity, lineages, social fission, social complexity and sedentary communities in such an early period of Stone Age Atlantic Europe, suggesting that in SW Iberia the rise of complex sedentary communities precedes the introduction of cereals and stock-rearing.

Ample evidence from settlement sites with standing stones calls into question traditional assumptions of primary diffusion, agricultural intensification, trade, and land irrigation as explanations for territoriality and population concentration, being therefore an exemplar model to explain some of the aspects of the genesis of social complexity. This is reinforced by the pristine character of the SW Iberian model as describing the origins and disarticulation of a society as an independent historical process not biased by interrelations with political centralized civilizations.

References

AIKENS, C.M., 1981, The last 10,000 years in Japan and Eastern North America: Parallels in Environment, Economic Adaptation, Growth of Social Complexity and the Adoption of Agriculture. In Koyama, S. & Thomas, D.H. (eds.) *Affluent Foragers. Pacific Coast East and West.* Osaka 1979. SENRI Ethnological Studies, 9, p. 261-273.

BARTH, F., 1966, *Models of Social Organization.* Royal Anthropological Institute Occasional Papers, n°23.

BARTH, F., 1969, Introduction. In Barth, F. (ed.) *Ethnic Groups and Boundaries: The Social Organization of Culture Difference.* Oslo: Universitetsforlaget.

BATEMAN, M., 2002, *Quartz Optical Dating Report. Quinta da Queimada Project.* SCIDR. University of Sheffield. (Unpublished report).

BAYMAN, J.M., 2002, Hohokam Craft Economies and the Materialization of Power. *Journal of Archaeological Method and Theory*, 9, p. 69-95.

BENDER, B., 1978, Gatherer-hunter to Farmer: A Social Perspective. *World Archaeology*, 10/2, p. 204-222.

BRUNFIELD, E.M. & EARLE, T.K., 1987, *Specialization, Exchange and Complex Societies.* Cambridge and New York: Cambridge University Press.

BRÖGGER, J., 1977, Socio-economic Structures and the Form of Religion. *Thenemos*, III, p.

BRÖGGER, J., 1983, *Belief and Experience. A Case Study of Social Action and System of Thought among the Sidamo of SW Ethiopia.* University of Trondheim.

BUXÓ, R., 2004, La explotación de los recursos vegetales de la cueva de El Toro: aproximación arqueobotánica a la agricultura de la época neolítica. In Martín-Socas, D., Cámalich, M.D. & González, P., (eds.) *La Cueva de El Toro (Sierra del Torcal, Antequera-Málaga). Un modelo de ocupación ganadera en el territorio andaluz entre el VI y el II milenios ANE.* Sevilla.

CÁCERES, I., 2002, Estudio de los restos óseos de la fauna terrestre en el asentamiento de "El Retamar". In Ramos, J. & Lazarích, M. (eds.) *El asentamiento de "El Retamar" (Puerto Real, Cádiz). Contribuición al Estudio de la Formación Social Tribal y a los inícios de la economía de producción en la Bahía de Cádiz.* Universidad de Cádiz.

CALADO, D., 2000, Poblados con menhires del Extremo SW Penínsular. Notas para sú cronología y economía. Una aproximación quantitativa. *Revista Atlántica-mediterránea de Prehistoria y Arqueología Social (RAMPAS)*, III, p. 47-99.

CALADO, D., CÀMALICH, M.D., FRINK, D.S., MARTÍN-SOCAS, D., NIETO, J.M., NOCETE, F., PINILLA, A., & RAMOS, J., 2003, Distribution Pattern of the Settlement Sites with Menhirs in SW Atlantic Europe and the Inference of the Socio-economic Organization of Their Builders. Paper presented at *The 5th World Archaeological Congress.* Washington.

CALADO, D., NIETO, J.M. & NOCETE, F., 2003a, Quinta da Queimada, Lagos, Portugal. Datação do momento de erecção de um monumento megalítico através de luminescência óptica de cristais de quartzo (OSL). *V Congreso Ibérico de Arqueometría. Libro de Resúmenes de Actas*, p. 167-168. Puerto de Santa María–Cádiz.

CALADO, D., NIETO, J.M. & NOCETE, F., 2003b, Menires, símbolos e organização social. O Extremo SW Peninsular. In Calado, M. (ed.) *International Conference Megaliths and Rock Art.* Évora 2003.

CALADO, D., NOCETE, F., CÀMALICH, M.D., MARTÍN-SOCAS, D., NIETO, J. M., ALEX, E., & BAYONA, M., 2004, Los Poblados con Menhires del Algarve Ocidental: Nuevas Perspectivas para la Explicación del Origen y Implicaciones Históricas sobre las Primeras Sociedades Sedentárias en el Suroeste Penínsular. In *Sociedades Recolectoras y los Primeros Productores. Jornadas Temáticas Andaluzas de Arqueología.* Sevilla.

CALADO, M., 2002, Standing stones and Natural Outcrops. The Role of Ritual Monuments in the Neolithic Transition in Central Alentejo. In Scarre, C. (ed.) *Monuments and Landscape in Atlantic Europe.* London.

CHANG, K.C., 1981, The Affluent Foragers in the Coastal Areas of China: Extrapolation from Evidence on Transition to Agriculture. In Koyama, S. & Thomas, D.H. (eds.) *Affluent Foragers. Pacific Coast East and West.* Osaka 1979. SENRI Ethnological Studies, 9, p. 177-186.

DRISCOL, S.T., 1988, Power and Authority in Early Historic Scotland: Pictish Symbol Stones. In Gledhil, J., Bender, B. & Larsen, M. (eds.) *State and Society: The Emergence and Development of Social Merarchy and Political Centralization.* London: Unwin Hyman.

DUPRE, G. & REY, P., 1973, Reflections on the pertinence of a Theory of Exchange. *Economy and Society*, 2/2, p. 131-163.

FITZHUGH, B., 2003, *The Evolution of Complex Hunter-Gatherers. Archaeological Evidence from the North Pacific.* Interdisciplinary Contributions to Archaeology. New York: Springer.

FORTEA, J. 1973, *Los Complejos Microlaminares y Geometricos del Epipaleolítico Mediterraneo Español.* Universidad de Salamanca.

FRIEDMAN, J., 1977, Tribus, Estados i Transformaciones. In Bloch, M. (ed.) *Análisis Marxistas y Antropología Social.* Barcelona.

FRIGOLÉ, J. *et al.*, 1986, *Las Razas Humanas.* Barcelona.

GAILEY, C.H. & PATTERSON, T., 1988, State formation and uneven development. In Gledhill, J., Bender, B. & Larson, M.T. (eds.) *State and Society: The Emergence and Development of Social Merarchy and Political Centralization.* London: Unwin Hyman.

GOMES, M.V. & CABRITA, L.M., 1997, Dois novos povoados neolíticos, com menires, no barlavento algarvio. *Setúbal Arqueológica*, XI-XII, p. 191-198.

GONZÁLEZ-VILA, F. *et al.*, 2003, Biomarker patterns in a time-resolved Holocene / terminal Pleistocene sedimentary sequence from the Guadiana river estuarine area (SW Portugal / Spain border). *Organic Geochemistry*, nº 34, p. 1601-1613.

JOHNSON, A.W. & EARLE, T., 1987, *The Evolution of Human Societies: From Foraging Group to Agrarian State.* Stanford: Stanford University Press.

KENT, S., 1989, Cross Cultural Perceptions of Farmers as Hunters and the Value of Meat. In Kent, S. (ed.) *Farmers as Hunters.* Cambridge & New York: Cambridge University Press.

LEBLANC, M., MORALES, J.A., BORREGO, J., & ELBAZ-POULICHET, F., 2000, 4500-Year-Old Mining Pollution in Southwestern Spain: Long-term Implication for Modern Mining Pollution. *Economic Geology*, 95/3, p. 655-662.

LILLIOS, K.T., 1991, *Competition to Fission: The Copper to Bronze Age Transition in the Lowlands of West-central Portugal (3000-1000 BC).* Thesis. Yale University.

LYONS, W.H., GLASCOCK, M.D. & MEHINGER, P.J., 2003, Silica from Sources to Site: Ultraviolet Fluorescence and Trace Elements Identify Chert from Lost Dune, Southeastern Oregon. *Journal of Archaeological Science*, 30/9, p. 1139-1159.

MARTÍN-SOCAS; CÁMALICH; BUXÓ; CHÁVEZ; ECHALLIER; GONZÁLEZ; GOÑI; HERNÁNDEZ; MAÑOSA; OROZCO; PAZ; RODRÍGUEZ; TUSELL and WATSON (2004) – La Cueva del Toro (Antequera, Málaga). Una comunidad ganadera en Andalucía, entre el VI y el III milénio ANE. In *Sociedades Recolectoras y los Primeros Productores. Jornadas Temáticas Andaluzas de Arqueología.* Sevilla.

MARTÍN-SOCAS, D., CÁMALICH, M.D. & GONZÁLEZ, P. (*eds*) – *La Cueva de El Toro (Sierra del Torcal, Antequera-Málaga). Un modelo de ocupación ganadera en el territorio andaluz entre el VI y el II milenios ANE.* Sevilla.

MATEUS, J.L., 1992, *Holocene and Present-day Ecosystems of the Carvalhal Region, Southwest Portugal.* Thesis. University of Utrecht.

MEILLASSOUX, C., 1977, *Mujeres, Graneros y Capitales.* Siglo XXI. México.

NADEL, D. & WERKER, E., 1999, The Oldest Ever Brush Hut Plant Remains from Ohallo II, Jordan Valley, Israel (19,000 BP). *Antiquity*, 73/282, p. 755-764.

NOCETE, F., 1984, Jefaturas y território. *Cuadernos de Prehistoria de la Universidad de Granada*, 9, p. 289-304.

NOCETE, F. *et al.*, 1996, Refutaciones al mundo arquograficamente organizado de los neolíticos del SW. *I Congrés del Neolitic a la Península Ibérica*, vol. II, p. 853-862. Gavá, Bellaterra.

NOCETE, F. *et al.*, 1997, *Cabezo Juré. 2500 a.C. Alonso, Huelva.* Alosno.

NOCETE, F., 2001, *Tercer milénio antes de nuestra era. Relaciones y contradiciones centro/periferia en el Valle del Guadalquivir.* Barcelona.

NOCETE, F., *et al.*, 2005, *Andévalo. Patrimonio Arqueológico.* Huelva.

OKADA, Y., 2003, Jomon Culture of Northeastern Japan and the Sannai Maruyama Site. In Habu, J., Savelle, J., Koyama, S., & Hongo, H. (eds.) *Hunter-Gatherers of the North Pacific Rim.* CHAGS 8. Aomori and Osaka. SENRI Ethnological Studies, 63, p. 173-186.

de OLIVEIRA, J., 2000, O megalitismo de xisto na Bacia do Sever (Montalvão–Cedillo). In Gonçalves, V.S. (ed.) *Muitas Antas, Pouca Gente.* Actas do I Colóquio Internacional sobre Megalitismo. Reguengos de Monsaraz 1996, p. 135-158. Lisboa.

ORIHUELA, A., 1999, *Historia de la Prehistoria: el Suroeste de la Peninsula Ibérica.* Huelva.

PLOG, S., 1990, Agriculture, Sedentism and Environment in the Evolution of Political Systems. In Upham, S.

(ed.) *The Evolution of Political Systems. Sociopolitics in Small-scale Sedentary Societies.* Cambridge & New York: Cambridge University Press.

PRICE, T.D. & BROWN, J.A., 1985, *Prehistoric Hunter Gatherers: The Emergence of Cultural Complexity.* New York: Academic Press.

RAMOS, J., 2000, El problema historiográfico de la diferenciación Epipaleolítico–Neolítico como debate conceptual. *SPAL*, 9, p. 279-292.

RAMOS, J.; LAZARÍCH; CASTAÑEDA; PÉREZ; HERRERO and GARCIA (2002, Contribuición de "El Retamar" al conocimiento del modo de producción, de los modos de vida y valoración socioeconómica de la formación social tribal. In Ramos, J. and Lazarích, M. (eds.), *El asentamiento de "El Retamar" (Puerto Real, Cádiz). Contribuición al Estudio de la Formación Social Tribal y a los inícios de la economía de producción en la Bahía de Cádiz.* Universidad de Cádiz.

SAXE, A.A. & GALL, P.L., 1977, Ecological Determinants of Mortuary Practices: the Temuan of Malaysia. In Wood, W. (ed.) *Cultural-Ecological Perspectives on Southeast Asia: A Symposium.* Athens: Ohio University Centre for International Studies.

SCOTT, J.C., 1985, *Weapons of the Weak: Everyday Forms of Peasant Resistance.* New Haven: Yale University Press.

SHARP, L., 1964, Technical Innovation and Culture Change: An Australian Case. In Hammond, P.B. (ed.) *Cultural and Social Anthropology: Selected Readings.* New York: Macmillan.

SOARES, J., 1996, Padrões de povoamento e subsistência no Mesolítico da costa sudoeste portuguesa. *Zephyrus*, 49, p. 109-124.

STRAUS, L., ALTUNA, J., FORD, D., MARAMBAT, L., RHINE, J., SCHAWRCZ, J., & VERNET, J.L., 1992, Early farming in the Algarve (Southern Portugal): A Preliminary View from Two Cave Excavations near Faro. *Trabalhos de Antropologia e Etnologia*, 32, p. 141-162.

THOMAS, D.H., 1981, Complexity among the Great Basin Shoshoneans. The World's Least Affluent Hunter-Gatherers? In Koyama, S. & Thomas, D.H. (eds.) *Affluent Foragers. Pacific Coast East and West.* Osaka 1979. SENRI Ethnological Studies, 9, p. 19-52.

TURÓN, J., LÉZINE, A. & DENÈFLE, M., 2003, Land-sea Correlations for the Last Glacial Inferred from a Pollen and Dynocist Record from the Portuguese Margin. *Quaternary Research*, 59/1, p. 88-96.

WALLACE, A., 1966, *Religion: An Anthropological View.* New York: Random House.

WOBST, M., 1977, Stylistic Behavior and Information Exchange. In Cleland, C. (ed.) *Research Essays in Honor of James B. Griffin.* Ann Arbor: University of Michigan Museum of Anthropology.

WOLF, E.R., 1990, Distinguished Lecture: Facing Power—Old Insights, New Questions. *American Anthropologist*, 92/3, p. 586-596.

TIME AND SIGNS: SOUTHERN PORTUGUESE MEGALITHIC ART DIACHRONY

Mário Varela GOMES

History Department, Faculdade de Ciências Sociais e Humanas, Universidade Nova de Lisboa, Av. de Berna 26 C, 1069-061, Lisbon, Portugal

***Abstract**: Southern Portuguese megalithic art is usually understood as a single, wide diachrony phenomenon, stretching from the early food producer societies with domesticates (Early Neolithic, 6th millennium BC) to the appearance of the metallurgical communities at the end of the 4th millennium BC and mainly in the 3rd millennium BC. However, the data relating to engravings and certain paintings shows pertinent iconography and symbolic evolution over more than 2500 years. Infrequently found in funerary monuments, the preferred supports for such manifestations were menhirs and menhir-stelae. They offer not only thematic transformations but also changes, associations, superimpositions and erasures of figures, creating complex palimpsests. The symbolic alterations over time reflect the changes in the ideological and behavioural patterns of the local communities, who progressively adapted the monuments to diverse new contexts. The two major iconographic renovation periods were the 4th millennium BC, when many standing stones were anthropomorphized and turned into menhir statues, and the 3rd millennium BC, when sun iconography, possibly allusive to a Mediterranean mother-goddess with solar eyes, was widely brought into use.*

***Key-words**: Megalithic Art; Neolithic; Chalcolithic; Southern Portugal*

CONCEPTS AND READINGS

The understanding of time by contemporary societies is, above all, related to the concept of Past and the attempt to quantify it by structuring the creation of historical models of past human communities and decisively marking their physical, economic, social, technological and ideological evolution.

'What time does this place date from? And this artifact?' These continue to be the primary questions archaeologists normally ask when confronted with unknown evidence. And what about nowadays? Can we conceive of an archaeology without absolute dates?

As happens with many academics who study sites containing graphic or artistic manifestations known as rock art, Southern Portuguese megalithic art is mainly considered to be a wholly contemporary phenomenon. Nevertheless, the data corresponds to a wide diachrony and to different cultural stages (the same happens with megalithic architecture), at least from the first food producer communities with domesticates, in the middle of the 6th millennium BC to the beginnings of metallurgical societies from the end of the 4th millennium but mainly from the 3rd millennium BC.

However, we wish to demonstrate, backed by secure and systematic data gathered over the last thirty years, that Southern Portuguese megalithic art presents a significant figurative and symbolic evolution which it is important to understand.

In fact, despite some apparent formal continuities, megalithic iconographic speech changed profoundly within this time, reflecting and following the historical process and especially the cognitive aspects of societies.

Contrary to those in the North of Portugal and Galicia, megalithic funerary monuments in the South show rare artistic evidence. The Southern examples reveal sets of cup-marks carved in the cover stones of passage graves, with many of them certainly produced in a "post-functional" chronology of such monuments. A circle was also engraved on the inner surface of a stone from the Freixo passage grave, identified by the French archaeologist, E. Cartailhac, in the late 19th century, and remains of paintings were detected in two other similar monuments.

The preferred supports for artistic manifestations of megalithic art in Southern Portugal, composed of engravings and reliefs, were the standing stones, or menhirs, and menhir-*stelae*, which sometimes display thematic and technological variations as well as changes, associations and superimpositions of images, thereby forming a kind of palimpsest where the erasure of figures and the volumetric transformation of some stones has also been acknowledged.

Such behaviour reveals changes in the meaning and functions of the above-mentioned monuments, with their being adapted successively to new cultural and ideological contexts.

Despite recognizing the scientific merit and the effort made by some researchers in producing earlier dates for menhirs in Southern Portugal, dating them to before the presence of the first food producer societies with domesticates, the experimental level and the degree of fallibility of the methodologies applied as well as the initial stage of the theoretical framework developed do not permit us to accept such chronologies, mainly in a generalized way.

As we have tried to demonstrate with archaeological arguments for some thirty years, the first Southern

Portuguese menhirs were erected, at least, in the second half of the 6th millennium. However, social and religious activity increased in the following years and during the whole Neolithic period, with some menhirs even being transformed during the 4th millennium, but rarely staying upright during the 3rd millennium BC. Some were very sporadically reused in the 2nd millennium (Bronze Age) – two such examples being São Martinho and Alfarrobeira, both of which were transformed into Bronze Age funerary *stelae* (Calado, 2000; Gomes, 1993, 1994, 1997, 1997a, 1997b, 2002, 2003; Gomes *et al.* 1997).

ARCHAEOLOGICAL DATA

In the Algarve, where many menhirs were reused during Prehistory, the Pontais 2 menhir (h= 2.46 m), belonging to a former stone alignment with at least four monoliths and chiselled in local red sandstone, displays a phallic shape. The first decorative program has a gland-belt in relief and a small cup-mark at the top, reaffirming the obvious phallic symbology, and two relief parallel wavy lines occupying the center of the main face and ending in the upper part in spirals with a lozenge form between them. Traces of other wavy lines can still be seen on the lateral faces of this monument (Fig.3.1-A).

This iconography is similar to that found in many other Algarve menhirs dating, at least, from the second half of the 6th and the first half of the 5th millennium BC (Early Neolithic times), where reliefs were the exclusive representational technique. In spite of this, we have detected traces of red paint in a menhir from Caramujeira (Lagoa).

The second decorative program of the Pontais 2 menhir was revealed by the representation, in relief, of three shepherd's crooks. Two engraved images of axes, a rectangular figure, a possible idol, shield form or box symbol, may represent a third moment of iconographical production.

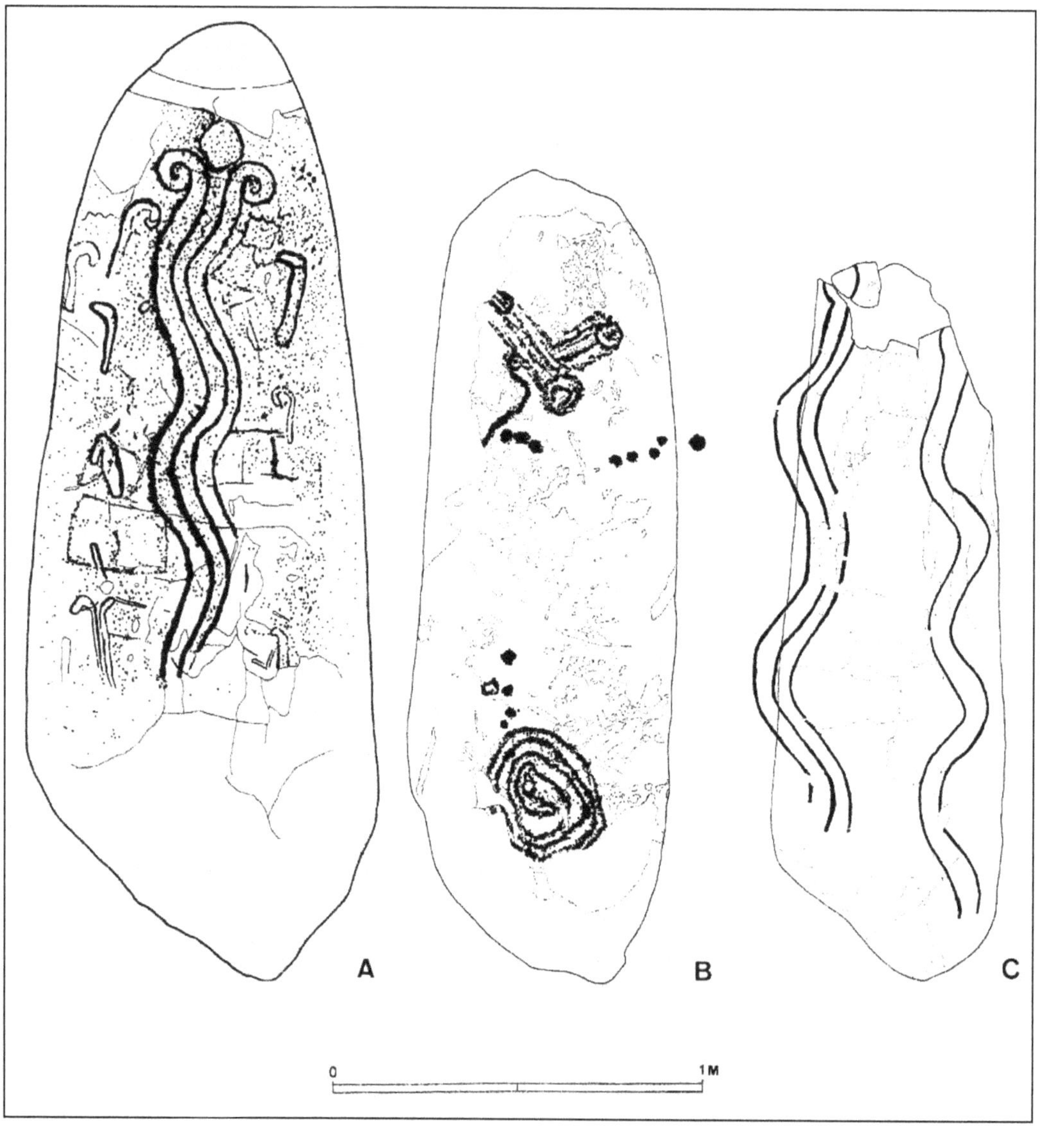

Fig. 3.1. Menhirs 2 (A), 1 (B) and 3 (C) from Pontais (Silves, Algarve) (after M.V. Gomes)

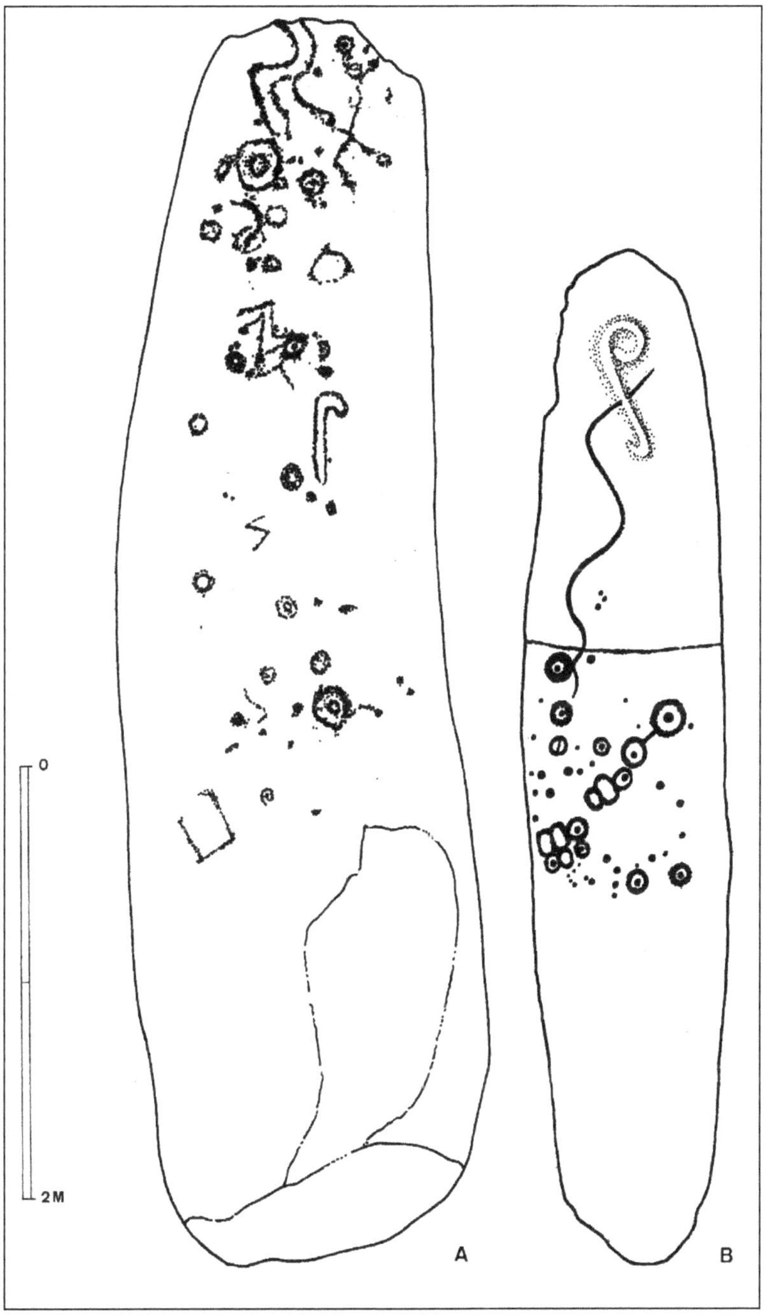

Fig. 3.2.Menhir-*stelae* from Herdade do Barrocal (A) and Monte da Ribeira (B) (Reguengos de Monsaraz, Évora) (after M.V. Gomes)

The Pontais 1 menhir (h = 2.12 m), also chiselled in red sandstone, has a phallic form and was erected during the Early Neolithic. This does not show any decoration from that period. However, probably during the second half of the 4th millennium (Late Neolithic), it was transformed into an anthropomorphic stele, as shown by the necklaces engraved on its upper part. Later, when it was already lying on the ground, two sets of aligned cup-marks were engraved, maybe during the 3rd millennium B.C., and afterwards, on its lower part, a huge serpent figure with a very realistic head was carved. This has been dated to the 2nd millennium BC (Bronze Age) by parallels with open air rock art (Fig. 3.1-B).

Another monument from the Algarve, discovered in the 19th century, is the Cerro das Pedras menhir, which has a phallic form and relief decoration. It belongs, at least, to the 6th or 5th millennia (first Neolithic times), but during the 3rd millennium a solar image was engraved and later, a set of cup-marks.

In the Alto Alentejo, tall menhir-*stelae*, such as the one found in the center of a stone enclosure at Barrocal (h = 5.72 m) which we studied ten years ago and the one in Monte da Ribeira (Gonçalves, Balbín-Behrmann, Bueno-Ramírez, 1997), both in the Reguengos de Monsaraz area, are true palimpsests (Fig. 3.2). On both monuments an

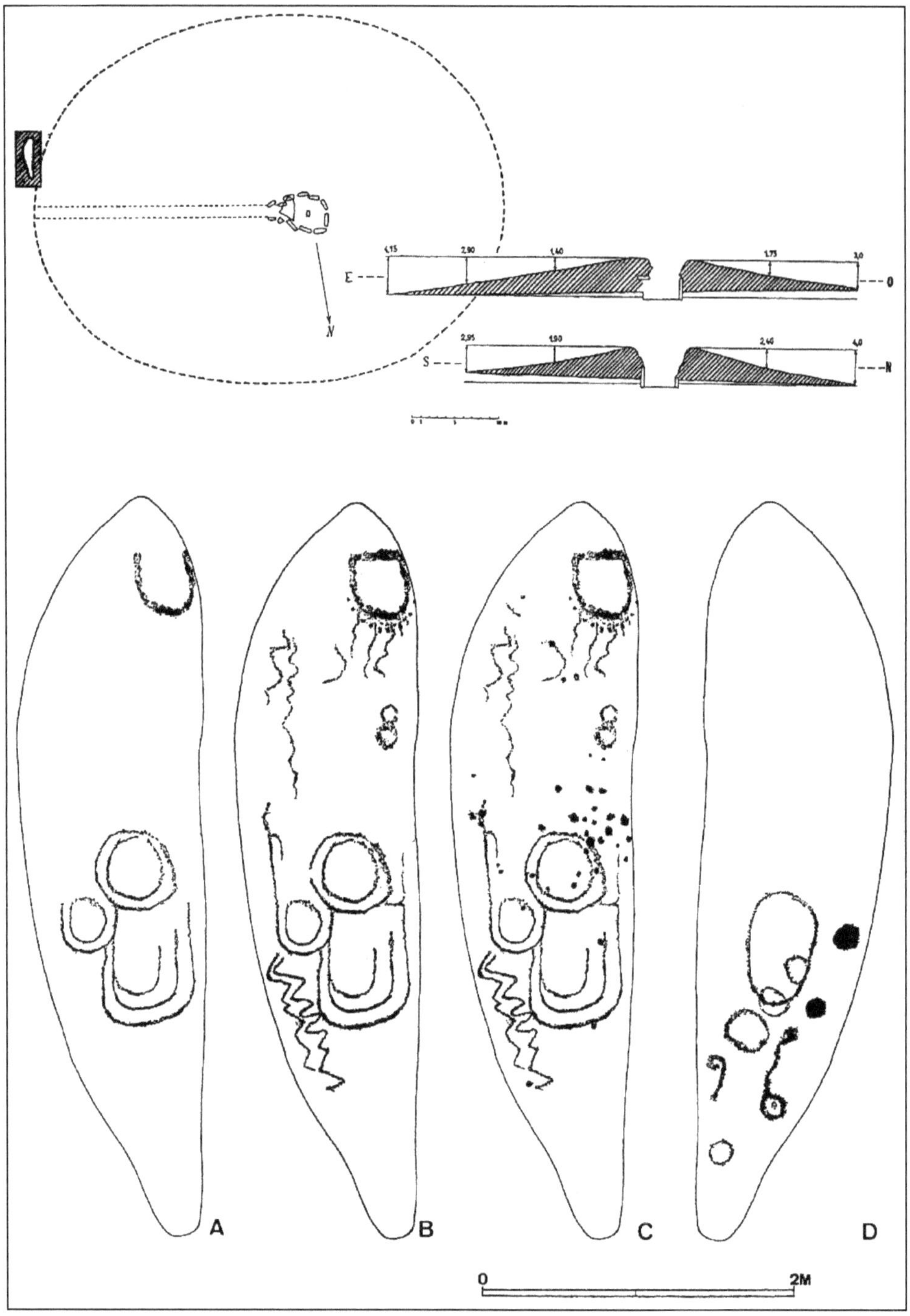

Fig. 3.3. Vele-de-Rodrigo (Évora). Barrow and menhir-stele (faces A and B) (after M.V. Gomes)

older period characterized by wavy lines was identified. Other periods were also recognized – one of them was identified by long crooks from the second half of the 5th to the middle of the 4th millennia BC (Middle Neolithic), and the next by short crooks from the second half of the 4th millennium, (Late Neolithic). Circles, cup-and-ring marks, concentric circles, one spiral and other iconography, all belonging to the 3rd and 2nd millennia BC, were also recorded.

A set of zig-zags, from the late 4th or early 3rd millennium BC (Late Neolithic or Chalcolithic times), can be seen on the Herdade do Barrocal menhir-stele. Both monuments show numerous cup-marks from later times (Fig. 3.2 –A).

In Vale de Rodrigo (near Évora), a menhir-stele found close to the barrow of a passage grave, transformed into a false dome monument just like the 3rd millennium BC funerary buildings named *tholoi*, shows a significant iconographic succession from at least three main periods (Fig. 3.3).

Corresponding to the first period is one of the surfaces with big concentric circles, U-shaped figures, some of

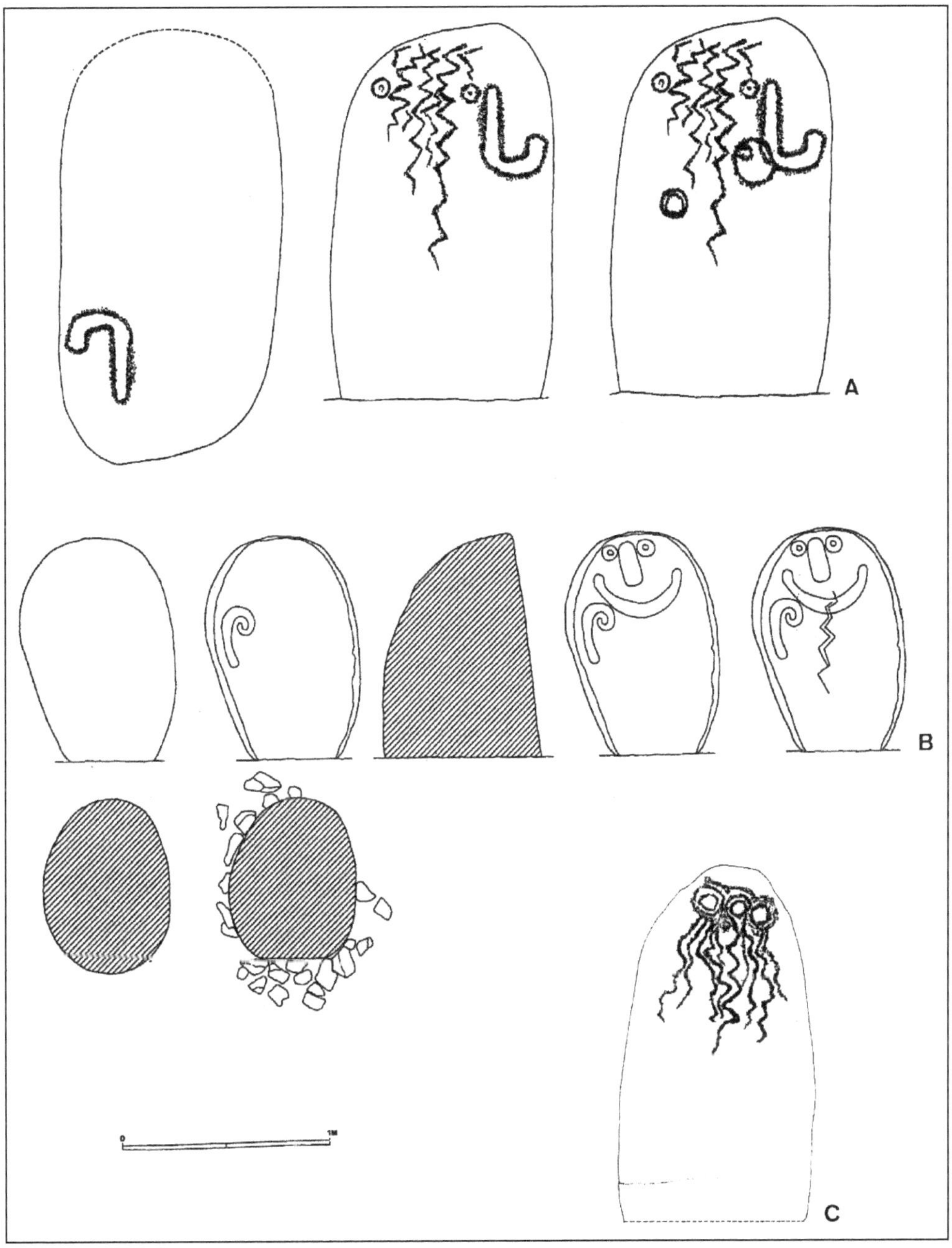

Fig. 3.4. Menhir 83 (A), 89 (B) and 58 (C) of the Almendres cromlech (after M.V. Gomes)

them also concentric and suggesting a kind of shield form, and two twin circles. On the opposite face an oval figure, five circles and a crook can be seen. However, this surface was partly pecked during Prehistoric times, thereby erasing the pre-existing figures.

Similar iconographies are to be found in the Almendres cromlech menhirs and also in the megalithic art of the European Atlantic front. They can be dated from the end of the 5th millennium BC or from the beginnings of the 4th millennium BC.

In the next decorative moment, the big U engraved near the top of the stone was closed, creating a circular form. In the lower part, wavy lines alternated with little cup-marks, depicting a radiating image with a solar symbolic meaning. The same face was engraved with wavy lines as well as a serpent form superimposed on the previous shield image (Fig. 3.3-B). On the opposite face, a wavy line and a circle with a central cup-mark was also detected (Fig. 3.3-D). This iconography should be dated around the end of the 4th millennium BC and from the 3rd millennium BC when Chalcolithic societies appeared in the area.

Around the same time, the passage grave with which the menhir-stele was associated was transformed into a false dome grave. Finally, several small cup-marks were engraved on both sides and superimposed on the earlier decorations. They were possibly made when the monument had already fallen to the ground. It is interesting to note that this monument was chiselled out of a kind of granite that is only found some 10 km from the place where it lies.

Relevant iconographic evolution can be seen in menhir 83 from the Almendres cromlech (Évora), which shows a rare change in its original position. In a second moment, it was turned upside down (Fig. 3.4-A). When the menhir was standing *in situ,* its south-facing side had a relief crozier representation and the remains of other eroded motifs. Later, after the upper part of the stone was buried in the ground, five zig-zag vertical lines were engraved, flanked by two circles with small central dots. Similar figures can be found in southern Portuguese rock and mobile 3rd millennium (Chalcolithic) art, and especially in menhir 58 of the same cromlech (Fig. 3.4-C). Finally, a simple circle and two concentric circles were engraved on menhir 83.

To end our main archaeological arguments on the evolution of the megalithic art of the menhirs and menhir-*stelae,* and recognizing this as a *longue durée* phenomenon, it is important to describe a patterned behaviour we found some years ago in the great Almendres and Portela de Mogos stone circles, lying 10 km apart. At both sites, the egg-shaped menhirs were transformed into menhir-statues and the sun-facing side flattened *in situ.* The blocks cut during that action remained there and were found during the archaeological diggings. Long noses, eyes, crescent-shaped moon elements and other attributes were engraved on the new surfaces, thus creating anthropomorphic representations possibly connected to ancestor cults (Gomes, 1997b).

Some of these monoliths still preserve traces of the primitive iconography, as is the case of a Portela de Mogos cromlech menhir where a long crook can be identified.

Menhir 76 from Almendres, the decoration of which can be dated to the second half of the 4th millennium (Late Neolithic), presents a relief circle on its lateral side and was flattened in a later moment when it was transformed into a menhir-statue. It shows a relief crook, and later a relief anthropomorphic face accompanied by a crescent-shaped moon element and, at the end of the iconographic production, vertical zig-zag lines were engraved (Fig. 3.4-B).

Some menhir-statues, initially without any sexual determination, were given female characteristics while still in the Late Neolithic through the engraving of breasts, thus showing a diachrony relating to the primitive iconography in relief (Fig. 3.5).

CONCLUSIONS

We believe we have demonstrated through the examples presented that megalithic art, even when represented on the face of one single monument, is frequently composed of several symbols that should not be taken as a generic whole of a certain historical period but are sometimes almost without a specific time. On the contrary, such data is the result of a succession of specifically created iconographic programs, which respond to social, economic and religious manifestations of the communities responsible for their existence.

Southern Portuguese megalithic art shows a complex evolution from, at least, the first producer societies with domesticates (Neolithic times) of the second half of the 6th millennium BC, when an innovative iconography linked to fertility and the stimulation of Nature was imposed without any known Iberian precedents.

At a second moment, with increased agriculture and husbandry and economic and cultural interaction, an iconography related to Atlantic megalithism was developed, presenting similarities with the Iberian Northwest and the art of Brittany. However, the second half of the 4th millennium BC marks the high point in the success of rural Neolithic economies, thanks to certain technological innovations such as the use of ploughs and chariots with ox traction. This led to deep social and ideological transformations as well as to iconographic changes as revealed by the first anthropomorphic menhir-statues we referred to.

At the end of the 4th millennium BC but, especially during the 3rd millennium BC, when Chalcolithic societies developed, a profound iconographic renovation was observed. Solar or sun-related images were frequently engraved, probably connected to the idea of a super female goddess with Euro-Mediterranean diffusion who, for the sake of convenience, has been called the "mother-goddess of the solar eyes".

Still in that period, many menhirs were decorated on their exposed faces with abundant cup-marks and circles after they had fallen down. In the 3rd millennium BC, or even a little later, the Chalcolithic societies marked the end of megalithism and its art.

Although already lying on the ground, some menhir-*stelae* continued to be a part of social and religious activities during the following millennia, receiving Bronze Age or even Late Bronze Age engravings. This was the moment when some of them were reused and transformed into decorated funerary *stelae.*

It seems, at this point, possible to conclude that Neolithic menhirs and menhir-*stelae* were taken to be symbols with different meanings along the ages. Reliefs and engravings were associated to their forms. The shape of these monuments shows a longer survival phenomenon, stimulating the interest of human societies in them until nowadays. The same has not happened to the rich diachronological iconography on their surfaces, which has been subjected to transformation, superimposition and to oblivion.

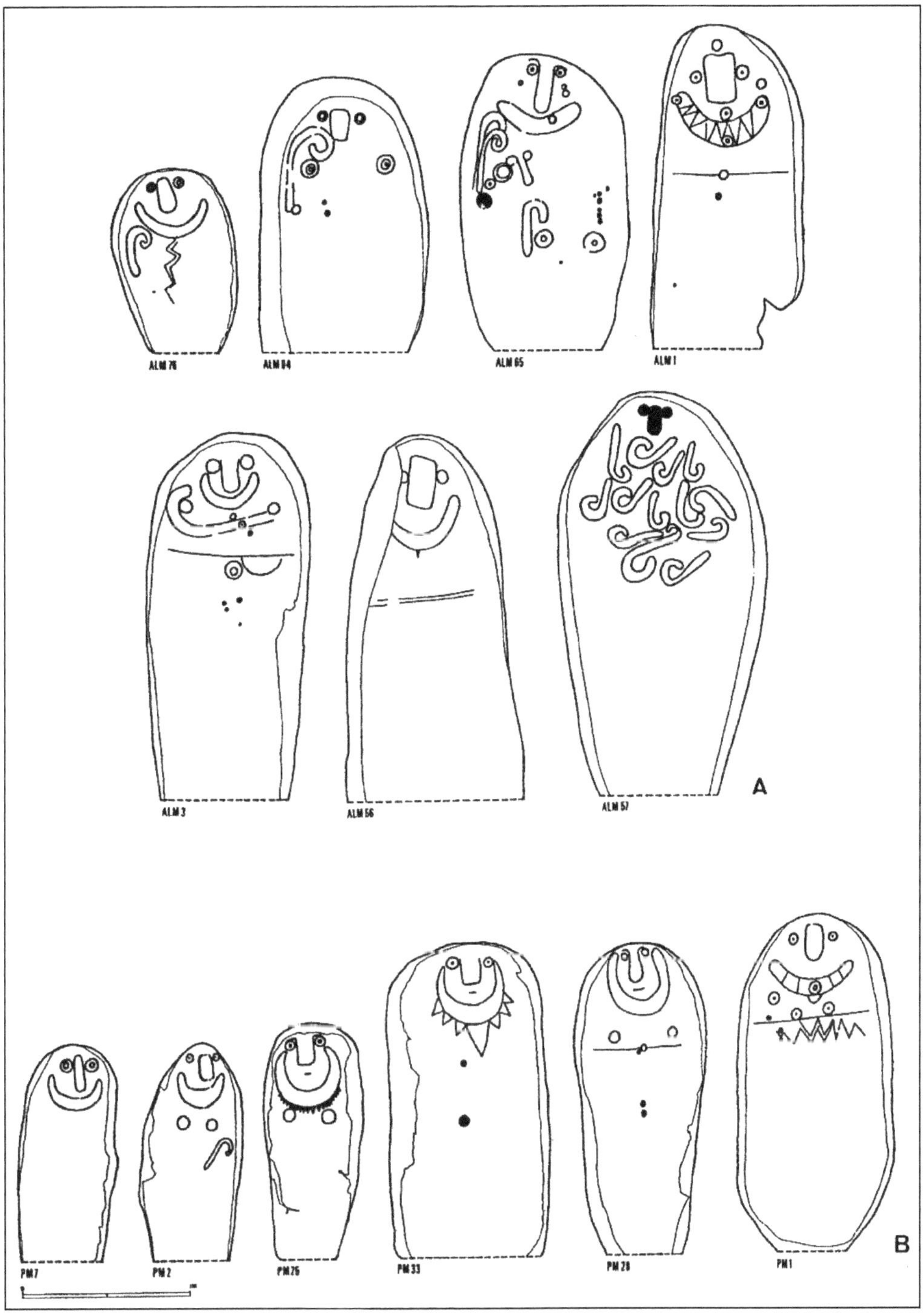

Fig. 3.5. Menhirs transformed into menhir-statues from Almendres (A) and Portela de Mogos (B) (after M.V. Gomes)

References

CALADO, D.C., 2000, Poblados con menhires del Extremo SW Peninsular. Notas para su cronologia e economía. Una aproximación cuantitativa, *Revista Atlántica-Mediterránea de Prehistoria y Arqueología Social* 3, p. 47-99.

GOMES, M.V., 1993, O Marco da Anta ou a estela-menir da Caparrosa (Tondela-Viseu), *Estudos Pré-Históricos* 1, p. 7-27.

GOMES, M.V., 1994, Menires e cromeleques no complexo cultural megalítico português – trabalhos recentes e estado da questão, *Estudos Pré-Históricos* 2, p. 317-342.

GOMES, M.V., 1997, O menir da Herdade das Vidigueiras (Reguengos de Monsaraz, Évora). Resultados dos trabalhos efectuados em 1988, *Cadernos de Cultura de Reguengos de Monsaraz* 1, p. 17-37.

GOMES, M.V., 1997a, Megalitísmo no Barlavento Algarvio – Breve síntese, *Setúbal Arqueológica* 11-12,

p. 147-190.

GOMES, M.V., 1997b, Estátuas-menires antropomórficas do Alto-Alentejo. Descobertas recentes e problemática, *Brigantium* 10, p. 255-279.

GOMES, M.V., 2002, *Cromeleque do Xarez. A Ordenação do Caos.* Monsaraz: Fundação Convento da Orada.

GOMES, M.V., 2003, *Cromeleque dos Almendres. Um Monumento Sócio-Religioso Neolítico.* Lisboa: Universidade Nova de Lisboa.

GOMES, M.V. & CABRITA, L.M., 1997, Dois novos povoados neolíticos, com menires, no Barlavento Algarvio, *Setúbal Arqueológica* 11-12, p. 191-198.

GONÇALVES, V.S., BALBÍN-BEHRMANN, R & BUENO-RAMÍREZ, P., 1997, A estela-menir do Monte da Ribeira (Reguengos de Monsaraz, Alentejo, Portugal), *Brigantium* 10, p. 235-254.

MEGALITHS AS ROCK ART IN ALENTEJO, SOUTHERN PORTUGAL

Manuel CALADO & Leonor ROCHA

Abstract: *This paper is based on the available evidence concerning standing stones, as well as broadly contemporaneous rock paintings and carvings in Alentejo. Instead of the traditional perspective, which treats those manifestations as ontologically different—though, on some occasions, tries to compare them or find specific links between them—rock art and megaliths are here considered as parts of the same complex of the Neolithic "packet", expressed by the development of symbolic devices, and interconnected by a system of beliefs around the validation of the role of man against nature, and, iconographically, mainly built upon schematic ways of representing the human figure. Actually, we can argue that the very concept of "megalithic art", creating a common ground between both megaliths and rock art, implies a restrictive view, because it highlights the most obvious similarities but hides the fact that, even when they have no carvings or paintings, standing stones are still rock art. We argue that in some sense, those symbolic and ritual manifestations share the same similarities and differences as painting, engraving, and sculpture in modern western art.*
Key-words: *Megaliths – Rock Art – Menhirs*

INTRODUCTION

In Alentejo, as well as in other European prehistoric areas, carvings, paintings and standing stones can be, on one hand, related with different historical contexts; but, on the other, they seem to be different adaptations of the very same purposes to diverse geographical conditions.

Actually, in Alentejo, standing stones exhibit an obvious dependence on the flat granite landscapes, carvings are only found on schistose water-eroded panels (in the main river bottoms), and paintings are restricted to quartzite rockshelters (in mountainous landscapes).

In rock-art interpretations, it is well established that panels were meaningful on their own. Beyond technical qualities such as the smoothness of the surface, other aspects including colour, shape, position, and kind of rock were not selected at random. Finally, the landscapes where the panels are inscribed seem to be decisive for locations of so-called rock-art sanctuaries (Bradley 1997a, 1997b, Ouzman 1998, Scarre 2003). It is clear, in Alentejo as elsewhere, that special points in the landscape were selected, together with peculiar shapes and types of stone.

Of course, conceiving of the standing stones as a development of rock art implies a link going back to the Upper Palaeolithic, in a process of continuity (the Alqueva complex spans from the Palaeolithic until Iron Age) (Collado 2003, Calado 2003) and change (from a naturalistic style displaying mostly animals, to a schematic style representing mostly human figures).

Rock art, including megaliths, may be thought of as the result of a complex way of creating and negotiating a system of symbols, or, in other terms, a graphic language that conveys differing ideologies and social formations. Though sharing the same mental ambiance as the rock art *tout court*, and eventually serving similar purposes, standing stones imply an important innovation in the way of graphically expressing ideas: they are three-dimensional and large-scale symbols that herald later developments of the statuary and, in some ways, the development of true megalithic architecture (e.g., dolmens).

The anthropomorphic nature of standing stones and the diverse ways they may be arranged together make them appropriate symbols for ritualising and performing social messages, in a process of increasing social and ideological complexity. The symbolic potential of standing stones, meaningfully dispersed on the landscape—frequently arranged in articulation with conspicuous topographic and astronomic features—is, in some cases, amplified by the carved motifs displayed on them.

Finally, and in modern terms, rock art, including standing stones, may be included in the category of landscape architecture or, better yet, *land art*.

IN THE BEGINNING…

In the last decade, the idea that standing stones are the oldest megalithic monuments in Europe has received significant attention, and a great deal of evidence has been found supporting this assumption. Confirmation during the 1980s of the reuse of broken menhirs in some Breton dolmens opened a Pandora's box of new questions. Results from the subsequent observations and studies addressing these questions appear to all be pointing in the same direction. The current list of menhirs that appear to have been reused in the dolmens of Brittany sums up to several-dozen instances, thus leaving little room to doubt the relative antiquity of standing stones, at least in that particular area (Cassen *et al.*, 2000).

In Iberia, partly as a result of the discoveries in Brittany, the revision of old data together with fresh excavations guided by new insights and methodologies has revealed a

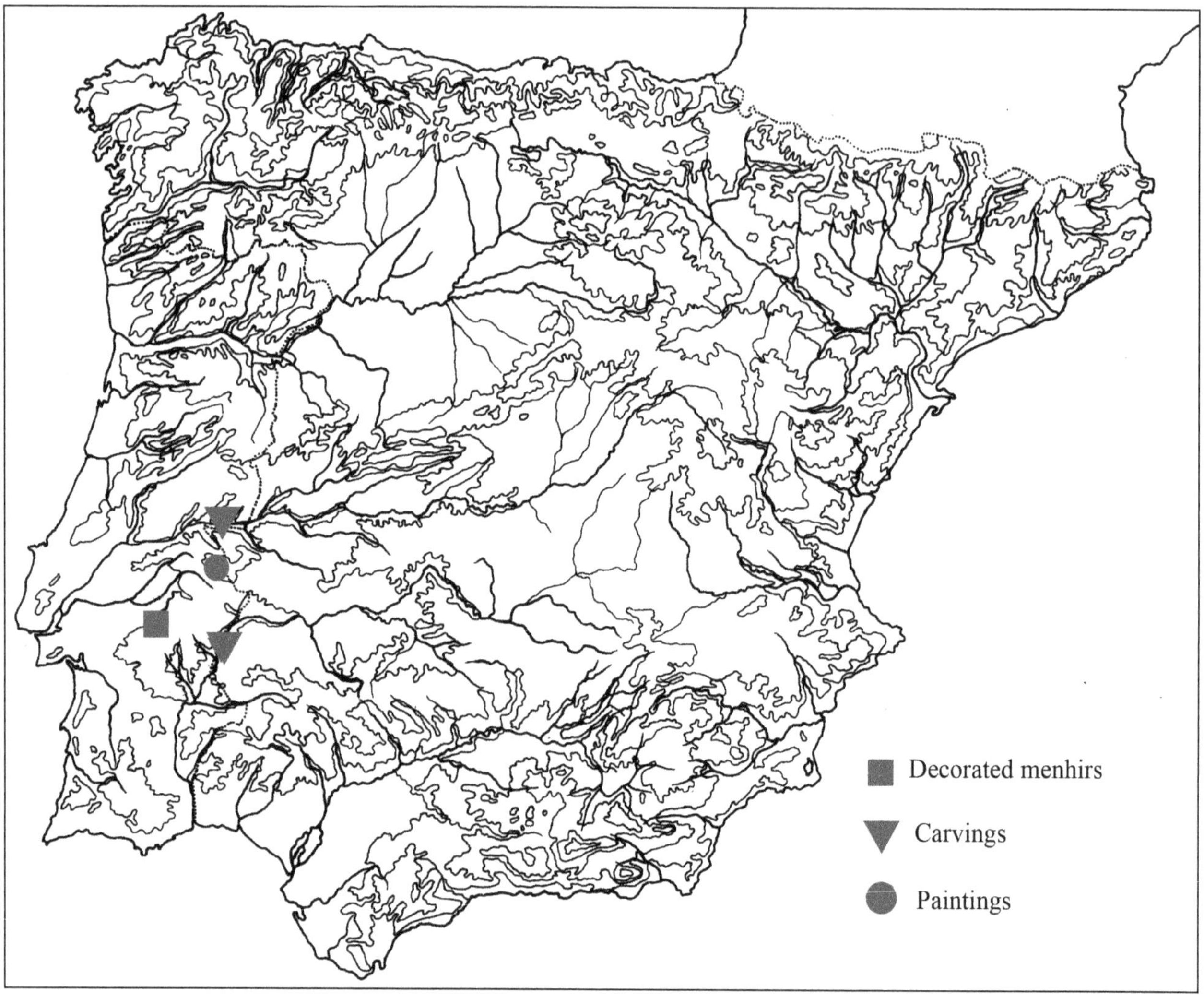

Fig. 4.1. Distribution of menhirs and rock art in Alentejo

similar situation. Thus, Iberian menhirs appear to have been, as in Brittany, reused for the construction of dolmens (Calado 2004). Further, those few absolute dates available, some obtained through analyses of materials embedded inside menhir sockets, tend to confirm the early existence of these monuments (Oliveira 1997, Gomes 1994, 1996, Calado D., *et al.*, this volume). This means that, at least in Brittany and Iberia, if standing stones (either alone or grouped) are one manifestation of megalithic architecture, they must be placed in the very beginning of the development of such architecture. In other words, when the first menhirs were erected, the concept of a dolmen had probably not yet been conceived.

THE CONTEXT

Menhirs seemingly arose during a period when significant changes were taking place throughout Atlantic Europe. The last communities of hunter-gatherers were experiencing the impact of a revolution in almost all aspects of their lifeways (economic, technological, and ideological). This revolution was but one stage in a sequence that had started some one-thousand years earlier in the eastern Mediterranean. Although the main domesticates (cereals and ovicaprids), pottery, and polished stone tools were certainly brought from that nuclear area, some of the most distinctive features of the western Neolithic seem to have no counterparts in the eastern Mediterranean. Among those features that appear native to Western Europe, menhirs are the most striking.

One of the most well-known aspects of the Neolithic revolution is the importance of anthropomorphic motifs. Such motifs contrast starkly with the zoomorphic figures that dominated previous periods (i.e., the Palaeolithic and Epipalaeolithic). In the Levant, those anthropomorphic representations are typically in the form of clay or stone figurines. Such figurines are quite rare in the central and western Mediterranean. Lime-plaster statues, also common anthropomorphic figures in the Levant, are completely absent elsewhere in the Mediterranean. In Iberia, painted and pecked rock-panel motifs, broadly attributed to the Neolithic or the Early Bronze Age, reference the human figure. Usually such motifs are schematic images associated with geometric motifs (mostly circles and

Fig. 4.2. Painted anthropomorphic motif in the rock shelter of Gaivões (Arronches)

wavy lines). Although anthropomorphic pillars have been found at a few sites in the Anatolian Peninsula (Cauvin 1999, Verhoeven 2002, Lewis-Williams 2005), menhirs seemingly have no parallels in the East.

Another important feature of most Neolithic cultures is the emergence of monumentality, expressed in many different ways. The cultic buildings of the Near East and earthen funerary structures in Western Europe share two basic similarities with menhirs. They involve a significant amount of labor to be built, and they reflect a strong sense of distinctiveness and power once constructed.

QUESTIONS OF MEANING

There is no general agreement about the meaning or the function of menhirs. Most authors accept that they are, in some way, anthropomorphic figures. This idea is reinforced by comparisons with the statue-menhirs that spread into different parts of Europe during the subsequent millennia until the Iron Age (D'Anna 2002a, 2002b, 2002c, Philippon 2002, Bueno & Balbín 2002, 2003). Actually, it is possible that all menhirs were basically conceived of as statues, with more or less explicit anthropomorphic details. Of course, reference to the human body does not contradict other meanings and functions frequently attributed to the menhirs, such as territorial markers, religious constructions, or mnemonics that substantiated social structures.

Fig. 4.3. Carved anthropomorphic motifs of the Alqueva Rock art complex

Whatever meanings these features had—and it is quite possible that they conveyed different messages in different regions and times—we assume that they, in ways similar to rock-art motifs, were primarily symbols. As anthropomorphic symbols, menhirs may have even related to ancestor cults, possibly as a result of the establishment of lineages in a society experiencing ever-increasing complexity.

MENHIRS AS ROCK ART

We suggest that menhirs arose as a peculiar development in the tradition of rock art, the origin of which can be traced back, at least in the European world, to the Upper Palaeolithic. In fact, likely precursors for the three-dimensional character of menhirs may be found in European Palaeolithic art. Feminine (Venus) figurines or, in a broader sense, some mobile art artefacts may be reasonably considered examples of such. If we conceive of menhirs as anthropomorphic symbols, an obvious difference between such symbols and those of earlier periods is the noticeable absence of a naturalistic character, an innovation shared by most Neolithic rock-art motifs.

The most significant innovation during the dawn of the Neolithic was, however, the scale of menhirs. The size of these monoliths has frequently led investigators to classify them as some kind of architecture which can be compared with megalithic enclosures. But this classification does not work well when we are faced with megalithic alignments or with single menhirs. We must remember, however, that architecture and sculpture are modern classifications, and menhirs could be, from our point of view, entities that bridge between these

Fig. 4.4. The single standing stone of Monte da Ribeira (Reguengos de Monsaraz)

classificatory concepts. The chronological sequence of megaliths observed in some European megalithic areas, specifically Brittany, Alentejo, and Algarve, begins with menhirs and ends with dolmens. This sequence could be translated as a development from sculpture to architecture, although some of the basic implications and meanings appear to have been retained.

The amount of necessary labour implied by the size of some menhirs and dolmens evokes another important feature of the Neolithic cultures—monumentality. This aspect has a close relationship with a newly emerging set of attitudes towards nature that are manifest in the Neolithic economy and that resulted from changes in the social use of the natural resources. These behaviors and attitudes appear to be directly related to an emerging trend toward changing landscapes and the need to establish anchors in space.

In contrast with other forms of Neolithic monumentality, megaliths involve the use of raw stones, suggesting a peculiar validation of the materiality itself and thus keeping a strong link with an important feature of rock art (Scarre 2003). Although conceived as symbols on their own, menhirs could also be used as canvases to paint or carve other symbols. As we shall see, groups of menhirs could also be arranged on the landscape to build large-scale sets of symbolic features. On such a level, menhirs evoke geoglyphs.

ALTERNATIVE SYMBOLS, ALTERNATIVE LANDSCAPES

Menhirs are not ubiquitous manifestations. Contemporaneous societies that shared similar developments did not invest in the same types of monuments. These different choices may be explained in some cases by differences in availability of raw materials; however, there are many situations where such explanations do not appear likely. In the case of menhirs in Central Alentejo, the notorious cultural specificity of the phenomenon within the context of Iberia can be attributed to a specific cultural background, substantiated on the Sado-Tejo late Mesolithic communities (M. Calado 2002, 2003, 2004). Though menhirs were not present in the Sado and Tejo estuaries—areas without available stone blocks—some evidence exists that wooden posts were used in the construction of ritual structures. These structures show some formal similarities to the layout of Alentejan megalithic enclosures (Calado 2004).

If the scope of inquiry is expanded, some poorly understood intra-regional singularities are identified that may address other questions. In Alentejo, menhirs seem to be restricted to granite outcrops, with virtually no exception. In the schistose landscapes, we find only stone carvings that are, interestingly, confined to the valley bottoms of main rivers (Calado 2003). In areas of quartzitic bedrock, artistic manifestations are reduced to paintings. Rockshelters located in mountainous environments appear to have been the preferred mediums for such symbolism (Oliveira 2003).

This panorama allows us to stress the roles of landscapes, and the different symbolic meanings they could convey, as active partners in the genesis of rock art. Carving, painting, and sculpture appear dependent on different raw materials, and therefore on landscapes, although it would also be possible to find alternate historical developments in these differences. When we map this observations we can easily conclude that they are not perfectly adjacent. In Alentejo, we find large areas that were occupied prehistorically that appear devoid of menhirs, carvings, or paintings, thus suggesting that at least some regions may have been incorporated in large territories where appropriate natural conditions were not available. For the moment, only the rock-art complex of the Guadiana (in parallel with the Tagus) seems to have begun during the

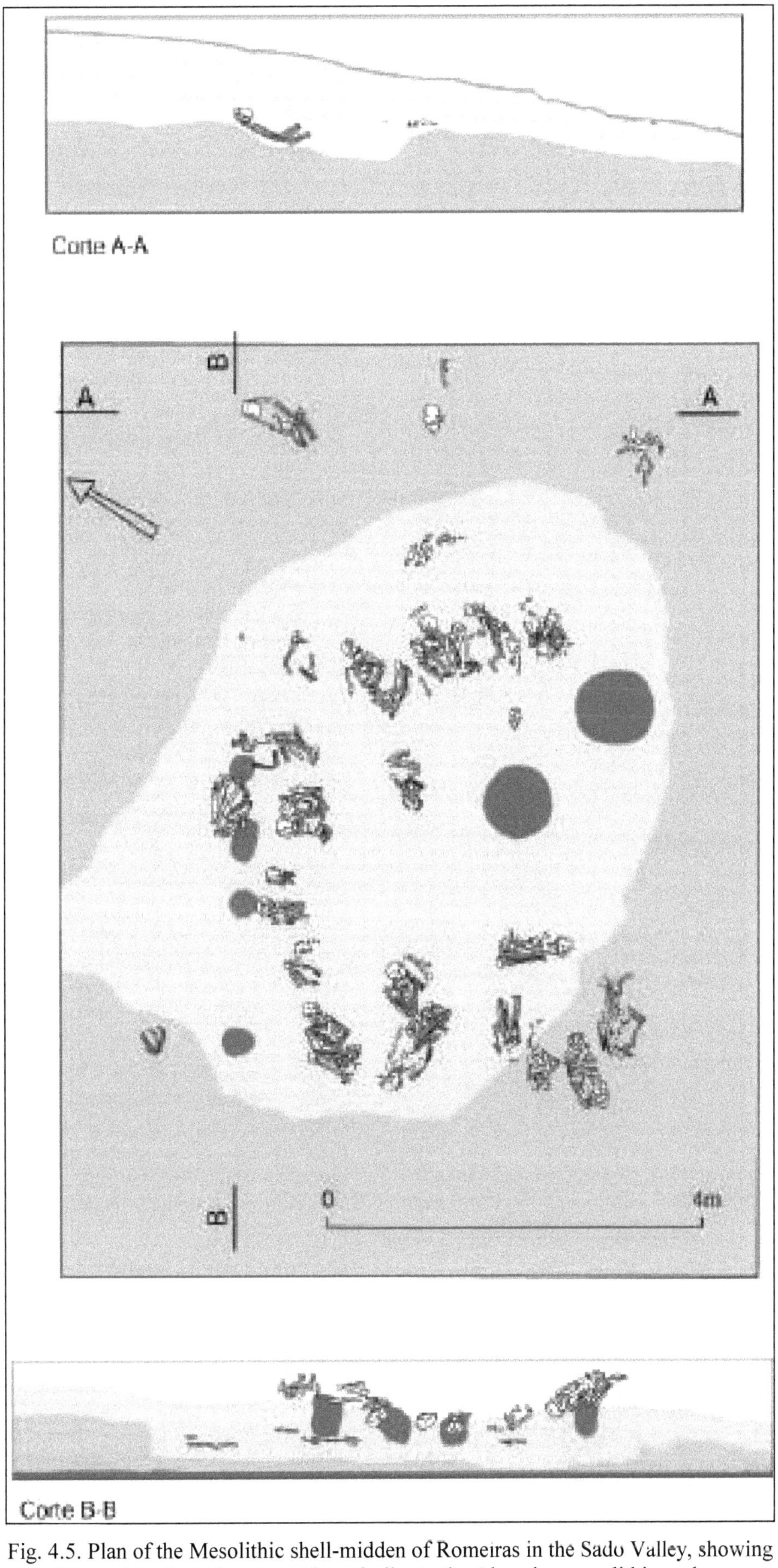

Fig. 4.5. Plan of the Mesolithic shell-midden of Romeiras in the Sado Valley, showing the horse-shoe shaped stone setting, similar to the Alentejan megalithic enclosures

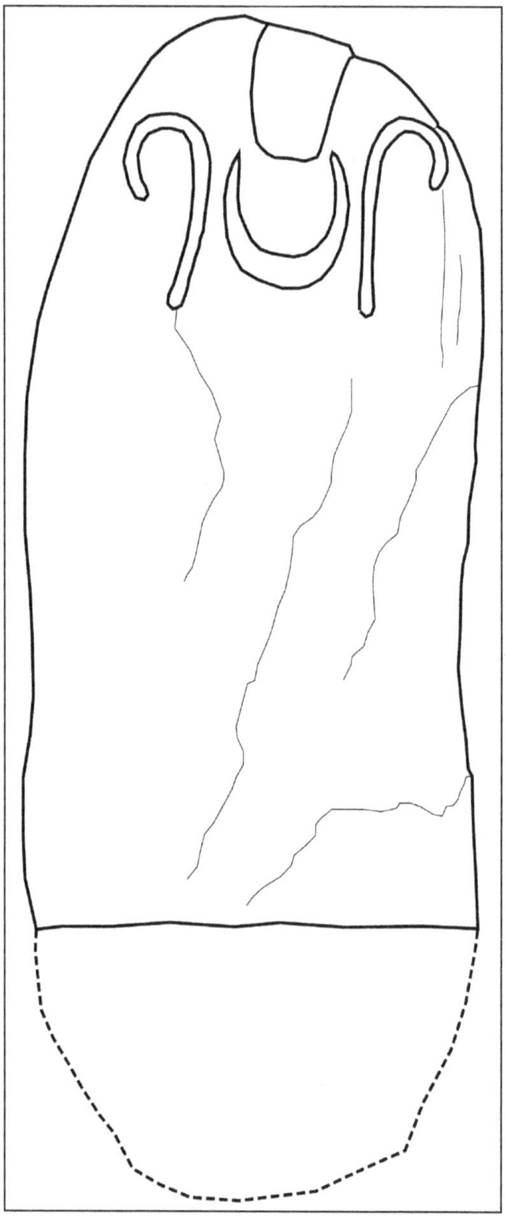

Fig. 4.6. Bas-relief motifs carved on a menhir from the enclosure of Vale Maria do Meio (Évora)

Palaeolithic. Here, appearances of paintings and menhirs are likely to be more limited within specific times and cultures.

Curiously, and somewhat contradictorily, we find almost no similarities between motifs carved on menhirs and those that are carved or painted in the other contexts. We previously suggested a Late Mesolithic genesis for part of the peculiar set of motifs, reinvented and amplified in a process of social fission, responsible for regional Mesolithic-Neolithic transitions (Calado 2003, 2004). Further suggesting the cultural specificity of each rock-art "kingdom" or territory is the virtual absence of Neolithic rock art in Escoural cave, despite the facts that the cave was occupied during the Early and Late Neolithic, and that is located only a few miles from Almendres.

References

BRADLEY, R., 1997a, *Rock Art and the Prehistory of Atlantic Europe: Signing the Land.* London: Routledge.

BRADLEY, R., 1997b, Symbols and Signposts—Understanding the Prehistoric Petroglyphs of the British Isles. In Renfrew, C. & Zubrow, E. (eds.), *The Ancient Mind. Elements of Cognitive Archaeology*. Cambridge: Cambridge University Press, p. 95-106.

BRADLEY, R., 1998a, Architecture, Imagination and the Neolithic World. In Mithen, S. (ed.), *Creativity in Human Evolution*. London: Routledge.

BRADLEY, R., 1998e, *The Significance of the Monuments*. London: Routledge.

BRANDHERM, D., 1995, Os chamados "báculos". Para uma interpretação simbólica-funcional. Trabalhos de Antropologia e Etnologia, Porto, 35, p. 89-94.

BUENO, R.P. & BALBÍN, B.R., 2002, L'Art mégalithique péninsulaire et l'Art mégalithique del a façade atlantique: un modèle de capillarité appliqué à l'Art post-paléolithique européen. *L'Anthropologie* 106, p. 603-646.

BUENO, R.P. & BALBÍN, B.R., 2003, Grafias y territórios megalíticos en Extremadura. Muita gente poucas antas? Origens, espaços e contextos do Megalitismo. *Actas do II Colóquio Internacional sobre Megalitismo.* Lisboa: IPA, p. 407-448.

CALADO, M., 2003, Entre o Céu e a Terra. Menires e Arte rupestre no Alentejo Central. In Calado, M. (ed.), *Sinais de Pedra.* Évora: Fundação Eugénio de Almeida.

CALADO, M., 2004, Menires do Alentejo Central: génese e evolução da paisagem megalítica regional. Lisboa: Faculdade de Letras da Universidade de Lisboa (Tese de doutoramento policopiada).

CASSEN, S., BOUJOT, C., & VAQUERO-LASTRES, J., 2000, Eléments d'architecture. Exploration d'un tertre funéraire à Lannec er Gadouer (Erdeven, Morbihan). Constructions et reconstructions dans le Néolitique morbihonnais. Propositions pour une lecture symbolique. Chauvigny: Association des Publications Chauvignoises.

CASSEN, S., & L'HELGOUAC'H, J., 1992, Du Symbole de la Crosse: chronologie, répartition et interprétation. *Revue Archeologique de l'Ouest.* Rennes 5, p. 223-235.

CAUBET, A., 2002, Naissance de la grande statuaire dans l'Orient ancien. In Philippon, A. (dir.), *Statues-menhirs, des enigmes de pierre venues du fond des ages*. Rodez: Éditions du Rouergue, p. 224-239.

CAUVIN, J., 1999, The Symbolic Foundations of the Neolithic Revolution in the Near East. In Kuijt, I. (ed.), *Life in Neolithic Farming Communities.* New York: Kluwer Academic, p. 235-261.

D'ANNA, A., 2002a, Les statues-menhirs: des dieux ou des homes? In Philippon, A. (dir.), *Statues-menhirs, des enigmes de pierre venues du fond des ages*. Rodez: Éditions du Rouergue, p. 252- 257.

D'ANNA, A., 2002b, Les statues-menhirs en Europe à la fin du Néolithique et au début de l'Âge du Bronze. In Philippon, A. (dir.), *Statues-menhirs, des enigmes de pierre venues du fond des ages*. Rodez: Éditions du Rouergue, p. 196-223.

D'ANNA, A., 2002c, Statues-menhirs? Stèles? Dalles anthropomorphes? Ou simplement sculptures préhistoriques? In Philippon, A. (dir.), *Statues-menhirs, des enigmes de pierre venues du fond des ages*. Rodez: Éditions du Rouergue, p. 52-53.

D'ANNA, A., & LEANDRI, F., 2000, Les alignements de menhirs du Sartenais. *Préhistoire Anthropologie Méditerranéennes* 9, p. 123-131.

D'ANNA, A., MARCHESI, H., & TRAMONI, P., 2000, Le site mégalithique de Renaghju à Sartène. *Préhistoire Anthropologie Méditerranéennes* 9, p. 141-146.

GOMES, M.V., 1994, Menires e cromeleques no complexo cultural megalítico português – trabalhos recentes e estado da questão. *Actas do Seminário "O Megalitismo no Centro de Portugal"*. Viseu, p. 317-342.

GOMES, M.V., 1996, Megalitismo do Barlavento Algarvio – Breve Síntese. *Setúbal Arqueológica* 11-12, p. 147-190.

LEWIS-WILLIAMS, J. & PEARCE, D., 2005, *Inside The Neolthic Mind: Consciousness, Cosmos and the Realm of the Gods*. London: Thames and Hudson.

OLIVEIRA, J., 1997, Datas absolutas de monumentos megalíticos da Bacia Hidrográfica do Rio Sever. In Balbín, R. & Bueno, P. (eds.), *Actas do II Congreso de Arqueologia Peninsular. TII-Neolítico, Calcolítico y Bronce*. Zamora: Fundación Rei Afonso Henriques, p. 229-239.

OLIVEIRA, J., 2003, A arte rupestre no contexto megalítico Norte-Alentejano. In Calado, M. (ed.), *Sinais de Pedra*. Évora: Fundação Eugénio de Almeida.

COLLADO GIRADO, H., 2003, Un nuevo ciclo de arte prehistórico en Extremadura: el arte rupestre de las sociedades de economía cazadora recolectora durante el Holoceno inicial como precedente del arte rupestre esquemático en Extremadura. In Calado, M. (ed.), *Sinais de Pedra*. Évora: Fundação Eugénio de Almeida.

OUZMAN, S., 1998, Towards a mindscape of landscape: Rock-Art as Expression of World-Understanding. In Chipindale, C. & Taçon, P. (eds.), *The Archaeology of Rock-art*. Cambridge: CUP, p. 30-41.

PHILIPPON, A., 2002, L'Homme en Grand. In Philippon, A. (dir.), *Statues-menhirs, des enigmes de pierre venues du fond des ages*. Rodez: Éditions du Rouergue, p. 8-17.

SCARRE, C., 2003, Monumentos de pedra "rude" e pedras troféu: a relação com os materiais nos megalitos da Europa ocidental. In Calado, M. (ed.), *Sinais de Pedra*. Évora: Fundação Eugénio de Almeida.

VERHOEVEN, M., 2002, Ritual and Ideology in the Pre-Pottery Neolithic B of the Levant and Southeast Anatolia. *Cambridge Archaeological Journal* 12/2, p. 233-258.

ZVELEBIL, M., 1998, What's in a Name: the Mesolithic, the Neolithic, and Social Change at the Mesolithic-Neolithic Transition. In Edmonds, M. & Richards, C. (eds.), *Understanding the Neolithic of North-Western Europe*. Glasgow: Cruithne Press, p. 1-36.

"THE-TEETH-UNDER-THE-SKY": MOUNTAIN STELES AND GREEN STONE WORKINGS IN THE KUZNETSKII ALATAU, SOUTHERN SIBERIA (KHAKASSIA, RUSSIA)

S. CASSEN

CNRS (Unité Mixte de Recherche 6566), Laboratoire de Préhistoire et Protohistoire de l'Ouest de la France, Université de Nantes, BP 81227, 44312 NANTES cedex 3 (France)

serge.cassen@univ-nantes.fr

W.M. TORGUNAKOV

Novokuznetsk, Kemerovo State University (Russia)

P. PÉTREQUIN

CNRS, Laboratoire de Chrono-écologie, Besançon (France)

B. LASNIER

Laboratoire de Gemmologie, Université de Nantes (France)

"Les-dents-sous-le-ciel": stèles de montagnes et exploitation de roches tenaces dans le Kuznetskii Alatau en Sibérie méridionale (Khakassie, Russie)

***Résumé**: A l'extrémité méridionale du massif montagneux Kuznetskii Alatau, au nord du village de Balyksu en Khakassie, plusieurs stèles en granite, érigées à une date inconnue puis chutées, ont été découvertes sur les monts Taskil, à 1500 m d'altitude. La découverte de filons de roche éruptive (vaugnerite de couleur vert sombre à vert clair) exploités par l'homme à une époque indéterminée, mais probablement ancienne dans la mesure où ce sont des ébauches de lames de hache qui furent ici préparées, laisse penser que cette juxtaposition de faits dans un environnement inhabitable en dehors de la courte saison d'été n'est pas le simple fruit du hasard...*

***Mots-clés**: Stèles, lames de haches, vaugnerite, Sibérie méridionale*

***Abstract**: At the southernmost end of the Kuznetskii Alatau mountain range, to the north of the village of Balyksu in Khakassia, in the Taskyl mountains, several fallen granite steles (up to eight meters in height), erected at an unknown date, were discovered at an altitude of 1500 m. The discovery of human workings in veins of volcanic rock (vaugnerite, from dark green to light green in colour) from an uncertain period, (but probably prehistoric since there are rough-hewn outlines of axe heads here) allows us to think that this juxtaposition of artifacts in an environment uninhabitable apart from the short summer season is not the fruit of mere chance.*

***Key words**: Stèles, lames de haches, vaugnerite. Steles, axe heads, vaugnerite*

THE PROBLEM

The study of the first monumental architecture (funerary, "symbolic systems", etc.) in the Western Europe merges gradually with the astonishing development of the perennial structures of stones, historically tied together under the term megalithic.

Much of this architecture is understood in terms of nature and function related to megalithic tombs, one of the greatest enigmas of European prehistory remains the "fields of menhirs" (*Champs de menhirs* in 19th century terms). Carnac is today the primary example of such menhirs. It presents a spectacular sight, consisting of single erect stones in multiple rows. These alignments are ill understood prehistoric symbols. Simultaneously they represent a symbol of the failure of western archaeology, which has been unable to deepen the understanding of these structures since the first interpretations were made at the beginning of the 19th century. Therefore, our first objective is to look at the basic questions through the cognitive sciences. The aim of the research to correct the predictive aspects of a model and prepare a theory on these alignments.

The erection and alignments of a monoliths or a monoxyles is a structural constant in many societies all over the world, sometimes even in strongly distinct social contexts. The alignment of standing stones is an additional architectural fact common to many different areas and different periods. The archaeologist interested in the Neolithic seeing these complexes may compare the Breton menhir alignments with those which are not immediately related (Tibet, Altaï, Turkey, Choukotka, Peru, etc.).

This article focuses on a vast geographical area (Khakassia, Altaï, Kazakhstan, western Mongolia – Fig. 1) and the discovery of an area where the *stele* remains an object of worship, sometimes for millenia after its erection.

TASKYL: HISTORY OF A CURIOSITY

At the southernmost end of a mountainous region (Kuznetskii Alatau), the surroundings of the (recent) village of Balyksu are well-known for their old mine workings in this very complex geological zone, and also for rivers abounding in fish (the proper name of the village), for their forests full of game, and for the beauty of their landscapes. There is a total apparent absence of archeological sites containing steles or some famous kurgans. These sites are more to the east and south-east, a few hours distant by car, towards the valley of the Askiz River and the Abakan (Fig. 5.1).

The trip towards the summit of Taskyl (1505 m) – the khakas form – *Tashyl*, variable *Taskyl*, from the old Turkish origin is composed of two words: *tas* – the mange, baldness, the empty place (in the tuvin languages – *tas* means also flat, smooth), ground without vegetation (in areas of Khahasia, Tuva, Altaï) and *Hyr/kyr* – mountain, height. One can say that *Tashyl* means the collection of snow-covered peaks, the tops of the mountains (crest line, summit) stripped of vegetation (Murzaev 1984) requires 5 to 6 hours walking over difficult terrain after the last houses in the valley (400 m). The dense forest of coniferous and leafy trees progressively gives place to more and more squat coniferous trees, before finally disappearing on the surrounding tops of which some exceed the 2000 m, a few kilometers in the north of Taskyl. It is on the ridge as one passes from the south-western to the north-eastern slope, on a track used by hunters (and collectors of wild berries), between the two prominences which mark the end of this chain, while arriving since the south, that we had noticed in 2003 a long recumbent block whose length and aspect seemed to be out of place with the surrounding blocks. Just beyond this site on the col, there were two other standing and leaning stones which attracted our attention on this same slope. After we had taken some photographs and made a quick visit of the top, our lack of equipment obliged us to begin our descent down the Tierentsu valley which river, at Balyksu, join the Chora and Balyksu rivers to form the Tom, as first a mountain torrent and then as a large river which flows northwards and later joins the Ob which flows into the Arctic Sea. And moreover, this small chain of Tegri Tichi (or Tegir Tich) is the group of celestial teeth, "the-teeth-under-the-sky" in the Russian variation. There are three "teeth" in Kouzntski Alatau – the Large, the Middle and Higher, all three of which form a range which the native population, the Chortsi, call *Tegri Tichi* (Murzaev 1984). Tegri-Tichi – formed by *tegri* from Chorsk-Turkish origin (an alternative *tengri*) – which means "the sky, celestial" and from the Chorsk *tich* "tooth". Mongolian *téngèr* may also be translated as the sky, celestial (Chabalin 1994, p. 177). The Russian topographic map shows this ethnic name as Tiger Tich. Teren Kazirskii (Teren – Kazyr) is from the Chorsk *Teren* meaning "deep", and *Kazyr* "river", that is to say the deep, impetuous river (Chabalin 1994). This small mountain chain called "The-teeth-under-the-sky" which comes to its end at is located at the end of the line of the watershed between these two immense rivers, the Ob and the Yenisei, which are among the longest in the world. An extraordinary site (Pereladova *et al.* 1997).

A second expedition in 2005 allowed us to carry out a precise survey of the large stele and the slabs whose positions did not appear natural to us. Their positioning and their morphology confirmed our first impression that the site had been fashioned by man. Such an idea, such an architectural project, if not inappropriate in the wider context of Khakassia and within the main or adjacent valleys, give rise to astonishment at the top of these mountains without special attraction in our current field of references, except the hunting of wild goat (*Ovis ammon* and *Capra sibirica*), siberian roe deer (*Capreolus capreolus pygargus*), carnivores (*Canis lupus, Vulpes vulpes* and *Otocolobus manu*) and Asian brown bears (*Ursus actros*). Even these activities however do not give sufficient motivation, in ethnographic literature, for the erection of stones of such a nature.

Guided by a worked intuition which would like to connect two apparently unconnected phenomena:

- on one hand the studies directed by P. and A.M. Pétrequin in New Guinea (1993) and in the Alps (Pétrequin *et al.* 1997, 2002) which have shown the interest that reveals a direct access to certain types of rocks in mountain within the framework of manufacture and of exchanges of socially developed ("prestige") goods like axe heads or ornamental objects,
- and on the other hand the firmly established relationship of a greater density of these artifacts in a region of Europe (Morbihan, France) where the most colossal worked standing stones are concentrated (Boujot, Cassen 1992), we started a search of the ground to seek possible indicators able to contribute to an "explanation" of such a monumental presence in an impossible place. Considerable heaps of stone splinters were rather quickly providing us with interesting replies…

OBSERVATIONS ON MONOLITHS

In a rocky environment which cannot however be compared with the granitic chaos visible on the slopes, in a dense lawn of vegetation developed on a ground covered with sufficient earth to allow rodents and lagomorphs (*Ochotona alpina*) to dig their burrows, there are four blocks located on the col, one lying, two upright, the fourth leaning at a great angle, with a last stone upright on the eastern slope of the summit itself. These stones were respectively numbered from 1 to 5 (Fig. 5.2).

The rock employed is from the local substratum, a leucocratic rock with fine grain (some mm), with grainy structure. On a petrographic slide, the mineralogical

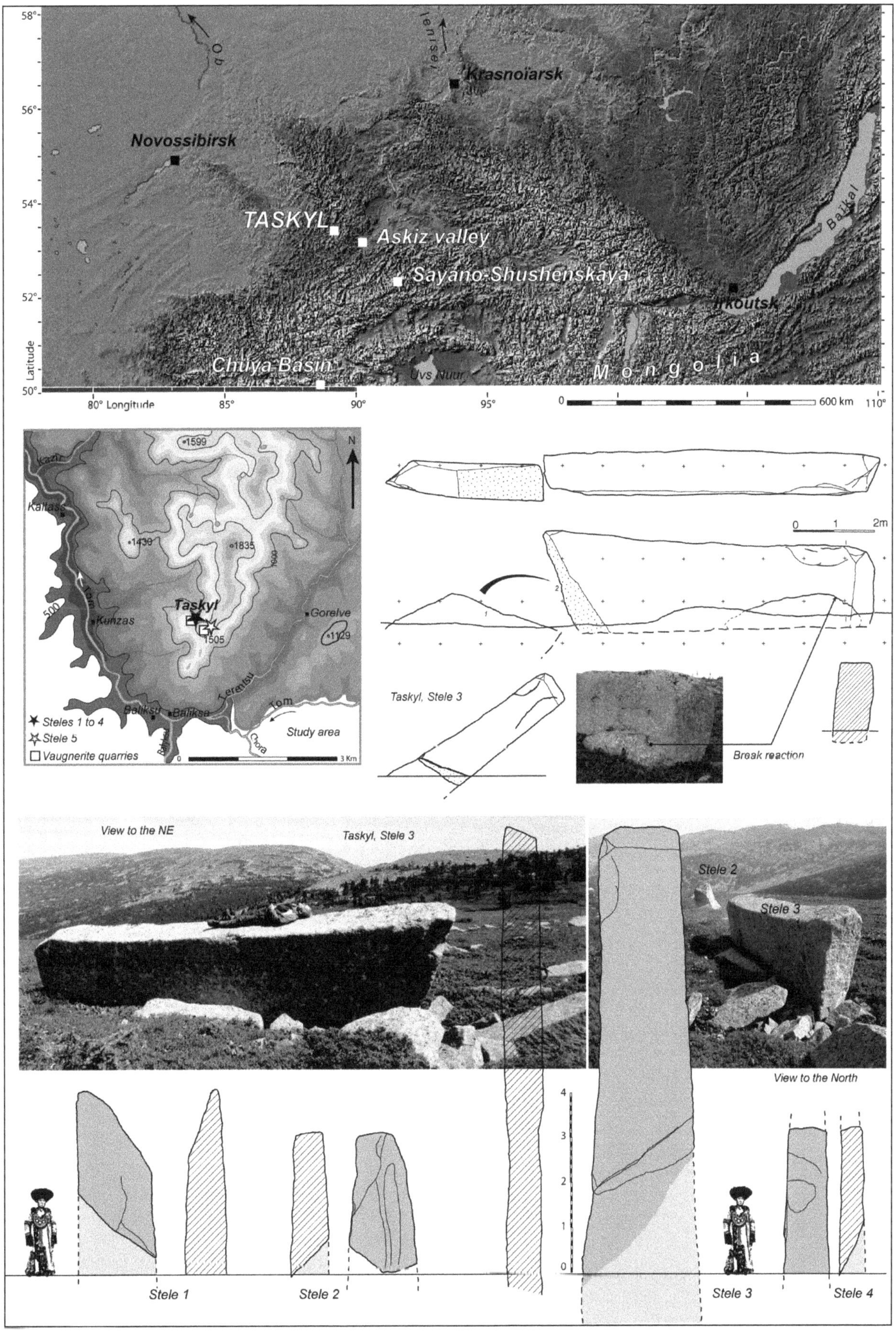

Fig. 5.1. Situation of Taskyl montain, south of Kuznetskii Alatau (map after Ray Steiner, John Hopkins University 1993) plan and elevation of stele 3, with simulation of erected position

composition is plagioclase dominating; orthoclase (microcline maximum); biotite; hornblende; sphene, as well as minerals of transformation of plagioclases (pidotes, chlorites ...). Therefore, it is a granitic volcanic rock with a grano-dioritic tendency.

In spite of spending one night spent in this spot, our stay was very short and we therefore chose to make the survey of the four stones in a group on the basis of two orthonormalized axes framing the site. We measured the site with a portable infra-red distance-meter (Leica Disto Classica) placed on a light photographic tripod. We made manual surveys which were on a scale of 1:20 and related to the steles only.

Stele 1

Stele 1 is a slab with trapezoidal section (Fig. 1), with a very sharply pointed tip, leaning markedly towards south-west, in accordance with the direction of fall which we know in Brittany for steles of such size established on a steep slope, the centre of gravity of the stele having been slightly shifted towards interior of the slope to ensure the stability of the monolith (Cassen, Vaquero 2003).

A wedge is still highly visible at the base. A control excavation around the bottom of the wedge could help archaeologists decide on its definitive status.

Stele 2

This stone with quadrangular section has a roughly triangular form, there again also markedly leaning towards the top of the slope, and supported by another block wedged in the ground. So close that one could ask whether it could be the same natural structure, simply cracked, eroded and open. It is none of these; the two faces in contact have no common point, and none of the surfaces can adapt to any other in their current positions: these blocks are quite separate from each other, and without doubt the one which interests us has been erected. On the other hand, it is difficult at the present time to be able to imagine that the block hidden in the ground at the base can be the root of the stele. An control excavation at the base could again help us decide on its final status.

Stele 3

Stele 3 is the first stele encountered when crossing over the col coming from south-west it offers the obvious elements of proof against a natural outcrop (Fig. 5.1):

- its unusual, lengthened and parallelepipedic form
- the presence of a crack, "recent" in the geomorphological history of the stele, visible towards its distal end, which may have been caused by a percussive shock coming up from the ground
- a concave top testifying a possible erosive process while in the vertical position
- finally, and most of all, at the base of its proximal end, the presence of another implanted block whose uppermost surface is the exact negative counterpart of the sharp break observable at the widened base of this 8 m long monolith.

The thickness of the stone could be measured by the means of small probes which give a depth from 15 to 20 cm before finding the opposite edge, depression caused more by the growth of vegetation and the settling of sediments.

If the monolith were restored to its connection with its foot, it would virtually give a shape leaning in the oblique direction of the slope, in this place less marked than with steles 1 and 2. Originally, stele 3 must have had at least 10 m showing above ground.

Stele 4

Stele 4 is a naturally regular parallelepiped (Fig. 2), broken at its distal end, erected but very markedly leaning in the exact direction of the slope at this place. One observes a basin shaped erosion on its southern edge, of course in a position having no function, proof of a displacement and reversal of the original stone.

Pseudo-stele 5

Planted in a rocky chaos on the eastern slope of Taskyl, the "stele" characteristic is not obvious in the same manner as for its neighbours set up on the col. Although from observation of the blocks in the rocky scree we did not expect to find this type of erection, we do not discount that it might indeed be a natural phenomenon. Its exposed site, however, just at the bottom of the worked vein of vaugnerite and its very visible setting both when ascending from the Terensu river and when ascending from the north from the Kunzass river, give rise to the idea that it might have been erected by humans, and might be comparable with the *inuksuit* of the north Canadian societies (Nunavut), stones raised and/or heaped which, according to their disposition, show the way, a cache of meat, a good place to hunt, etc (Hallendy 2001)...

Observations on the worked mineral veins

Western vein

Some 30 m to the west of the group of four steles described above, a bedrock may be distinguished from the surrounding granite, partly by its color – dark on the weathered surfaces, green where freshly broken – and partly by its very fine grain. It seems to come to the surface, exposed by erosion, in the form of long blocks emerging from the granite. There is no visible trace to make us think that the site could have been worked by man but the survey in this direction was too limited by the execrable climatic conditions prevailing at the time of our arrival for us to take up a definitive position on this subject.

Fig. 5.2. Stele 3 with indication of a basin of erosion in the granite, in a non functional position two specimen of axe rough-out in vaugnerite picture of a workshop on the top of Taskyl, directly on the vaugnerite source comparisons with steles from Khakassia and Altaï (photos S. Cassen and Novossibirsk Regional Museum)

One notable fact must be mentioned. A recumbent parallelepipedic block, taken from this bedrock, is upright on a granitic outcrop. It is clearly not a natural formation the sedimentation and the revegetation at the base of this small "stele" do not give evidence either that it might have been recently erected by a visitor.

The samples taken from this location made it possible to recognize:

- a microgrenue rock with subdoleritic structure
- plagioclases damouritized in interlaced slats
- some rare ouralitized clinopyroxenes
- the presence of chlorite.

It is a volcanic rock with vaugnerite type veins.

East vein

We are at the topographic summit of Taskyl (Fig. 5.2). A broad vein of the same rock, coloured from grey to sustained green where freshly broken, appears in inclusion in the granite. This time there are obvious traces of working, and it is possible to count positions where stone cutting took place at the top and on the northern slope and there is a collection of thousands of fragments over 3 to 4 m^2 and the early stages of rough hewing, showing extraction and the first working of the rock for the manufacture of axe blades (the various manufacturing processes will not be described here and we can limit them to summary knapping).

The cutting cannot be attributed to any metal instrument, but on the other hand we did not collect any lithic hammers. Working this very hard stone was obviously facilitated by the type of vaugnerite intrusions which can be extracted in bars of 50-70 cm in length, suitable to be cut along the natural sidelong grain of the stone, also avoiding later sawing (the cutting is however very difficult, carried out in experimentally and very hastily on the spot with the aid of other vaugnerite blocks, the granite being evidently useless). However, we undertook no sampling nor did we survey this sector which would have been an immense task. We took care to draw one rough hewed shape (Fig. 5.2), a rare piece no other object was taken except the rock samples.

Vein of Tegri Tichi

On right bank of Kazir river and forming part of the Tegri Tichi mountains which had been visible since Taskyl, we discovered an enormous bed of vaugnerite of a very beautiful green colour under the cover of vegetation as a result of recent ground slippage caused by the driving of a track for the purpose of exploiting forest resources and a talc quarry. It would be necessary to prospect this new source, eventually located at a higher and accessible altitude as an outcrop, to determine if it could be profitable.

ARCHAEOLOGICAL DIAGNOSES

Two archaeological entities are juxtaposed in a space and a place offering no obvious evidence of a previous human establishment, and no current occupation by people (either Russian speakers or native). The exception is the evidence of hunters′ and gatherers′ tracks and the addition of a geodetic point made of wood during the Fifties.

A space covered by snow in long winter, accessible in short summer only.

The blocks detached from the local substrate, without obvious displacement from their place of extraction, were erected at an unknown date, and are today either leaning or fallen these are human work these steles have a "function" unknown to us since the funerary character that it is usual to attribute to such steles in neighbouring areas is not apparent in the site of today, because it is without low mounds or cairns.

The veins of vaugnerite accessible at the surface on the summits were worked at an unknown time, and most probably for the making of axeheads, which would lead us to place the period of extraction at some time in regional Prehistory ("Neolithic").

If there is nothing to connect these two facts – the steles on the one hand and the working of hard rock on the other hand, because we have neither control excavations nor regional reference points – their juxtaposition in an improbable area puzzles the observer, *a fortiori* because they are in a geographical area without known archaeological antecedent, either in the valleys already cited, or of course at altitude.

ANALOGICAL CONNECTIONS AND PERSPECTIVES

The studies on carvings in central Asia, particularly in the Russian Federation (Kubarev 1987, 1988, 1997 Tcheremisinee 1993) and recent surveys carried out both on the Ykok plateau and in the basin of the rivers Katun and Chuya some 400 km to the south in Altaï (Bourgeois *et al.* 2003 Molodin *et al.* 2004), or older studies only 80 km to the south-east of Balyksa in the valley of Askiz, or Minusinsk basin (Kovaleva 2006), showed the dynamic development of the cultures (generally recognized as dating from the Bronze Age) which gave origin to these systems of erected stones, which are generally integrated with funerary complexes of mounds and cairns grouped together in necropolises.

The unusual dimensions of stele 3 could give rise to doubt about the authenticity of human intervention, particularly because the neighbouring stones (steles 1, 2 and 4) are difficult to distinguish from those blocks in the chaos of debris or those standing out from the outcrops as a result of wind erosion giving rise to this vision of natural architecture.

We however recall a narrative of an expedition made in what is now Kazakhstan, in the 1850s, in the Kora valley, 800 km to the south, where a group of steles marked the spirits of travellers as well as of the inhabitants of these mountains since the group was the object of strongly held beliefs and living legends when they were discovered by Thomas Witlam Atkinson. The astonishing dimension of the largest stele (76 imperial feet, around 22 m), unknown to this day in the literature, gives the impression however, on first reading, that it was the object of an obvious exaggeration, even though the illustration emphasises the size of the stones (Fig. 5.1), like the contemporary romantic illustrations of the megalithic sites of western Europe. But the author is also an attentive and creditworthy commentator on historical, geographical and political issues, and about those referring to human habits and settlements, and so one does not see why his evaluations and description of the site would be false, or entirely erroneous, when he has already observed and described in the steppes the different kurgans and other steles whose dimensions are reliable and verifiable today. We believe that there is something to redetermine there on the ground (mountainous but in valley), and to rediscover what can still be kept from the statements of this traveller; perhaps with smaller dimensions.

However this may be, the perennially of the "occupation" of the same spaces over many centuries is an outstanding character pointed out by many observers in Central Asia and Siberia, and particularly in connection with these wood or stone steles (Egorov 1987 Kubarev 2004 Seleznev 2000). It is noticeable that a certain part of the population holds in veneration these steles as well as paintings and engravings in their shelters and on the rock cliffs (Fig. 5.2). This veneration brings us back to the situation in Brittany, which is the object of our research, and makes us bracket together in a common reality these analogous functions of the human imagination, which may be able to throw light on the question which we are trying to solve in Morbihan.

Isolated standing stones, stones set up vertically or lengthways and deliniating the mounds of tumuli, lines of steles connecting structures however diachronic, all situations should be relevant to observers who want to understand the enigmas of Neolithic alignments of western Europe. Here in Khakassia, on grounds scarcely touched by culture and ceremony, archaeology *in the landscape* is a given whose meaning is arrived at only through analysing the objects themselves, in other words a promising way to test a guiding principle. This could be our first objective for the future.

The working at altitude of hard, green stone for polishing axeheads is another unexpected subject for investigation. Current investigations in France and Italy were quickly related albeit distantly (Pétrequin *et al.* 2005). Of course, these areas have a geology comparable with the European Alps and hard, green stones are not absent from their riverbeds (rock strata are also very difficult to detect and to access under the cover of dense forest). But these riverstones would not be held in high regard by societies who valued the difficulty of access to untouched remote sources, their eventual establishment privileged in the mythical and distant topography of the landscapes, and in a given system of beliefs, as well as the length of the blades and the intrinsic quality of the rock to be cut, then to be polished. Blades of such value, socially speaking, are known in the vast space of Siberia, in universally attractive stones like nephrite or jadeitite a "jadeite" which traversed nearly 1800 km to arrive in the tombs of 5th and 4th millenia BCE Europe, or to constitute deposits hidden in other improbable places. A rare jadeite on the planet – except the famous deposits worked in South Mandalay in Burma, another source is known in Russia, at Pysyerka in the north of the Urals with several tens of known outcrops (Dobretsov, Ponomareva 1965), and another in Kazakhstan, at Itmurundy, close to the Chinese border, a site besides not very far away from the large stones, possibly steles, described by W. Atkinson – a rare jadeite but the bed of which was discovered in West Sayan and in the banks of the Ieniséi (Dobretsov 1963), some 200 km to the south-east of Balyksu, is today the only one in commercial exploitation in Siberia and in this part of Central Asia for the great benefit of the Chinese consumers (Hughes *et al.* 2000, Hughes, Kouznetsov 2000).

In the case of Taskyl, one can wonder about the qualities of this stone which cannot bear comparison with the jadeitite or nephrite which was so highly valued. However, vaugnerite is not a common stone (Montel 1998), and one will remember that in Grandrieu, Lozère (France), to limit ourselves to a field that we ourselves know and can immediately compare, a very hard, dark green "syenite" was mined – in fact an intrusion of vaugnerite (lamprophyres group) in the granite of Margeride – which was used historically and famously for making stones for tombs, lending itself to a polished surface much admired by the tastes of the XXe century (Perrier 1996).

Neither does one know what type of instrument could be transferred or exchanged at a distance of some tens or hundreds of kilometres from there (recut blades? finely polished?). There is much to be done in the study of the regional collections scattered through the museums of several cities (Bysk, Barnaul, Novokuznetsk, Novos-sibirsk, Abakan, etc. as well as the Mongolian or Chinese part of the area of study). One suspects that there must have been very strong reasons to overcome the great difficulties of access to the stone deposits at Taskyl, going well beyond the strict use of material for making tools of usual size and ordinary polishing. Ethno-archaeology on polished axes concluded that it is the social context (and male competitiveness), which establish the value of these polished tools in relation to their sites of extraction, and the ability of these tool-symbols to cross cultural boundaries, irrespective of the manufacturing techniques used (Pétrequin *et al.* 2002). The presence of axe representation – even metallic arms/tools – on standing stones in the Yustyd valley (Altaï – Fig. 5.2) belongs to the same family of explanations.

In the European Neolithic, the problem also seems to be connected with complex and ritually-charged techniques, and the resulting axeheads have formed part of competitive exchanges between individuals in stratified societies, where the axe as a tool has a powerful social significance, and is seen as a material expression of the power of the elite, and of ancestral power (Cassen 2000 Pétrequin *et al.* 2005). One cannot nevertheless conclude that we are observing a working at altitude which marks the beginning of the chain of the exchanges and circulation of socially developed goods, still indicated by the "prestige" which surrounds them (while they generally take part of payments of marriage or compensations, etc.). In any case, "richness" and wealth are not absent in the regional history of this area, as shown by the gigantic tombs and sometimes impressive steles which are a characteristic of Central Asia, without mentioning here the Chinese tombs within the "Jade kingdoms" or in particular the remote maritime culture of Longshan, where blades (with a perforated extremity) in nephrite and jadeitite, some of which are considered to originate from the lake Baïkal area in Russia including our West Sayan region (Cf. the jadeitite sources from Sayano-Shushenskaya dam – Mirsky 1965 Thorp, Vinograd 2001 Liu, Li 2004 – Of course, nephrite stone occurs naturally in Jiangsu and Zhejiang Chinese provinces, particularly in the areas near Lake Tai), and were accumulated from the 5th millenium onwards in a manner so similar to the Morbihan deposits.

Steles and axeheads sometimes take on other roles, sometimes exchanging their anthropomorphic status, or their sexual character – male (often) or female – and play on the three ages of human construction, marking the thresholds between past and future. It is the reason why the badly understood juxtaposition of, on one hand the famous Er Lannic stele hemycircles in Morbihan, and on the other hand rare and beautiful sawn and polished fibrolite on the same site (Le Rouzic 1930), is enlightened by the briefly described situation in Taskyl while in another time, for another space, other steles in line, along the banks of Lake Neuchâtel in Switzerland (Joye, Grau, Bitterli 2005), are still taken as a reference point for work on stone for the manufacture of axeheads, several centuries after the introduction of the alignment of menhirs …

To compare the incomparable is simply the risky and promising way for those who want to understand the basic music. Green and hard rocks, rare because inaccessible under the sky… Mother-rocks located in mountains and commemorated by steles, maybe one of the origins of monumentality…

Appendix

"Having travelled onward several miles, I arrived at a part of the valley where the Kora makes a bend toward the cliffs on the north, leaving, a space of about 200 yards in width, between the base of the rocks and the river. As I approached this spot, I was almost induced to believe that the works of the Giants were before me, for five enormous stones. were standing isolated and on end, the first sight of which gave me the idea that their disposition was not accidental, and that a master mind had superintended the erection--the group being in perfect keeping with the scene around. One of these blocks would have made a tower large enough for a church, its height being 76 feet above the ground, and it measured 24 feet on one side and 19 feet on the other. It stood 73 paces from the base of the cliffs, and was about 8 feet out of the perpendicular, inclining towards the river. The remaining four blocks varied from 45 to 50 feet in height, one being 15 feet square and the rest somewhat less. Two of these stood upright, the others were leaning in different directions, one of them so far that it had nearly lost its equilibrium.

A sixth mass of still larger dimensions was lying half buried in the ground; on this, some young pieta trees had taken root and were growing luxuriantly. About two hundred yards to the eastward, three other blocks were lying, and beneath one was a cavity many a family in Kopal would have considered a splendid dwelling. Not far from these stood a pile of stones undoubtedly the work of man, as a great quantity of quartz blocks had been used, with other materials, in its construction. It was circular, 42 feet in diameter and 28 feet high, shaped like a dome: a circle of quartz blocks had been formed on the ground, enclosing a space ten feet wide all round the tomb. Finding such a tumulus in this valley surprised me greatly; it could not have been the grave of a chief of the present race, but was as ancient as those I had found on the steppe." (Atkinson 1860, p.117)."

References

ATKINSON, THOMAS W., 1860, Travels in the Region of the Upper and Lower Armour and the Russian Acquisitions on the Comfits of India & China; With Adventures with Mountain Kirghis and the Manjoors, Myanmars, Toumzamtz, Gold, and Gelyaks, the Hunting and Pastoral Tribes. Reprint. Delhi: Asian Educational Services, 2001.

BAUER, M., 1895, On the jadeite and other rocks from Tawmaw in Upper Burma, *Records of the Geological Survey of India,* vol. 28, pp. 91-105.

BOUJOT, C., CASSEN, S., 1992, Le Développement des premières architectures funéraires monumentales en France occidentale. In: *Paysans et Bâtisseurs. L'émergence du Néolithique atlantique et les origines du Mégalithisme.* Actes du XVIIe colloque interrégional sur le Néolithique. Vannes 29-31 octobre 1990. Rennes: Revue Archéo. de l'Ouest, Supp. n° 5, 1992, p. 195-211.

BOURGEOIS, I., L. CAMMAERT, C. MASSART, J.H. MIKKELSEN & W. VAN HUELE, 2000, *Ancient Nomads of the Altai Mountains. Belgian-Russian Multidisciplinary Archaeological Research on the Scytho-Siberian Culture*. Bruxelles: Royal Museums of art and History, Monographs in General Prehistory 5.

CASSEN, S., 2000, Terminaison. In: Cassen (dir.), Eléments d'architecture (Exploration d'un tertre funéraire à Lannec er Gadouer, Erdeven, Morbihan. Constructions et reconstructions dans le Néolithique morbihannais. Propositions pour une lecture symbolique). Chauvigny: Editions chauvinoises, Mémoire 19, p. 737-752.

CASSEN, S., VAQUERO, J., 2003, Les Marches du Palais. Recherches archéologiques sur alignements de stèles et tertres funéraires néolithiques autour de la baie de Quiberon (Morbihan, 2000-2002). Nantes: Ed. Taskil – Laboratoire de Préhistoire, Université de Nantes, 166 p., 135 fig., 4pl coul.

CHABALIN, V.M., 1994, Les Secrets des noms de la terre de Kouznetsk (in russian). Kemerovo.

DOBRETSOV, N.L., 1963, Mineralogy, petrography and genesis of ultrabasic rocks, jadeites, and albitites from the Borus Mountain Range (the West Sayan), *Proceedings of the Institute of Geology and Geophysics* (Academia Scientifica USSR, Siberian Branch), vol. 15, 1963, pp. 242-316.

DOBRETSOV, N.L., PONOMAREVA, L.G., 1965, Comparative characteristics of jadeite and associated rocks from Polar Ural and Near-Balkhash Region, *Institute of Geology and Geophysics* (Academia Scientifica USSR, Siberian Branch, Trudy), vol. 31, 1965, pp. 178-243.

EGOROV, G.M., 1987, *Altaïskii kraï*. Moscou: Profizdat (Touristckie rayoni CCCP).

HALLENDY, N., 2001, *Inuksuit. The Silent Messengers of the Arctic*. Vancouver: Ed. Douglas & McIntyre.

HUGHES, W., KOUZNETSOV, N., 2000, From Russia with Jade. *GemKey Magazine* , Vol. 3, No. 1, pp. 58–66.

HUGHES, W., GALIBERT, O., BOSSHART, G., WARD, F., OO, T., SMITH, M., THYE SUN, T., HARLOW, G., 2000, Burmese Jade: The Inscrutable Gem. *Gems & Gemology*, Vol. 36, No. 1, pp. 2–26.

JOYE, C., GRAU BITTERLI, M.-H., 2005, Produire des outils polis en contexte mégalithique: les deux structures excavées de Bevaix/Treytel-A Sugiez (poster 43). *In: 28e Colloque interrégional sur le Néolithique (Internéo)*, 1 et 2 octobre 2005, Université de Neuchâtel.

KOVALEVA, O.V., 2006, Petroglyphs of the Barsuchy Log Mound. *Archaeology, Ethnology & Anthropology of Eurasia* 1 (25), p. 110-116.

KUBAREV, V.D., 1987, *Antropomorfnye khvostatye sushestva altaiskikh gor*. Pervobytnoie iskusstvo. Antropomorfnye isobrazenia. Novosibirsk.

KUBAREV, V.D., 1988, *Drevnie rospisi Karakola*. Novosibirsk.

KUBAREV, V.D., 1997, *Kamennye izvayaniya Altaya: Kratkii katalog*. Gorno-Altaisk: Ak-Chechek.

KUBAREV, V.D., 2004, Ancient steles and sculptures in the ceremonies and superstitions of central asian peoples. *Eurasia* 1 (17), p. 28-38.

LE ROUZIC, Z., 1930, Carnac. Restaurations faites dans la région. Les Cromlechs d'Er Lannic, commune d'Arzon, de 1923 à 1926. Vannes: Imp. Lafolye, 1930.

LIU, LI, 2004, *The Chinese Neolithic: Trajectories to Early States*. Cambridge: Cambridge University Press.

MIRSKY, J., 1965, *The Great Chinese Travellers*, London: Allen & Unwin.

MOLODIN, V.I., PALASMAK, N.V., NOVIKOV, A.V., BOGDANOV, E.S., CLIUSSARENKO, I.Y., TCHEREMISINE, D.V., 2004, *Arkheologitcheskie pamiatniki ploskogoria Ykok (Gorni Altaï)*. Novossibirsk: Izdatelstvo Instituta arkheologii i etnografii SO RAN.

MONTEL, J.M., 1988, Première découverte d'une vaugnérite à orthopyroxène: pétrographie, géochimie et conséquences pour la genèse des vaugnérites. *Comptes-Rendus de l'Académie des Sciences* (Paris), 306, 985-990.

MURZAEV, E.M., 1984, The dictionary of the popular geographical terms (in Russian). Moscow: Ed. "Misl".

PERELADOVA, O., V. KREVER, and M. WILLIAMS, (Ed.). 1997, Biodiversity conservation in central Asia – Analysis of Modern Situation and Project Portfolio. WWF.

PERRIER, R., 1996, Les roches ornementales du Languedoc-Roussillon. *Mines et Carrières*, vol. 78, août-spt. 1996, p. 65-75.

PETREQUIN, P., PETREQUIN, A.-M., 1993, *Écologie d'un outil: la hache de pierre en Irian Jaya (Indonésie)*. Paris: Éditions du CNRS, Monographie du CRA 12, 1993.

PETREQUIN, P., CASSEN, S., CROUTSCH, C., WELLER, O., 1997, Haches alpines et haches carnacéennes dans l'Europe du Ve millénaire. *Notae praehistoricae*, 17, 1997, p. 135-150.

PETREQUIN, P., CASSEN, S., CROUTSH, C., D'AMICO, C., ERRERA, M., 2002, La Valorisation sociale des longues haches dans l'Europe néolithique. In: Guilaine (dir.), *Matériaux, productions, circulations du Néolithique à l'Age du Bronze. Séminaires du Collège de France*, Ed. Errance, p. 67-98.

PETREQUIN, P. et A.M., ERRERA M. CASSEN, S., CROUTSCH, C., KLASSEN, L., ROSSY, M.,

GARIBALDI, P., ISETTI, E., ROSSI, G., DELCARO, D., 2005, Voltri, Viso et Valais. Beigua, Monviso e Valais. All'origine delle grandi asce legivate di origine alpina in Europa occidentale durante il V millennio. *In*: *Materie prime e scambi nella Preistoria italiana.* XXXIX Riunione scientifica dell'Istituto Italiano di Preistoria e Protostoria (Firenze, 25-27 novembre 2004), *Revista di Scienze Preistoriche*, LV, p. 265-322.

SELEZNEV, A.G., 2000, Le syncrétisme islam-paganisme chez les peuples türks de sibérie occidentale. *Cahiers du monde russe*, 41/2-3, avril-septembre 2000, pp. 341-356.

TCHEREMISINE, D.V., 1993. K isucheniu posdnikh petroglifov Gornogo Altaia Sovremennye problemy isuchenia petroglifov. Kemerovo.

THORP, R.L., VINOGRAD, R.E., 2001, *Chinese Art and Culture*. New York: Harry N Abrams, Inc.

NEOLITHIC ROCK ART AT THE AVEBURY STONE CIRCLES IN SOUTHERN ENGLAND

Terence MEADEN
Oxford University, Department of Continuing Education, Rewley House, Wellington Square, Oxford, OX1, 2JA
Email: terence.meaden@torro.org.uk

Kate PRENDERGAST
Oxford University
Email: member@brodgar.fsnet.co.uk

Di PATTISON
Email: di@pattison-artwork.co.uk

L'art rupestre néolithique des cercles en pierre d'avebury au sud de l'angleterre

***Abstract**: There is strong academic research on a range of different rock art traditions in Neolithic Britain. In particular, extensive work has explored the rock art associated with the passage-graves of Ireland and Scotland, and the open-air rock art of Northern Ireland, Scotland and northern England. These traditions, some of which appear to be related to Breton rock art, span much of the Neolithic era, and represent a major expressive medium for these societies. This paper argues that comparable rock art also exists in Neolithic Wessex, specifically at the Avebury stone circles in southern England. It presents evidence for dressed and carved stones and suggests that potential meanings associated with such carvings are integral to the wider ritual and symbolic uses of the monument. Hence it signifies a major, hitherto unrecognised, regional rock art tradition in Neolithic Britain.*
***Keywords**: Avebury, megalithic art, rock art, Neolithic Wessex*

INTRODUCTION

The existence of developed rock art traditions across the European Neolithic is well established. In a recent summary, Bradley, Chippindale and Helskog identified the range and extent of regionally based traditions (2001). Although these traditions draw on particular influences, follow their own trajectories, and have important differences, nevertheless most seem to be associated with the introduction of agriculture and house-based settlement. The proliferation of rock art across Europe after the onset of agriculture may be part of a wider set of responses to agriculture, both in terms of indigenous Mesolithic groups already resident in outlying areas of western and northern Europe, and of the ways in which Neolithic economic and social systems developed across Europe until the introduction of metallurgy.

A major consequence of the arrival of agriculture was the emergence and development of monuments (Bradley 1998). Much of the earliest Neolithic rock art in Europe is associated with monuments. This should be seen as an integral part of the developing skills involved in dressing and positioning great megaliths in the landscape. The rapid evolution of monumental forms from ca. 4500 BC in areas where Mesolithic populations were well established (including Scandinavia, Iberia, Brittany, Ireland and Scotland) would indicate indigenous influences on monument building (Bradley 1998: 51-67). In these areas we see the development of new forms of monument: chambered long barrows and passage graves, and the emergence of a rich megalithic art associated with them.

MONUMENTAL ROCK ART IN NORTHERN BRITAIN AND IRELAND

In Britain, whereas chambered long barrows have a distribution that includes central southern England, round passage-graves have an exclusively western and northern distribution. Passage-graves appear to originate in Iberia and Brittany, and along with the simpler portal dolmens, spread relatively rapidly to Cornwall, Ireland, Wales and Scotland. Monumental rock art in Brittany is associated with passage-graves: intensely elaborate examples of passage-grave art exist, for example at the Gavrinis passage-grave. It is also associated with decorated menhirs, sometimes singly, sometimes with individual or groups of monuments. Some are explicitly anthropormorphic, as for example carved standing stones like La Gran'mere du Castel (Guernsey), Prajou Menhir (Cote-du-Nord) and Laniscar (Finistere).

In Ireland, rock art is closely associated with passage-graves. Large passage-grave cemeteries, as at Loughcrew, County Meath, are associated with the emergence of a distinctive art form (Sheridan 1986: 23-27). This was superseded by the seemingly authoritative sets of engravings found at the Boyne valley passage-graves Newgrange, Knowth and Dowth. Comparable art with similar motifs are found in passage-graves in northern Scotland, and at open-air rock-art sites across northern Britain and Ireland. Interpretations are ongoing, and include those that explicitly link the Loughcrew and Boyne Valley art to astronomical properties of the monuments (Brennan 1983, O'Brien 1988, Prendergast 2004).

In northern Britain the later Neolithic is typified by new forms of monument: henges, stone circles and related types. Rock art is frequently associated with such monuments. Bradley (1997) has argued that open-air rock art has direct associations with these monumental forms: distribution patterns indicate that such art becomes more elaborate the closer it is to a ceremonial site.

MONUMENTAL ROCK ART IN SOUTHERN ENGLAND

Whereas the Neolithic megalithic and rock-art traditions of northern and western Britain have been well researched, less work has been done out on rock art in southern England. This is partly because the evidence is not as abundant or obvious as in the north and west. Little investigation has been undertaken for evidence of rock art at the chambered long barrows of the earlier Neolithic in southern and central England, so our understanding of stone-carving traditions in these areas remains limited (MEADEN 1999).

In southern England earlier Neolithic monuments came to be replaced by great ceremonial sites centred on impressive timber and stone circles. The largest, and one of the most elaborate of such ceremonial centres was at Avebury in Wessex. The sheer scale and complexity of the later-Neolithic megalithic landscape in Avebury is astonishing. In total, about 600 sarsen megaliths were erected at Avebury in complex arrangements comprising stone circles, avenues and Coves, during a time span approaching five centuries: ca. 2900-2400 BC.

Comparable ceremonial monuments were erected across Wessex during the same time span. The most famous is Stonehenge. Yet, despite the scale and elaboration of megalithic culture at these sites, little recent work has been undertaken on the stone-working methods used to dress the sarsens. At Stonehenge, the working and dressing of the sarsen stones is undeniable. It is common knowledge that woodworking traditions are echoed in the lintel joints, and research is being carried out on the early Bronze Age rock art (depicting daggers and axes) evident on some stones (Goskar 2003). But little attention has been given to the extent and detail of the late-Neolithic working of the sarsens. Even less work has been done at Avebury, and most archaeologists assume that, unlike at Stonehenge, the sarsens at Avebury are in their natural state (but see Meaden 1999). In this paper we argue that many of Avebury's megaliths are not only worked in ways typical of many megaliths in the western-European Neolithic, but that there is deliberate and complex imagery carved into many of the standing stones.

EVIDENCE FOR ROCK ART AT AVEBURY

Of the original standing stones at Avebury's circles and avenues, only 80 out of 600 can be seen today. A few dozen more remain buried; hundreds have been destroyed. Avebury's sarsen stones were brought a short distance from nearby sarsen beds on the Marlborough Downs. This was also the origin of the sarsens that were taken to Stonehenge 30 km distant. Sarsen is a very hard siliceous sandstone of Lower Eocene date, the result of cementation of sand beds overlying the Cretaceous Chalk at a time when they lay beneath the sea, and at some early period the sandstone beds cracked through shrinkage into their characteristic polygonal forms. Subsequently, following geological uplift, the sarsen beds were raised to their present heights on the chalk hills of the Marlborough Downs. The hardness of sarsen varies greatly, from a friable sandstone to the fully-developed sarsen variety known as quartzite.

The dressing of the Stonehenge megaliths was examined by earlier generations of archaeologists in Wessex. Herbert Stone (1924: 75-98) was among the first to do so. His manuscript notes (at Devizes Museum) illustrate his research into various stone-working methods, including energetic mauling, and abrading or polishing and gentler activities, like scaling by using shallow, carefully-controlled firing and hammerstone-beating. Eyewitness accounts of these methods in contemporary use in other countries together with Stone's conversations with elderly Avebury stonebreakers are recorded and discussed in personal correspondence. Stone (1924: 49) nevertheless stated of Stonehenge that in its quartzite form sarsen "is extremely hard and cannot be scratched, or even marked, with a hard steel tool." The Neolithic stonemasons of Stonehenge therefore chose the hardest quartzite boulders for their mauls to define the initially-desired form. In India, Stone watched how granite was quarried by this method. After repeated use, the 20 kg mauls (being thrown from head-height to crack a target stone on the ground) increasingly wore to their characteristic football-size form. The finer work at Stonehenge was achieved by abrading the surface with a rubbing stone over a scatter of wetted sharp flint grit—a much-discussed and very laborious process not far different from modern wet-and-dry grinding methods.

In contrast Herbert Stone noted in his manuscript that shallow firing (by stoneworkers boiling water for their tea beside a stone) sometimes resulted in the outer skin of a stone flaking away in a localised area. This also browns the skin of the stone—a phenomenon observed by Passmore at Avebury in 1919-1920 and recorded in his manuscript (MS. 1920: Pt 4, p. 9). Stone's manuscript includes an eyewitness account of an African woman rhythmically and relatively gently beating a stone to shape it with a cricket-ball-sized (ca. 80 mm) hammerstone. The result at the edge of a shallow-fired zone would be a well-defined edge separating the burnt and hammered surfaces—i.e., a lower surface on the hammered side and a characteristic pattern of small arcs and rounded hollows left by the tool. This sharp contrast of brown and the natural stone colour, and an irregular line between the two surfaces, was noted at Avebury by Passmore who concluded the surface had been intentionally removed—and we avow the same thing.

At Avebury, Keiller and Piggott had no doubt that the stones had been dressed. Writing in *Antiquity* (1936: 420): "The stones...have hitherto been erroneously referred to as 'rough unhewn blocks of sarsen'. Actually these megaliths have been dressed, and very carefully dressed, although not, it should be noted, to the flat surface obtained at Stonehenge. Moreover there can be no question but that the stones were dressed deliberately to conform to certain required shapes, and to this end were in the first place selected as near to the required form as possible, with a resultant economy in the labour of the final dressing."

Keiller and Piggott (1936: 417-27) specifically argued that the lozenge and "long phallic" pairs of stones located in the Kennet Avenue had been explicitly selected and shaped to symbolically represent male and female. Ironically, despite the lack of recent study and the generally prevailing *assumption* that the Avebury stones were not worked, Keiller and Piggott's observation about an intended lithic sexuality is widely acknowledged to be correct.

Similar techniques to those known for Stonehenge were used at Avebury. Mauls at Stonehenge helped define the rectilinear blocks of trilithon uprights and lintels upon which distinguishing tell-tale scoop-marks remain visible to this day. It was used, as Herbert Stone observed, in the manner of flint-knapping on a giant scale. An example is the bladed below-ground section of re-erected trilithon Stone 30 carefully drawn by the Office of Works and reproduced by M. Pitts in *Hengeworld* (2001: 216) featuring a group of 19 concoidal fractures, five of which are about a metre long, with the smallest group about 30 cm in length.

Similar concoidal fractures on Avebury's sarsens must be seriously considered as artificial because hard sarsen stone rarely breaks like this through natural causes. They are surely deliberate when the evidence points to an ordered or specially placed group, as in the blade formation, a group of uniform size and depth, or a group resulting in a special silhouette shape.

In discussing Avebury, Pitts referred to his observations of "artefactual scarring" on some stones without specifically referring to the tool or particular examples, and he does comment that this is worthy of further study (personal communication, 2001: 214). We believe that these large shell-shaped fractures help define some of Avebury's classic silhouettes. They can be seen occurring in groups just above ground level on certain stones (e.g., Avebury Stone 26A, Stone 8) and appear to be good evidence for mauling.

At Stonehenge the matching mortises and tenons were *carved,* and the tenons stand up to 120-150 mm proud of the body of the stone. Bladed hard-stone chisel-like tools were used extensively at Avebury, leaving vast numbers of characteristic v-cuts at the terminals of frequently-grouped linear incisions. These are visible to the naked eye in bright directional sunlight. Blade angles can be measured on photographs, and templates can be made from tracings that can be tested for fit against neighbouring marks. This demonstrates the fact of deliberate carving activity, and the number and contrasting blade profiles of the tools. From this and other evidence, such as the cutting direction, the handedness, expertise and stance of the carver, even the time spent working can be potentially determined.

At Stonehenge abrading and polishing techniques are well understood. At Avebury the technique was limited to stones having either special significance due to their size and location (e.g., the inner face of the blocking stone at nearby West Kennet Long Barrow) or those featuring the most advanced sculpture as with Stone 26A in the Kennet Avenue. An example of what may be wedge-splitting is visible on Avebury's Stone 4, among others. If the regularly-spaced marks are not natural, then part of the stone was split using a technique similar to that inferred at Stonehenge and Stanton Drew, e.g., lintel 154 at Stonehenge shows regular wedge marks evenly spaced. Although we may be unsure as to how they did it, nonetheless at Stonehenge and Stanton Drew it was certainly done—and very likely at Avebury too.

At Avebury the fervent destruction of megaliths by villagers using intense fire and cold water was famously witnessed by William Stukeley in 1720. However four millennia earlier the monument builders had used this very method with a positive and possibly ritualistic intention. Maud Cunnington (1931) found scorched and fractured sarsen blocks in many post holes at the Sanctuary. In discussing this evidence Dames (1996: 76) concluded that "no explanation of the scorching has been advanced to date. Wood fibre from post bases was found uncharred, so the stones were not burned in a general conflagration. Instead, they were submitted to intense heat *before* the timbers were erected." Intense heat—when quenched by water—fractures sarsen uniformly and scorches a brown-red colour more deeply into the body of the stone. Keiller and Piggott's observations may relate to this practice. Burl rejects any possibility that the burnt sarsens at the Sanctuary were due to stone-burning in more modern times because they had been in the ground for so long and earthen material had been deliberately placed over them. He suggests (Burl 2002: 42) a ritualistic purpose commenting that "similar scorching is known in other southern tombs: among them Belas Knap, Tinkinswood, Nympsfield, Rodmarton, Stoney Littleton...it was a widespread Neolithic practice." In 2006 excavations at stoneless Woodhenge revealed local deposits of burnt sarsen too.

While it is clear that some Avebury stones were worked, in this paper we extend the arguments of Stone, Keiller,

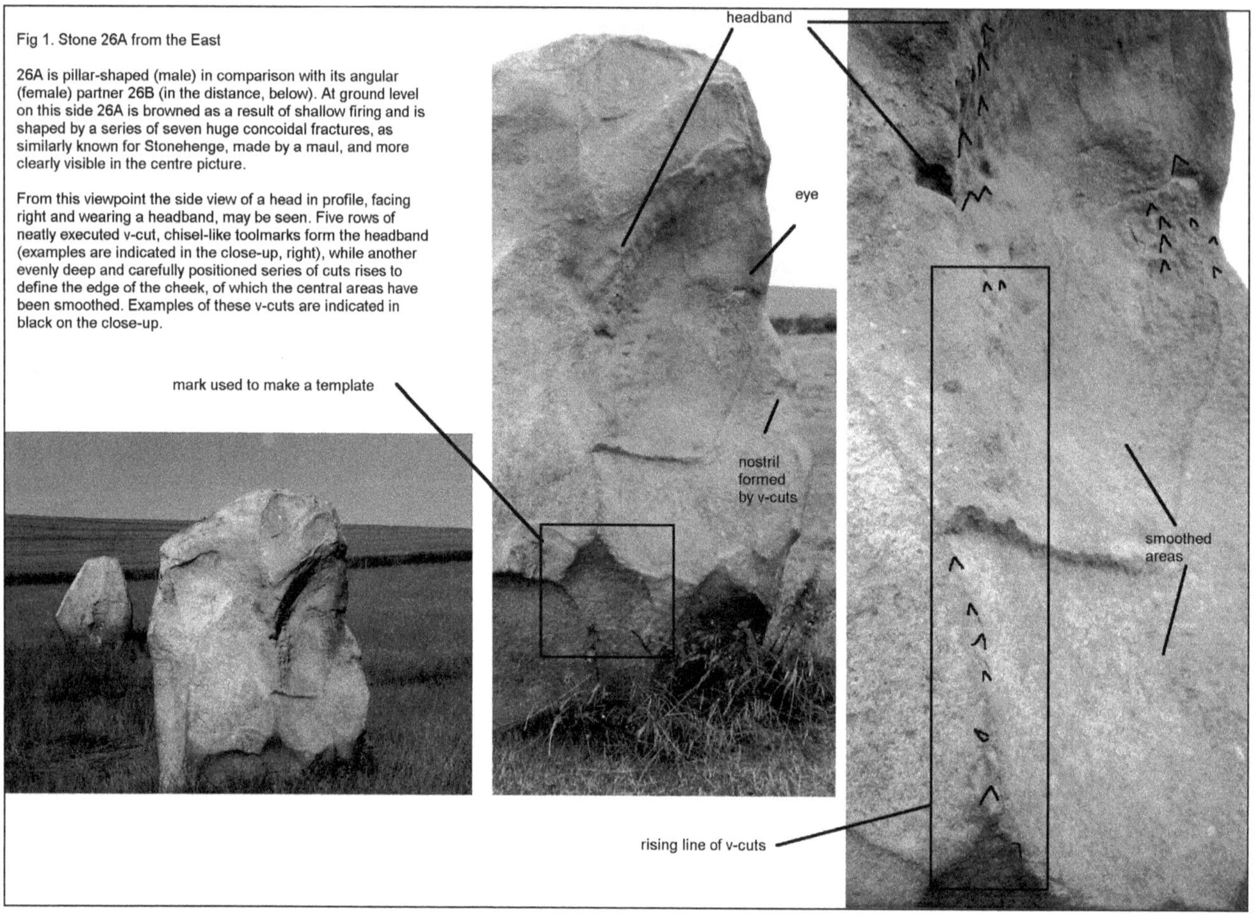

Fig. 6.1. Stone 26A from the East

Piggott, Passmore and Pitts, to suggest that they were also *artistically* carved, and on a scale and in quantity and quality commensurate with the grandeur and singular nature of this monument complex. The resulting images are a major feature of the whole and would have played an essential part in its ritual and ceremonial purposes, conceived as they must have been during the stone selection and erection process. They are absolutely not an afterthought, an incidental inclusion, or prehistoric graffiti. The execution of these carvings was skilful and time-consuming, often involving a series of increasingly specialised and creative activities that had to be directed and mastered—these techniques would surely have been passed on and developed from generation to generation.

In this paper, for reasons of space, we present evidence from only two stones as examples of figurative carvings: Stone 206 in the north-circle setting and Stone 26A on the Kennet Avenue.

AVENUE STONE 26A

The whole of the eastern side of this anthropomorphic megalith was carved to create a human head in profile facing right (Fig. 6.1). This straight-sided stone, three metres high, comes under the Type A or male category of Keiller and Piggott. The head, which is adorned with a headband or diadem, looks northwards to the Avebury stone circles. Black lines on the photograph indicate the marks of a chisel and the 'v' profile of its stone blade. A broad area may have been smoothed using the abrading and polishing technique described earlier. As this is a softer, sandier stone, this area may later have been subject to erosion, which is not evident generally on most of the sarsens. Stone 26A is very expertly worked. At its base it is coloured brown, indicating some localised and deliberate—but not vandalistic—firing. At the base is a series of plainly visible concoidal maul-marks. They are neatly grouped and regularly spaced having even depth and uniformity, as known for some stones at Stonehenge. From a photograph a template of one of these marks can be made and fitted against its neighbours, establishing that a single tool of a particular size having both rounded and sharper sections was responsible for all the shaping at the base of this eastern side of the stone. It is consistent with the carving skill evidenced on Stone 26A that extra time was taken for the final smoothing. Evidence of the care in the chisel work is in the line of tiny v-cuts rising at the junction of two key maul marks. Moving right and facing the narrow end of this stone from the north, a second face comes into view with a mouth very cleverly worked under the cheek area when studied as a three-quarter back view. The headdress featured on this stone suggests that the subject of this carving was perhaps a personage of status and/or veneration, someone worthy of so much effort. This profile is so well sculpted and so realistic that one may suggest that the image may possibly be a portrait.

STONE 206

This splendid megalith weighs about 22 tonnes. A fine human head in south-east right-facing profile is visible from the east (Fig. 6.2). Most obvious is the well-carved nose, mouth and chin but there is an exquisitely sculptured twisting horn too that rises from the right temple. The eye is a natural feature, and perhaps the major reason that inspired the Neolithic artist to develop the image on this scale at this location. The sculpture is more than a restricted profile because the horned head holds good through about 40 degrees of arc between 205 and 245 degrees east of north. This horned image is one of a small group of surviving sculptures combining the characteristics of animal-human hybrids with the grossly accentuated facial features and iconic motifs of what we recognise as *archetypes*. Was this figure a hunting deity manifest in human imagery? Close examination reveals a series of v-shaped indentations and linear grooves created by the sculptor's tool (Fig. 6.2). They are best identified by inspecting the shapes of shadows and the patterns of lichen growth, the lichen having developed in the micro-environment of the cut marks. Natural hollows and protuberances were accentuated to further enhance this form.

CONCLUSION

This introduction to the evidence for abstract and figurative rock art at Avebury demonstrates the reality of a developed rock art tradition in southern England, hitherto unrecognised. The presence of such art has significant implications in terms of extending our understanding of Neolithic rock art in Britain.

First, the artwork would have been closely related to the ritual uses and symbolic understandings.

associated with the monument. The creation of art-forms may have been linked to initiation ceremonies into the secrets of the stones, whether mythological or spiritual. The lozenge and the pillar or long stone were interpreted by Keiller and Piggott in terms of gender symbolism. Burl, Meaden and other writers have related this very specifically to fertility veneration, centrally important in this early agricultural context.

Second, explicitly anthropomorphic motifs may add to other evidence for a Breton influence on late Neolithic Wessex, and may represent a cultural sphere of influence comparable to the passage-grave zone further to the west (e.g., Burl 1999: 158-167).

Third, the rock art at Avebury extends our understanding of ceremonial centres in late Neolithic societies, of art history, and of some peoples' actual clothing, hairstyles and possible appearance. Figurative subject-matter reflects an interest in groups and types of characters including fictitious identities, archetypal figures, possible supernatural beings and deities, animals, animal-human hybrids and individual men and women of all ages including children.

Individually and collectively, the sculptures are integral to their setting. The figures could have communicated visually and metaphorically to reinforce deeply held beliefs and experiences. By their gazes and gestures they react to other features of the human-made environment and to the viewer. By their positioning they are deliberately intended to be revealed and concealed by the moving sun as well as by the approach route or by the angle of view adopted by the beholder. The sculptures and the entire monument are intentionally placed to interact with, and communicate an essence of central importance about, the wider cosmos. As at Stonehenge so at Avebury there are astronomical functions associated with the positioning of certain megaliths, indicating that awareness of the sun and seasons was built into the monument. Moreover, some carved faces at Avebury stare either vertically to the sky or at a very sharp angle towards the heavens. An example of each is located on the topmost part of the inner and outer surfaces of Stone 206.

Avebury's magnificent rock art testifies to, and is on a scale commensurate with, the obsessions of monument-building groups. It evidences monumental, freestanding, stone sculpture and a superlative technical skill and creative innovation of a regional school of artists that developed their expertise over many generations (Meaden 2007). In the language of contemporary art, Avebury's circles and avenues are a site-specific land-art installation. Successive generations of artists and craftspeople selected specific materials from that landscape to devise sculpture that responds to and metaphorically communicates something mysterious, esoteric, about that place and the beliefs of that community. We can see how the art is conceptual in being interactive and four-dimensional, the moving sun and the gender imagery playing a central role. Notions of a female deity and a polytheistic tradition can again be openly debated. This, the acceptance within archaeology of the importance of prehistoric rock art, as well as modern observation and recording techniques may help explain why we are only now able to identify and appreciate this highly innovative artwork for what it is.

References

BRADLEY, R., 1997, *Rock Art and the Prehistory of Atlantic Europe*, Routledge: London.

BRADLEY, R., 1998, *The Significance of Monuments*, London: Routledge.

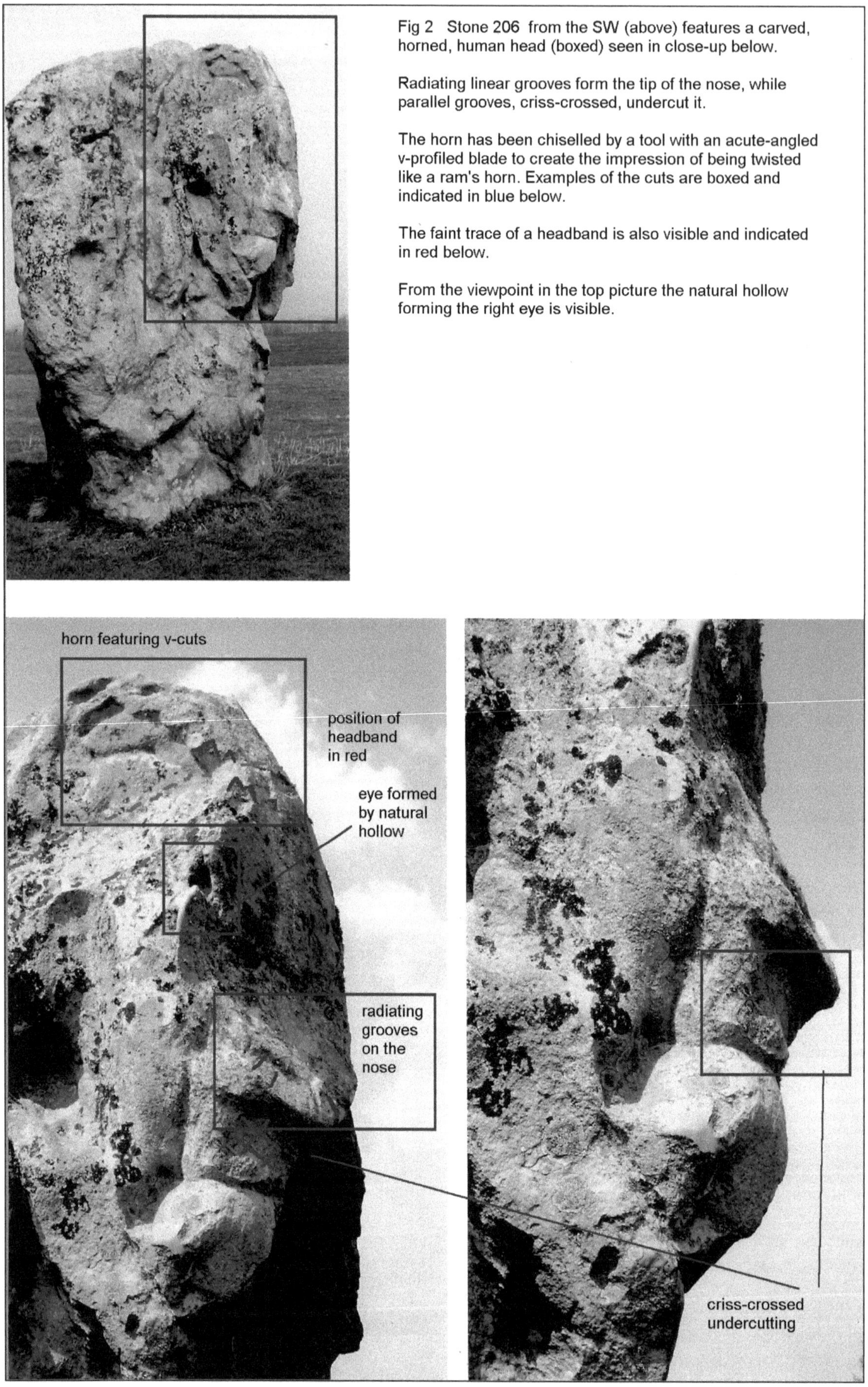

Fig. 6.2. Stone 206 from the SW (above) features as carved, horned, human head (boxer) senn in close-up bellow

BRADLEY, R., CHIPPINDALE, C. & HELSKOG, K., 2001, Post-Palaeolithic Europe. In D. Whitley (ed.), *Handbook of Rock Art Research*, Beverly Hills: AltaMira Press, p. 482-529.

BRENNAN, M., 1983, *The Stars and the Stones*, London: Thames & Hudson.

BURL, A., 1999, *Great Stone Circles*, New Haven & London: Yale University Press.

BURL, A., 2002, *Prehistoric Avebury*. 2nd Ed., New Haven & London: Yale University Press.

CUNNINGTON, M., 1931, *Wiltshire Archaeological Magazine* 45, p. 314.

DAMES, M., 1996, *The Avebury Cycle*, 2nd Ed., Thames & Hudson: London.

GOSKAR, K., 2003, The Stonehenge Lasershow, *British Archaeology* 73.

KEILLER, A., & PIGGOTT, S., 1936, The Recent Excavations at Avebury, *Antiquity* 10/40, p. 417-427

MEADEN, G.T., 1999, *Secrets of the Avebury stones*, London: Souvenir Press.

MEADEN, G.T., 2007, Circles and cupmarks in British Neolithic art with particular attention to triangular portable stones each with a cupmark at the apex, *Proceedings of the UISPP, XV Congress, and Rock Art Conference, Session W34. Lisbon. September 2006*, British Archaeological Reports, Oxford: BAR Publishing.

O'BRIEN, T., 1988, Winter solstice decoration at Newgrange, *Riocht Na Midhe* 8/2, p. 50-59.

PITTS, M., 2001, *Hengeworld*, London: Arrow Books.

PRENDERGAST, K., 2004, Caves of the winter sun. Synthesising the evidence for astronomical orientation at the Boyne Valley passage tombs, *Riocht Na Midhe* 15, p. 12-25.

SHERIDAN, J.A., 1986, Megaliths and megalomania: an account, and interpretation, of the development of passage tombs in Ireland, *Journal of Irish Archaeology* 3, p. 17-30.

STONE, E.H., 1924, *The Stones of Stonehenge*, London: Robert Scott.

CIERTOS ASPECTOS FUNERARIOS EN LA NECROPOLIS DEL III MILENIO DE VALENCINA-CASTILLEJA (SEVILLA)

Rosario CRUZ-AUÑON
Universidad de Sevilla
Email: rcab@us.es

Francisco NOCETE
Universidad de Huelva
Email: nocete@uhu.es

Juan Carlos MEJIAS
Universidad de Sevilla

Some funerary aspects of the third millennium BC necropolis of Valencina-Castilleja (Sevilla)

Abstract: *During the 3rd millennium BC the Valencina-Castilleja settlement site grew to spectacular dimensions. Due to its rapid growth the political leadership were unable to cope with the fast economic changes that generated internal social contradictions within the society and likely to be expressed at the ideological level. The aim of this work is to present a global vision of the settlement site's necropolis and understand its historical circumstances.*
Key words: *Sociedad clasista, necrópolis, calcolítico, enterramientos de cámara y corredor, ajuares, antropología*

INTRODUCCIÓN

El asentamiento de Valencina de la Concepción-Castilleja de Guzmán (Sevilla), se ubicó a orillas de la gran ensenada marina en la que durante el III milenio a.C. desembocaba el Río Guadalquivir (Arteaga *et al.* 1995). El sector noroccidental estaba configurado por un escarpe donde se encontraba una amplia penillanura (el Aljarafe) donde se desarrollaban esporádicas elevaciones o cabezos, cuya altitud media ronda los 140 mts. y una cota máxima de 165 mts. Litológicamente, el material sobre el que realizaron sus construcciones corresponden a limos arenosos y margas. En ellos se crearon, y se crean actualmente frecuentes vertientes, cauces o zonas de acumulación de agua puntuales.

LAS INTERVENCIONES ARQUEOLÓGICAS EN VALENCINA-CASTILLEJA

El yacimiento de Valencina-Castilleja se viene excavando desde 1868, año de la primera actuación de carácter arqueológica en el Dolmen de la Pastora; hasta la actualidad se han realizado 90 intervenciones arqueológicas en 75 lugares distintos del yacimiento.

Durante los primeros 87 años (1868-1955) tan sólo se llevaron a cabo 6 intervenciones, que suponen el 6,5% del total. El gran boom de las excavaciones se desarrolló en las décadas de los 70', 80' y 90' (71 intervenciones en 25 años), coincidiendo con el momento en el que los municipios de Valencina y Castilleja van a crecer indiscriminadamente, pasando de 18,41 y 5,26 ha. (en 1956) respectivamente hasta las 205,96 y 27,99 ha. En las 90 intervenciones se ha documentado arqueológicamente 9,85 ha. que van a significar tan sólo 21,46 ha. para el total de superficie en la que se ha llevado a cabo algún tipo de actuación. Es decir, en 50 años ambos municipios crecen 210 ha. pero sólo se realizan análisis arqueológicos en 58,51 ha, de las que se han documentado arqueológicamente 21,46 ha, "olvidando" de llevar a cabo análisis en al menos 151,49 ha., que han quedado baldías de información.

Es muy significativo que en los últimos 25 años se han producido las transformaciones urbanísticas de mayor envergadura. Hasta finales de los años 70' las intervenciones se realizaron en pequeñas parcelas del centro histórico de los municipios o en su entorno inmediato, mientras que a partir de la década de los 80' las transformaciones se llevan a cabo en el perímetro más exterior de los municipios, en grandes bolsas de suelo urbanizadas.

Pero aún hay un aspecto especialmente negativo, tal cantidad de actividades ha desembocado en un compendio de investigaciones inconexas que precisan ser articuladas continuamente para así poder acceder a una visión general del asentamiento, su entidad crono-cultural, el modelo ocupacional, establecimiento de pautas de actuación y protección, y como no, examinar su papel en relación con otros enclaves poblacionales en un marco territorial más amplio.

VALORACIÓN DEL ASENTAMIENTO

Valencina-Castilleja responde al modelo de gran asentamiento de la estructura territorial jerarquizada del Valle del Guadalquivir del III milenio a.C., con capacidad de centralización de la circulación de productos críticos a pesar de la lejanía de sus áreas de procedencia, y una capacidad también para liderar la centralidad política. Se trata de unas tendencias de ordenación del territorio, definidas en el Valle del Guadalquivir desde los inicios del IV Milenio a.C., que culminan en las diversas formas de jerarquización entre los asentamientos, que convergen en la consolidación de los primeros centros de carácter comarcal a inicios del III Milenio a.C. y que se denomina "Territorio Modular Prístino del Valle del Guadalquivir" (Nocete 2001).

Su ubicación periférica en el territorio de la sociedad clasista inicial, y su proximidad a áreas fuente de recursos mineros, etc., lo convierten en una "puerta de entrada" con capacidad de articular y controlar tanto la concentración de recursos mineros como su distribución. Esta condición va a marcar su desarrollo posterior, hasta la destrucción como centro primado hacia el 2200 a.C. coincidiendo con la desmantelación de la periferia minera occidental a causa del desarrollo de otros ámbitos mineros en la periferia minera oriental, en un proceso complejo, de indudable naturaleza política de fragmentación y reordenación territorial, donde la traslación de los centros políticos al interior del valle, también implicó una mayor intensificación de la explotación agraria (Nocete 2001).

Respecto a su modelo ocupacional, varias han sido las propuestas, siendo las más recientes:

La apreciación más reciente del modelo ocupacional distingue una probable Área Nuclear con dos ámbitos, el de ocupación habitacional y el de producción (donde se depositarían los excedentes agropecuarios acumulados, tanto en campo de silos como en cierres de ganado (Cruz-Auñon, Arteaga 1999); además de barrios artesanales, caso del metalúrgico y otra exclusiva de Necrópolis, siendo la máxima extensión conjunta 468,80 hectáreas (Vargas 2004).

ASPECTOS FUNERARIOS DE LA NECRÓPOLIS

Como ya hemos señalado, el yacimiento precisaba de una valoración global, y su necrópolis especialmente, ya que contamos únicamente con referencias bibliográficas de carácter puntual y/o cruzado.

La estrategia seguida para iniciar una valoración global de su necrópolis parte de entenderla como la plasmación ideológica de las relaciones económico-sociales en las que los individuos de sus grupos internos se involucraron durante su vida. Una tumba, de forma recurrente, mediante su arquitectura y los ajuares, responde a las intencionalidades de los vivos, pues son ellos quienes manipulan y dictaminan el cómo, el dónde, el cuándo, de su ejecución, de los seres humanos que la han de albergar y el tratamiento que van a recibir.

Aunque analicemos los aspectos formales de las tumbas, la valoración global del asentamiento de Valencina, antes expuesta, es la que nos va a ayudar a explorar y explicar las particularidades de su necrópolis.

Análisis formal

Barajado las diferentes técnicas constructivas con las dimensiones de cada tumba, y añadiendo el componente de la existencia de túmulo o no, es decir el aspecto formal del "continente", intentaremos observar intencionalidades, expresadas unas veces con cierta espectacularidad y otras con notable precariedad.

El punto de partida es que se ha podido definir un Área exclusiva de Necrópolis en la que no se han hallado otro tipo de registros y en el que todas las estructuras funerarias responden al tipo de tumba de cámara circular y corredor, si bien con marcadas variables constructivas. Mientras, las otras referencias a restos humanos inhumados localizadas en silos, zanjas, estructuras habitacionales, etc. se adscriben al Área Nuclear, siendo excepción la tumba de falsa cúpula del Cerro de La Cabeza y las estructuras funerarias de Cerro Mármol y Sitio de Valencina, las dos primeras mirando hacia el Valle del Guadalquivir pero en el extremo norte del poblado, y la segunda más hacia en interior.

Todas las estructuras funerarias conocidas y relativamente conservadas, han presentado el mismo trazado en planta, cámara circular y corredor, siendo sus únicas diferencias arquitectónicas el efecto de la mayor o menor inversión de fuerza de trabajo en su construcción. Así, las más espectaculares y de mayor tamaño serían las de mampostería, con corredor largo y cubierta de ortostatos bajo túmulo (claramente los dólmenes de La Pastora y Matarrubilla, y el dolmen de Montelirio donde sólo conocemos la cubierta de ortostatos); le seguirían las de mampostería de corredor medio y sin túmulo individualizado (7 tumbas en el Señorío de Guzmán); las de lajas en cámara y corredor (varios ejemplos en el Señorío de Guzmán, dolmen de los Veinte, Mataherrera, etc.); o algo más precarias, donde las lajas solo intervienen de forma puntual (algunas tumbas de El Roquetito, Nª Sra. De los Reyes, Manuel Muñoz A, etc.); y por último los casos en los que claramente las paredes no se revistieron y tampoco llegaron a utilizarse (Manuel Muñoz B y al menos dos tumbas en el Roquetito).

Existen otras variables arquitectónicas que suelen ser casos aislados, por ejemplo los vestíbulos de la Pastora, el Roquetito I y Manuel Muñoz A. Tan solo hay dos y de trazado angular, además del vestíbulo semicircular de Ontiveros, que se arrastra en la bibliografía al respecto, y que descartamos pues pensamos se trata de parte de la cámara. Más exclusivos aún han sido un pequeño corredor y subcámara adosados a la estructura principal en Manuel Muñoz A, la hornacina de La Pastora y la pila de Matarrubilla, circunstancias destacables por su singularidad dentro del conjunto.

En cuanto a las posibles capacidades de las cámaras, el diámetro oscila entre 1 mts. y los 4,4 mts., siendo su valor modal 2 mts. Las grandes tumbas de mampostería, como La Pastora y Matarrubilla, no son precisamente las más amplias, alcanzan 2,60 y 2,80 mts. respectivamente, mientras que el mayor diámetros registrado hasta la actualidad corresponde a la tumba 1 de Montelirio construida con lajas de pizarra y que comparte el túmulo del Dolmen de Montelirio. En general comprobamos como las tumbas de lajas verticales son las únicas que ocasionalmente superan los 3 mts. aunque no siempre, circunstancia que no ocurre con las de mampostería. Como casos significativos, la sepultura con el más elevado número de individuos, El Roquetito I, presenta una cámara de tan sólo 2,20 mts., así como entre las menos espaciosas, algunas de El Roquetito y del entorno de Montelirio, donde en ambos casos intervienen las lajas verticales, oscilan entre 1,55 mts. y 1,70 mts.

Para los corredores las cifras oscilan desde 45,65 mts. hasta 1 mts., coincidiendo los más largos con las estructuras de mampostería y bajo túmulo.

El otro elemento significativo son los túmulos. Ya de por sí, llaman la atención en el paisaje de penillanura los cabezos naturales, algunos de ellos manipulados por los seres humanos a lo largo de la historia. La manipulación y construcción artificial de los túmulos supone la inversión de una gran cantidad de mano de obra y que define la construcción de un paisaje que persigue inmortalizar un sistema social de relaciones desiguales al restringir su acceso a un grupo reducido de la comunidad y utilizar, para su construcción, la fuerza de trabajo del un conjunto social que no tiene acceso a su uso.

En total hemos contabilizado al menos 9 túmulos, si bien con seguridad 5 de ellos cubren tumbas del III milenio a.C., los restantes, sin excavar, pueden o no corresponder a dicho periodo prehistórico o bien tratarse de enterramientos de época tartésica (Arteaga *et al.* 2001). Esos 5 túmulos se refieren a La Pastora, Matarrubilla, Ontiveros, Montelirio y Antiguo Depósito de Castilleja.

Al analizar arquitectónicamente el tipo de tumba merecedora de tan espectacular cubierta nos encontramos con lo siguiente:

> La Pastora y Matarrubilla, ambas de mampostería, son de las tumbas más espectaculares, pero sus respectivos túmulos (de 45 y 30 mts. de diámetro) están si explorar, por lo que es posible que aún estén pendientes de descubrirse tumbas anexas a ellas.

Montelirio cubre una tumba espectacular con cubierta de ortostatos pero se desconoce su paramento. Posee una segunda tumba, de lajas y más sencilla y cuyo corredor queda dentro del túmulo (36 mts. de diámetro).

El Antiguo Depósito de Castilleja, también cubre dos tumbas, siendo siempre una de lajas más sencilla con el corredor dentro del túmulo, y otra de mampostería sin excavar, y que debió de tratarse de la principal.

La descubierta en Ontiveros también es de lajas además de que nosotros interpretamos como cámara lo descrito como vestíbulo; su corredor también transcurre hacia el interior del túmulo. Por todo ello, posiblemente no es la tumba principal de éste túmulo, al igual que ocurre con el Antiguo Depósito.

La presencia de estructuras adjuntas en estos túmulos, a falta de dataciones y estudios arqueológicos que nos permitan definir bien que las diferentes estructuras funerarias implican un proceso diacrónico, y por tanto el túmulo mostraría el desarrollo de dinastías; o bien la posibilidad de su contemporaneidad , lo cual nos permitiría inferir relaciones clientelares en el seno de las clases dominantes, dado que la mayoría de la población no se inhuma en estos cementerios.

Análisis del ajuar

Una vez expuesto los aspectos formales de las tumbas pasamos a articularlos con el contenido material: los ajuares. Debe existir una relación estrecha entre esos aspectos formales, reflejados principalmente en la arquitectura, y los ajuares, con el status y categoría adquirido por familias o individuos propietarias de las tumbas. Los análisis antropológicos realizados en algunas tumbas, en cuanto a las relaciones de edad y sexo, nos permiten inferir tanto familias simples como extendidas, dependiendo de cronometría interna, aparte de enterramientos individuales.

Desde su nacimiento y en el transcurso de su vida, no obstante serán los vivos quienes ejecuten la materialización de la cualificación, y por lo tanto, el ajuar como referente, ocasionalmente se ve condicionado a la decisión de los que quedan y es así como puede que, una tumba y su contenido no reflejen siempre la intencionalidad de magnificar aún más a aquellos para quienes se construyó.

Revisando la información del ajuar, llama la atención el hecho de ser relativamente pobres en cantidad, aunque variados o expresivos en cualidad. A pesar de esta afirmación existen excepciones en cuanto a la cantidad:

> Matarrubilla se trata de una de las tumbas más espectaculares arquitectónicamente, en donde las dos inhumaciones realizadas están en el corredor, con material asociado de momentos campaniforme y como la cámara no llegó a usarse. Ahora bien, todo el material se documentó en el corredor sin especificar lo que pertenecía a rellenos postdeposicionales y lo que formaba realmente parte del ajuar de los enterrados. Destacan numerosos vasos cerámicos y algunos platos, con decoración campaniforme en algunos, además de material lítico, óseo, marfil, metal, oro. También queremos llamar la atención sobre los adornos hallados, oro y marfil adscritos de manera individualizada para cada uno de los inhumado.

El Roquetito I con 15 vasos y un ajuar bastante variado: varios útiles de metal, material lítico, óseo, y un recipiente calizo. Este ajuar, sin embargo, se corresponde con la mayor cantidad de inhumaciones realizadas en la misma tumba de esta necrópolis, un total de 31, siendo además una de las tumbas más precarias arquitectónicamente con dimensiones medias entre los valores de esta necrópolis.

También abundante, aunque en menor medida, la Tumba 5 del Señorío de Guzmán, con arquitectura excepcional de mampostería y 10 inhumaciones, donde destacan 6 vasos, entre ellos algunos campaniformes, y cierta variedad de otros artefactos, entre las que llaman la atención 600 cuentas de collar de caliza.

Junto a ello debemos señal que:

> Las construcciones de mampostería presentan material con decoración campaniforme, siendo la excepción la Tumba de La Pastora, en la que por lo demás contenía un ajuar muy escueto, destacable tan solo dos útiles de cobre, y documentado todo exclusivamente en el corredor.

Manuel Muñoz A, tumba de lajas, presentaba un enterramiento de un guerrero con un puñal y varias puntas de tipo Palmela, claramente estratificado sobre el nivel múltiple y sucesivo, aunque en el mismo espacio funerario, documentado claramente como una reutilización.

El número de individuos no implica una cantidad de ajuar mayor. A pesar de la singularidad de el Roquetito I, la tumba A de Manuel Muñoz presenta en su nivel múltiple más de una decena de individuos y tan solo un vaso cerámico como ajuar. O el caso de el Roquetito II con 14 inhumaciones y tan solo 2 vasos y 5 útiles entre líticos y óseos.

El Cerro de la Cabeza, de lajas, con 1 sólo individuo, muestra un ajuar escaso si consideramos tan sólo lo registrado en el nivel del enterramiento, mientras que el resto pertenece a efectos postdeposicionales, incluido un vaso polípodo hallado en el túmulo, que nos llevaría a otro tipo de explicaciones y no a lo referente al ajuar del inhumado.

La presencia de útiles de cobre, aunque en un número reducido de tumbas, suele ofertar una rica variedad y cantidad, marcando diferencias entre los grupos de inhumados y a su vez demostrando la posibilidad de acceder a este producto, ocasionalmente realizado en el mismo poblado, cuando no de procedencia externa (Rodriguez 2006).

Remarcamos de momento que a pesar de alguna excepción, el número de individuos no se corresponde con la cantidad de ajuar. El rito de incluir ofrendas no es un condicionante para cada inhumación. Pero ocurre ocasionalmente todo lo contrario, que se personaliza al individuo a base de adornos personales, lo cual siempre coincide con la presencia de items campanifomes, aparte de objetos exóticos demostrativos de una sociedad clasista, destacando al individuo dentro de un colectivo social y sus relaciones de parentesco.

Si relacionamos la cantidad con el tipo de estructura no existen diferencias notables entre los de mampostería, los de lajas verticales o los de cámaras sin revestir, circunstancia que difiere algo, aunque no sustancialmente, en cuanto a la calidad, resultando las de mampostería ocasionalmente más significativos en este último aspecto.

Análisis antropológico

A los datos expuestos hasta ahora hay que sumarle la información antropológica, ya que realmente son los inhumados los responsables de provocar un tipo de arquitectura en un espacio determinado y un trato singular o no en su ajuar. Al respecto tan solo hemos podido manejar indicaciones respecto al número de individuos, edad y sexo (aspectos que consideramos insuficientes), y sólo para algunas tumbas, dando como resultado de momento 7 modelos: 1) tumbas con 1 o 2 individuos; 2) con 3 o 4; 3) entre 10 y 14; 4) de más de 20 individuos; 5) sin utilizar; 6) reutilizaciones y 7) en estructuras no funerarias.

1) Tumbas con 1 o 2 individuos. Ocurre en las estructuras más monumentales de esta necrópolis, como La Pastora y Matarrubilla, por ejemplo. Para la Pastora tan solo se habla de restos de 1 individuo en el contacto entre la cámara y el corredor, y dado que el corredor estaba sellado intencionadamente, indicaría este hecho que las tumbas habrían cubierto su fin social. En Matarrubilla, la cámara no se utilizó como depósito funerario, documentándose las inhumaciones (acompañadas de items campaniformes) exclusivamente en el corredor. Otras sepulturas, éstas de lajas, como Ontiveros, El Cerro de La Cabeza y en el entorno de Montelirio, presentaron la misma circunstancia en cuanto a pocas evidencias funerarias.

Cabría considerar que para quién, o quienes, fueron o iban a ser destinadas estas estructuras, no llegaron a ser merecedores de tal status social, político o ideológico; o bien lo perdieron, o se segregaron de la estructura "jerárquica" a la que pertenecían, lo que en sí se presenta como una contradicción en relación con los espacios sociales funerarios.

2) Tumbas con 3 o 4 individuos. En tumbas como las de el Señorío de Guzmán resulta evidente la troncalidad familiar, dando lugar siempre a una pareja de adultos de distinto sexo y un infantil, y/o un pre-adulto, lo que sería, en cualquier caso, representativo de la promoción ancestral. Las tumbas son de lajas de pizarra en dos casos y en uno de mampostería con material claramente campaniforme, por lo que la intencionalidad de marcar la identidad unifamiliar, ocurre en el seno de una sociedad con desigualdades, en este caso materializado en la arquitectura funeraria y en el ajuar.

3) Tumbas entre 10 y 14 individuos. En tumbas del Roquetito, Manuel Muñoz A y el Señorío de Guzmán, todas de lajas excepto una de mampostería, ofertaron un

porcentaje bastante igualado entre los adultos de ambos sexo, por lo que cabe pensar en un osario, que además viene remarcado por un menor número de individuos de corta edad, pre-adultos o infantiles, indicativo de una posible relación "paterno-filial". Ahora bien, en la de mampostería con 14 individuos, a falta de indicadores concluyentes, resulta difícil discernir sobre una posible complejidad generacional o si corresponden a miembros de una familia ampliada, ya que en el ajuar y en el mismo nivel arqueológico se asocian decoración campaniforme marítima y continental.

4) Tumbas que superan la veintena de individuos. El número máximo en esta necrópolis en una tumba es de 31 individuos (Roquetito I). A pesar de la falta de otros indicadores, podemos suponer que albergara familias ampliadas. Ocurre, por otra parte, que su arquitectura es de las más precarias, dado que apenas algunas lajas intervienen en el revestimiento de los paramentos y tampoco la dimensiones responden a las mayores. Así pues, la cantidad de individuos, tampoco implica un mayor cuidado arquitectónico.

5) Tumbas sin utilizar. Casos en el Roquetito y Manuel Muñoz B nos permiten asegurar la ausencia total de registros humanos, garantizado por el proceso de excavación al que fueron sometidas, del que fuimos partícipes. Estas tumbas evidencian el carácter "preventivo" de sus construcciones como ya indicamos anteriormente.

6) Tumbas reutilizadas con enterramientos posteriores. Ya señalamos como en Matarrubillas, siendo una estructura espectacular, aparecieron sólo dos individuos y espaciados entre sí, de época campaniforme y ubicados en el corredor, excluidos de acceder a la cámara. En otras tumbas Roquetito II y Manuel Muñoz A, claramente aparecen estratificados sobre el nivel colectivo, siendo el segundo caso excepcional, con un guerrero con puñal y puntas de tipo Palmela, sobre el que se establecería encima otro enterramiento femenino. La reutilización de ciertas tumbas y además con carácter individual, nos lleva a inferir la emergencia en el seno de esta comunidad de un cambio de rito por motivos socio-económicos, además de apreciaciones referente a la secuencia diacrónica del asentamiento.

7) Enterramientos en estructuras no funerarias. Se refiere siempre a inhumaciones individuales o dobles, y aunque en alguna estructura siliforme se llegó a 7 inhumaciones, aparecen claramente estratificadas. Obviamente se adscriben a espacios habitacionales o de actividad donde fueron originariamente construidas tales estructuras. La ausencia de ajuar o de indicadores cronológicos ha generado apreciaciones diferentes. De momento resulta evidente la existencia de este recurso funerario con un matiz degradador de la categoría del individuo y trato que recibió en el momento de su inhumación, lo que viene a ser una evidencia más de la complejidad social y de las contradicciones en el seno de esta comunidad.

CONSIDERACIONES

Este asentamiento, que llegó a alcanzar tan espectaculares dimensiones y categoría en un espacio de tiempo relativamente corto dentro del III milenio a.C., generó claras contradicciones sociales internas en el ámbito social, susceptibles de materializarse en niveles ideológicos, consecuencia o causa de ciertos cambios económicos en las periferias mineras occidental y oriental dentro del territorio modular de la sociedad clasista inicial, y/o de su propia gestión política frente a este hecho. Hemos pretendido con este trabajo acceder a una visión global de la necrópolis, y captar en ella manifestaciones de esas circunstancias históricas.

Dentro de este espacio-necrópolis podemos asegurar que las tumbas se construyen de forma "preventiva", ya que en determinados casos no se terminaron de erigir o no se llegaron a utilizar. Además, antes de construirlas se les asignan unas ubicaciones espaciales selectivas, según su categoría arquitectónica, de hecho comprobamos como las más precarias, caso las del Roquetito, forman un conjunto, las de mampostería y las de lajas verticales en el Señorío de Guzmán se asocian formando grupos separados, que no se alternan indiscriminadamente, y todo ello como consecuencia de la categoría social de quienes en el futuro ocuparían dichas tumbas.

Contamos pues con la existencia de sepulcros posiblemente individuales, y otros numéricamente más complejos, y aunque los análisis paleopatólógicos nos llevan a entrever filiaciones entre individuos, la falta de estudios de ADN nos impide precisar con mayor rigidez este aspecto, a la hora de determinar el tipo de relaciones familiares.

La preparación y utilización, o no, de sepulcros para el enterramiento de parientes obedece a una intencionalidad social diferente. Unos serán más tradicionales, manteniendo las "normas" del culto colectivo ancestral, mientras que otros al desmembrarse algún miembro de la familia para "formar" nuevas unidades "de procreación", construirán nuevos panteones familiares, identificadores de su voluntad de segregación, afirmando y negando de manera contradictoria la estructura social en que se operaba su emergencia. Así en la misma progresión en que una "clase" de individuos hacía permisible la identificación emergente de la "familia" propia, otras "clases" de individuos continúan más "conservadoras". El nuevo "modelo" de formación familiar se gesta en el seno de una sociedad clasista inicial, y ésta a su vez en un emergente "modelo" de Estado.

Las fechas absolutas existentes para Valencina-Castilleja en el momento de máxima importancia dentro de la Sociedad Clasista Inicial marcan un espectro temporal entre el 2772+/-50 y el 2575+/-50 B.C., pero ninguna ha sido tomada para la necrópolis. Además, las descripciones de las secuencias estratigráficas se refieren a contextos cerrados y/o de cada excavación en sí. Basándonos en los registros arqueográficos, difícilmente podemos pronunciarnos sobre la temporalidad y diacronía de las tumbas, ya que las de mampostería, con material campaniforme propio de los últimos momentos del "Calcolítico", pueden incluso ser coetáneas a otros enterramientos en tumbas de lajas, o incluso en estructuras no funerarias.

Con lo expuesto creemos aproximarnos a una visón global de la necrópolis de Valencina-Castilleja en sí, pero por otra parte quedan problemas al respecto sin resolver:

La articulación o relaciones entre los distintos grupos clasistas materializado en las tumbas.

Si tal diversidad es susceptible de manifestarse cronológicamente.

Explicar el comportamiento de las tumbas de mampostería ya que creemos que son éstas las que jugarán el papel como items del cambio social.

Obtener una visión de cómo los distintos y distantes asentamientos del III milenio a.C. jerarquizados en el Valle del Guadalquivir manifiestan el transcurso de su historia en el trato a sus difuntos.

Para ello es obvio que necesitamos más excavaciones competentes, pero dado el grado de destrucción al que está sometido el asentamiento por el acoso urbanístico, cada vez se accede a menos espacios a excavar, por lo que consideramos altamente necesario proyectar investigaciones intensificando analíticas sobre los registros.

References

ARTEAGA, O., ROOS, A., 1995, Geoarchäologische Forschungen im Umkreis der Marismas am Río Guadalquivir (Niederandalusien), *Madrider Mitteilungen* 36, p. 199-218.

ARTEAGA, O., CRUZ-AUÑON, M.R., 2001, Las nuevas sepulturas prehistóricas (tholoi) y los enterramientos bajo túmulos (tartesios) de Castilleja de Guzmán (Sevilla). Excavación de urgencia de 1996, *Anuario Arqueológico de Andalucía 1996* III, p. 640-651.

CRUZ-AUÑON, M.R., ARTEAGA, O., 1999, El sector funerario de Los Cabezuelos (Valencina de la Concepción, Sevilla). Resultados preliminares de una excavación de urgencia., *Anuario Arqueológico de Andalucía 1995* III, p. 589-599.

NOCETE, F., 2001, *Tercer milenio antes de nuestra era. Relaciones y contradicciones centro/periferia en el Valle del Guadalquivir*, Barcelona: Bellaterra.

RODRIGUEZ, M., 2006, La invetigación de la actividad metalúrgica durante el III milenio a..n.e. en el suroeste de la Península Ibérica (Tesis Doctoral, inédita).

VARGAS, J.M., 2004, Carta Arqueológica Municipal de Valencina de la Concepción. In Junta de Andalucía (eds.), *Arqueología. Monografías*, Sevilla.

ESTUDIO GEOARQUEOLÓGICO DEL CONJUNTO DE LOS DÓLMENES DE ANTEQUERA (MÁLAGA, ESPAÑA)

Francisco CARRIÓN MÉNDEZ, José Antonio LOZANO RODRÍGUEZ, David GARCÍA GONZÁLEZ, Teresa MUÑIZ LÓPEZ, Paulo FÉLIX, Carmen Fátima LÓPEZ RODRÍGUEZ, José Antonio ESQUIVEL GUERRERO, Israel MELLADO GARCÍA

Abstract: *A geoarchaeological approach to the Antequera monuments enabled to identify the used lithologies and their provenance, also contributing for the understanding of the building techniques.*
Key-words: *Geo-Archaeology – Antequera – Megaliths*

Résumé: *L'approche géo-archeólogique auz monuments d'Anquera a permis d'identifier les lithologies utilisées ainsi que leur provenance, tout en contribuant a la compréhension des techniques de construction.*
Mots-clés: *Géo-archéologie – Antequera – Mégalithes*

INTRODUCCIÓN

El conjunto arqueológico objeto de estudio se encuentra situado en las inmediaciones de la ciudad de Antequera, al sur de la Península Ibérica (Fig. 8.1). La comarca de Antequera, que se extiende por el norte de la provincia de Málaga, se sitúa en el denominado Surco Intrabético constituyendo un paso clave hacia las campiñas del Guadalquivir. Por el sur, queda separada de la zona meridional de la provincia por las sierras del Valle de Abdalajis, Chimenea, Pelada, Cabras y Camarolos; al este, las sierras de Gibaltón y de Los Pedrosos la separa de las depresiones interiores granadinas, mientras que, por el norte, la zona en la que el limite de la comarca de Antequera queda menos definido, la sierra de los Caballos marca el paso a las campiñas sevillanas; por ultimo, al oeste, la sierra de Cañete sirve de frontera occidental (Guarnido 1977, Carvajal, Ruiz 1984).

El conjunto está formado por los dólmenes de Menga y Viera, muy próximos entre sí, y por el *tholos* del Romeral, que dista unos dos kilómetros de los anteriores. Los dólmenes fueron descubiertos en los primeros años del siglo XX por los hermanos Viera, aunque las referencias escritas al sepulcro de Menga se remontan al siglo XVI (Mitjana 1847, Gómez 1905, Márquez 2000, Ferrer *et al*., 2004).

En el dolmen de Menga podemos distinguir tres zonas: un atrio, un corredor y una enorme cámara. La longitud de todo el conjunto alcanza los 27,5 metros. El atrio de entrada es el que se encuentra en peor estado de conservación, por la pérdida de alguno de sus elementos estructurales o la rotura de los que aún conserva. El segundo tramo, con una planta rectangular, está formado por seis ortostatos y una losa de cobertura con una altura de unos 2,50 metros. El primero de los ortostatos que conforma esta estancia presenta una serie de grabados: las últimas investigaciones apuntan a que se trata de elementos relacionados con una sacralización del espacio por la población cristiana a partir del siglo XVI. La cámara presenta las dimensiones más grandes, con una longitud de 16,10 metros y una altura que va aumentando desde la entrada hasta el final de la cámara, donde alcanza los 3,30 metros. Está formada por quince ortostatos cubiertos por cuatro losas. A su vez, presenta tres pilares, que se sitúan en la unión de las losas de cobertura.

El dolmen de Viera está formado por un largo corredor de unos 19 metros que da paso a la cámara a través de una puerta perforada. En la parte inicial de este corredor se han perdido las losas de cobertura y el dintel de la puerta perforada que daba acceso a su segundo tramo. La cámara es un espacio cuadrangular de 1,6 metros de anchura por dos de altura.

En cuanto al Romeral, se configura como un *tholos* formado por un corredor con paredes de mampostería de piedra y cubierta de losas que da acceso a una cámara a través de una puerta adintelada. La cámara, de forma circular y un diámetro de 5,20 metros, se cierra con una cúpula conformada por la técnica de aproximación de hiladas. La altura total de la cámara es de unos cuatro metros. Tras esta, existe un segundo corredor conformado al igual que el primero, con paredes de mampostería y losas, que da paso a una segunda cámara con las mismas características arquitectónicas que la primera, pero de dimensiones mucho mas reducidas, destacando la existencia de una gran losa de unos 20 centímetros de espesor.

Las primeras investigaciones acerca del dolmen de Menga aparecen hacia mitad del siglo XIX (Mitjana 1947) y se intensifican a lo largo todo el siglo XX (Gómez 1905; Mergelina 1922; Leisner, Leisner 1943; Giménez 1946). Ya en la década de 1990 se llevan a cabo una serie de actuaciones que incluyen la realización de numerosos cortes arqueológicos a cargo de la Universidad de Málaga (Ferrer *et al*., 2004). A su vez, el territorio que circunda los monumentos megalíticos ha sido objeto de estudio de numerosos proyectos de investigación que han podido definir la ocupación de la zona durante la Prehistoria (Márquez *et al*., 1987; Sanchidrían, Gracia 1987, Muñoz 1992, Suárez *et al*. 1995; Marquéz *et al*., 2004). De esta

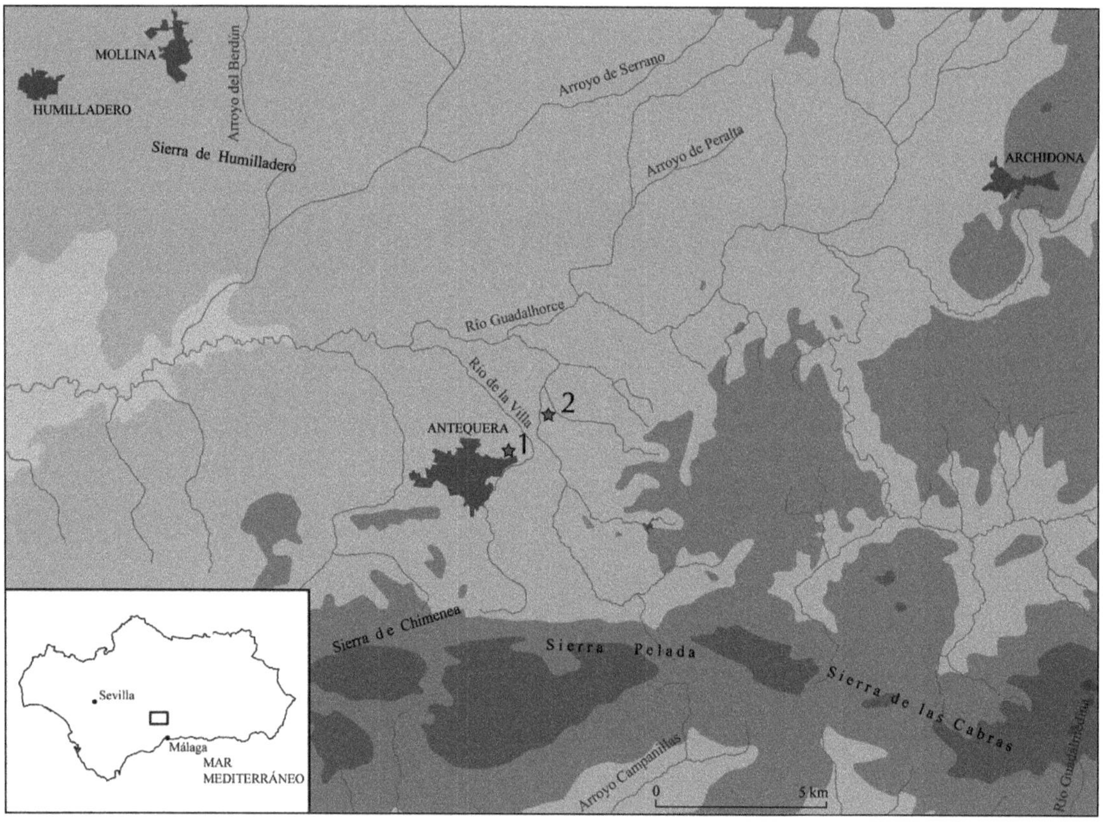

Fig. 8.1. Ubicación de los monumentos

forma, en lo que respecta a los indicios mas antiguos de ocupación, estos se sitúan sobre algunas terrazas del Guadalhorce, donde se ha documentado industria lítica.

Durante el Neolítico, encontramos yacimientos en cueva, sobre todo en la zona del Torcal, de los que podemos mencionar la cueva del Toro, la sima del Tambor y de la Mujer (Martín, Cámalich, González 2004). Por su cercanía a los dólmenes de Menga y Viera, destaca el Cerro de Marimacho, las intervenciones llevadas a cabo en él dieron como resultado la documentación de un poblado calcolítico con estructuras excavadas en la roca y planta ligeramente oval (Marquéz *et al.*, 2004). La secuencia de Marimacho debe comenzar hacia un Cobre Pleno y vería un momento de auge durante el Cobre Tardío y Final con la llegada de influencias campaniformes, continuando su vigencia al menos durante las primeras fases del Bronce, en las que compartiría su influencia en la zona con el cercano poblado de la Peña de los Enamorados (Marquéz *et al.*, 1987). En cuanto a las necrópolis, hay que destacar, además del complejo dolménico de Menga, Viera y Romeral, las del Tardón, Ferradores, Alameda y Alcaide.

OBJETIVOS DEL PROYECTO DE INVESTIGACIÓN

Por encargo de la Dirección General de Bienes Culturales de la Junta de Andalucía, en el mes de mayo de 2005 se proyecta para su ejecución el "Estudio Geoarqueológico de los Sepulcros de Cueva de Menga, Viera y Romeral". Los trabajos de investigación de campo y laboratorio han sido llevados a cabo íntegramente por personal investigador del Instituto Andaluz de Geofísica y del Departamento de Prehistoria y Arqueología, pertenecientes ambos a la Universidad de Granada.

El objetivo general de esta investigación ha sido el de contribuir al estudio e interpretación histórica del conjunto megalítico. Por lo tanto, el estudio geoarqueológico estuvo encaminado al conocimiento del medio geológico local y regional así como al estudio de los soportes líticos empleados para la manufactura de grandes ortostatos y losas de cobertura que conforman la arquitectura de los dólmenes de Menga y Viera y el *tholos* del Romeral. A su vez, el estudio del origen de la materia prima lítica y de los sistemas de aprovisionamiento, involucrando la explotación de canteras para la construcción de los dólmenes, han constituido también objetivos prioritarios de este proyecto de investigación.

Para ello, se han desarrollado trabajos destinados a clasificar, estudiar, reconocer y cartografiar el medio geológico desde diversas perspectivas (sedimentológica, paleontológica, tectónica, estratigráfica, geomorfológica, hidrogeológica, etc.). Se han estudiado y clasificado las diversas litologías presentes en cada una de los megalitos desde una perspectiva petrológica, sedimentológica, estratigráfica, micropaleontológica, tectónica, etc., habiéndose obtenido una cualificada, numerosa y diversificada información.

El objetivo de estos estudios era comprobar si existe relación entre los materiales calcareníticos y brechas del Tortoniense superior empleados en el sistema constructivo de los sepulcros, con los afloramientos naturales presentes tanto en el entorno como en las proximidades de la necrópolis. El estudio de estas relaciones entre necrópolis y afloramientos nos ha conducido, finalmente, a la determinación de las distancias desde las fuentes de suministro, la tecnología de extracción de bloques y el transporte de ortostatos y losas de cobertura hasta el lugar de emplazamiento de los dólmenes.

Para la materialización de estos objetivos se han llevado a cabo las siguientes propuestas:

a. Una aproximación al contexto geográfico y geológico en el marco de la escala local y regional, mediante:
   - El estudio geológico de los entornos de la ciudad de Antequera con la realización de una cartografía geológica de detalle a escala 1:10.000.
   - La obtención de una litoteca de referencia que ha sido georreferenciada mediante GPS.
   - La elaboración de una memoria explicativa de la cartografía geológica.
   - La ejecución de estudios petrográficos, petrológicos y micropaleontológicos.

b. El estudio geológico de los dólmenes de Menga y Viera y el *tholos* de El Romeral, mediante:
   - El estudio detallado de la petrología de los tres megalitos.
   - La toma de muestras litológicas.
   - La realización de estudios específicos a nivel micropaleontológico.

c. El estudio detallado de las probables áreas de captación de materiales líticos empleados en la construcción de los dólmenes.

d. El estudio geométrico del dolmen de Menga, con la realización de mediciones y cálculos matemáticos sobre todos y cada uno de los elementos estructurales que conforman el dolmen de Menga, determinando volúmenes y cálculos relativos al sistema constructivo.

e. Por último, el estudio geotécnico del dolmen de Menga, con la finalidad de:
   - Caracterizar las propiedades mecánicas del material sobre el que se asientan los ortostatos, para determinar la carga de hundimiento y los asientos inducidos.
   - Establecer las características físicas de los ortostatos (densidad aparente, la densidad seca, el peso específico de las partículas sólidas, la porosidad, la humedad y el grado de saturación).
   - Estudiar las propiedades mecánicas de los ortostatos tales como la resistencia a compresión simple, la resistencia a la tracción, el módulo de elasticidad, etc.
   - Determinar las solicitaciones de esfuerzos a las que están sometidos los distintos ortostatos, debido tanto a su propio peso como a la sobrecarga de tierras del túmulo.
   - Explicar el origen de las grietas que presentan algunos de los ortostatos y losas de cubierta.

MÉTODOS Y TÉCNICAS APLICADAS A INVESTIGACIÓN GEOARQUEOLÓGICA DE LOS DÓLMENES DE MENGA, VIERA Y *THOLOS* DEL ROMERAL

El estudio petrográfico y mineralógico de los materiales líticos que conforman los elementos estructurales de los dólmenes constituyó la base de partida. Para la posterior identificación de áreas de captación de materias primas, se identificaron macroscópicamente y a través de métodos petrográficos y geoquímicos los distintos materiales líticos presentes en la construcción de estos monumentos megalíticos. De la misma forma que entre ellos presentan diferencias en cuanto a sus dimensiones, arquitectura y técnicas de construcción (aunque los dólmenes de Menga y Viera se encuentran más próximos respecto a estos aspectos que el *tholos* del Romeral), las litologías empleadas en cada uno de ellos son también distintas. Por lo tanto, los métodos de identificación mineralógica y petrológica se adaptaron a estas premisas, así como a los distintos agentes, de naturaleza antrópica o natural, que dificultaron en ocasiones esta labor de análisis.

Una primera fase de identificación de los materiales que componen los elementos estructurales de los megalitos mediante medios macroscópicos fue complementada con la imprescindible analítica de precisión, utilizándose técnicas tales como la lámina delgada. Paralelamente a este análisis litológico, se llevó a cabo un estudio geotécnico del dolmen de Menga orientado a determinar las propiedades del material geológico sobre el que se asienta el sepulcro, así como las características físicas y mecánicas de los ortostatos, pilares y losas de cobertura.

El siguiente paso consistió en la planificación de la fase de campo. El trabajo se inició con la aproximación al marco geológico y geográfico mediante el estudio de la bibliografía especializada, de la cartografía geológica y geográfica y de la fotografía aérea y satélite disponible. Esta información formó la base documental sobre la que se trazó el área y los diversos diseños de prospección.

La cartografía base de nuestro estudio fue la editada por el Instituto Geominero de España, en la escala 1:50.000: sin embargo porque nuestro trabajo suponía analizar en detalle la totalidad de las facies geológicas presentes en la región, hubo necesidad de recurrir al tradicional trabajo de campo, a escalas algo más sensibles. Para ello, hemos empleado la cartografía topográfica a la escala 1:10.000 publicada por el Instituto Cartográfico de Andalucía (hoja 1023-44), escala que permitía abarcar todas las litologías presentes en las losas y las distintas facies presentes en ellas y explicar todos los fenómenos de génesis y posterior transformación de las unidades geológicas por procesos tectónicos o erosivos.

Los estudios previos nos ayudaron a delimitar el área de estudio, a través de la definición de una serie de criterios como son las características geológicas de la zona y la naturaleza de los soportes utilizados en la elaboración de sepulcros megalíticos. Con todo, conforme el desarrollo de la fase de campo fue avanzando, esta delimitación previa se fue viendo sujeta a transformaciones que recomendaban su limitación. Este factor se debió a la corroboración sobre el terreno de la inexactitud de la información geológica publicada y al volumen de datos que iba generando la investigación de campo.

Aun así, la zona delimitada para la prospección presentaba una serie de problemáticas, la mayoría relacionadas al elevado índice de antropización encontrado: es necesario no olvidar que el conjunto dolménico se encuentra en el límite del casco urbano de la ciudad de Antequera, en un área que hoy día presenta un alto grado de urbanización. Las lagunas que ofrece el terreno, debido a la trama urbana, han sido subsanadas con un análisis detallado de las zonas visibles y el apoyo de las distintas obras, públicas y privadas, que se efectuaban en ese momento y que permitieron, a través de los rebajes mecánicos, poder analizar el material geológico presente y corroborar determinados aspectos del proceso de investigación.

En resumen, se ha llevado una labor de prospección muy sistemática, motivada por la escala elegida, que permitió cartografiar afloramientos de pocos metros. Esta prospección geoarqueológica presentó varias fases:

a. Prospección Selectiva: estuvo encaminada al conocimiento de las unidades geológicas existentes en el área de estudio. Se ha contrastado la información aportada por la cartografía geológica publicada observándose que, en ocasiones, ésta no respondía a la realidad litológica o bien los límites de las distintas unidades no se encontraban bien definidos.

b. Prospección Intensiva: destinada a cartografiar de forma precisa las distintas unidades geológicas, haciendo hincapié en aquellas relacionadas directamente con las litologías presentes en los dólmenes de Menga, Viera y Romeral. Por lo general, las cartografías geológicas disponibles ofrecen una perspectiva muy general sobre la disposición de rocas y minerales (1:50.000 IGME), utilizando criterios de economía y rentabilidad actual a la hora de definir la descripción geológica y que no responde a las necesidades de la investigación geoarqueológica. Por consiguiente, fue fundamental la elaboración de cartografías de detalle que pudiesen mostrar todas las fenomenologías relativas a la disposición geológica de los materiales en una escala mucho más cercana a nuestros intereses, donde se incluyesen actividades económicas de aprovisionamiento de materias primas.

c. Toma de Muestras: ésta permitió la elaboración de una litoteca con las muestras seleccionadas procedentes de las unidades descritas. Para la preparación de la litoteca el muestreo que se realizó fue de carácter sistemático, en que cada muestra obtenida directamente de las diversas formaciones y unidades geológicas fue posicionada en la cartografía disponible mediante GPS con coordenadas UTM. Además se incluyó una documentación fotográfica del área donde se ha obtenido y un sistema de registro para su informatización en una base de datos. Una parte del material se reservó para la determinación petrográfica y geoquímica.

Por último, se ha aplicado un Sistema de Información Geográfica (SIG), que ha permitido organizar de forma eficiente todo el volumen de información obtenido, tener un rápido acceso a todas las capas y generar mapas que relacionan las distintas variables que nos interesan en cada momento resaltar. Otro aspecto interesante que incluyen estos sistemas informáticos es la posibilidad de agregar modelos digitales de elevación. Esta cartografía en tres dimensiones intenta aproximar más aún la representación del mapa a la realidad. Una vez creado un modelo digital, se puede utilizar esta información en nuestra investigación. En el caso que nos ocupa, fue de vital importancia definir las probables áreas de cantería usadas para la extracción de los bloques y la situación topográfica de éstas respecto a los conjuntos megalíticos, ya que el gran volumen de algunas de las losas dificultaría mucho el transporte de las mismas en una orografía con fuertes desniveles y largas distancias.

RESULTADOS

Geología y geomorfología

Desde el punto de vista de la geología, los dólmenes de Menga y Viera se localizan sobre materiales sedimentarios de *facies de delta* de edad Tortoniense superior (Mioceno), abundando las arenas poco o nada cementadas y gravas poligenéticas y heterométricas, así como algún que otro bloque de considerable tamaño y niveles de lutitas de escasa potencia. El *tholos* de El Romeral, por el contrario, está al parecer ubicado sobre materiales del Jurásico (según el IGME, tal vez por la cercanía de estos materiales y la situación sobreelevada del túmulo con respecto a los materiales cuaternarios que lo circunscribe), si bien no hemos podido confirmarlo en este sitio en concreto (Fig. 8.2).

La geomorfología es consecuencia directa de los materiales geológicos que forman la zona: la paleodirección de

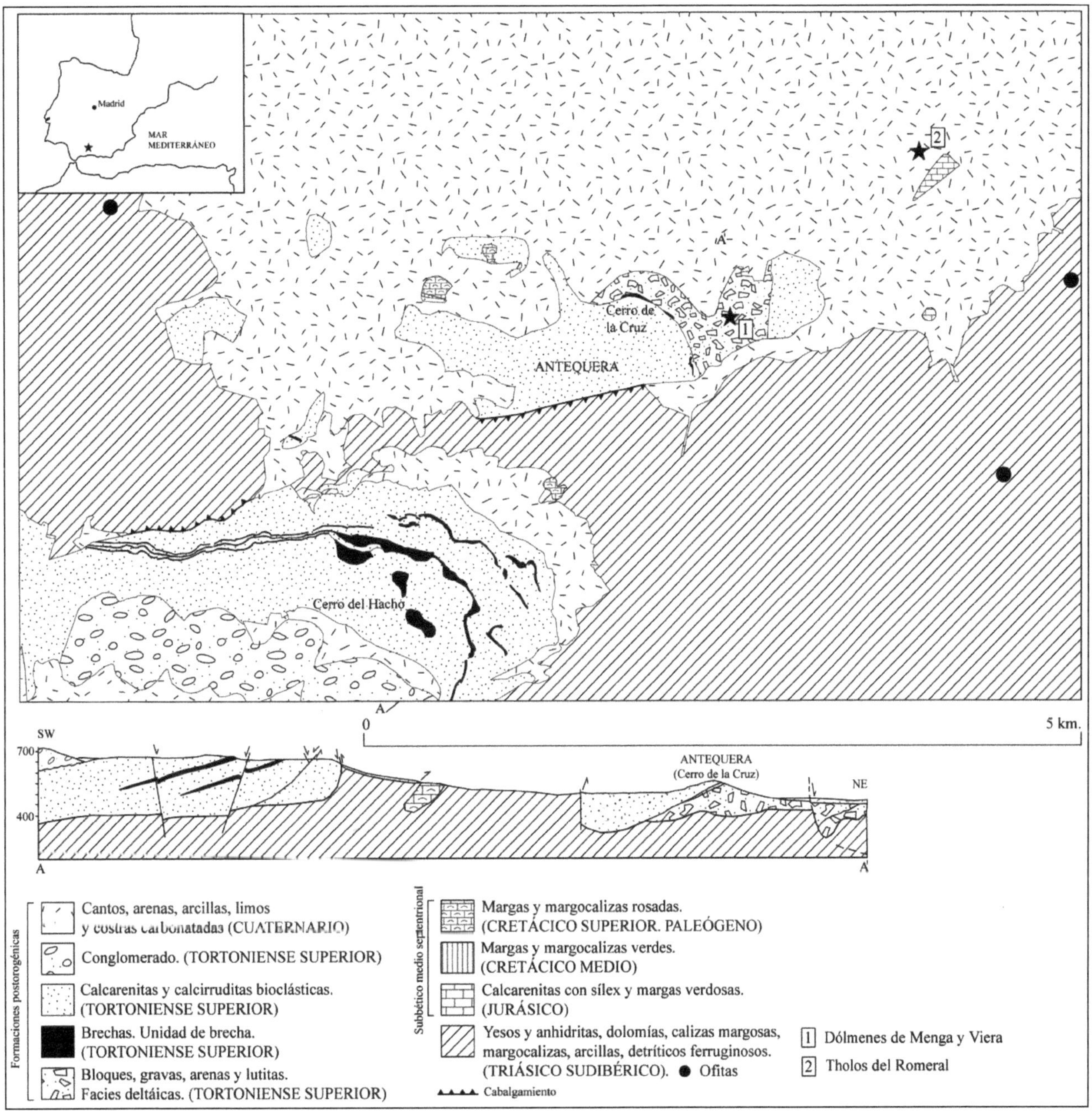

Fig. 8.2. Litologias

progradación de las facies litológicas condiciona una topografía alomada y no muy abrupta, con caída en todas direcciones en torno a los 25-30 metros hasta la llanura cuaternaria, salvo por una zona estrecha de 10 a 25 metros, a modo de península, en la parte suroeste, por donde se sale del pequeño cerro donde se ubican Menga y Viera. Esta salida está marcada por las cabeceras de dos pequeños arroyos que discurren en direcciones enfrentadas. La morfología de este entorno en la época de construcción de los dólmenes no debió de ser muy diferente de la actual, aunque, atendiendo al tiempo transcurrido y a la tasa de degradación específica del material de base, se ha de pensar que las cabeceras de los arroyos se han encajado un poco más, erosionando algunos metros en el pasillo natural.

Ubicación de las canteras de materia prima para la construcción de los dólmenes de Menga y Viera

Las investigaciones geológicas plasmadas en el ámbito de este proyecto implicaron la realización de una cartografía detallada en la escala 1:10.000 sobre la hoja topográfica 1023-44. Esta labor posibilitó la identificación de cuatro series estratigráficas de materiales del Tortoniense superior (Serrano 1979) teóricamente compatibles con los materiales utilizados en la construcción de los monumentos megalíticos de Menga y Viera.

El conjunto más antiguo está definido por las series de Marimacho, Cerro de la Cruz y Barrio de los Remedios, todas ubicadas muy cerca del emplazamiento de los dólmenes: la serie del Marimacho consiste en una facies de playa y plataforma en donde se aprecian movimientos relativos del nivel del mar de pequeño orden y termina a techo con facies deltaicas. Estos deltas presentan litologías propias de materiales de edad triásica, cretácica y del *Complejo del Campo de Gibraltar*, que eran los terrenos elevados en esa época. Posteriormente, se produce una transgresión marina, colocándose encima de los deltas las facies de playa. Éstas presentan eventualmente abanicos aluviales que transportan materiales entre los acantilados marinos, proporcionando un material grosero propio de playas conglomeráticas. Esta cuenca sigue evolucionando con otras dos transgresiones, estabilizándose a techo de la serie con una progradación.

La serie topográficamente más alta es la del Hacho de Antequera, localizada al sur de la ciudad: la secuencia de areniscas puede tener aquí unos 170 metros de espesor y presenta desde facies de rodolitos de algas rojas de zona de factoría hasta facies turbidíticas e, incluso, niveles de ostras (*Ostrea clasistrea gryphoides* y *Ostrea lamellosa*). Existe una *Unidad de Brecha* intercalada en esta serie, poligénica, común en la mayoría de las cuencas terciarias, para esta misma edad (Martín, Braga, Betzler 1996), que responde a una paleoplaya retrabajada en parte por las mareas y el oleaje, con depósitos en forma de lóbulos, aunque en su origen fue posiblemente portada por conos de deyección desde el continente. Debido a sus características, es posible que esta brecha se hubiese originado en un paleorrelieve de acantilados y playas. Pero lo más importante de esta serie del Hacho es la presencia de terrígenos de litología distinta de la presente en las demás series y estructuras sedimentarias no correlacionables: abundan las ostras con respecto a los pectínidos, así como los cantos redondeados y fracturados de carbonatos del Lías, nódulos de sílex, etc., de origen fluvial. Se trata, por lo tanto, de una paleogeografía con rellenos procedentes de áreas diferentes y separadas, posiblemente, por un Triásico que se eleva a modo de diapiro debido a la tectónica y a su contenido en sales y yesos.

Las litologías que configuran los elementos estructurales del dolmen de Menga y de la mayor parte del de Viera responden a rocas sedimentarias detríticas formadas en un contexto marino costero de carbonatos templados, de edad tortoniense superior. Las diferentes unidades litoestratigráficas existentes en la geología local compatibles *grosso modo* con aquellos elementos arquitecturales afloran en el Hacho, en el Cerro de Marimacho y en el Cerro de la Cruz, continuando este último afloramiento hacia el SSW bajo la ciudad de Antequera. Otros pequeños enclaves de la misma tipología y edad geológica se encuentran al oeste y noroeste, cabalgados por el Triásico Sudibérico. Con todo, podemos descartar cualquier posibilidad de que las canteras prehistóricas se ubicasen en el Hacho por absoluta incompatibilidad litológica. Restan las series de Marimacho/Cerro de la Cruz qué, por otra parte, tienen la ventaja de estar mucho más cercanas respecto a los monumentos.

Estratigráficamente, este Tortoniense superior está constituido por unos materiales detríticos deltaicos en la base, de 30 metros de potencia, seguidos por facies de playa (*foreshore*) de no más de dos metros de espesor. Encima aparece una brecha de a veces más de siete metros (*Unidad de Brecha*), pasando a *facies de shoals* muy potentes (10-15 metros) y terminando a techo con una alternancia de margas y areniscas en paquetes de 3-5 metros de potencia con un suelo de alteración. Tanto la Unidad de Brecha como la *facies de foreshore* se acuñan, no estando presentes en todos los cortes geológicos. Por otro lado, las *facies de factoría* pertenecientes a la plataforma carbonatada templada, son observables en un único corte geológico, puesto que también se acuñan o cambian lateralmente de facies.

Hay que recordar que, de las litologías señaladas, el dolmen de Menga está compuesto por *facies de factoría* en su gran mayoría, *Unidad de Brecha*, microconglomerado con abundancia de bivalvos y un ortostato de *facies de foreshore*. En el caso del vecino sepulcro de Viera, predominan los materiales de esta última facies. Con el estudio estratigráfico y paleogeográfico que hemos realizado se ha podido reconstruir la ubicación en el terreno de las unidades litoestratigráficas pertinentes, mediante la obtención de una serie de medidas estadísticas de paleocorrientes en las estructuras internas de las *facies de shoals*, así como la abundancia relativa de terrígenos en las *facies deltaicas* e, incluso, la cantidad de pisolitos en la *Unidad de Brecha*. Con todo esto, se pudo llegar a la conclusión de que la paleolínea de costa para un momento determinado del Tortoniense superior, presentaba una dirección más o menos NW-SE para esta latitud. A partir de aquí fue posible establecer la ubicación de algunas de las distintas partes de la paleoplaya y de la paleoplataforma.

De este modo, situaríamos la *zona de factoría*, la *Unidad de Brecha* y la *facies de shoals* en una franja estrecha comprendida entre el Cerro de la Cruz y el Barrio de los Remedios, con dirección W-NW (Iglesia de la Santísima Trinidad, único lugar donde aparece la *zona de factoría*). De los componentes de Menga, en el Cerro de la Cruz sólo aparece la *Unidad de Brecha*, ubicándose ésta directamente sobre las *facies de delta*. Un análisis en detalle de la litología de esta brecha nos demuestra que presenta menor contenido en pisolitos que los existentes en el dolmen. En el Barrio de los Remedios surgen igualmente las *facies de shoals* y la *Unidad de Brecha*, estando esta última a su vez sobre las *facies de foreshore* y éstas sobre las deltaicas. Por otro lado, hay que anotar que aquí la *Unidad de Brecha* presenta mucha más matriz terrígena que la presente en Menga.

En definitiva, creemos es posible asegurar que los materiales utilizados en la edificación de los sepulcros megalíticos de Menga y Viera no proceden de los

Fig. 8.3. Ubicación de los dólmenes conm respecto al Cerro de la Cruz

afloramientos de areniscas y conglomerados carbonatados del Hacho de Antequera. La ubicación de las canteras explotadas por los constructores prehistóricos no es conocida con precisión absoluta, pero los datos litoestratigráficos que poseemos indican, con una probabilidad muy elevada, para los afloramientos de la serie Cerro de la Cruz/Barrio de los Remedios (Fig. 8.3), si bien es casi seguro que los ortostatos y losas de cubierta de material brecha no se extrajeron en el Cerro de la Cruz propiamente dicho, al contrario de lo que afirma la tradición local. La cantera o canteras deberían de haberse localizado en un área o banda muy estrecha comprendida entre el Barrio de los Remedios y las inmediaciones del Cerro de la Cruz, es decir, muy cerca de la ubicación final de los sepulcros.

El dolmen de Menga

Litología y conservación

En el estudio litológico del dolmen de Menga se ha podido diferenciar, a grandes rasgos, tres tipos distintos de rocas (Fig. 8.4): calcarenitas/calcirruditas bioclásticas (procedentes de *facies de factoría* y de *foreshore*), una brecha plana poligenetica con matriz calcárea muy cementada (*facies de foreshore* – como consecuencia de abanicos aluviales que superan paleoacantilados marinos) y, por último, un microconglomerado con bivalvos (también de *facies de foreshore*). Hay que señalar que dentro de la *facies de factoría* hemos encontrado materiales de dos subfacies: una correspondiente a fauna de bivalvos y briozoos y otra de bivalvos, briozoos y algas rojas (a 5-7 metros más profunda sobre el nivel del mar Tortoniense Superior que la primera).

Desde el punto de vista de la paleofauna se observan especies típicas de carbonatos templados de plataforma y playa: briozoos, bivalvos (*Clamys*, Pectínidos, etc.), algas (rojas, Dasycladáceas, etc.), espinas de erizo, foraminíferos (Nummulites, Amphisteginas, Globigerinas, Operculinas, etc.) y algún braquiópodo.

Los ortostatos y las losas de cobertura del dolmen presentan algunos problemas de conservación que pueden suponer, a medio plazo, graves problemas de estabilidad. El más delicado está constituido por la fracturación que se observa en todos los componentes estructurales del monumento, pero de modo más importante en las losas del techo, con fracturas en forma de diaclasa e incluso con pérdida de masa (Losa 3). Su génesis se debe a procesos microtectónicos (movimiento lento de los materiales del Triásico que subyacen a los de edad miocénica que forman el substrato en donde se asienta el dolmen), actuantes con carácter más significativo en la Losa 3 por ausencia de un pilar de sustentación necesario para reducir este efecto. Muchas de las fracturas son recientes, puesto que algunas de ellas cortan las costras calcáreas y oscuras.

Otros problemas de conservación están formados por la erosión de la parte baja de los ortostatos (probablemente en consecuencia del rozamiento del ganado, incrementado por un mayor contenido de humedad de estas zonas) y por alteraciones químicas de tipo concreciones y disoluciones.

La alteración química más importante se ha producido por reiterados procesos de combustión realizados dentro del monumento, que provocaron el desarrollo de un costra oscura constituida por sulfatos cálcicos hidratados en forma de cristales de yeso, creciendo entre los elementos estructurales de la piedra, con distintos hábitos y tamaños, con la consiguiente disminución superficial de la permeabilidad de la roca, disgregación, pérdida de masa y, finalmente, su disolución.

La segunda clase de alteración superficial de los ortostatos y losas de techo de Menga lo constituye la formación de una costra calcárea. Esta capa de carbonato

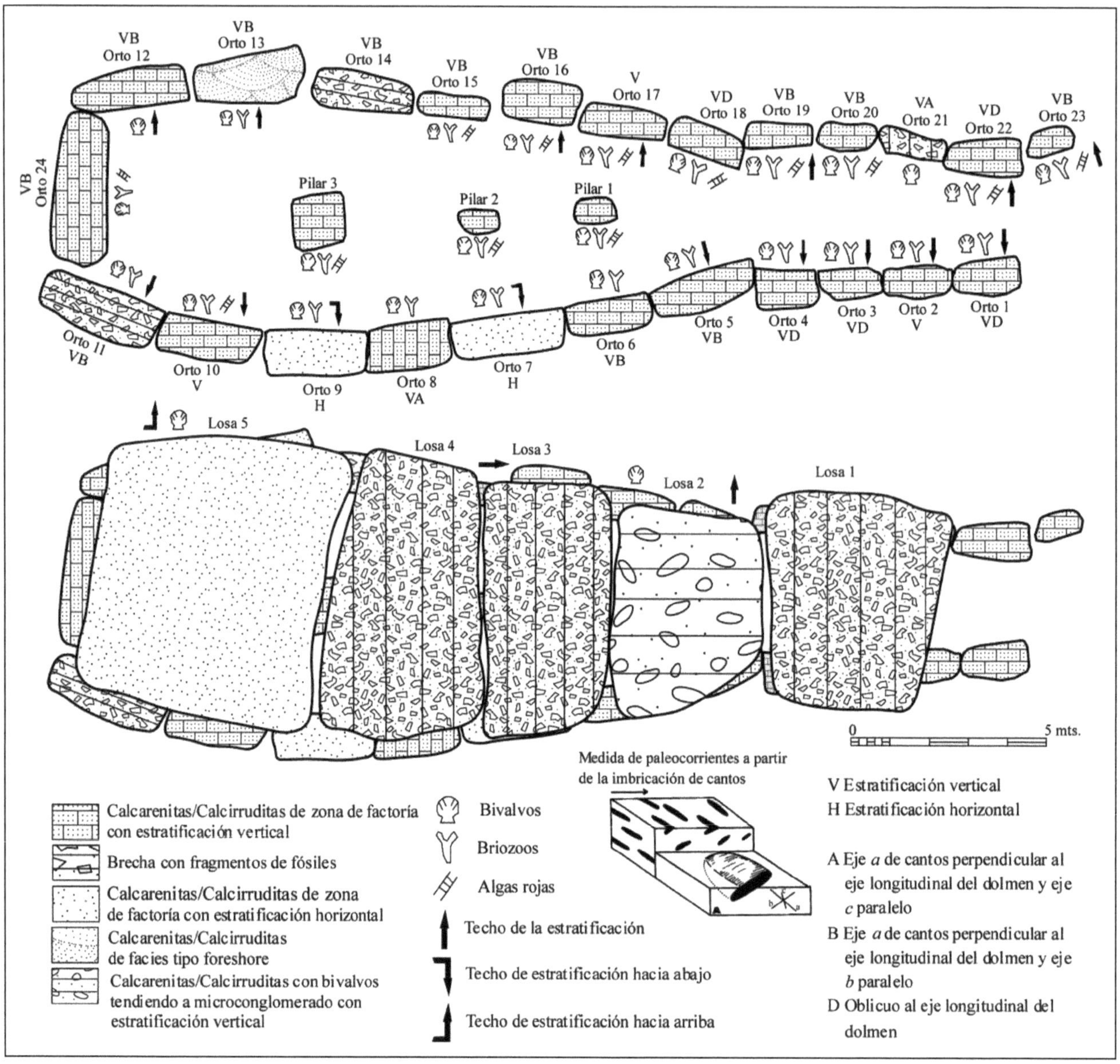

Fig. 8.4. Estudio litológico de detalle. Dolmen de Menga

cálcico se origina a partir de la actividad microbiológica y de su interacción con el oxígeno y los componentes minerales elementales de la roca, generándose principalmente nitratos que se transforman en ácido nítrico y disuelven el carbonato cálcico, produciendo óxido cálcico. Este producto, mediante la reacción posterior con el dióxido de carbono, crea un precipitado de carbonato cálcico.

Además de las costras antes descritas, existen algunas eflorescencias de nitrato potásico, identificadas con DRX y F-Tir, estando también presente una cantidad significativa de cloruros, puestos de manifiesto en el microanálisis con SEM-DEX (Espinosa 1998).

Finalmente, se aprecia un fenómeno importante de deformación de tipo mecánico, visible sobre todo en el Ortostato 13: este elemento estructural del dolmen pertenece litológicamente a la *facies de foreshore* y está compuesto por unas estructuras internas consistentes en estratificaciones planares que facilitan el pandeo, por sobrepeso en la vertical, ya que el ortostato ha extraído de la cantera paralelo a la estratificación y a la laminación y su colocación en el dolmen se ha realizado con estas estructuras orientadas paralelamente a la dirección de los esfuerzos.

Estudio geotécnico del dolmen de Menga

Se ha realizado un estudio geotécnico completo del dolmen de Menga, cuyos objetivos fueron los siguientes:

a. Caracterizar las propiedades mecánicas del material sobre el que se asientan los ortostatos, determinar la carga de hundimiento y los asientos inducidos.

b. Determinar las características físicas de los ortostatos, al menos de sus litologías representativas, entre las que podemos destacar la densidad aparente, la densidad seca, el peso específico de las partículas sólidas, la porosidad, la humedad y el grado de saturación.

c. Estudiar las propiedades mecánicas de los ortostatos tal como la resistencia a compresión simple, la resistencia a tracción, el módulo de elasticidad, etc.

d. Determinar las solicitaciones de esfuerzos a las que están sometidos los distintos ortostatos debido tanto a su propio peso como a la sobrecarga de tierras situadas sobre los laterales y la cubierta.

e. Explicar el origen de las grietas que presentan los ortostatos en función de las solicitudes indicadas anteriormente.

La elevada capacidad portante del terreno y las pequeñas presiones ejercidas por los ortostatos sobre el mismo han asegurado la estabilidad del dolmen a lo largo de los siglos. En cuanto al análisis estructural, cabe decir que las grietas observadas en las Losas 1 y 2 no se han producido por el momento flector debido al propio peso de la roca y a la sobrecarga de tierras sobre la misma, puesto que la tracción inducida por dicho momento es bastante inferior a la resistencia a tracción de la roca. En el resto de las losas de cubierta, la tracción ocasionada por el momento es menor pero próxima a la resistencia a tracción de la roca e incluso pudo haber sido superado en el pasado con una mayor sobrecarga de tierras en el túmulo. Tal era la conciencia de tal efecto que por esta razón se colocaron los pilares centrales de forma que dicho momento sufriera una reducción considerable.

Las grietas que se observan en los Losas 1 y 2 se han debido producir por movimientos sísmicos con un grado de magnitud superior a 6,8. Al efecto de estos movimientos sísmicos hay que añadir el momento flector máximo que actúa permanentemente en el eje central de las losas, el cambio de momentos flectores que sufrieron estas losas cuando se eliminó el soporte central fue el causante de la presencia de discontinuidades internas.

Por último, cabe comentar que el lajamiento que se observa en el Ortostato 13 se ha producido por pandeo debido a la presión vertical ejercida sobre el mismo abarca la altura total de la pieza con un espesor de apertura comprendido entre los 8 y los 15 centímetros.

Geometría del dolmen de Menga

A partir de la planimetría y los datos de campo se han establecido unas conclusiones importantes acerca de las dimensiones del monumento, el diseño arquitectónico, el planteamiento previo al diseño, el análisis energético, etc., que proporcionan una información de gran importancia acerca de la construcción del dolmen y de sus constructores.

En primer lugar, toda la construcción se ha realizado pensando en cómo se va a visualizar el monumento desde el interior del mismo, por ello los aspectos estéticos se establecen para ser llevados a cabo exclusivamente en el interior. Así:

a. Las dimensiones del monumento mantienen unas proporciones casi perfectamente regulares a partir de las partes visibles del mismo: altura visible y anchura visible.

b. Los ortostatos y las losas que conforman la cubierta están bastante alisadas y se mantienen en un plano paralelo al suelo, sin inclinaciones laterales. Y puesto que el suelo mantiene una pequeña inclinación, existe una variación de las alturas visibles en tres partes, lo que permite mantener el paralelismo de las losas de la cubierta.

c. Existen tres partes respecto a las alturas visibles que constituyen conjuntos independientes: 1) formada por los cinco primeros ortostatos a partir del central, 2) el resto de ortostatos excepto los dos pequeños de la parte final, y 3) una parte muy residual distinta del resto del dolmen formada por los dos pequeños ortostatos del final.

d. Los análisis previos indican que otras variables no visibles no están previamente determinadas. Así, el grosor, la anchura, la altura total (en los casos en los que se ha podido establecer) son muy variables. Además, la parte oculta de los ortostatos verticales no tienen relación con respecto a la parte visible, es decir, son independientes.

Existe una simetría general respecto a la planta del monumento bastante clara, incluyendo los pilares del centro; sin embargo, un análisis detallado muestra que existen bastante diferencias entre los ortostatos de la parte izquierda y los de la parte derecha (mirando hacia el interior desde la entrada); los ortostatos de la izquierda siguen una curva continua bastante acusada, mientras que los ortostatos de la derecha siguen una línea bastante más recta que los anteriores.

El volumen interior al dolmen se ha calculado en 270 m^3, un valor bastante grande que no solamente indica las dimensiones volumétricas del mismo, sino que permite afirmar que si la técnica de construcción exigía rellenar el interior de arena para posteriormente poder colocar la cubierta y eliminar dicho relleno, el gasto energético sería el correspondiente a mover 540 m^3, cantidad muy importante que es necesaria tener en cuenta, si se considera cierta alguna teoría constructiva que incluya este proceso. Además, habría que contar con el gasto energético necesario para vaciar los cimientos y para construir el túmulo, ambos muy difíciles de estimar en este estadio de la excavación.

Estas consideraciones inducen la existencia de un patrón arquitectónico bien definido basado en la geometría, indicando que ya en el periodo de construcción del

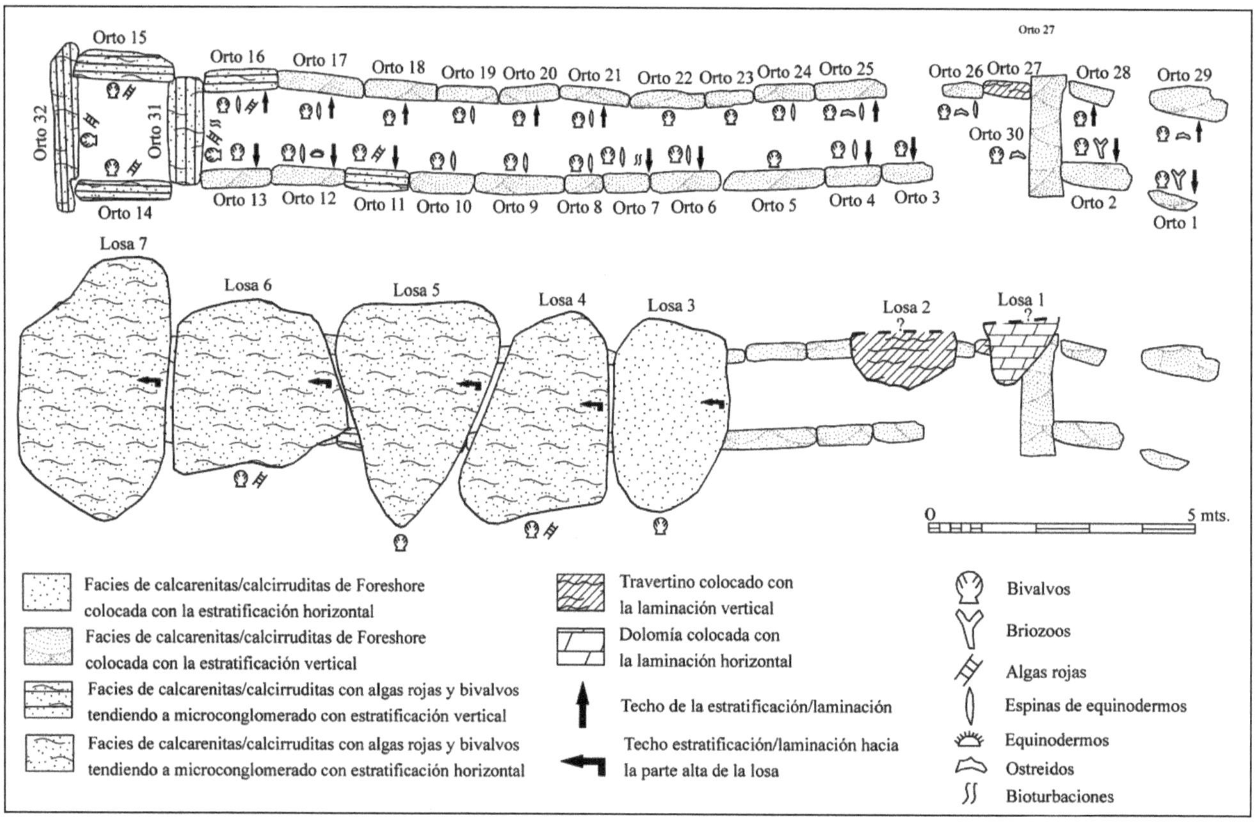

Fig. 8.5. Estudio litológico de detalle. Dolmen de Viera

dolmen, los habitantes de la zona de Antequera conocían conceptos y términos métricos y geométricos, como se ha constatado en Los Millares y otras zonas del sureste durante el Calcolítico (Esquivel, Navas 2005, 2007).

El dolmen de Viera

Este monumento es bastante más homogéneo que el de Menga en cuanto a la litología que constituye sus elementos estructurales. Está compuesto sobre todo por materiales de la *facies de foreshore*, exceptuando algún que otro componente formado por calcarenitas y calcirruditas con algas rojas y bivalvos que tienden a microconglomerado, dos elementos de travertinos cuaternarios y uno formado por una dolomía de edad triásica (Fig. 8.5).

Tanto en las calcarenitas como en las calcirruditas aparece, a grandes rasgos, la misma fauna que en el dolmen de Menga, propia de los carbonatos templados de playa y plataforma del Tortoniense superior, con la diferencia de que pertenecen mayoritariamente a la *facies de foreshore*. El medio de formación es muy energético, propio de las zonas de playa y se ve reflejado en los bioclastos bastante fracturados, siendo también normal ver alguna que otra bioturbación.

En este monumento, los elementos arquitectónicos poseen estructuras internas bien visibles (superficies de discontinuidad) que favorecen la fracturación y/o el pandeo si su colocación coincide con la dirección del esfuerzo producido por las losas de cubierta y el material del túmulo. Sin embargo, los ortostatos de Viera resisten bastante bien esos esfuerzos, sin duda debido a los menores tamaños de sus piezas estructurales cuando son comparadas con las de Menga. No obstante, algunas de las losas de techo han llegado a fracturarse a pesar de estar colocadas con la estratificación interna orientada perpendicularmente a los esfuerzos de carga, con fracturas en cruz presentes en el centro y en el lateral de algunas de las losas. Al igual que en Menga, esta fracturación se debe a la microtectónica, aunque es posible que este monumento pudo verse afectado por algún seísmo con magnitud tal que pudiera mover elementos estructurales en este caso de dimensiones más pequeñas.

Estos elementos no presentan tanta erosión física ni meteorización cuando en comparación con los de Menga; son observables rubefacciones por alteración térmica en muchos de sus ortostatos, pero no se aprecian gran número de costras carbonatadas o de sulfato cálcico, probablemente debido al hecho de que este dolmen ha sido sometido a diversas fases de conservación y restauración.

El *tholos* de El Romeral

La composición litológica de este monumento es bien diferente de las anteriores: presenta mayor variedad de materiales, predominando las rocas sedimentarias de

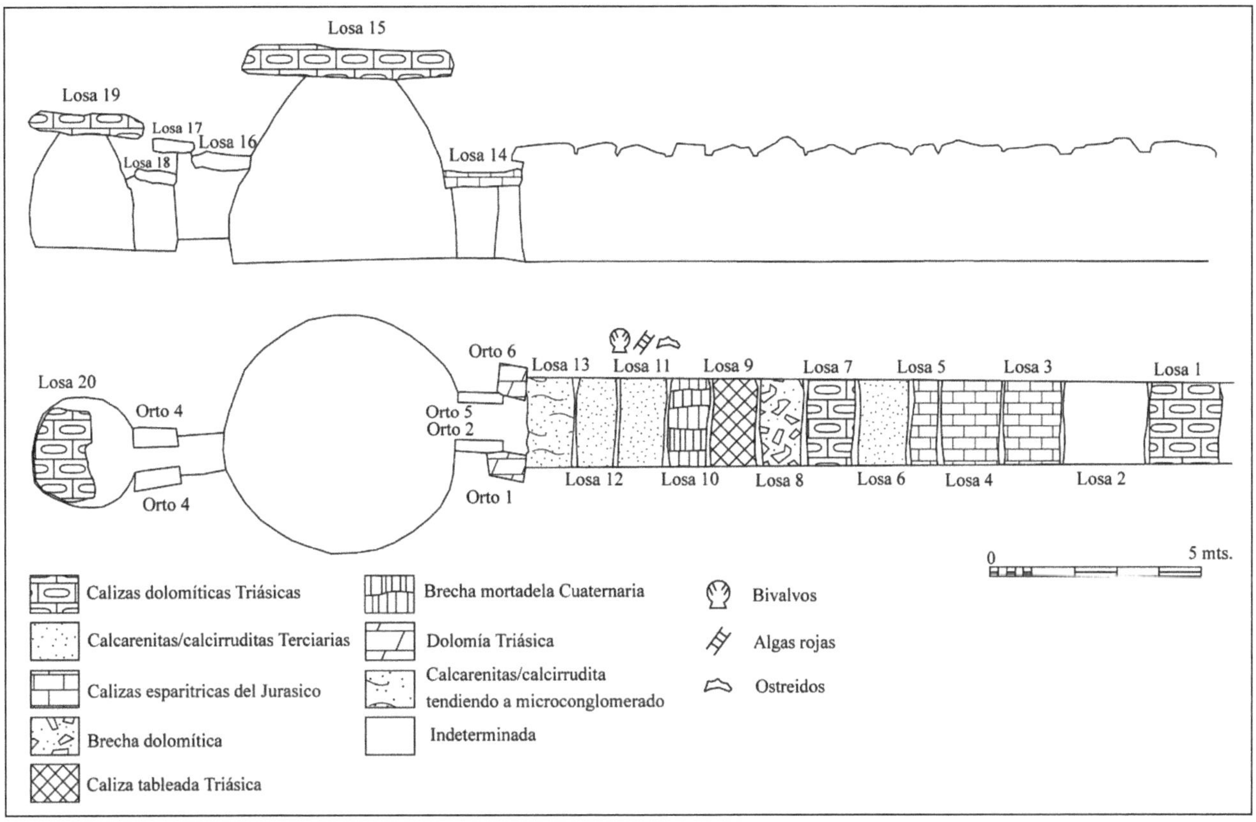

Fig. 8.6. Estudio litológico de detalle. Tholos de Romeral

precipitación química (calizas, dolomías y calizas dolomíticas del Triásico y del Jurásico), además de calcarenitas bioclásticas del Tortoniense superior y brechas del Triásico y del Cuaternario. La losa 11, del corredor, es la única que presenta fauna observable, correspondiendo a la propia de plataformas carbonatadas templadas, con bivalvos, briozoos, foraminíferos, etc., de edad tortoniense (Fig. 8.6).

El *tholos* de El Romeral es el monumento del conjunto de Antequera más perjudicado por la fracturación, con fracturas que se presentan de modo vertical tanto en las losas de techo como en las rocas que componen la mampostería de las paredes y dinteles. El número de estas fracturas es muy elevado, estando distribuidas por la totalidad del sepulcro y son muy visibles en las dos cámaras de falsa cúpula por haber tenido menos intervenciones de restauración. El dintel que marca el acceso a la primera cámara presenta igualmente fractura vertical, con la peculiaridad de afectar a un caliche con génesis posterior a la edificación del *tholos*. Además, la fractura no ha finalizado su recorrido alrededor del dintel, lo cual nos hace pensar que muchas de ellas son activas. Algunas de la losas del techo fueron intervenidas en campañas de restauración anteriores por presentar fracturas completas con basculamiento.

La erosión y meteorización afecta tan sólo a la losa de arenisca carbonatada, por ser una roca poco cementada y muy porosa y sobre todo, al barro utilizado para fijar y sellar la mampostería. Por otra parte, se observan pocos caliches en el interior del sepulcro, aunque los que se aprecian presentan características típicas de concreciones carbonatadas por precipitación.

CONCLUSIONES

La aplicación de una metodología geoarqueológica al estudio del conjunto monumental de los dólmenes de Antequera ha permitido establecer una serie de conclusiones acerca de las litologías empleadas en la edificación de los sepulcros megalíticos y de la definición de las posibles áreas de captación de las materias primas que constituyen sus elementos estructurales. Además, este enfoque ha contribuido al avance en el conocimiento de los procesos de construcción de los monumentos y, en el caso de Menga, el estudio geotécnico ha aportado valiosos datos sobre la caracterización de las propiedades físicas y mecánicas de sus ortostatos y losas de cobertura, a la vez que contribuye a la planificación de estrategias de conservación.

Los dólmenes de Menga y Viera están construidos sobre materiales de facies deltaicas que, por sus características geológicas, presentan una morfología propia de cerro testigo. A su vez, es posible encontrar muy cerca materiales con unas características litológicas muy óptimas para levantar monumentos megalíticos con las dimensiones que exhiben. Esas propiedades no son otras que la gran resistencia a los esfuerzos, la capacidad para ser trabajada y un peso específico no muy alto.

En una primera fase del proyecto, se identificaron de un modo lo más preciso posible las diversas litologías de las cuales están constituidos los diferentes elementos estructurales de los dólmenes. En seguida se elaboró una cartografía geológica a una escala que nos posibilitara la ubicación teórica de la zona o zonas de extracción de los bloques utilizados en la construcción de los sepulcros, la zona que hemos determinado tendrá que situarse dentro de una franja muy estrecha comprendida entre el Barrio de los Remedios y las inmediaciones del Cerro de la Cruz, en el área norte de la ciudad de Antequera, muy cerca de la ubicación de los monumentos megalíticos.

Las facies sedimentológicas identificadas en los elementos estructurales de los dólmenes pertenecen a tres zonas bien diferenciadas del medio costero: por un lado, la correspondiente a una brecha propia de una playa conglomerática; por otro lado, la correspondiente a la *facies de foreshore*; y, por último, las que proceden de las facies de plataforma de tipo *zona de factoría*. De esta última zona hemos podido reseñar dos de las tres subfacies que la constituyen: la de briozoos y algas rojas y la de bivalvos y briozoos.

Es muy probable que la extracción tanto de los componentes estructurales del interior como los correspondientes a las rocas que forman el túmulo, se realizaran aprovechando superficies de discontinuidad previamente existentes como consecuencia de procesos puramente geológicos. Esto se deduce del hecho de observar en algunos laterales, recrecimiento radial de calcita cristalina propia de disolución de carbonato cálcico y precipitación en fracturas ya preexistentes. La presencia de este mineral carbonatado indica la existencia de una fractura anterior a su precipitación, siendo por aquí el lugar por el cual se favorece su extracción.

En relación a las alteraciones documentadas, la causa fundamental de la aparición de una costra oscura sobre algunos de las losas y ortostatos es el hecho de haber realizado combustión en el interior de la cámara, generándose una serie de reacciones químicas en la roca carbonatada que llegan a generar yeso hidratado. Respecto a la costra carbonatada, se debe a un proceso de precipitación química por disolución de parte de la roca de la que están compuestos los sepulcros, fundamentalmente por cambios de presión y temperatura.

En referencia a la fracturación que presentan algunas losas de cobertura, en un principio se barajó la posibilidad de que ellas fuesen producto de un gran movimiento sísmico. Tal hipótesis fue desechada a medida que observábamos datos en contra de esta suposición inicial. En primer lugar, tendríamos que tener en cuenta que para poder mover tanto tonelaje como el compuesto por la suma de todas las losas de techo tendría que haber existido un terremoto de magnitud mayor a 6,8, en torno a 0,5 G de aceleración. Tal terremoto dejaría en el campo un escarpe de falla tan grande que se tendría que apreciar netamente y haber dejado constancia en la memoria histórica de los pueblos colindantes. Es más probable pensar en el hecho probado de movimiento a modo de diapiro del Triásico, que se mueve bajo el material Terciario en el que están ubicados los dólmenes. Con el agravante de la ausencia de un pilar, en el caso del dolmen de Menga, las losas de techo se fatigan y fracturan lentamente en el centro por pandeo.

El tercer sepulcro del conjunto monumental de Antequera es el *tholos* de El Romeral que, obviamente, posee una arquitectura y un sistema de construcción totalmente diferentes al resto. Presenta un largo corredor que lleva a una primera cámara circular con falsa cúpula y de aquí, por medio de un pequeño pasillo, a una última cámara mucho más pequeña, también con falsa cúpula y algo escorada con respecto a la primera. Se encuentra situado lejos de los dos anteriores en una pequeña elevación posiblemente de edad jurásica, rodeado de materiales de edad cuaternaria como consecuencia de llanuras de inundación y abanicos aluviales. Está compuesto por una variedad litológica muy representativa de todos los materiales que aparecen en el entorno. Mientras en Viera y Menga la litología que los compone es mucho más homogénea, en El Romeral la heterogeneidad es un dato característico: son mayoritariamente calizas tableadas, calizas dolomíticas y brecha dolomítica del Triásico, calizas esparíticas de edad jurásica y, por último, "brecha mortadela" del Cuaternario. De todos los sepulcros, este *tholos* es el que presenta señales más preocupantes de deterioro, sobre todo por fracturación de casi la totalidad de los bloques usados en el sistema de mampostería. Si bien fue intervenido en diversas ocasiones, la última de las cuales en los años 40, su estado de conservación sigue siendo muy delicado, presentando evidentes señales de problemas de estabilidad.

Por último, cabe destacar que este estudio geoarqueológico se viene complementado con una serie de intervenciones arqueológicas tanto en el interior como en el túmulo del dolmen de Menga. Cuando estas finalicen se dispondrá de un gran conjunto de datos que ayudarán a la interpretación de los distintos procesos de construcción de este sepulcro megalítico.

Bibliografía

CARVAJAL, M.C., RUIZ, J.D., 1984, La depresión de Antequera. In Alcobendas, M. (ed.) *Málaga. 1: Geografía.* Málaga.

ESPINOSA GALVÁN, J., 1998, Estudio petrográfico de los materiales de los Dólmenes de Antequera. *PH, Boletín de Instituto Andaluz del Patrimonio Histórico.* Sevilla. 25, p. 80-88.

ESQUIVEL, J.A., NAVAS, E., 2005, The geometry used in the enclosure "Fortín 1" at Copper Age site of Los

Millares (Almería, Andalusia). *Journal of Archaeological Science*. London. 32, p. 1577-1586.

ESQUIVEL, J.A., NAVAS, E., 2007, Geometric architectural pattern and constructive energy analysis at Los Millares Copper Age settlement (Santa Fe de Mondújar, Almería, Andalusia). *Journal of Archaeological Science*. London. 34, p. 894-904.

FERRER PALMA, J.E., MARQUÉS MERELO, I., BALDOMERO NAVARRO, A., AGUADO MANCHA, T., 2004, Estructuras tumulares y procesos de construcción en los sepulcros megalíticos de la provincia de Málaga: La necrópolis megalítica de Antequera. *Mainake*. Málaga. 26, p. 177-210.

GARCÍA PÉREZ, A., RODRÍGUEZ VINCEIRO, F.J., BARRERA POLO, M., FERNÁNDEZ RODRÍGUEZ, L.E., VON THODE MAYORAL, C., SUÁREZ PADILLA, J., La Peña de los Enamorados de Antequera (ladera oeste): Un Importante Enclave en la Ruta del Genil hacia Andalucía Oriental. In *Actas del XXI Congreso Nacional de Arqueología*. Zaragoza. Vol. 1, p. 73-84.

GIMÉNEZ REYNA, S., 1946, *Memoria arqueológica de la provincia de Málaga hasta 1946*. Madrid: Comisaría General de Excavaciones Arqueológicas.

GÓMEZ MORENO, M., 1905, Arquitectura tartesia: la necrópolis de Antequera. *Boletín de la Real Academia de la Historia*. Madrid. 47, p. 81-132.

GUARNIDO, V., 1977, *La depresión de Antequera*. Málaga.

LEISNER, G., LEISNER, V., 1943, *Die Megalithgräber der Iberischen Halbinsel. I: Der Süden*. Berlin: Walter de Gruyter.

MARTÍN, D., CÁMALICH, M.D., GONZÁLEZ, P., 2004, *Cueva del Toro (Sierra del El Torcal, Antequera, Málaga): Un modelo de ocupación ganadera en el territorio andaluz entre el VI y II milenios A.N.E.* Sevilla: Junta de Andalucía.

MARQUÉS MERELO, I., AGUADO MANCHA, T., BALDOMERO NAVARRO, A., FERRER PALMA, J.E., 2004) – Proyectos sobre la Edad del Cobre en Antequera (Málaga). In *Actas del II-III Simposios de Prehistoria Cueva de Nerja*. Málaga: Fundación Cueva de Nerja, p. 238-260.

MÁRQUEZ, J., MORALES, A., 1987, Prospección superficial en la Sierra de Camorra (Mollina, Málaga). *Anuario Arqueológico de Andalucía*. Sevilla. 1985:2, p. 29-32.

MÁRQUEZ ROMERO, J.E., 2000, *El Megalitismo en la provincia de Málaga: breve guía para su conocimiento e interpretación*. Málaga: Universidad de Málaga.

MERGELINA, C. de, 1922, La necrópolis tartesia de Antequera. *Boletín de la Sociedad Española de Antropología, Etnografía y Prehistoria*. Madrid. 4, p. 37-90.

MITJANA, R., 1847, *Memoria sobre el templo druida hallado en las cercanías de la ciudad de Antequera*. Málaga.

MUÑOZ VIVAS, V.E., 1992, Las manifestaciones pictóricas del abrigo del Cortijo de la Escardadera. *Zephyrus*. Salamanca. 44, p. 497-510.

SANCHIDRIÁN, J., GRACÍA, M., 1987, Material cerámico de la Sima Hoyo del Tambor (El Torcal, Antequera). *Mainake*. Málaga. 8-9, p. 89-104.

SERRANO, F., 1979, *Los foraminíferos planctónicos del Mioceno Superior de la Cuenca de Ronda y su comparación con los de otras áreas de las Cordilleras Béticas*. Málaga: Universidad de Málaga.

MORE THAN BIG STONES! PERIPHERAL AND CONFINED OR RESISTANT LINEAGE SOCIETIES IN THE PRISTINE CLASS-SOCIETY TERRITORIAL FRAMEWORK OF THE SOUTH-WESTERN IBERIAN PENINSULA (2900-2000 BC)

Francisco NOCETE
Department of History I, University of Huelva, Huelva, Spain 21071
Email: nocete@uhu.es

Ana PERAMO

(Translated by Catherine T. Boulanger)

***Abstract**: In the first inter-settlement hierarchical framework of the South of the Iberian Peninsula (3rd millennium BC), a singular phenomenon of territorial and social exclusion in south-western Iberia (which is it, South of the Iberian Peninsula or south-western Iberia? can be observed: the mountain-inhabiting nomad herdsmen social units from the Andévalo region, living surrounded by the large agricultural centers from the Guadalquivir Valley and the coastal polities mining/metallurgical inland factories. Their cemeteries, in the Andévalo, are located at the geographical and political centre of a complex funerary network, that define and delimit a 2000 km² territory situated in between the Tinto and Odiel Rivers, where small peripheral tombs dot each of the access points, defining an ideological as well as a territorial boundary. In their large megalithic necropoli (Pozuelo, Villar, Gabrieles, Buitón), the biggest tombs are located at the centre of the cemetery, commanding and dominating the smaller tombs dotted around them. Their position in the overall layout is indicative of their hierarchical importance. The chronological evidence (¹⁴C dates) reveals that for over a century, rituals involving bonfires and the breaking of ceramic vessels were carried out on a regular basis at the central tomb locations. These practices seem to have been performed along the same pathways, establishing a form of ceremonialism involving processional rituals. These megalithic cemeteries became the main ideological instrument of these social units, justifying through ancestor worshiping their incipient internal inequality as well as defining their territorial and ideological boundaries. We understand the dispersion pattern of these monuments as a result of peripheral formations of confined and/or resistant lineage societies as an effect of core/periphery relations and of the internal contradictions of the early society of classes.*
***Key-words**: Core/Periphery relationships, Resistance, Lineage Societies, Iberian Peninsula, Third Millennium BC*

***Resumen**: En el primer armazón intersocial jerárquico del Sur de la Península Ibérica (Tercer Milenio ANE), puede observarse un fenómeno territorial singular de exclusión social en el Suroeste: los grupos nómadas de la región del Andévalo que coexistieron entre los grandes centros agrarios del Valle del Guadalquivir y las factorías minerometalúrgicas. Los cementerios del Andévalo, localizados en el centro geográfico y político de un complejo armazón funerario, definen y delimitan un territorio de 2000 km² situado entre los ríos Tinto y Odiel con pequeñas tumbas periféricas en cada uno de los accesos al territorio, mostrando una frontera ideológica y territorial. En sus grandes necrópolis megalíticas (Pozuelo, Villar, Gabrieles, Buitrón), sus tumbas mayores se localizaron en el centro de los cementerios, dominando las tumbas pequeñas situadas a su alrededor. Su ubicación y complejidad de construcción señala su importancia jerárquica. Las dataciones radiocarbónicas (¹⁴C) muestran la continuidad, durante mas de cien años, de prácticas rituales con fracturación de vasos cerámicos y fuegos alrededor de ellas mediante un ceremonialismo que incluyó rituales procesionales. Esos cementerios megalíticos se convirtieron, así, en un instrumento ideológico fundamental de las unidades sociales, justificando, a través de los antepasados su incipiente desigualdad interna a la par que su límite territorial e ideológico, sugiriendo, que fueron el resultado de una formación periférica de sociedades de linaje marginales o resistentes y un efecto de las relaciones y contradicciones centro/periferia de la primera sociedad de clases.*
***Mots clés**: Relations Centre/Périphérie, Résistence, Sociéte du Lignage, Péninsule Ibérique, IIIème millénaire BC*

PREAMBLE

On the threshold of the 3rd millennium AD—the millennium of the global village—it is no coincidence that one of the most powerfully evocative vehicles for reflection about our present comes from the history of societies living during the 3rd millennium BC in the southwestern corner of Europe. The short, but nevertheless vast, history of these societies is taking on new significance in a place traditionally regarded as marginal in the context of Old World archaeology. Study of these societies highlights the need to overcome some of the contradictions that exist in our society, such as those that cause societies to vie with nature, men to vie with women, and one society to vie with another.

In the 3rd millennium BC, western Europe was not a place where people waited eternally for civilization to arrive from elsewhere. On the contrary, it was the scene of significant independent economic and social development. Furthermore, it was during then that some of the contradictions that still affect us today first appeared. It is therefore conceivable that an analysis of how they arose may show us a way to overcome them. In fact, the study of the 3rd millennium BC can show us what may happen to people whose social dependence prevents them from being masters of their own history.

The potential of a better future is dependent upon an understanding of the present, and the present can only be understood through a scientific analysis of the past. Key

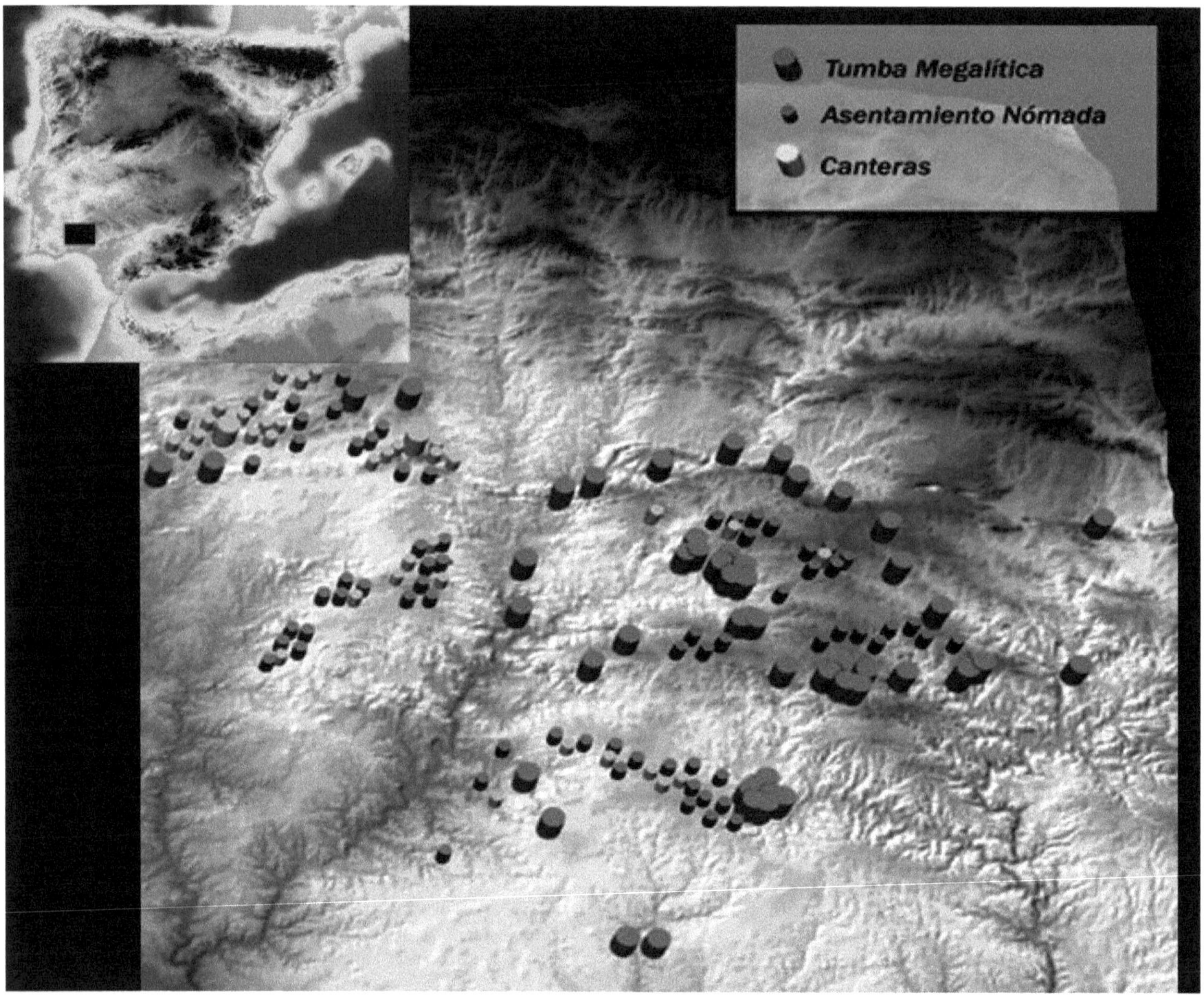

Fig. 9.1. Ordenación del territorio en el Andévalo Central

to this issue is the pursuit of history documented in the physical legacy of the past—archaeological remains. Once the necessary scientific research has been completed, our focus must be shifted away from individual archaeological sites towards their history and the factors that explain them. Doing so allows archaeological treasures, often converted into decontextualized icons, to acquire their true meaning, to become understandable, and to become socially useful. In this way, our ruins can contribute to ensuring that our future is not ruinous.

The region of the Andévalo (Huelva, Spain) provides the setting for one of the foremost examples of 3rd millennium BC historical processes. During that time, the Andévalo was home to one of the most technologically advanced societies in the western world. These societies developed specialized copper mining techniques and complex metallurgical processes. Curiously, El Andévalo was also home to societies that purposely avoided metallurgy. It was these societies that constructed one of the area's most lasting and significant archaeological legacies—the megalithic tombs of the nomadic herdsmen.

Now, 5000 years later, the legacies and histories of these Iberian megalithic tombs are in danger of disappearing forever. A comprehensive research project was therefore designed to recover and to preserve these archaeological treasures. Above all, this project aims to ensure that the possibility of imminent disappearance of these monuments will never again arise.

A necessary first step in this project was to clear and delimit the tombs. This program also allowed researchers to determine which monuments needed to be protected and how to prevent continued deterioration. Following this first step, a strategy was developed to recover and analyze the archaeological record. This strategy provides us, for the first time, with the information necessary to begin explaining the history of these monuments.

INTRODUCTION

Throughout the ages, a distinctive feature of societies characterized by social inequality, is their tendency to express territoriality. These societies also justify their internal relations by altering the natural landscape with the construction of prominent and lasting monuments. Such monuments first appeared in southwestern Europe over 9000 years ago in the form of stone monoliths (menhirs). These menhirs were erected to identify the territories and totemic lineages of influent "leaders" of those middle range communities. The megalithic phenomena in the SW Atlantic Europe culminated, four thousand years later, with the construction of complex monumental cemeteries of dolmens and tholoi. Through these constructions and the practice of ancestor worship, great stones became one of the primary markers of differentiation and a means of justifying and legitimizing a new form of inequality—the division of society into classes. This explanation embraces a wide variety of cemeteries differing in terms of constructive features and conception. Variations stemmed from differences in the level of inequality existing in the societies that built these cemeteries, as well as from the geographical position they occupied.

In terms of both number and variety of tomb construction techniques, the Andévalo region is the most complex in the megalithic area of the southern Iberian Peninsula. This complexity is attributed to the fact that the Andévalo borders with the territories of the early class society of the Guadalquivir and Guadiana River valleys areas. The coexistence of traditionally nomadic communities of the Andévalo with the small coastal colonies of copper miners and metallurgists in the Guadalquivir and Guadiana River valleys led to a significant social and economic diversity in a relatively small area.

The Andévalo megalithic cemeteries are concentrated between the Tinto and Odiel Rivers, forming a unique, closed territorial network encompassing a ca. 2000 km^2 central territory delimited by five large funerary sites.

The fossil pollen record and plant remains recovered from tombs of the Andévalo suggest that, with the exception of the river banks, regional vegetation cover, between 2900 and 2000 BC, was very sparse. This, in spite of the fact that the climate was more humid than at present. Trees, mainly helm, oak, and wild olive, seemed to have covered approximately 10% of the total surface area. Undergrowth was composed primarily of meadows of rock rose (*cistaceae*), mastic trees, and narrow-leaved *phillyrea*.

One of the factors that previously contributed to the enigmatic interpretation of the megalithic constructions is the absence of human remains in the archaeological record. However, systematic research carried out at the Las Palomas tomb has allowed us to determine that earlier conclusions concerning the absence of human remains were reached because data collection was not sufficiently thorough. Initial tests determined that soil at the burial site has a pH of 5.52, indicating that any possible skeletal remains were likely to be in a delicate state of preservation. We therefore designed a microspatial collection system that enabled us to determine, beyond all doubt a funerary purpose for the site. Furthermore, this strategy resulted in the recovery of human remains that, for the first time, give us an idea of the physical characteristics of the people living in the area.

Beyond their purely funerary purpose, these megalithic cemeteries became the main ideological instrument that societies used to justify an incipient form of internal inequality. Monuments were also used to define territorial boundaries. For these megalith builders, the interment of bodies was only one aspect of a complex reutilization of ancestors. Radiocarbon dating of material from La Venta reveals that rituals were carried out on a regular basis over a period of approximately 100 years. These rituals appear to have involved breaking ceramic vessels and construction of bonfires. These practices were performed along the same two pathways surrounding the chamber and seem to have established a form of ceremonialism involving processional rituals. The first ritual itinerary was between the entrance to the tomb and the menhir positioned opposite it, which is aligned with the rising sun. The constant repetition of this ritual practice wore a path there. The second ritual itinerary followed paved paths around the perimeter of the site of the tomb.

The large necropolis of La Venta, El Villar and El Pozuelo, were not just isolated cemeteries. Petrographic and chemical analyses of burial artifacts reveal a multilevel pattern of origin involving several scales. Artifacts found at the sites can be traced to distant communities in the southern Iberian Peninsula. Territorial distribution of similar artifacts suggests that these long-distance relationships were laid upon a foundation of regional exchange between the Guadalquivir and Guadiana Rivers, which in turn rested upon local-scale distribution between the Tinto and Odiel Rivers.

These large cemeteries are located at the geographical and organizational center of a complex funerary network defining and delimiting, in ideological terms, a territory situated between the Tinto and Odiel Rivers. This territory is dotted with small peripheral tombs at access points. One purpose of these constructions seems to have been to create and express a mechanism of resistance to early class society of the Guadalquivir Valley. This expresses a singular phenomenon of territorial and social exclusion in the core/periphery relationships that seems to imply the existence of peripheral formations of confined and/or resistant lineage societies (Dupré & Rey 1973, Gailey & Patterson 1988, Meillassoux 1977, Nocete 2000, 2001, Plog 1990, Rey 1975).

LA ORDENACIÓN DEL TERRITORIO MEGALÍTICO EN EL ANDÉVALO (HUELVA, ESPAÑA)

En las tierras del interior de la actual Provincia de Huelva, el tamaño, ubicación y distribución de los asentamientos muestran como, de un territorio donde coexistieron pequeños y grandes emplazamientos durante el VI y V

Fig. 9.2. Tumbas centrales de las necrópolis megalíticas de El Labradillo, Las Palomas, La Venta, Los Gabrieles y El Pozuelo

Milenios A.N.E., el poblamiento pasa a ordenarse, desde inicios del IV Milenio A.N.E., mediante una dispersión de pequeños emplazamientos en las altiplanicies, que nos permiten inferir, inicialmente, sistemas económicos de énfasis silvo-pastoril. La ausencia de estructuras constructivas emergentes, la pequeña entidad de los sitios, la escasez de restos cerámicos, la escasa incidencia de la producción laminar de manufacturas talladas y una reiterada distribución lineal de los asentamientos con ubicaciones donde la potencialidad productiva del suelo para articular formas de producción agrícola no presentan regularidad, nos sitúa ante un modelo arqueológico representativo de formas de vida nómada (Cribb 1991). En este riguroso modelo de dispersión e isometría de pequeños asentamientos, sólo destaca la reiterada presencia de lugares de aprovisionamiento de materias primas para las manufacturas talladas poco intensificados y claramente compartidos, así como la irrupción del fenómeno megalítico.

En esta continuidad histórica del patrón disperso, no jerarquizado y nómada de los asentamientos, la sustitución histórica los sitios de concentración poblacional del VI-V Milenios A.N.E. por las necrópolis megalíticas en el III Milenio A.N.E., cuyas primeras manifestaciones se erigirán sobre estos enclaves, nos permite inferir no sólo el fortalecimiento de los linajes a través de la monumentalización del espacio desde los antepasados, sino la forma en que esto ocurrió.

La función social que las concentraciones (¿estacionales?) poblacionales del VI-V Milenios A.N.E. ubicadas en el límite territorial de estas comunidades pudieron ejercer en un sistema disperso y nómada (defensa, circulación de productos, de hombres y mujeres, etc.), en el III Milenio A.N.E. queda mediatizado, vía antepasados, desde grupos de parentesco identificados y, posiblemente, restringidos de una comunidad territorial (linajes) que asumen el control de los medios de reproducción social.

Una exploración del patrón locacional de estos monumentales cementerios y su relación con la dispersión de los asentamientos, nos permite iniciar la exploración de un proceso con cuatro niveles espaciales:

- El primero se materializa en la distribución perimetral de un conjunto de 22 tumbas aisladas de similar tamaño (túmulos de 12 metros de diámetro) y localización que, ubicadas en cada uno de los accesos a las plataformas interiores del Andévalo Central y en su posición de dominio visual (construidas para ser percibidas desde el exterior), delimitan una distribución perimetral fronteriza entre los ríos Tinto y Odiel que circunscribe la distribución de los asentamientos y las plataformas con suelos aptos para el desarrollo de las actividades agropastoriles, generando una territorialidad ideológicamente disuasoria uniforme y unitaria.
- En segundo se materializa en la distribución longitudinal y exterior de asociaciones pareadas de túmulos,

Fig. 9.3. Necrópolis de El Pozuelo. Programa de limpieza y delimitación 1988

de similar tamaño que los anteriores que, desde este territorio se proyectan a lo largo de los cauces fluviales, marcando vías de comunicación hacia el Oeste y hacia el Sur.

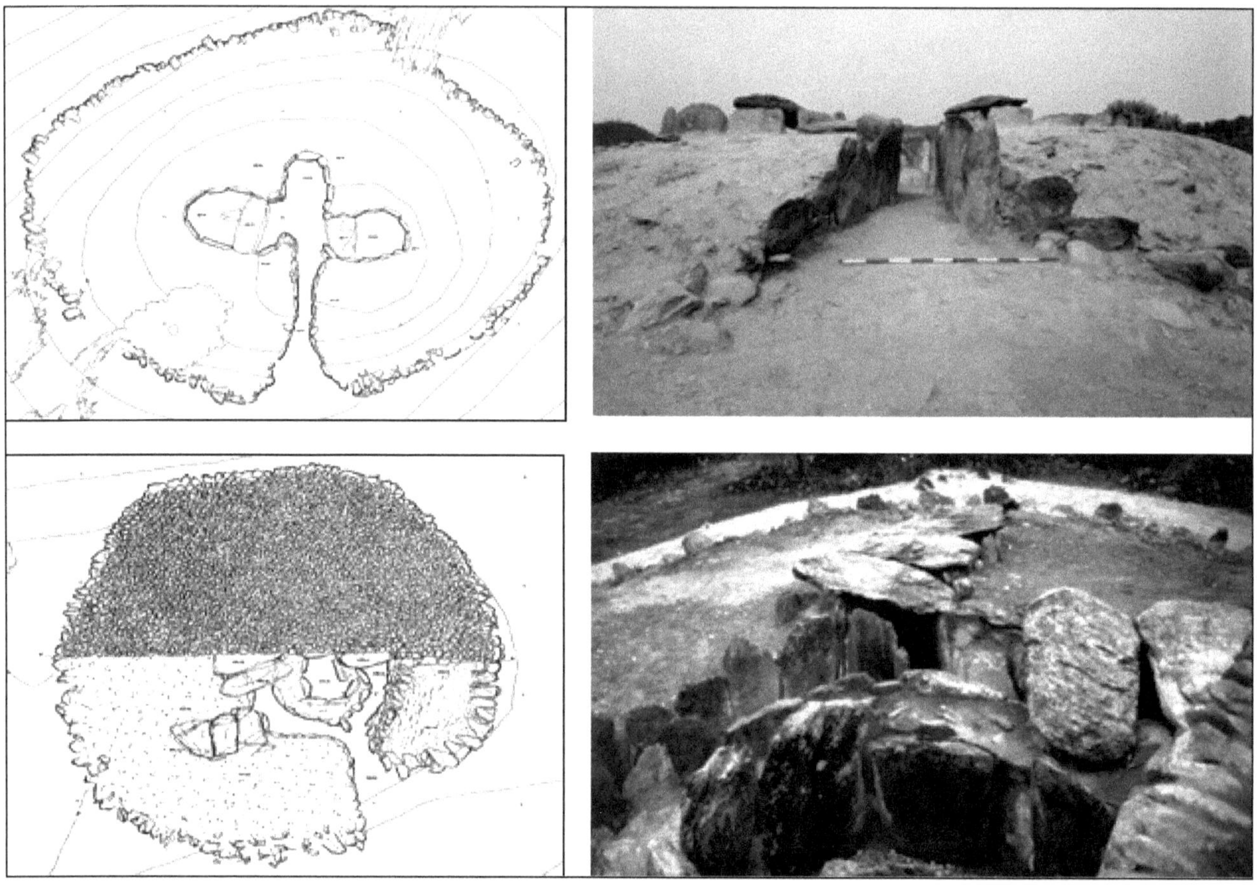

Fig. 9.4. Necrópolis de El Pozuelo. Programa de documentación arqueológica 1988

- El tercero se materializa en la distribución interna de cuatro concentraciones megalíticas (Villar, Pozuelo, Buitrón y Gabrieles) distanciadas y aisladas en el espacio bajo una estructura de *modularidad* (Nocete 1989, 1994) territorial, donde se ubican las construcciones funerarias de mayor tamaño (túmulos de más de 22 metros de diámetro). Éstas discriminan cuatro unidades productivas con sus respectivas ordenaciones territoriales que muestran, tras la aparente dispersión poblacional, la existencia de cuatro grupos locacionales al interior del territorio unitario y sin aparente jerarquización entre ellos.
- El cuarto se materializa en la asociación constante, al interior de cada una de estas cuatro concentraciones funerarias interiores, de una disimetría que enfrenta a grandes tumbas ubicadas en posiciones visualmente dominantes (túmulos de más de 22 metros de diámetro), frente a pequeñas tumbas (túmulos de menos de 12 metros de diámetro) ubicadas en posiciones visualmente subordinadas a su alrededor que determinan la existencia de disimetrías sociales internas al interior de cada grupo locacional.

LOS CONTEXTOS FUNERARIOS DEL ANDÉVALO

Sin embargo, sustantivar la especificidad de la estructura social que se halla tras esa peculiar ordenación del territorio, requiere contar con niveles de evaluación empírica más poderosos (contextos de prácticas sociales en asentamientos y necrópolis). Para ello, la excavación de una de las tumbas centrales de El Pozuelo (Nocete, Lizcano, Bolaños 1999), y dos de las tumbas centrales de El Villar (La Paloma y La Venta) (Nocete *et al.* 2004), tras definir que la ausencia o precariedad de restos humanos en sus contextos, lejos de ser el efecto del expolio o practicas de inhumación secundarias, fue la consecuencia del efecto destructor del ph ácido de los suelos (Nieto, Nocete, Sáez, Franco 2002); tras proporcionar una secuencia cronológica fiable de estas cementerios megalíticos sobre dataciones radiométricas de materia vegetal, habida cuenta que la incidencia del ph de suelo imposibilita el uso de dataciones basadas en el colágeno de restos óseos, que sitúa sus orígenes a inicios del III Milenio ANE y su final a inicios del II A.N.E. (Nocete *et al.* 2004); y tras contrastar mediante análisis antracológicos y polínicos la conducta pastoril de sus constructores, ofrecieron una información crucial de las practicas sociales.

La intervención arqueológica en estas tumbas, más allá de garantizar un registro de las entidades constructivas y muebles, pretendía recuperar el registro arqueológico contextualizado de las prácticas sociales que envolvieron los cementerios mediante una documentación miscroespacial de los contextos exteriores e interiores relativos a:

Fig. 9.5. Necrópolis de El Pozuelo. Programa de restauración y puesta en valor 1999

- La deposición prefuneraria de las prácticas sociales relativas a la construcción de la tumba, contrastando sus indicadores con los procedentes de la intervención previa en otros dólmenes del conjunto.
- La deposición pre y posfuneraria que se articula alrededor de la tumba, y especialmente junto a su entrada, a fin de caracterizar las prácticas sociales que envuelve el mantenimiento de las conductas rituales y de culto a los antepasados.
- La deposición funeraria de los enterramientos, contextualizando los niveles sincrónicos y diacrónicos de los cadáveres y sus respectivos ajuares.
- La deposición posfuneraria dentro de la cámara (limpieza, mantenimiento, ofrendas y actividades de culto permanentes).

Una vez descartadas las unidades sedimentarias de origen posdeposicional (respecto al uso funerario), los contextos interiores de las tumbas centrales, tras su registro microespacial, y tomado como ejemplo la tumba central de Las Palomas en la necrópolis del Villar, nos permiten identificar tres conductas netamente diferenciadas:

1. De un lado que la deposición funeraria de estas grandes y centrales tumbas se articuló sobre un escaso número de inhumados (frente a la recurrencia de múltiples inhumaciones en las de pequeño tamaño ubicadas en una posición subordinada a estas). En el caso de la tumba central de las Palomas, la deposición funeraria se articuló en torno a dos concentraciones de productos y huesos humanos que identifican dos enterramientos con una regularidad en la asociación de productos (cuentas de variscita/puntas de flecha/cuchillo de caliza oolítica/vasos cerámicos, etc.). Estos productos, a su vez, identifican tres escalas de circulación:

- La primera de carácter local y comarcal, y afecta tanto a los productos cerámicos como a la mayoría de los pétreos, pues tanto las pizarras sobre las que se fabricaron las placas decoradas, como la arenisca en la que materializó al hacha, o el cristal de cuarzo, se halla en las inmediaciones de la tumba. Igualmente, la mayoría de las puntas de flecha están realizadas sobre materias primas del entorno (66,6%), empleándose para su elaboración rocas volcánico-sedimentarias de la Faja Pirítica bien representadas en toda la comarca: riolitas, dacitas, tufitas ácidas, chert, jaspe, etc. Dada la recurrencia de estas materias primas en la región, resulta difícil precisar sus áreas de procedencia. Sin embargo, podemos reconocer las fuentes de aprovisionamiento de las tufitas en las canteras de Valdelamusa y Cerro del Andévalo (Nocete 2004), revelando un suministro de carácter comarcal. Otras puntas de flecha se realizaron sobre una riolita sedimentario-magmática muy peculiar que se encuentra en las inmediaciones de la aldea del Villar (Zalamea la Real, Huelva) y muy próxima al dolmen de La Paloma.

- La segunda, de carácter regional, queda ejemplificado en las cuentas de collar, pulidas y perforadas. De éstas, dos se han elaborado sobre una materia prima peculiar: variscita, cuyo centro de producción/suministro más próximo se encuentra a unos 70 km., al noroeste de la provincia de Huelva, en el término municipal de Encinasola (Nocete 2001).
- La tercera, de carácter suprarregional y, tal cono ocurría en las tumbas centrales (Dólmenes 5 y 6) de El Pozuelo, se focaliza sobre la asociación de un determinado producto (hojas talladas) y una materia prima (caliza oolítica silicificada) cuyo origen dista más de 150 km y fue fruto de un proceso de circulación a gran escala con un desigual reparto territorial de la producción que desciende a lo largo de las redes jerárquicas del poblamiento del Sur de la Península Ibérica (Nocete *et al.* 2005).

Frente a estos productos, la ausencia de artefactos metalúrgicos en los contextos funerarios, así como de las representaciones antropomorfas y ginemorfas que caracterizaron a las formaciones sociales situadas a su alrededor, definen un bloqueo ideológico de los constructores de megalitos respecto a la sociedad clasista inicial del Valle del Guadalquivir y sus formas periféricas.

2. De otro, las conductas asociadas a la deposición funeraria que se articulan a la entrada del corredor se caracterizan por un producto no asociado al contexto previo (placas decoradas), y por un tratamiento del mismo diferenciado: la fracturación. Frente a la deposición completa y no alterada de cuentas, puntas o cuchillos de caliza, junto a los cadáveres, las placas decoradas han sido fracturadas a la puerta de la tumba.

3. Por último, el hecho de que todos los vasos cerámicos asociados a la deposición sean mitades de recipientes completos (tal y como registramos en El Pozuelo 6), cuyos homólogos no se hallen en el interior de la tumba, revela que estos forman parte de una práctica social donde la fracturación sobrepasa los niveles de la deposición funeraria y se traslada al exterior.

Con independencia de las implicaciones que estos registros poseen para identificar practicas sociales de ritualización de/en los espacios funerarios (Chapman 2000) las interpretaciones sobre la fracturación de productos en contextos funerarios del Megalitismo europeo), cuya magnitud volveremos a contrastar en los contextos exteriores del dolmen de La Venta o en El Pozuelo 6, y de la posibilidad de discriminar las practicas de deposición funeraria y las asociadas a ellas en función de la presencia (formas de fracturación/no fracturación) de los productos en la tumba, el carácter portable (adornos y armas) y el origen lejano de los productos asociados al ajuar de los escasos difuntos de las grandes tumbas centrales (caliza oolítica, variscita) también revela que nos hallamos ante una formación social creadora de excedentes para articular el consumo disimétrico de productos lejanos. La regularidad espacial de esta práctica social (Dolmen de La Paloma y Dólmenes de El Pozuelo) y la asociación de estos productos a las tumbas de mayor tamaño, que implicaron un mayor esfuerzo para su construcción, y de una posición dominante en el entramado de las necrópolis, ubicadas para ser vistas y servir de referencia, y que, paradójicamente, incluyen un número de individuos inversamente proporcional al esfuerzo de su construcción respecto a las ubicadas a sus pies, donde los productos de procedencia externa no están presentes, no solo revela una práctica social que trasciende a los individuos enterrados, sino que ésta está orientada a materializar unas relaciones de desigualdad en el seno de la comunidad. Las disimetrías de los contextos de esta dualidad funeraria señala que los individuos enterrados en estas tumbas dominantes se beneficiaron de un esfuerzo social (construcción de la tumba, acceso a productos lejanos) del que desconocemos su contrapartida.

Respecto al contexto exterior, los registros del Dolmen de La Venta nos permiten discriminar otras dos conductas netamente diferenciadas:

4. La primera se articula en dos contextos asociados a la construcción de la tumba. Uno, situado alrededor del túmulo, se caracteriza por la presencia de mazos y martillos e indican que los trabajos de formateo final de las losas de cubierta y paredes de la cámara funeraria se desarrollaron en el lugar destinado para la ubicación de la tumba. Otro, situado en los afloramientos de pizarra que rodean el emplazamiento de la tumba, vuelve a caracterizarse por los residuos de mazos y, también, por las huellas de extracción. Ambos vuelven a reiterar un modelo de cantería y prácticas constructivas que ya fue identificado en el caso de El Pozuelo (Nocete, Lizcano, Bolaños 1999).

5. La segunda se articula en un amplio conjunto de conductas prolongadas a lo largo del tiempo en que se uso esta tumba (confirmado por las diferencias cronológicas entre el interior de la cámara y la rampa de acceso en el interior de la misma) y que determinaron la creación de un espacio exterior afín y una frecuentación periódica de la tumba regida por prácticas de ritualización. Ello determinó la morfología y tamaño del túmulo, el cual se restringe a la parte central de la tumba, con un diseño longitudinal que arropa la cámara relegando un espacio perimetral delimitado por un anillo de lajas inclinadas. En torno a este, se definió un espacio abierto y plano transitable y materializado por dos circuitos perimetrales empedrados. Uno interno y otro externo. Por último, el ámbito dominante y principal se articulo delante de la puerta de la cámara. Este condicionó una morfología

Fig. 9.6. Contextos internos. Necrópolis de El Villar. Tumba de Las Palomas. Excavación microespacial y productos

Fig. 9.7. Contextos externos de menhires en tumbas centrales. Necrópolis del Villar (1,2,3 Tumba de la Venta). Necrópolis de El Pozuelo (4 Tumba Pozuelo 2, 5 Tumba Pozuelo 6)

cóncava en la delimitación del acceso desde el túmulo, señalando un acceso en rampa y empedrado a la cámara y creando un espacio transitable de recurrente uso, donde la presencia de restos muy fracturados de productos y materia orgánica (carbón) revela el desarrollo de actividades permanentes y diferenciadas de las asociadas a la deposición funeraria. Aunque este espacio ya estaba representado en el dolmen de La Paloma, bajo similares características, en el caso de La Venta adquiere una mayor complejidad. Así se desprende de la delimitación de un pasillo rehundido y alineado entre la puerta de la tumba que se oculta formando una rampa hacia el interior de la cámara, y un menhir situado en la proyección de la misma respecto al anillo perimetral exterior con una clara orientación de ambos, en un eje, hacia oriente que ya registramos en la tumba 2 de el Pozuelo.

La materialización de un espacio externo orientado a la realización de diversos recorridos, con la presencia de restos fracturados de recipientes cerámicos, señala la complejidad de una ritualización de los espacios funerarios que amplia la simple visión de contenedores de productos desde los que han sido interpretados y que han condicionado formas de registro arqueológico que redundaron en esa explicación, al focalizar el interés en la recuperación de los productos interiores de las tumbas.

La recurrencia de estos registros en El Pozuelo (asociación de menhir-tumba en Pozuelo 2), no solo señala la contemporaneidad de ambas necrópolis, sino que muestra la generalización de estas prácticas en el origen de los grandes cementerios de inicios del III Milenio A.N.E. Adicionalmente, nos permite explicar el desarrollo posterior de los grandes dólmenes de la segunda mitad del III Milenio A.N.E. (Pozuelo 6) con sus múltiples cámaras, y la presencia de contextos de fracturación en los pasillos y entradas de las mismas (Pozuelo 6), en una continuidad de prácticas de frecuentación de los recintos funerarios donde, la traslación de estas al interior de unas construcciones, cuyo mayor tamaño y altura, permitieron, frente a La Venta y La Paloma, o Pozuelo 2, en la primera mitad del III Milenio A.N.E., "ocultarlas" a inicios del II Milenio A.N.E.. Con esta continuidad, concentración y "ocultación" de las prácticas "rituales" asociadas al ámbito funerario, se consolidó una regularidad ideológica orientada a crear un instrumento efectivo de expresión y ratificación de unas relaciones sociales que, no olvidemos, sustentan la disimetría social. El hecho de que esta relación se exprese y materialice desde los antepasados, muestra, adicionalmente, la vía y contradicciones de su reproducción social (Nocete 2001).

DISCUSIÓN FINAL

La introducción de los antepasados (intermediación) en la delimitación externa (distribución perimetral de tumbas megalíticas) e interna (distribución del poblamiento en torno a cuatro necrópolis) del territorio, en las prácticas ceremoniales, la circulación de productos y, en definitiva, en la reproducción física de la sociedad que se refleja tras la sustitución de los puntos perimetrales de concentración poblacional del VI-V Milenio A.N.E. por tumbas megalíticas a iniciaos del III Milenio A.N.E., y la articulación en su entorno de complejas y periódicas prácticas rituales (fracturación, procesionalidad, alineación astronómica, etc.), unido al énfasis y monumentalización de los ancestros, no representa sólo un desarrollo cuantitativo de los procesos sociales que lo preceden, ya que, no olvidemos, muestran, y justifican, la existencia de disimetrías internas.

Los contextos arqueológicos de la distribución espacial de las necrópolis megalíticas (frontera común, grupos locacionales, disimetrías internas) unidos a los relativos al proceso de su construcción, inhumación y frecuentación sistemática, etc., más allá de las prácticas socioparentales (antepasados, parentesco restringido) y económicas (nomadismo, explotación grupal de recursos, acceso restringido a productos de origen externo, etc.) que implican, muestran un entramado sociopolítico de relaciones clasistas iniciales que se orientan y sustentan en la disposición de la fuerza de trabajo directa (construcción de tumbas) e indirecta (excedentes que garanticen, por ejemplo, el consumo restringido de productos de procedencia externa) y muestra una trayectoria constante en el control restringido (fijado a través de segmentos parentales) de los medios de reproducción social, donde la propiedad colectiva de los recursos, el bajo desarrollo del nivel técnico, el nomadismo, etc.. conducen a la disposición de fuerza de trabajo a través del control de los medios de reproducción social, como única vía de reproducción de la desigualdad (Nocete 1999),característico de una Formación Social de Linaje con tendencia a la verticalización interna de sus segmentos a lo largo de todo el III Milenio A.N.E.

Al final del proceso, a inicios del II Milenio A.N.E., la desaparición de tres de los grandes cementerios situados al interior del territorio y la permanencia de solo uno de ellos (El Pozuelo), coincidiendo con la fase de mayor construcción monumental en el mismo, y las transformaciones en el proceso ritual que la acompaña (ocultación al interior de la tumba de las prácticas de ritualización), unido a las mayores disimetrías en el conjunto de la necrópolis, señalan el camino a la distinción de los linajes con la concentración de funciones supragrupales (territorial) y la aparición de relaciones de dependencia (¿clientelas?) que, posteriormente, se desarrollarán en las necrópolis del II Milenio A.N.E. en el suroeste peninsular (Nocete 2001).

Sin embargo, este proceso en ningún caso fue autónomo y prístino, dado que se construyó en la periferia física, temporal e histórica de la sociedad clasista inicial del Valle del Guadalquivir y su desarrolló dependió de los ritmos de esta. Así:

- El origen de los grandes cementerios centrales del Andévalo, a inicios del III Milenio A.N.E. y su red de delimitación fronteriza del territorio mediante los antepasados, fue posterior a la aparición de las primeras redes jerárquicas del Valle del Guadalquivir, y coincide con el período de máxima expansión de las contradicciones de esta sociedad clasista inicial y el establecimiento de periferias mineras directas en los márgenes territoriales de estas comunidades, lo que determinaría tanto el inicio de un sistema de organización supragrupal de territorialidad marcada, como el fortalecimiento de algunos de sus linajes y su configuración como una forma de resistencia (Nocete 2001).
- Su posterior desmantelación de la red perimetral de cementerios periféricos y la desaparición de cuatro de los cinco grandes concentraciones funerarias a favor del fortalecimiento de una de ellas (El Pozuelo), a finales del III Milenio A.N.E., que señalan el periodo de la máxima concentración de poder y de verticalización de los linajes que precede a las necrópolis clientelares del II Milenio A.N.E., coincide, con el colapso y desmantelción del jerarquizado armazón territorial de relaciones de dependencia de la sociedad clasista inicial del Valle del Guadalquivir (Nocete 2001).

Con ello, el registro de las comunidades megalíticas del Andévalo ejenplifica uno de los procesos de formación secundaria de sociedades clasistas que C.H. Gailey y T. Patterson (Gailey, Patterson 1988) definieron con el término de *Formas de Linaje* (Meillassoux 1977; Dupre, Rey 1973; Rey 1975; etc.) y del que señalaron su emergencia en la periferia inmediata de los estados tributarios como formas de jerarquización inestables que se organizan como sistemas resistentes forzados a defender su autonomía frente a los deseos de injerencia de sus vecinos (conquista, anexión, pillaje, captura de esclavos, etc.). Por ello, a pesar de que las unidades de trabajo, producción y tenencia de la tierra y/o ganados previas se mantienen, se restringen a lo largo de líneas de parentesco para impedir que las unidades territoriales se atomicen, garantizando el desarrollo de formas de cooperación militar estables. De ahí que sus manifestaciones territoriales se caractericen por el dominio de unas formalizaciones funerarias de tal magnitud (frente a los asentamientos) que expresan y reproducen, desde los ancestros, la formación de grupos clánicos cerrados, competitivos y territoriales (Plog 1990).

References

CRIBB, R., 1991, *Nomads in Archaeology*, Cambridge: Cambridge University Press.

CHAPMAN, J., 2000, *Fragmentation in Archaeology. People, Places and Broken Objects in the Prehistory of South Eastern Europe*, London: Routledge.

DUPRE, G., & REY, P., 1973, Reflections on the Pertinence of a Theory of Exchange, *Economy and Society* 2/2, p. 131-163.

GAILEY, C.H., & PATTERSON, T., 1988, State Formation and Uneven Development. In J. Gledhill, B. Bender, & M.T. Larson (eds.), *State and Society: The Emergence and Development of Social Hierarchy and Political Centralization*, London & Boston: Unwin Hyman, p. 71-90.

MEILLASSOUX, C.L., 1977, *Mujeres, Graneros y Capitales. Economía Doméstica y Capitalismo,* México: Siglo XXI.

NIETO, J.M., NOCETE, F., SAEZ, R., & FRANCO, M., 2002, Cambios Mineralógicos en Restos Óseos en Función de las Condiciones de pH del Suelo, *Geogaceta* 31, p. 189-193.

NOCETE, F., 1989, *El Espacio de la Coerción. La transición al Estado en las Campiñas del Alto Guadalquivir (España). 3000-1500 A.C.*, B.A.R. International Series 492, Oxford: British Archaeological Reports.

NOCETE, F., 1994, Space as Coercion: The Transition to the State in the Social Formations of la Campiña, Upper Guadalquivir Valley, Spain. ca. 1900-1600 B.C., *Journal of Anthropological Archaeology* 13, p. 171-200.

NOCETE, F., 1999, Las relaciones y Contradicciones Centro/Periferia de la Sociedad Clasista Inicial. Hacia la definición de una Unidad Arqueológica para la Evaluación Empírica de los Estados Prístinos, *Boletín de Antropología Americana* 34, p. 39-52.

NOCETE, F., 2001, *Tercer Milenio antes de Nuestra Era. Relaciones y Contradicciones Centro/Periferia en el Valle del Guadalquivir*, Barcelona: Bellaterra.

NOCETE, F., 2004, *ODIEL. Proyecto de Investigación Arqueológica para el análisis del Origen de la Desigualdad Social en el Suroeste de la Península Ibérica*, Monografías de Arqueología n 19, Sevilla: Consejería de Cultura. Junta de Andalucía.

NOCETE, F., 2006, The First Specialized Copper Industry in the Iberian Peninsula: Cabezo Juré (2900-2200 BC), *Antiquity* 80/309, p. 646-657.

NOCETE F., LIZCANO R., & BOLAÑOS, C., 1999, *Más que Grandes Piedras. Patrimonio, Arqueología e Historia desde la Primera Fase del Programa de Puesta en Valor del Conjunto Megalítico de El Pozuelo (Zalamea la Real, Huelva),* Sevilla: Consejería de Cultura de la Junta de Andalucía.

NOCETE, F., ALEX, E., NIETO, J.M., SÁEZ, R., & BAYONA, M.R., 2005, An Archaeological Approach to Regional Environmental Pollution in the South-Western Iberian Peninsula Related to 3rd millennium BC Mining and Metallurgy, *Journal of Archaeological Science* 32, p. 1566-1576.

NOCETE, F., SAEZ, R., NIETO, J.M., CRUZ, R., CABRERO, R., ALEX, E., & BAYONA, M.R., 2005, Circulation of Silicified Oolitic Limestone Blades in South-Iberia (Spain and Portugal) During the 3rd Millennium BC: An Expression of a Core/Periphery Framework, *Journal Of Anthropological Archaeology* 24, p. 62-81.

PLOG, S., 1990, Agriculture, Sedentism and Environment in the Evolution of Political System. In S. Upham (ed.), *The Evolution of Political Systems. Sociopolitics in Small-Scale Sedentary Societies,* Cambridge: Cambridge University Press, p 177-199.

MOON, SPRING AND LARGE STONES – LANDSCAPE AND RITUAL CALENDAR PERCEPTION AND SYMBOLIZATION

Catarina OLIVEIRA
CIIPC – Centro de Investigação e Informação do Património de Cacela,
Santa Rita P- 8900-059 Vila Nova de Cacela, Portugal
Email: oliveiracatarina@gmail.com

C. Marciano da SILVA
UNL – Universidade Nova de Lisboa, Monte da Caparica P-2829-516 Caparica, Portugal
Email: cms@netvisao.pt

***Résumé**: Nous avons étudié plusieurs sites mégalithiques dans l'Alentejo Central pour relever les orientations astrales et nous avons reconnu une possible célébration cultuelle de l'Equinoxe, et sa relation avec le début du printemps. La Lune y tient un rôle essentiel qui parait avoir été repris, plusieurs millénaires après, de façon assez semblable pour fixer la célébration liturgique pascale. L'évidence d'un rapport clair entre la Lune, la perception du paysage et le calendrier rituel, apparemment matérialisé pour la première fois par les monuments mégalithiques, nous rend sensible à l'identification de signes cachés dans la mémoire collective, se rapportant à l'idée de la Lune comme représentation symbolique de la vie. La recherche conduite jusqu'à présent a révélé des indications pertinentes, non seulement dans l'Alentejo Central où le phénomène mégalithique est important, mais aussi dans d'autres régions du pays où cette association – matérialisée par d'anciens lieux de dévotion, des rituels et des pratiques liturgiques – demeure encore significative.*
***Mots-clés**: Equinoxe Mégalithique, Lune du Printemps, Pâques*

***Abstract**: We have surveyed several megalithic sites in Central Alentejo in order to evaluate astral orientations, and have identified a possible cultual celebration of the Equinox and its relationship to the onset of Spring. The Moon plays an essential role in this association, in a very similar manner to that of the Moon in the Paschal liturgy developed several millennia later. The evidence of a clear connection between the moon, landscape perception, and the ritual calendar, apparently first materialized in megalithic monuments, alerts us to signs, hidden in collective memory, that refer to the idea of the Moon as a symbolic representation of life. The investigation developed so far has unveiled relevant indications, not only in Central Alentejo, where the megalithic phenomena seem prominent, but also in other parts of the country, where that association – materialised in ancient places of devotion, rituals and liturgical practice remains significant.*
***Keywords**: Megalithic Equinox, Spring Moon, Easter*

INTRODUCTION

The awareness of the cosmic order beyond the immediate cycles of the Sun and the Moon may have been a result of the process of becoming sedentary. The line separating one's own territory, where one was able to stand, from the space above where those dominating luminaries appeared to move, and where one could not step, would have necessarily provided a cosmic view of the surrounding universe. That line, separating these two united realities, may have assumed an important symbolic meaning; for it was there that those bodies would emerge or disappear every day, following a long arch in the sky.

The landscape, which now includes the celestial bodies (Ruggles 1998), introduces an extra dimension in the structure of the symbolic dialogue between man and nature, resulting in the sacralisation of space and the ritualisation of time.

The representation of the cosmos and of the cosmic order, in permanent structures built in one's own territory, seems to be an appropriation of the forces of nature as perceived through the empirical association of events with the emergence of the Sun or the Moon in the landscape. The archaeological record shows an increasingly complex collection of construction practices and decorations that precede the megalithic manifestations. Megalithism, then, as observed in the Central Alentejo, is perhaps an example of the early representations of the cosmic order that regulate the cycles of life.

Building with durable material of great monumentality was decisive for the creation/recreation and production/ reproduction of space. The resulting monuments ensure that the ritual and the mythological significance of a particular place will not be forgotten, and are useful to stabilise both the cultural memory of the place and the relationship between places (Tilley 1994: 204). It is generally accepted that the megaliths may also have been territorial symbols, i.e. socially active markers in the landscape, chosen in terms of a symbolic perception and importance of a social memory. The monumentality of the megaliths, therefore, appears to be associated with the celebration of the place and the surrounding cosmic order. This can be regarded as the progressive establishment of a dialogue between people and the external forces that they cannot control.

Documenting social and ritual practices in the megalithic period is probably beyond the reach of present-day research. Little information exists other than artefacts deposited in megalithic tombs and engravings, often depicting astral motifs, particularly the sun and the moon. Altogether, these seem to add some measure of plausibility to the idea of a society in the process of becoming conscious of the cosmic order, however crude this consciousness may have been.

Later, however, when the record becomes more legible, we find apparent references made to the intermediate period. This may indicate that the cult of celestial bodies, particularly the Moon, can plausibly be regarded as an impetus for regular festivals that would eventually carry concepts such as the "Spring Full Moon" across successive periods. References to such concepts exist in Sumerian and Canaanite sources before the Phoenicians. It is likely that similar celebrations were common to the many groups of people who inhabited Iberia before the Romans arrived.

Strabo (58 BC – 25 AD), referring to Iberia in his "Geographika," describes the widespread custom of the local people: "They, the 'Gaelics,' have no cult images and are reverent to a nameless divinity which families feast in nights of Full Moon dancing until dawn, in the open, outside their homes" (Geographika, III 4, 6). Presumably this divinity was not named because everybody knew it, and saw it when it was cyclically present. This rite could still be observed in Galicia at the beginning of the twentieth century, close to the border with Trás-os-Montes, as described by N. Tenorio (Espirito-Santo 2004:191).

The present paper tries to explore the continuation of that ritual dialogue, on the assumption that it may not only be represented in the archaeological record, but may have survived in modern beliefs and practices.

Earlier results are reviewed together with information accumulated in the meantime. As a complementary approach, this study searches for continuities in the ritual celebrations relating the Moon and Spring to the symbolisation of time and space. Although centred between the Neolithic period and the emergence of literate societies, the study takes into account the eventual identification of related old sanctuaries and of ritual practices, religious or simply festive that may have persisted up to the present day.

Aware that the religious phenomenon has, at all times and places, revealed itself as an "inherited conglomerate," (Ribeiro 2002a: 9) the present study tries to understand how people have appropriated the Moon, especially the Spring Moon, and integrated it in magico-symbolic structures. These structures mediated their relationship with space and time, in the light of specific space-time contexts, movements of people, and religious syncretism and assimilation phenomena.

CENTRAL ALENTEJO MEGALITHISM – THE EARLIER EQUINOX EVIDENCE

Although we can find megalithic monuments all over Iberia, it is in the Southwest, and particularly in Central Alentejo, where their concentration is greatest.

We have surveyed several megalithic sites in Central Alentejo for astral orientations (Da Silva 2000, 2003a, 2003b), and seem to have identified a possible cultual commemoration of the Equinox, and its relationship to the onset of Spring. It should be stressed that, as opposed to the solstices, which are characterized by standstill celestial events, therefore providing a nearly stationary mark in the horizon; the observation of the equinox does not have a fixed celestial reference mark. Its use in symbolic terms may represent an abstract concept that reflects a deeper understanding of the cosmic order.

Perhaps the most significant megalithic sites are the enclosures of Almendres and Vale Maria do Meio, which seem to incorporate internal arrangements for the observation of the passage of the Sun midway between the solstices, both in time (Spring/Autumn) and space (East quadrant of the horizon). The similarity of some related construction details in the layout of Vale Maria do Meio seems to suggest that it could have been a precursor of Almendres, since this one appears to embrace the rising Sun close to the vernal equinox, adding great symbolic significance to this observation.

No less significant are the similar observations that can be made of the rising Sun over the conspicuous hill of Monsaraz (a possible "sacred mountain") from the megalithic sites of Perdigões, Monte da Ribeira and Barrocal. The east-west alignment of these three sites, between themselves and with the Monsaraz profile, seems to suggest more precise observations due to the longer base-line involved.

This growing accumulation of data supports the idea of the existence of a culture conscious of the celestial order in this region, and eventually, a cultual practice of celebrating the Equinox.

However, the funerary megalithic monuments best represent this symbolic association with the onset of Spring, as their orientation seems to provide the firmer empirical evidence for a redefined "Megalithic Equinox" associated with the rising Spring Full Moon (Roslund *et al.* 2000, Da Silva 2003b). When regular and meticulous measurements of the geographical orientation of the dolmen's corridor were recently made (Hoskin 1998), we were able to demonstrate the preferential corridor orientation of approximately 8° south of East, an excellent correspondence between the range of the rising Spring Full Moon azimuths and the distribution of the dolmen's orientations. The Spring Full Moon is then defined as the point where the rising Sun/Full Moon cross over on the horizon (Da Silva 2004), a definition that turns out to be

Fig. 10.1. Full Moon directly on the symmetry axis of the horseshoe enclosure at Vale d'elRei (Pavia)

essentially the same as that of the present day Full Moon that determines Easter, i.e., the first Full Moon after the vernal equinox.

NEW SPRING FULL MOON DATA AND SPRING EQUINOX CELEBRATION

It has long been noticed that most enclosures found in Central Alentejo are generally located at the top of a gentle slope facing east, and that a large menhir is regularly found close to the west top, slightly north of the axis of symmetry. A close inspection of several sites (Almendres, Vale Maria do Meio and Portela de Mogos) has revealed distinct internal features that, when observed from the large menhir, seem to lie in the appropriate direction of the average Spring Moon azimuth. Additionally, Almendres seems to have a clear corridor in the northern arm of the enclosure, which is oriented in the same direction and incorporates a truncated monolith.

Among the horseshoe-shaped enclosures (e.g., Tojal, Cuncos, Sideral, etc), the best preserved is Vale d'el Rey near Pavia. Calado (M. Calado 2004), in order to precisely locate the megaliths' sockets and replace the stones that have been removed, recently excavated this enclosure. A careful topographical survey has shown that the symmetry axis of the horseshoe points also in the direction of 98°, and therefore that the open arms seem to be intended to embrace the rising Spring Full Moon in the otherwise featureless horizon (Fig. 10.1). Although the menhirs of this enclosure are small, no one exceeding one meter above ground, its precise layout seems to suggest a cultual or ritual use more than any other site, except perhaps Almendres at the rise of the equinoctial Sun.

In addition, isolated large menhirs seem to have been placed in some locations so as to confer a precise meaning on the landscape. Some involve prominent and close hill profiles as in the case of Montemor and Monsaraz, while others relate to conspicuous undulations (usually a distant hill) in the flat horizon (Fig. 10.2). We have surveyed the large menhirs of Póvoa & Meada (Castelo de Vide), and recently of Outeiro and Barrocal near Monsaraz. In these, as in other cases (Courela das Casas Novas and Casbarra, first pointed out to us by M. Calado), we find that the conspicuous or prominent marks in the landscape all lie close to 100°, as does an average Spring Full Moon rise (Table 10.1).

SPRING FULL MOON: SYMBOLIC LANDSCAPE AND RITUAL CALENDAR

In the Neolithic, the widespread cult of Mother-Goddess was clearly related to the vital cycles of nature, including the agricultural ones, and to the calendar naturally based on the moon phases. The Moon and the Great Neolithic

Fig. 10.2. Ondulations on the horizon, relevant to the observation of the "Spring Full Moon" rise (Outeiro, Monsaraz)

Mother-Goddess seem to coexist in the magico-symbolic systems; however, the connection between them or with the megalithic monuments, especially the funerary ones, is not easy to comprehend.

Symbolically, the moon's disappearance might have represented death. For three nights the sky becomes dark. But, as the moon reappears also the dead resurrect, initiating a new life. In many cultures it is believed that the buried dead go to the moon to regenerate in a new existence (Eliade 1992: 224-225). Perhaps the concept of life after death is rooted in man's consciousness of his own possible continued existence, as conveyed by the successive phases of the moon in its cycle of birth, death, and resurrection (Belmonte 2003:37).

Having lost direct evidence of the rituals associated with the megalithic monuments, we must turn to megalithic art and artefacts. The importance of the Moon in the magico-symbolic contexts of the Neolithic-Chalcolithic is recognised not only in the Spring Moon orientation of the funerary monuments, but also in its representation in megalithic engravings (in relation to the Sun, rectangle, staff, etc.) in votive artefacts (ex. limestone lunules), and linked to other groups with figurative associations with fertility (rabbits, hares) and to the Mother-Goddess. Of some significance is the presence of limestone lunules found in megalithic monuments, in particular in the region of Lisbon (Gonçalves 2003), where the "Serra de Sintra" is prominent in the sacred geography of this region, associated with the cult of the Moon and of the great Mother-Goddess (Pereira 2005: 132).

More recently, cult objects were found with the shape of the Moon Crescent (lunules), very often in silver or in some other bright metal, and most frequently embedded in the icons of "Our Lady" of particular devotions (Nª Srª da Conceição regularly stands on a celestial starry sphere with a white moon crescent behind). In Garvão, the use of such small crescent moons still survives today as amulets to invoke the protection of Stª Luzia, and can be acquired from local goldsmiths. Evidence was found of such use in protohistory in a recent excavation of the Iron Age site at Garvão (Beirão *et al.* 1985).

M. Calado (pers. comm.) also brought it to our attention that Neolithic/Chalcolithic rock art at the "Lapa dos Gaivões" (Arronches) might have some lunar referents. In fact, although the anthropomorphic and serpent images are predominant, there is a group of marks that seem to represent a tally. A detailed examination shows four rows of seven individual linear marks, as if to represent the full cycle of the Moon with its four phases of approximately seven days each.

From the evidence of a clear connection between the moon, landscape perception, and ritual calendar, apparently first materialised in megalithic monuments, we

Tab. 10.1. Compilation of observed relevant sites and events
(Note: possible equinoctial and Spring Moon sites, and plausible continuities)

Type	Site	Significant orientation	Event and Azimute
Sun Equinoctial Megalithic Sites	Almendres	Symmetry axis	Sunrise 090°
		Truncated monolith	Sunset 270°
	Vale Maria do Meio – encl.	"Symmetry" axis	Sunset 270°
	Perdigões – Monsaraz	Menhir Alignment	Sunrise 090°
	Mte da Ribeira – Monsaraz	Enclosure	Sunrise 090°
	Barrocal – Monsaraz	Isolated Menhir	Sunrise 090°
Spring Moon Megalithic Sites	Póvoa e Meada – menhir	Horizon Undulation	Moonrise 085-115
	Outeiro – menhir	Horizon Undulation	Moonrise 085-115
	Casas Novas – menhir	Horizon Undulation	Moonrise 085-115
	Barrocal – Monsaraz	Hill Profile	Moonrise 085-115
	Vale d'elRei – enclosure	Horseshoe axis	Moonrise 098
	Almendres – enclosure	Large menhir line	Moonrise 098
	Vale Maria do Meio – encl.	Large menhir line	Moonrise 098
	Cuncos – enclosure	Large menhir line	Moonrise 098
	Tojal – enclosure	Large menhir line	Moonrise 098
Sanctuaries	Srª da Penha/Luz–Marvão	ConspicuousHill	Moonrise 098
	SrªdaLuz(Lagos)–Coast line	Land's edge	Moonrise 098
	Arcelis	Horizon Undulation	Moonrise 085-115
Traditions	Lagoa de Albufeira	Lagoon axis (E-W)	Opening to the Sea
	Praia de S. Julião		Mussel pickup
	Easter Monday – Alentejo		Oudoors Easter Celebration
	Easter Monday – Minho		Family Celebration

begin to become aware of signs hidden in the collective memory, across time, guided by the idea of the Moon as a symbolic representation of life. Relevant indications have been unveiled, not only in Central Alentejo, where the megalithic phenomena seem prominent; but also in other parts of the country, where that association – materialised in ancient places of devotion, rituals and liturgical practice — remains significant.

As mentioned above, in the Early Roman period Strabo (I BC – I AD) refers to the cult of the moon in Iberia. This is also observed in northwestern Iberia where the Gaelics devoted an island to the moon (Ptolomeo, I – II AD). The "Serra de Sintra" might have continued to be devoted to the moon. It is alluded to as *Mons Sacer* (Varrão, Rer. Rust., II, I; and Columela, Rer. Rust., VI, 27.7); *Promontorium Lunae* or *Mons Lunae* (Ptolomeo); and *Sintra Promontorio Sacrum* (Strabo). From the Roman Period on, we find reference to a sanctuary and inscriptions in Colares devoted to *Soli et Lunae* (Vasconcelos 1989: 364-367; Ribeiro 2002b: 235-239) and lunar representations in funerary stelae (Vasconcelos 1989: 407-446).

RITUAL CALENDAR AND SANCTUARIES

The continuity of religions is achieved through the ritual calendar and reutilization of old sanctuaries based on spatial collective memory. The rule for religious succession seems to be syncretism (Espirito-Santo 2004: 11).

A few millennia after the funerary megalithic monument orientations followed the rise of the Spring Full Moon, we witness the establishment of a liturgical practice based on this same Full Moon. The originating event may have been when Moses crossed the Jordan River on the low equinoctial tide of the 14th of Nisan. This is in fact our present-day Paschal Full Moon celebrated in the Jewish faith which, in that lunar calendar, is the first Full Moon past the vernal equinox. In the Christian faith Easter is celebrated as associated with Christ's resurrection on the following Sunday, as established in the First Nicaea Council of 325 AD, which also fixed the basic algorithm to find the Easter day that we still use today with minor adaptations.

It is interesting to note that the most genuine and popular Easter celebrations in some regions of Portugal occur on the Monday following Easter Sunday. We refer, in particular, to the widespread collective custom of going out to the countryside, in Alentejo, to eat the lamb (a possible reminder of a sacrificial lamb on the "moon day" (i.e. moon in Monday, "lune" in "lundi" in French, "lunes" in Spanish, etc). The blessing of bunches of flowers (which may include rosemary/ romerillo, laurel, olive branches, etc.) on Palm Sunday (in the past designated Flowery Easter), the use of flowers on Alleluia Sunday (ex. "Festas das Tochas" in S. Brás de Alportel, "Festa da Aleluia" in Tomar, among others), the festive gatherings and Paschal celebrations in the flowery fields, marking the arrival of Spring, seem to recall the initial meaning of the ancient equinox celebrations that, in many cultures, would signal the beginning of the year. In Babylon, the year would begin with the sight of the first lunar crescent in Spring, and the Roman calendar also started with the Spring Moon. In fact, the lunar month is the time unit most used as a calendar basis in almost every culture, progressively associated with the solar year, in attempts to stay in step with the agricultural cycles (Belmonte 2003:211-37).

The traditional and popular sanctuaries (springs, outcrops, chapels, etc.) have usually been built upon earlier ones, and the place usually converted to a new divinity. It is possible that the geographical location of some sanctuaries devoted to the Catholic faith may reflect an earlier Spring Moon orientation.

Among many of the sites visited, the sanctuary of Arcelis, between Mértola and Castro Verde, has a root name (*Ara Coelis*) that strongly suggests a relation with the sky. This sanctuary sits on top of a hill with a breathtaking 360° horizon view, and shares the same property of a fairly flat distant horizon with appropriate undulations in the approximate direction of 100°. The small chapel at the top is dedicated to Nª.Srª. da Conceição whose image always stands on a blue celestial sphere flanked by a white crescent moon, as mentioned above.

However, in the neighbourhood of Castelo de Vide, the small church of Srª da Luz stands at the base of a high hill in which top a sanctuary, Srª da Penha, provides a clear and impressive view of the distant horizon, particularly a prominent view of the fortified town of Marvão at the top of the mountain profile, at the regular azimuth of 100°.

In Algarve, the old fishing town and beach of Srª da Luz near Lagos still has in use the old chapel dedicated to "Our Lady", almost on the beach, from where we can observe a large distant promontory and the sea beginning at the appropriate azimuth. Also Srª da Luz near Tavira, and Stª Luzia nearby, may be related to an azimuth close to 100° when observed, respectively, from the hills of S. Miguel and Cabeça.

The devotion, in the Catholic faith, to "Our Lady of the Light" (N.ªSr.ª da Luz) as well as to N.ªSr.ª da Conceição and to N.ªSr.ª dos Prazeres, seems to be an appropriation of the old moon cult, and the lunar crescent under Our Lady's feet seems to be a survival of that old connection to the moon (Espirito-Santo 2004: 104-109).

We recognise traditions of particular relevance, still (or until very recently) in regular use, where this association of a ceremony of religious nature with an earlier practice dictated by the occurrence of the Spring Full Moon seems well established. Between Lisbon and Sesimbra the yearly opening to the sea of the Lagoon of Albufeira, closed during winter by the strong seas and winds, is scheduled for the day of the Full Moon in the Easter week. This event used to be preceded, on the same day, by a religious procession from the nearby village (Alfarim). This custom, brought to our attention by P. Alvim (pers. comm.), persists today although it is carried out by local administrative authorities as a measure of environmental conservation (J. Alexandrino, pers. comm.).

Also, near Ericeira there is an old custom of descending to the beach of S. Julião to pick up mussels at low tide on Good Friday. First pointed out to us by Rosário Fernandes (pers. com.), we have checked with local people and found that this custom extends north up the coast to the beach of Stª Cruz. It should be noticed that this coastline region is very close to well-known prehistoric middens, e.g. S. Julião (Sousa 2004). Nearby, at the mouth of the river Lisandro, there is a similar event on Ascension day.

It seems that Christianity still preserves elements of that association to the Moon, in the location of some sanctuaries, in Paschal liturgy and in devotions to Our Lady.

DISCUSSION

Almost everywhere, large stones – especially great blocks of granite, owing to their dimensions, durability, resistance, and visibility – have been used to build monuments to mark and define the territory and to anchor memories for the coming generations, in association with the concepts of centrality and axis-mundi. Erecting a stone in a territory makes it the centre of one's universe, which one knows and controls. Similarly, the equinox can be thought of as the midpoint between the solstices, both in space and time. This is a reinforcement of the symbolic value of that direction, and of that point in the landscape as the residence of the power that rules the cycles of nature, in a sense the centre of the mighty forces that people cannot control. For this reason relevant features of the landscape in that direction become important references in the religious framework, as they are also in the socio-economic and ritual cultural structure (Pereira 2004:99). That is probably why non-western views of the universe do not separate land and sky. Astronomy is found to be an integrating part of all native cosmologies, and this means that it is ill-advised to study sacred landscapes separately from the sky (Ruggles 1998: 208).

The analysis of several of the above sites is compatible with lunar observation and ritual practices. In particular, the Megalithic Equinox appears to be related to the Spring Full Moon, and this seems to be well supported by the orientation of funerary megaliths, as symbolic representations of resurrection, rebirth, or new life at the onset of Spring. Additional plausibility is provided by the frequent presence of astral decorative motifs engraved on the stones.

The above data on the megalithic monuments' geographical orientation, together with their decorative display of megalithic rock art (M. Calado 2004) discussed also by this author in the present Volume, and their association with symbolic artefacts, makes the megalithic monuments the first durable materialization of this relationship between the Moon, the landscape, and the ritual calendar. In this way the agro-pastoral communities of the Neolithic may have sought to influence, or control, the rhythms of nature in their favour, searching for protection in their harmonization with the unreachable cosmos.

All this is material evidence of religious thinking, traces and reminiscences of sacred gestures, which this study tries to retrieve. They are embedded in mythical structures that establish the relationship between humanity and the cosmos, assumed to be systems capable of creating "meaning" and mediating the individual, the collective, and the cosmogonic experience. They appear to be expressions of collective thought structures, determined by the unchanging aspects of the way the moon is represented or associated with other features, as their repetition throughout the Iberian space seems to anticipate.

Stones, Moon and Spring are, though, the main ingredients present in this relationship, associated with the perception and symbolization of the landscape (space) and of the ritual calendar (time). The megaliths would have then embodied a framework of astral and calendrical references and an understanding of the territory and its vital cycles. It is in the landscape that man observes the cyclical flow of time. The changing Moon is thus an expression of the cyclical transformation of the landscape, of nature and of humankind itself.

This relationship seems to have been perpetuated in time and in the collective memory, as recent data seem to suggest. The clear agreement that we can still observe today between the dolmen orientations and the direction of the Spring Full Moon rise, together with the close similarity with the present day definition of the Paschal Full Moon and the recognition that many present day cults (ex. Nª.Srª. da Conceição e da Luz) have originated in former cults of the Moon, suggests that the symbolic importance of the Moon persisted across time and found its way into the ritual and liturgical calendar of several religions.

However, its meaning was never equal or unchangeable for, as Mircea Eliade notes, the moon prompted diverse representations, personifications, symbols, and myths (Eliade 1992: 2-10). Constant change is the rule, but the heterogeneity of formulas that expresses this change is only apparent. The moon "divides", "flows" and "measures"; or "feeds", "impregnates", "blesses"; or "receives the soul of the dead", "initiates", "purifies" – for it is alive, and therefore, it is in constant cyclic change (Eliade 1992: 230-231).

Acknowledgments

We thank Calouste Gulbenkian Foundation for partial support of this work.

References

BEIRÃO, C., *et al.*, 1985, Depósito Votivo da II Idade do Ferro de Garvão. *O Arqueólogo Português* 4/3, p. 45-136.

BELMONTE, J.A, 2003, *As Leis do Céu.* Lisboa: Mareantes Editora. Orig. *"Las Leyes del Cielo-Astronomia y Civilizaciones Antiguas*", 1999, Madrid: Ed. Temas de Hoy, S.A.

CALADO, M., 1997, Vale Maria do Meio e as Paisagens Culturais do Neolítico Alentejano. In *Paisagens Arqueológicas a Oeste de Évora*, Évora: Câmara Municipal de Évora, p. 41-52.

CALADO, M., 2004, *Menires do Alentejo Central. Génese e Evolução da Paisagem Megalítica Regional.* Lisboa: FLUL (PhD. Thesis).

DA SILVA, C.M., 2000, Sobre o Possível Significado Astronómico do Cromleque dos Almendres. *A Cidade de Évora* II/4, p. 109-127.

DA SILVA, C.M., CALADO, M., 2003a, New Astronomically Significant Directions of Megalithic Monumentos in the Central Alentejo. *Journal of Iberian Archaeology* 5, p. 67-88.

DA SILVA, C.M., CALADO, M., 2003b, Monumentos Megalíticos Lunares no Alentejo Central. In Calado, M. (ed.), *Sinais da Pedra. Actas do 1º Colóquio Internacional sobre Megalitismo e Arte Rupestre na Europa Atlântica,* Évora: Fundação Eugénio de Almeida (CD-ROM).

DA SILVA, C.M., 2004, The Spring Full Moon. *Journal for the History of Astronomy* XXXV, p. 475-478.

ESPÍRITO-SANTO, M., 2004, *Cinco Mil Anos de Cultura a Oeste. Etno-História da Religião Popular numa Região da Estremadura*, Lisboa: Assírio & Alvim.

GONÇALVES, V.S., 2003, *Sítios, Horizontes e Artefactos. Estudos sobre o 3º milénio no Centro e Sul de Portugal*, Cascais: Câmara Municipal de Cascais.

HOSKIN, M., CALADO, M., 1998, Orientation of Iberian Tombs: Central Alentejo Region of Portugal. *Archaeoastronomy* 23, p. S77-82.

PEREIRA, P., 2004, *Paisagens Arcaicas,* Mem Martins.

PEREIRA, P., 2005, *Montes Sagrados, Altos Lugares e Santuários,* Mem Martins.

RIBEIRO, J.C., 2002a, Religiões da Lusitânia. *Loquuntur Saxa* In Raposo, L. (coord.), 2002, *Religiões da Lusitânia. Loquuntur Saxa*, Lisboa: Museu Nacional de Arqueologia, p. 9.

RIBEIRO, J.C., 2002b, Soli Aeterno Lunae. O Santuário. In Raposo, L. (coord.), 2002, *Religiões da Lusitânia.. Loquuntur Saxa*, Lisboa: Museu Nacional de Arqueologia, p. 235-239.

ROSLUND, C. *et al*., 2000, Portuguese Passage Graves in the Light of the Easter Moon. *Fornvännen* 95, p.1-11.

RUGGLES, C., 1998, Ritual Astronomy in the Neolithic and Bronze Age British Isles: Patterns of Continuity and Change. In Gibson, A. and Simpson, D. (eds.), *Prehistoric Ritual and Religion*, London: Sutton Publishing Limited, p. 203-208.

SOUSA, A.C. (coord.), 2004, *São Julião: Núcleo C do Concheiro Pré-Histórico*, Cadernos de Arqueologia de Mafra 2, Mafra: Câmara Municipal de Mafra.

TILLEY, C., 1994, *The Phenomenology of Landscape: Places, Paths and Monuments*. Oxford: Berg.

VASCONCELOS, José Leite, 1989, *Religiões da Lusitânia*, vol. II, Lisboa: I.N.C.M.

MEGALITHS, MEMORY AND THE POWER OF STONES

Chris SCARRE
Department of Archaeology, Durham University, Durham DH1 3LE, UK
Email: chris.scarre@durham.ac.uk

***Abstract**: The distinctive character of many of the stone slabs used in the construction of megalithic monuments in western Europe suggests that these slabs may have been intended to convey memories of the places from which they were taken. The appearance of the blocks (notably their shape, size, texture and colour) will have provided visual clues to the sources of origin. Some of the sources may have been recognised by the prehistoric builders as places of special power within the landscape, and the stones may have embodied those powers of place and their associations. Memories were also conveyed through the re-use of slabs taken from earlier monuments, a practice that has been documented at chambered tombs in Iberia, France and Britain. The visual clues provided by the megalithic slabs will, however, have been compromised by their inclusion within a covering mound or cairn, a feature that sparked 19th century antiquarian debate. These issues are discussed in the light of recent excavations at the Anta da Lajinha, a small megalithic tomb in inland Portugal north of the Tagus valley.*
***Key words**: megalithic monuments, memory, recycled stones, Anta da Lajinha*

***Résumé**: Le caractère particulier d'une grande partie des dalles utilisées pour la construction des monuments mégalithiques dans l'ouest de l'Europe nous amène à penser que ces blocs ont pu être destinés à communiquer le souvenir des endroits desquels on les a extraits. L'allure des ces blocs (notamment leur morphologie, leur taille, leur texture et leur couleur) aurait fourni des indices visuels de leur sources d'origine. Quelques-unes de ces sources avaient pu être déjà remarquées par les bâtisseurs préhistoriques qui les avaient considérées des lieux de pouvoir dans le paysage. Les blocs eux-mêmes concrétisaient peut-être les pouvoirs de ces lieux et les symbolismes associés. La mémoire des pierres avaient été communiquée également par le ré-emploi de dalles prises dans des monuments antérieurs, un phénomène qui a été mis en évidence dans les sépultures mégalithiques de la péninsule Ibérique ainsi qu'en France et en Grande Bretagne. Les indices visuels fournis par les dalles mégalithiques ont dû être entravé cependant par leur recouvrement d'un tumulus ou d'un cairn, ce qui a provoqué le débat méné par les antiquaires du 19e siècle. Ces questions seront discutés ici à la lumière des fouilles récentes à l'Anta da Lajinha, une sépulture mégalithique de dimensions modestes dans l'intérieur du Portugal au nord de la vallée du Tage.*
***Mots clés**: monuments mégalithiques, mémoire, pierres réutilisées, Anta da Lajinha*

The use of megalithic blocks in the prehistoric monuments of western Europe has both impressed and intrigued antiquaries and archaeologists for many years. The word implies the use of large stones, and indeed the blocks involved can weigh as much as 100 tonnes or more. Some have sought to deconstruct the concept of megalithic, and have quite rightly emphasized that megalithic monuments form but a part of a broader pattern of monument construction that involves timber, earth and dry stone. Yet, dependent though it is on the availability of local materials and the character of the local geology, it is difficult to believe that megalithic architecture was in any way opportunistic.

The very size of the blocks would have made them difficult to transport and use. The raising of these large masses of stone upon each other to create a chamber was not an easy option, but involved particular skills, a certain degree of danger, and—where megalithic blocks were involved—a large labour force. In some cases, particular blocks were brought from a considerable distance.

This suggests that the stones themselves, or the places they were taken from, were of especial importance. The contention can be backed up by evidence that within the burial chambers, the stones were in a sense on display. Thus in northern Europe, the dry-stonework was not only carefully adjusted to fit the contours of megalithic blocks, but it was sometimes picked out by use of differently coloured stone or by white paste or birch-bark infill between the stone courses (Dehn and Hansen 2006). In other areas of western Europe, the megalithic blocks themselves might be of different colours, and arranged in a controlled and patterned manner through the monument.

The use of megalithic blocks finds a close parallel in the use of massive timbers in other Neolithic monuments. Thus at Haddenham in eastern England, the burial chamber beneath one end of a long mound was constructed from what were essentially slabs of wood taken from large oak trees 300-400 years old and 1.5 m in diameter (Morgan in Evans & Hodder 2006: 116). The ritual or symbolic significance of major trees is reinforced by the discovery of the Holme-next-the-Sea timber circle on the east coast of Britain. Here, the lower part of an oak tree, complete with roots, had been inverted and raised upright in a socket at the centre of a circle of posts (Brennand & Taylor 2003). The circle has been dated to the end of the 3rd millennium BC, but the concept of sacred trees may have had a long prehistory.

The deployment of massive elements taken from nature, be they stone blocks or mighty oaks, seems thus to constitute a leading feature of the monuments built by prehistoric communities in western Europe during the 5th, 4th, and 3rd millennia BC. Large trees and prominent boulders or outcrops may have been considered to possess particular significance, or to be places of special power.

By taking their materials from these places, the builders of tombs were seeking perhaps to appropriate and incorporate the power and significance of those places in the monuments that they were creating. In this context, megalithic blocks may have had a particular rôle as visible and tangible links to important locations within the landscape. The shapes, textures, and colours of those stones may have constituted the enduring memory of those links, to those with the necessary knowledge.

The contention that megalithic monuments incorporate memories and associations of particular places from which the materials came may help to explain the West European–tradition of megalithic construction. The rocky landscapes of the Atlantic façade provided ample supplies of stone and a series of prominent landscape features that may have been places of mythical, symbolic, or cosmological significance. The appearance and texture of individual megalithic blocks will in themselves have provided an indication of the sources from which they were taken. In one of the earliest studies of its kind, Arthur Mourant distinguished seven varieties of stone among the megalithic slabs of La Hougue Bie on Jersey (Mourant 1933). Some came from places close to hand, but others were from sources on the opposite side of the island. There was also a particular connection with the coast: fifteen of the blocks from La Hougue Bie were visibly wave-worn, and others too were rounded; only 15 of the 65 blocks were angular, and though he observes that these must have been "in a broad sense" quarried, he adds that they too may have been obtained from rocks on the foreshore (Mourant 1933: 220).

In other cases, megalithic monuments incorporated stones that had previously functioned as standing stones or as parts of other megalithic structures. Once again, these stones will often have presented visual clues that disclosed their earlier history. A classic example is the passage grave of Maes Howe on Orkney, where the passage walls are formed by long monolithic blocks. These closely resemble in form the standing stones of the nearby Stenness stone circle, and the discovery of stone holes in the platform beneath the mound of Maes Howe strongly suggests that the long stones in the passage had originally been part of a stone circle that was dismantled to make way for the Maes Howe passage grave (Richards 1996, 2003).

The Maes Howe stones are impressive both in their size and in their distinctive shape, tapering to acutely angled points that reflect natural fault lines of the Orkney sandstone. These visual cues were retained when the monoliths were incorporated into the sides of the passage. In most passage graves, however, the visual appearance of the original megalithic blocks would have been partially or indeed predominantly obscured by their incorporation in a chambered structure that was ultimately covered by a mound. In the 19th century there was considerable debate as to whether all chambered tombs had originally been covered by a mound, or whether, conversely, some had been left free-standing so that the megalithic blocks—in particular the capstones—remained visible. In his famous *Essai sur les dolmens*, the Baron de Bonstetten divided tombs of megalithic construction (dolmens) into "dolmens apparents" and "dolmens recouverts d'un tumulus" (Bonstetten 1865). The argument was taken up by James Fergusson in *Rude Stone Monuments* (1872). Fergusson argued that it was implausible that those who had built such impressive monuments had intended the visible proof of their skill to have been hidden from view within a tumulus:

The mode of architectural expression which these Stone men best understood was the power of mass. At Stonehenge, at Avebury, and everywhere...they sought to give dignity and expression by using the largest blocks they could transport or raise—and they were right; for, in spite of their rudeness, they impress us now; but had they buried them in mounds, they neither would have impressed us nor their contemporaries. (Fergusson 1872: 169)

Others were unconvinced by these arguments. The Rev. W.C. Lukis, for example, maintained that free-standing megalithic chambers were merely the denuded remains of chambered barrows, and that all had originally been covered by mounds (Lukis 1864). Excavations since the 19th century have consistently demonstrated the presence of a mound or cairn, sometimes reduced to a faint outline, around the foot of these megalithic chambers. Yet the survival of the footings of a mound does not automatically imply that the mound completely covered and concealed the chamber. The portal dolmen of Pentre Ifan in southwest Wales provides a good example. A famous lithograph of 1865 shows mounted horsemen sheltering beneath the great capstone. The impressive character and appearance of the monument led some 19th century antiquaries (including James Fergusson) to argue that Pentre Ifan could never have been covered by a cairn. Yet in the brief account that accompanied the 1865 lithograph, Longueville Jones had observed that traces of a cairn might still be found at Pentre Ifan, "if the soil all around were carefully proved and examined" (Longueville Jones 1865: 285). This prescient observation was borne out by excavations undertaken in 1936 and 1937 which revealed that the chamber of Pentre Ifan stood at the centre of a deep semicircular forecourt, behind which had stretched a cairn 39 m in length (Grimes 1948).

The encasing of Pentre Ifan within a mound would result in a monument radically different in appearance from the denuded chamber that greets the visitor today. It also has serious implications for the symbolic significance of the massive tilted capstone. Tilley (1994) has argued that the capstone provided a direct visual link with the mountain crag of Carn Ingli some 3.5 km to the west. The burial mound of Pentre Ifan, like the crag, was oriented north-south. Furthermore, the capstone (like the crag) dips from north to south. Tilley concludes that "important architectural features of the monument seem to duplicate the outline of the mountain outcrop" (Tilley 1994: 105). Yet unless the form and height of the cairn can be demonstrated, it remains distinctly possible that the capstone of Pentre Ifan was intended to be entirely hidden from view. It has also been observed that the tilted placement of the Pentre Ifan capstone is not a feature unique to this monument but that sloping capstones are a common and distinctive feature of portal tombs as a whole (Fleming 1999: 121). One possibility is that the cairn at Pentre Ifan rose only to the height of the base of the capstone, leaving visible the capstone itself (Turner 1992: fig. 8). An alternative interpretation is that at portal dolmens in general the cairn was simply a low platform around the foot of the megalithic chamber (Kinnes 1975: 25, Cummings & Whittle 2004: 74, Whittle 2004).

Recent interpretations of the megalithic tombs of southwest England, across the Bristol Channel, have also tended to assume that the megalithic elements were externally visible. Tilley and Bennett (2001), building on earlier work (Tilley 1996, Bradley 1998), have compared the portal dolmens of West Penwith in Cornwall to the natural granite outcrops known as tors. In their eroded condition, the tors take the form of outcrops surrounded by stacks of detached blocks. Tilley and Bennett argue that prehistoric populations may have regarded the tors and other natural features as the petrified shapes of ancestral beings, or as the work of ancestors who sculpted the rocks. The portal dolmens were built of megalithic blocks taken from these stacks and outcrops, such that dolmens and tors came to resemble each other closely. Tilley and Bennett contend that the dolmens were built to imitate tors:

It is not that the tors look like dolmen chambers, but that the dolmens look like tors…The tors were not only their source of inspiration, but they were constructed in the form of tors. In elevating large stones, these people were emulating the work of a super-ancestral past. Furthermore, the stones from which they were built were taken from the tors. The dolmens, in effect, were the tors dismantled and put back together again to resemble their original form (Tilley & Bennett 2001: 354).

This interpretation makes no concession to the possibility that the portal dolmens of West Penwith were covered by or concealed within mounds. Nor is much attention paid to their traditionally assumed role as burial places, albeit (as in southwest Wales) the granitic geology has prevented the survival of any human remains. The implication, however, is that by taking blocks from the tors to construct tombs, and that by placing their dead within the resulting dolmens, prehistoric communities would have been burying them within artificial tors. The relationship was modified and finessed during the Early Bronze Age, when cairns for the dead were built among the tors themselves (Tilley & Bennett 2001: 354).

The proposal that megalithic tombs may represent the reconstitution of an exploded natural landform can be posited in other contexts outside Britain. Thus on the North European plain, where megalithic tombs are built of split glacial erratics, it is the smooth inner faces of the blocks that are turned to the inside, as if the dead were being buried symbolically within the erratics themselves. In Portugal, Vortisch and Dehn have demonstrated how constituent elements of Alentejan megalithic chambers can be traced back to specific parts of original granite outcrops (Dehn *et al.* 1991, Vortisch 1999). The concept works particularly well where the capstone retains the weathered and rounded upper surface of the outcrop, and where the orthostats have been extracted by exploiting vertical fissures in the outcrop. In such cases, the tombs might be taken symbolically to represent the outcrop, although the fact that tombs do not invariably follow this pattern should warn us against an overly symbolic interpretation. Technical considerations no doubt also played a part in guiding the placement of the megalithic blocks that were extracted from different parts of the rock outcrop.

A number of Alentejan tombs have cup marks on orthostats or capstones. Anta 1 at Paço das Vinhas had 16 cup marks on the upper surface of the capstone. They were also present on the capstones of Anta 1 at Casas do Canal, Bencafêde and Cabaconhitos (Gonçalves 1992, Dos Santos 1994). These probably represent the removal of slabs from outcrops on which cup marks had already been carved. At Olival da Pega 2, the two outermost passage orthostats had numerous cup marks on their outer faces, that would have been hidden once the cairn was built. It is possible that these two stones had originally been free-standing menhirs that were subsequently converted into orthostats (Gonçalves 1992: 263). At all events, the cup marks must have been carved before the slabs were placed in their final position within the tomb. Cup marks are also found on natural outcrops in the Alentejo region, and it may be that stones taken from such outcrops were considered especially powerful.

Once again, questions of visibility must be addressed. Some Alentejan tomb chambers may have resembled granite outcrops that had been reassembled, but most if not all were originally concealed within a mound. Substantial traces of the original mound still survive at monuments such as Anta 1 in the Vale de Rodrigo, Anta 1 at Paço das Vinhas, Anta Grande do Zambujeiro and Anta Grande da Comenda da Igreja. Equally, it has been suggested that Anta 3 in the Vale de Rodrigo may not have been covered by a mound (Kalb 1996: 685), so the practice may not have been universal.

In Galicia, too, it has been argued that in some cases, the chamber and capstone protruded above the surface of the mound. Felipe Criado and Fabregas Valcarce have suggested that visibility of the chambers within mounds varied over time, resulting from a dialectical tension between the two elements. As the mound became less important, chambers grew to attain lengths of seven or eight meters, and the upper part of the orthostats and capstone rose visibly above the surface of the mound

(Criado & Fabregas 1989: 687). At Dombate, the excavator concluded that the mound, measuring 24 m in diameter and preserved to a height of 1.8 m, would originally have covered the passage but not the chamber, and that the latter would have projected above the top of the mound. The space between the orthostats at the back of the chamber was carefully sealed by a vertical stone of regular size, and the interior surfaces were coated with white plaster and painted with red-and-black motifs in a pattern that covered not only the individual orthostats but also the spaces between them (Bello Dieguez 1996). Hence in this instance megalithic blocks may have been visible externally, but they were masked internally by plaster and paint.

THE ANTA DA LAJINHA

The issue of external visibility of orthostats and capstone has arisen again in the course of recent excavations at the Anta da Lajinha, a small megalithic tomb in the hill country of inland Portugal to the north of the River Tagus, 150 km upstream from Lisbon and 50 km from the Spanish frontier. The field project initiated here in 2006 by Durham University in conjunction with the Instituto Politécnico di Tomar seeks to understand the structure of the monument and in particular to establish its original environment in terms of vegetation and soils.

The tomb stands at the highest point of a spur projecting into the Vale de Pereiro. The ground falls away on all sides, but most steeply to north, east and west. The tomb is hence in a locally prominent position, although enclosed within a basin framed by higher ground on all sides. The remains are those of a passage grave constructed of schist orthostats at the centre of a circular mound some 10 m in diameter. The tomb had been heavily disturbed before the current excavations began. Some of this disturbance can be dated to the 20th century, since a brief description published in 1939 indicates a structure consisting of eight orthostats, whereas by 1967 only six of these remained, and of those only two were undisturbed (Silva Louro 1939, Horta Pereira 1970). There were scanty remains of an entrance on the eastern side of the chamber, though it was not possible to trace the plan of the passage. This was the condition of the monument when excavations began in 2006.

The chamber is of irregular oval plan and measures approximately 1 m x 1.2 m across. In addition to the two undisturbed orthostats at the rear (west) of the chamber, the positions of two others were revealed by stumps, and displaced fragments of two further orthostats survive on the northern and southern sides of the chamber. The surviving orthostats and the stumps all had a pronounced inward inclination, and of the two western orthostats the southernmost overlapped and rested against the edge of the northern stone. The original form of the chamber was hence clearly a series of eight orthostats leaning inwards, each resting against its neighbour for support. The capstone that once covered and completed this structure has long since disappeared. Of the passage that adjoined the chamber on the east, little remains in situ save a single massive block at the southern junction with the chamber. A second large block resting against it appears to be disturbed and might be a displaced orthostat or capstone from either the passage or the chamber. Excavation on the line of the passage revealed a confused jumble of stone fragments that may be the result of intentional destruction, though the interpretation of this deposit will need to await further excavation.

The two surviving undisturbed orthostats are substantial slabs of blue-grey schist. The photographs published in 1939 show that these were the largest of the orthostats (Silva Louro 1939: 12). They measure respectively 1.14 m and 0.83 m in maximum width, with a visible height of approximately 1.2 m. Both have been severely damaged by forest fires, and the laminar structure of the stones is encouraging active exfoliation of the surfaces. Examination of the surfaces does however reveal successive stages in the history of these blocks. In both cases, the surface of the lower part of the orthostat consists of a weathered light grey surface tending to brown or even green in places. This may be the original surface of the stone. Above this is an extensive area of uniform dark-grey appearance corresponding to a recent episode of exfoliation, where the newly exposed surface has not had sufficient time to weather. Between the ancient and recently exposed surfaces there is a third surface, most-clearly visible on the southern orthostat. This is blue-grey in colour. It covers the lower part of the southern slab and is preserved in patches at the top of the stone. The surface appears to correspond to a process of shaping which has given the upper profile of the orthostat a rounded shape, worked upwards from both front and back to a longitudinal keel. Other fragments of schist slabs with rounded and keeled edges were recovered lying loose on the surface of the site. It seems clear that the tops of the orthostats had been carefully shaped by the prehistoric builders.

The preservation of the worked surface at the top of the southern orthostat implies that this stone is preserved to its full height. Since it and its neighbour appear to have been the tallest orthostats, we are able to determine the height of the chamber as a whole. Adding an estimated 30 cm for the thickness of a missing capstone, we are hence able to estimate the original height of the megalithic structure as around 1.5 m. By contrast, the mound, a stone-free structure of silty decayed schist, survives today to a height of only 0.6 m against the rear of the chamber orthostats. Its original height is difficult to determine, but the absence of slip outside the kerb of the mound suggests that it may never have been substantially higher than it is today. If that is correct, then the upper part of the chamber orthostats and the capstone would have been left visible. This would have established a visual link between the material of the orthostats and the source from which they were derived.

The orthostats of the Anta da Lajinha do not come from the immediate vicinity of the site. The schist bedrock on which the monument stands is vertically bedded, heavily eroded, and brown/grey in colour. As a source of building material, it would furnish only small- to medium-sized cobbles. The wider area around the site is however punctuated by parallel rows of schist outcrops. These are prominent and, in some cases, spectacular landscape features, creating a series of natural monuments. Field survey identified one set of outcrops 1 km east of Lajinha that is associated with prehistoric surface material including a finely flaked hollow-based arrowhead of flint. This type of arrowhead is dated to the early Chalcolithic period (late 4th millennium BC). Further investigations will be undertaken to identify the nature of prehistoric activity at this location.

Closer to the Anta da Lajinha, some 200 m east of the site, a series of four parallel rows of schist outcrops extends obliquely down the hillside towards the Vale de Pereiro. These outcrops, though damaged by recent fires, attain heights of up to 3 m and are visually identical to the material of the intact orthostats of Lajinha. It is not possible to assert that the orthostats came from this precise location, but it highlights the likelihood that the orthostats were derived from prominent outcrops of the blue-grey schist that runs in bands across the landscape. Ethnographic evidence suggests that outcrops such as these would in themselves have been sufficiently intriguing to have been the subject of myths and stories by prehistoric populations. They may have been thought places of particular power. That contention finds support in the site of Jogada 5, in the Zêzere valley to the west of Lajinha, where a natural outcrop was monumentalized in the Chalcolithic period.

CONCLUSION

It is not my contention here to revive the 19th century debate on the presence or absence of covering mounds at megalithic tombs, but to emphasize rather the variability of the structural arrangements, and the implications that these may have had for the symbolic significance of the stones. In instances where the megalithic blocks were clearly visible in the external appearance of the monument, it is easy to contend that the tombs may incorporate the memories and associations of particular places from which those materials came. The rocky landscapes of the Atlantic facade provided both amply supplies of stone and a prominent series of landscape features that the builders of megalithic monuments may have been seeking to reference and imitate.

In this perspective, the megalithic blocks may have served as mnemonics, as visual reminders of other places in the landscape. Those places—the sources from which the stones were taken—may in some cases have been spectacular in themselves and may have constituted a kind of natural monument. The prominent schist outcrops around the Anta da Lajinha may have been just such natural monuments. In building the tomb of this material, direct reference was being made to landscape features that had probably been of special significance for generations. That reference would have been reinforced if these stones remained partially visible from outside even after the mound had been completed.

Direct visual links to natural monuments would have been obscured if a megalithic chamber was entirely covered by a mound. Other kinds of symbolic associations must be considered in these cases. One possibility is that the megalithic structure of the burial space reconstituted a natural feature that had been dismantled or exploded. Studies of megalithic tombs in the Alentejo have shown that the capstones are from the horizontal upper surfaces of the outcrop, and that the orthostats are from vertical fractures. Portal dolmens in southwest England may be granite tors dismantled and reassembled. In similar fashion, timber chambers beneath the long mounds of southern Britain are often bracketed between post holes that held twin D-shaped posts that may have been halves of a single tree trunk (Noble 2006). This once again draws attention to the likely significance of construction-material sources, be they massive trees several centuries old, or conspicuous cliffs or outcrops.

At the same time however, the proposal that megalithic architecture is driven by the identity and significance of individual stones does not depend entirely on their external visibility. Even if the shapes and sizes of individual slabs were partially occluded, and they were viewed only in flickering light of lamps or torches, their colours and textures would still have been visible from within the chambers. Furthermore, visibility itself may not have been essential to the conveyance of cultural meaning. Without any direct visual clues to the character or origin of the stone slabs, memory of these traits may have been sufficient to convey meaning. In some cases, the slabs were transformed by smoothing, shaping, carving, or painting, so that many features of their original form were removed or concealed. Whether covered or exposed, intact or reshaped, these slabs represented identifiable elements of the landscape that had been appropriated and exploited. That different communities chose to do this in different ways should hardly surprise us. What lies behind them all, however, is the materiality and identity of the megalithic blocks themselves.

Acknowledgements

The excavations at the Anta da Lajinha were funded by the British Academy with generous support from the museum and municipality of Mação and the Instituto Politécnico de Tomar. My special thanks go to Professor Luiz Oosterbeek for his invitation to undertake this fieldwork and for his assistance with the numerous practicalities; and for information about the site of Jogada 5.

References

BELLO DIEGUEZ, J.M., 1996, Aportaciones del dolmen de Dombate (Cabana, La Coruña) al arte megalitico occidental. In J. L'helgouach, C-T. L. Roux & J. Lecornec (eds.), *Art et Symboles du Mégalithisme Européen. Revue Archéologique de l'Ouest, Supplément no. 8*, p. 23-39.

BONSTETTTEN, A. DE, 1865, *Essai sur les Dolmens*, Geneva: Fick.

BRADLEY, R., 1998, Ruined Buildings, Ruined Stones: Enclosures, Tombs and Natural Places in the Neolithic of South-West England, *World Archaeology* 30, p. 13-22.

BRENNAND, M., & TAYLOR, M., 2003, The survey and Excavation of a Bronze Age Timber Circle at Holme-next-the-Sea, Norfolk, 1998–9, *Proceedings of the Prehistoric Society* 69, p. 1-84.

CRIADO BOADO, F., & FABREGAS VALCARCE, R., 1989, The Megalithic Phenomenon of Northwest Spain: Main Trends, *Antiquity* 63/241, p. 682-696.

CUMMINGS, V., & WHITTLE, A., 2004, *Places of Special Virtue. Megaliths in the Neolithic landscapes of Wales,* Oxford: Oxbow.

DEHN, T., & HANSEN, S., 2006, Birch Bark in Danish passage graves, *Journal of Danish Archaeology* 14, p. 23-44.

DEHN, W., KALB, P., & VORTISCH, W., 1991, Geologisch-petrographische Untersuchungen an Megalithgräbern Portugals, *Madrider Mitteilungen* 32, p. 1-28.

DOS SANTOS, A.P., 1994, *Monumentos Megalíticos do Alto Alentejo*, Lisbon: Fenda.

EVANS, C., & HODDER, I., 2006, *A Woodland Archaeology. Neolithic Sites at Haddenham*, Cambridge: McDonald Institute for Archaeological Research.

FERGUSSON, J., 1872, *Rude Stone Monuments in All Countries; Their Age and Uses,* London: John Murray.

FLEMING, A., 1999, Phenomenology and the Megaliths of Wales: A Dreaming too Far? *Oxford Journal of Archaeology* 18, p. 119-125.

GONÇALVES, V.S., 1992, *Revendo as Antas de Reguengos de Monsaraz*, Lisbon: UNIARQ.

GRIMES, W.F., 1948, Pentre-Ifan burial chamber, Pembrokeshire, *Archaeologia Cambrensis* 100, p. 3-23.

HORTA PEREIRA, M.A., 1970, *Monumentos Históricos do Concelho de Mação*, Mação: Câmara Municipal de Mação.

KALB, P., 1996, Megalith-Building, Stone Transport and Territorial Markers: Evidence from Vale de Rodrigo, Evora, South Portugal, *Antiquity* 70/269, p. 683-685.

KINNES, I., 1975, Monumental Function in British Neolithic Burial Practice, *World Archaeology* 7, p. 16-29.

LONGUEVILLE JONES, H., 1865, Pembrokeshire Antiquities. Cromlechs—Newton, Manorbier, St. David's Head, Pentre Ifan, *Archaeologia Cambrensis* 11, p. 281-285.

LUKIS, W.C., 1864, On Cromlechs, *Journal of the British Archaeological Association* 1864, p. 228-237.

MOURANT, A.E., 1933, Dolmen de la Hougue Bie: nature and provenance of the materials, *Bulletin Annuel de la Société Jersiaise* 12, p. 217-220.

NOBLE, G., 2006, *Neolithic Scotland: Timber, Stone, Earth and Fire,* Edinburgh: Edinburgh University Press.

RICHARDS, C., 1996, Monuments as landscape: creating the centre of the world in late Neolithic Orkney, *World Archaeology* 28, p. 190-208.

RICHARDS, C., (ed.) 2003, *Dwelling Among the Monuments: an examination of the Neolithic village of Barnhouse, Maeshowe passage grave and surrounding monuments at Stenness, Orkney*, Cambridge: McDonald Institute for Archaeological Research.

SILVA LOURO, H. DA, 1939, *Monografia de Cardigos*, Cucujãis: Escola Tipográfica do Seminário das Missões.

TILLEY, C., 1994, *A Phenomenology of Landscape. Places, paths and monuments*. Oxford: Berg.

TILLEY, C., 1996, The power of rocks: topography and monument construction on Bodmin Moor, *World Archaeology* 28, p. 161-76.

TILLEY, C., & BENNETT, W., 2001, An Archaeology of Supernatural Places: The Case of West Penwith, *Journal of the Royal Anthropological Institute* 7, p. 335-362.

TURNER, R.C., 1992, Pentre Ifan Burial Chamber, Pembrokeshire. The Story of the First Ancient Monument in Wales, *Transactions of the Ancient Monuments Society* 36, p. 99-118.

VORTISCH, W., 1999, Geologisch-petrographische Untersuchungen an megalithischen Monumenten–Beispiele aus Portugal. In K.W. Beinhauer, G., Cooney, C.E. Guksch & S. Kus (eds.) *Studien zur Megalithik. Forschunggsstand und ethnoarchäologische Perspektiven*, Weissbach: Beier & Beran, p. 275-288.

WHITTLE, A., 2004, Stones that Float to the Sky: Portal Dolmens and their Landscapes of Memory and Myth. In V. Cummings & C. Fowler (eds.), *The Neolithic of the Irish Sea. Materiality and Traditions of Practice*, Oxford: Oxbow, p. 81-90.

LANDSCAPE, ARCHITECTURAL AND RITUAL ASPECTS OF THE CHALCOLITHIC (CALCOLITHIC) SANCTUARIES IN THE LOMBARDY ALPS (ITALY)

Raffaella POGGIANI KELLER
Soprintendenza per i Beni Archeologici per la Lombardia, Via Edmondo De Amicis, 11 – 20123 Milano, tel. 02/89400555 – fax 02/89404430
Email: sop.arch.lomb@fastwebnet.it

***Abstract**: In Valle Camonica and in neighbouring Valtellina, during the 2nd half 4th and the beginning of 3rd millennium BC, as recent and wide excavations and surveys show, megalithic cult and ceremonial sites with steles and menhir-boulders engraved were founded. These sites, where a systematic survey was carried out to define the parameters of territorial choice, have a special significance in the landscape of the valley and constitute an expression and consequence of the density of occupation, extending from the valley floor to high altitudes, which developed from the Late Neolithic onwards, as an enduring expression of territoriality.*

Among the 29 sites found to date in the two valleys, at least 18 are in situ. The article provides a new information on these sanctuaries discovered in recent years in Valcamonica, at Ossimo-Pat and Cemmo, and in Valtellina, at Caven-Teglio.

***Key words**: Sanctuaries, megaliths, Calcolithic, Lombardy Alps*

***Résumé**: Environnement, architecture et aspects rituels des sanctuaires chalcolithiques de la Lombardie alpine (Italie. Dans la Vallée Camonica et la Valtellina, il y a un réseau extraordinaire de sites de culte et cérémoniaux, avec stèles et menhirs gravés, nés le long des parcours qui du fond de la vallée montent à haute altitude depuis la moitié du 4ème millenaire a.J.C. pendant l'âge du Cuivre et plusieurs fois continués, si même avec solution de continuité, dans l'âge du Fer et plus longtemps. Avec surveys systhématiques et fouilles on a examiné les caractères- morfologiques, geografiques, d'implantation, de relation, de fonction de chacun d'eux afin de repérer les paramètres de choix des sites, d'en comprendre les logiques. Des 29 sites découverts dans les deux vallées, 18 sont des contextes in situ. Ce article donne trois exemples des sanctuaires fouillés à Ossimo-Pat et Cemmo (Vallée Camonica) et à Caven-Teglio (Valtellina).*

***Mots clés**: Sanctuaires, megalithes, Chalcolithique, Lombardie alpi*

INTRODUCTION

In the Alpine Piedmont valleys of Lombardy one of the most important discoveries of recent years have been the megalithic sanctuaries. They were built from the Copper Age (mid-4th to 3rd millennium BC) through the Iron Age and beyond, although their use was not completely continuous over this long period of time. There are large standing stones, almost always with engravings, and other stone structures of varying form and function (platforms, tumuli and boundary walls), which articulate the space, history, and use of these complexes.

The sanctuaries are restricted to two Lombard valleys, Valle Camonica and Valtellina, which lie side by side (Fig. 12.1). There the Lombardy Superintendent's Office of Archaeology (*Soprintendenza per i Beni Archeologici della Lombardia)* has undertaken systematic field research since the early 1980s. These include surveys, mapping of engraved steles and rocks, which had not previously been positioned with precision. Research also focuses on the morphological, geographical and functional characteristics of each site and interrelationships between sites, so as to understand how they functioned. The research furthers strategies to protect them. In addition, when new discoveries were made, area excavations were carried out (De Marinis 1988; Poggiani Keller 1999, 2000 a and 2004), on by universities in the sites of Ossimo-Anvòia and Passagròp (Fedele 2006 with bibliography). New studies of monuments found in the past were published (Anati 1990 and Casini 1994).

Of the 29 sites yielding archaeological information 18 are original sites (13 in Valle Camonica and 5 in Valtellina). There are 16 new sites in Valle Camonica and 13 in Valtellina. We are therefore dealing with an extraordinary network of cult and ceremonial sites that grew up along ways that led from the valley floor to high ground. Their distribution corresponds to the dense occupation of the territory that developed in the Late Neolithic, presumably due to the search for lithic raw materials, copper, agricultural areas and animal herding. The total number of engraved monuments, whole or fragmentary is about a hundred, with unsurprising concentrations in areas where archaeological excavations have been conducted.[1]

The relationship between sanctuaries and settlements (the latter are only known at present in Valcamonica[2]) is not yet clear.[3] In Valcamonica, stable villages were founded in the 4th millennium along the main river in positions which offered strategic control of routes and resources.[4] They precede the cult and ceremonial sites by several centuries, which are distributed in two main groups, corresponding to two distinct geographical areas: the

[1] The Ossimo-Pat sanctuary, for example, has yielded 30 engraved stones.

[2] Bibliography in Poggiani Keller 2002.

[3] The only sanctuary near a settlement – not yet excavated – is Cemmo, see below.

[4] The Valcamonica settlements, which were founded in the Late Neolithic to early Copper Age (mid-4th millennium BC), show some characteristics of the Square-Mouthed Vase and Lagozza Cultures (indicated by the appearance of Breno-type stamped pottery) and remained on the same sites until the end of the Iron Age.

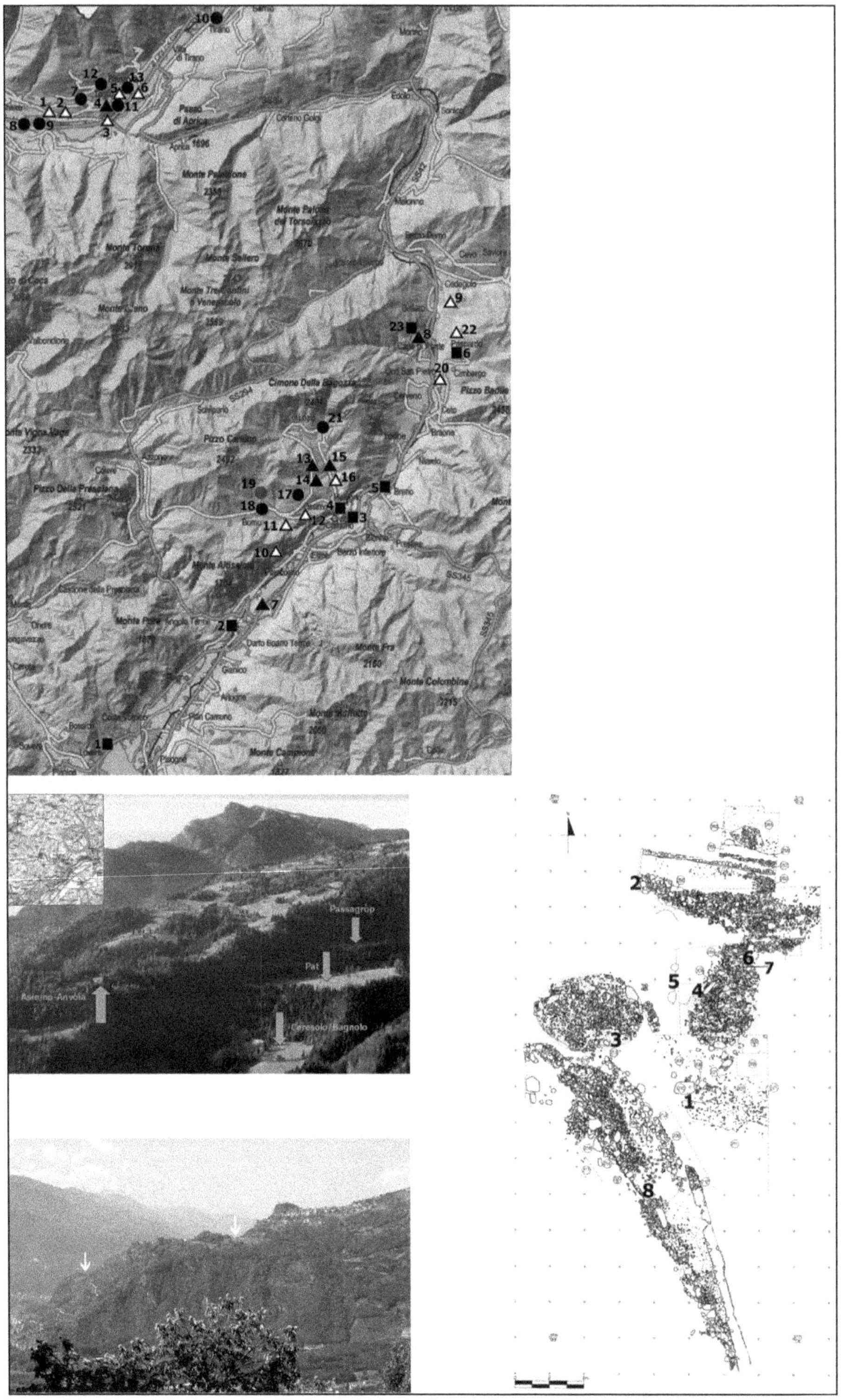

Fig. 12.1. 1. Lombardy map with megalithic sanctuaries (triangle), calcolithics monoliths isolated (point) and coevals settlements (square). The full symbol: original sites excavated; the empty symbol: the sites non investigated.
VALLE CAMONICA. Settlements: 1- Lovere, Colle del Lazzaretto; 2- Darfo Boario Terme, Luine; 3- Cividate Camuno, Via Palazzo; 4- Malegno, Via Cavour; 5- Breno, Castello; 6- Capo di Ponte, Dos dell'Arca; 23- Capo di Ponte, Seradina. Megalithic cult and ceremonial sites (nn. 7-16, 20-21) and isolated menhirs and steles (nn.17-19): 7- Darfo B.T., Corni Freschi; 8- Capo di Ponte-Frazione Cemmo, Pian delle Greppe; 9- Cedegolo, Campolongo; 10- Piancogno, Dassine; 11- Borno, Valzel de Undine; 12- Ossimo inferiore, centro/S. Rocco; 13- Ossimo superiore, Località Passagròp; 14- Ossimo superiore, Località Anvòia/Asinino; 15- Ossimo superiore, Località Pat; 16- Malegno, Località Ceresolo (già indicata come Bagnolo); 17- Ossimo superiore, centro abitato; 18- Borno, centro; 19- Borno, Località ignota; 20- Ceto, Foppe di Nadro; 21- Lozio, Camerata-Mulini; 22- Paspardo, Plas Capitello dei due Pini. VALTELLINA: 1- Teglio, Cornàl/Castelvetro; 2- Teglio, Vangione; 3- Teglio, Valgella; 4- Teglio, Caven ; 5- Teglio, Somasassa; 6- Teglio-Frazione Boalzo, Località Fugarola; 7- Teglio, Ligone; 8- Chiuro, centro; 9- Chiuro, Castionetto; 10- Tirano?; 11- Teglio, Boalzo- fiume; 12- Teglio, ...; 13- Teglio, Cànove

Ossimo-Borno upland, on the eastern slopes of the Orobic Alps (Fig. 1, Nos. 10-16), and the valley floor and lower slopes near the River Oglio (Fig. 1, Nos. 7- 9, 20).

Settlements occur in Valtellina (Anati 1967, Poggiani Keller 1989 pp. 40-46) and the sanctuaries, apart from the uncertain case of Tirano, are all located on the hills around Teglio, which dominate the junction of the Adda and Oglio valleys. All of the sites, with the exception of Valgella, which faces the river, are distributed between of 600 and 700 m above sea level in proximity to the clustered settlements of Teglio. They occur along the old paths leading up from the valley floor.

These long-lived open-air sanctuaries constitute clear territorial markers. They are visible by means of sighting corridors, either *ad hoc*, or created by the removal woodland areas, as in Valcamonica (Fig. 12.2). In other instances they make use of the natural morphology, as in the Teglio hills, where the sanctuaries (Fig. 12.3) are sited on hillside terraces overlooking the valley (Caven and Vangione). They are also located on hills, as in Cornàl.

For many sites in both valleys the vicinity to water is important. This includes streams, rivers, waterfalls (in Valtellina: Valgella and Boalzo; in Valcamonica: Darfo-Corni Freschi, Borno-Valzel de Undine, Ossimo-Pat and Lozio). In the sites of Cornàl and Caven (Valtellina) and in Foppe di Nadro Valcamonica and in Cemmo pools lakes are important, while other sites are close to springs.

Research has been carried out by the *Soprintendenza per i Beni Archeologici della Lombardia* in five megalithic sanctuaries, four in Valcamonica (Ossimo- Passagròp and Pat, Cemmo, Darfo-Corni Freschi) and one in Valtellina (Teglio-Caven). A sixth site was dug by Fedele in Ossimo-Anvòia (Fedele 2006). Whilst the three Ossimo sites were discovered in 1988-89 by G.C. and A. Zerla, the others have been known for decades and excavated between 1930 and 1965 (with generally insignificant results).

THE CAVEN, PAT AND CEMMO SANCTUARIES

By way of example I will describe the sites of Caven in Valtellina, Ossimo-Pat and Cemmo in Valcamonica. The three sanctuaries are important in for their long periods of use (prehistoric, proto-historic and later), complexity of the activities associated, as well as for their architectural features, numerous engravings and variety of iconography.

The sites are distinguished by their imposing alignments of steles, engraved rocks and/or for the various stone structures which give each its specific character. These include platform and boundary walls in Caven di Teglio, In Pat there is a platform and enclosures. Stone-built boundary structures surround the sacred area in Cemmo. Excavations in Cemmo and Pat indicate a progressive development from initial constructions in earth and wood to stone architecture. Furthermore, evidence of ritual practices has been found in two sanctuaries. Fires were lit and offerings of flowers, berries and shrubs were deposited in Pat. Finally, ritual plough furrows were made in the foundation layers in Cemmo.

In Teglio-Caven, the discovery in 1940 of three steles (bibliography: Poggiani Keller 1989) marked the beginning of a series of finds which have totalled a further 12 sites in Valtellina. None of which have been excavated.

Caven is situated in proximity to a spring on a terrace which steeply overlooks the Adda Valley. It is visible from far afield (Fig. 12.3) and is close to the "Rupe dell'alveo", a rock engraved with symbols from the 4th-3rd millennium. The excavation was conducted between 1998 and 2003 and covers an area of about 700 m^2. The sanctuary is estimated to occupy at least 2,000 m^2. No new steles came to light, but the excavation allowed us to understand the development and architecture of this cult site (Fig. 12.4).

At the beginning, an artificial terrace was constructed. The surface of was cobbled with small stones and featured large rocks. On one of these were several cup-marks (Fig. 12.4, 1). Subsequently, an enclosure was erected (Fig. 12.4, 2). One side contained two circular platforms, 6.0 m and 5.2 m in diameter and 2.5 m apart (Fig. 12.4, 3-4). The smaller of these was surrounded by a ring of isolated rocks (Fig. 12.4, 5). Around the platforms, patches of cobbled surface survived (Fig. 12.4, 6). One was associated with a post-hole which may have been a wooden marker (Fig. 12.4, 7).

Few finds were recovered from the excavated platform (Fig. 12.4, 4). These included fragments of undiagnostic prehistoric pottery, flint flakes and tiny charcoal fragments of Pinus sylvestris/P. mugo and Quercus robur, probably from fires, and a burnt seed or fruit fragment of Chenopodium hibridum, a plant which grows on waste ground or infests crops. Under the platform a previous occupation horizon was found; it was associated with a large pit that yielded no finds.

Caven's interpretation as a Calcolithic sanctuary is based thediscovery of three steles. In addition, it is its similarity to other Alpine megalithic sites, in particular that in Velturno- Tanzgasse (Province of Bolzano, Italy), where ceremonial platforms are associated with funerary remains of this period (Dal Ri *et al.* 2004).

After a period of disuse renewed activity occurred in the late Iron Age when a large wall was built on the Calcolithic terrace (Fig. 12.4, 8). Study of the stratigraphy suggests that the steles found in 1940 had probably been reused on the crest of this wall, traces of which were uncovered by a trench dug in 1941 on the spot where the steles were found. If this supposition is correct, the cult

focolare	15	GX-23006	2120±140 BP	550-250	BC
focolare	7	GX-31247	2640±70 BP	980-750; 900-760	BC
focolare	151	GX-31249	2660±70 BP	1000-750	BC
focolare	154	GX-31246	2670±70 BP	1010-750;	BC

Fig. 12.2. Ossimo area: four sanctuaries of Pat, Anvoia, Passagròp and Ceresolo-Bagnolo (G. Carlo Zerla photo)

Fig. 12.3. The Teglio hills: the sanctuaries (Caven and Somasassa) are sited on hillside terraces overlooking the valley

site was reused in the Iron Age. This date is in agreement with diverse evidence from other excavations in Valcamonica, where in proto-historic times and later, Calcolithic religious sites were re-occupied, clearly respecting for their traditional functions.

In Valcamonica, apart from a few cases on the valley floor, sites are concentrated on the Ossimo-Borno upland (Fig. 12.1). This is similar to the hilly area near Teglio. The Ossimo-Pat sanctuary is part of an unusual group of cult locations, sited about 400 m apart and each visible from the others, at an altitude of around 800 metres. At the time of their foundation in the Calcolithic period, the plateaus on which the sites are situated were "cut out" of wooded areas and cleared with the use of fire (Fig. 12.2). The site, under excavation since 1994, is composed of two main components. One group is a Calcolithic sanctuary in which cult activity was renewed at the end of the Bronze Age and continued throughout the 1st millennium BC. The other is a settlement of the *Camunni* people, composed of seven rectangular houses built in the late Iron Age, on the uphill side of the sanctuary.

The sanctuary covers over 4,000 m^2 at the eastern end of the Pat terrace facing the Inferno Valley, and includes an area of standing stone alignments, in between two zones with platforms[5] and enclosures (Figs. 12.5, 8). Its foundation is followed by various phases of use alterations, and abandonment commenced between the Late Neolithic and the Copper Age, around the mid-4th millennium BC. It lasted until the Early Bronze Age. At present, the excavation has brought to light the foundation level of the sanctuary in only the ceremonial area south of the aligned monoliths. There were three circular stone-built platforms and perimeter walls, occasionally having several courses, range in diameter from 5.0 m to 6.4 m. Structure A, is the only one excavated to date. It contained an oval of stones, divided into a series of niches where offerings, datable to the Copper Age, had been deposited. One niche contained a vase. In second a vase, above a wooden container decorated with studs made from copper sheet, a necklace with six strings of small bone rings had been placed. Two of the platform's perimeter stones ("Pat 8 and 9") bore so-called "topographic" engravings, serpentine motifs and cup-marks. These figures are comparable to those of the Late Neolithic/Early Copper Age. Underneath the structure, an earlier post-hole and pits were found. They may be evidence relating to the consecration of the area. For one of the pits (US 116) was full of charcoal from burnt branches of *Juniperus communis, Abies / Juniperus, Coniferae, Salix sp., Corylus avellana, Prunus sp., Laburnum sp.* and *Acer sp.* The ^{14}C date (GX-31248 4820±40 bp) yields 3700-3510 BC.[6] I.e. the Italian Late Neolithic/Early Copper Age. The two stones "Pat 8 and 9" reused the platform since they belong to the first phase of engraved monoliths from the sanctuary and reused the

[5] Thought at first to be barrows, these were found to be structures for the deposition of offerings, with no evidence of burials.

[6] GX-31248: 4820±40 BP yields 3660 BC (23.5%) 3620 BC, 3580 BC (44.7%) 3530 BC at 68.2% probability; 3700 BC (95.4%) 3510 BC at 95.4% probability, using atmospheric data from Reimer *et al.* (2004) and OxCal v3.10 (Bronk Ramsey 2005).

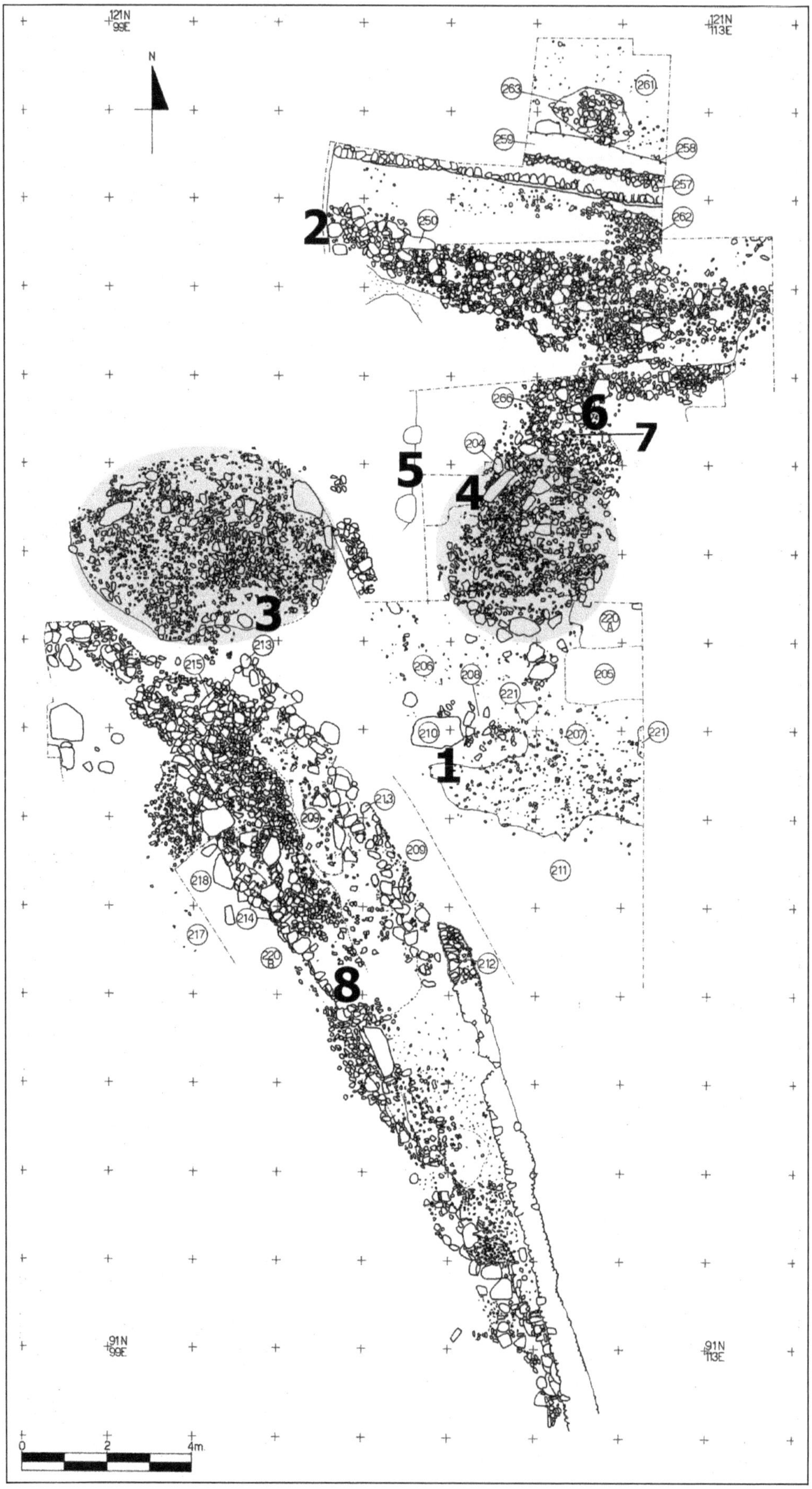

Fig. 12.4. Teglio-Caven. The development and architecture of this cult site

Fig. 12.5. Ossimo-Pat. The Copper Age platforms

platform. The area of the south platform was abandoned in the Early Bronze Age, reused during the 1st millennium BC when small fires were lit above the Calcolithic mounds, which by now were covered by colluvial deposits.

To the north of the features described above, a row of boulder-menhirs and engraved steles was present (Fig. 12.6). To date, 27 whole or partial monuments have been found, aligned N-S towards the mount Cimon della Bagozza. Each had a sun motif carved on the upper portion of the principal engraved face, looking eastwards. Some sit in foundation trenches with packing stones, whilst others are placed on rectangular platforms.

Thus fat, the excavation has reached layers deposited during the late Copper Age, but not yet those associated with the construction of the line of standing stones. The layers have been rebuilt more than once. There is stratigraphic evidence that the sanctuary passed through a number of construction and demolition phases, during which some monuments were removed and new ones erected. At least three phases may be recognised. During the final period of use, i.e. the Calcolithic – Early Bronze Age, several stones had already fallen over and were partially covered or broken. The "Pat 17" stele shows clear signs that wedges were used to break it up. Finds recovered from the trodden surfaces include half-moon flint pieces, arrowheads, sickle microliths, pot fragments, copper slag (Poggiani Keller 2006). These may have been purposely placed in this ceremonial area. The engravings on the standing stones also celebrate these activities and others, such as ploughing.

North of the standing stones there is a zone completely lacking evidence of the activities just noted. Instead, this it contains several circular enclosures (Fig. 12.8). The two so far excavated consist of double concentric stones circles partly built from reused stele fragments. The enclosures surround rectangular structures outlined with stones. They resemble tombs but contain only offerings. In one nine flint arrow points, and in the other, a vase and a bone bead necklace were found, indicating similar rituals as those found in the southern area.

After the site was abandoned in the early 2nd millennium BC, colluvial deposits gradually collected around the few still upright monoliths ("Pat 2, 10 and 22"). After a long

Fig. 12.6. Ossimo-Pat. Alignment N-S of boulder-menhirs and engraved steles, Early Bronze Age level

Fig. 12.7. Ossimo, Pat-excavation 2003. The votive fires in front of the monument "Pat 2"

period of abandonment, at use of the area recommenced at the end of the Late Bronze Age and continued throughout the Iron Age, until the 2nd – 1st century BC. This second period is dated through a few significant potsherds and a series of charcoal ^{14}C dates from over 30 hearths situated beside and on top of the monuments (Figs. 12.7, 9) and structures.

Palaeobotanical studies by Michela Cottini of the Como Civic Museum's Archaeobiology Laboratory have revealed the contents of several ritual fires in front of "Pat 2" (Figs. 12.7, 9) (unpublished). They date activities to the Late Bronze Age – Early Iron Age. US 154 was lit in spring judging from the small flowers or flower buds of *Crataegus monogyna*, mixed with fruits and branches of *Corylus avellana* and *Coniferae*. US 151 was lit in late summer based on rose hips and seeds of *Rosa canina* as well as *Fagus sylvatica* and *Corylus avellana* branches. The ritual character of these actions brings to mind the classical festival of *floralia*.

The monoliths vary in height from 0.40 to 2.95 m and may be classified as steles and boulder-menhirs. They consist of glacial erratics from the local fluvio-glacial deposits. Various phases of engraving may be distinguished during the Copper Age, clearly characterised by the details of the weapons portrayed. These include axes, axe-hammers, Remedello and Ciempozuelos-type daggers, as well as Villafranca-type halberds. The chronological sequences are confirmed by cases of over-carving. Combining the stratigraphic and iconographic sequences has made possible a more detailed analysis of the monuments' engraving phases during the 4th and 3rd millennia BC. A new first phase (with respect to 1994 chronological scheme of De Marinis) is distinguished by the Late Neolithic – early Calcolithic topographic designs.

The monoliths' iconography also raises the possibility of identifying different functions. Some engravings show more clearly anthropomorphic attributes and may be viewed as portrayals of ancestors, perhaps in the guise of "civilizing heroes". Others are densely engraved on generally large boulder-menhirs, covering the entire surface with sets of arms ("panoplies"), animals, ploughing scenes, "fringed rectangles", groups of dancing men etc., which seem to represent the community (or communities) that used the sanctuary.

Fig. 12.8. Ossimo, Pat. The circular enclosures north

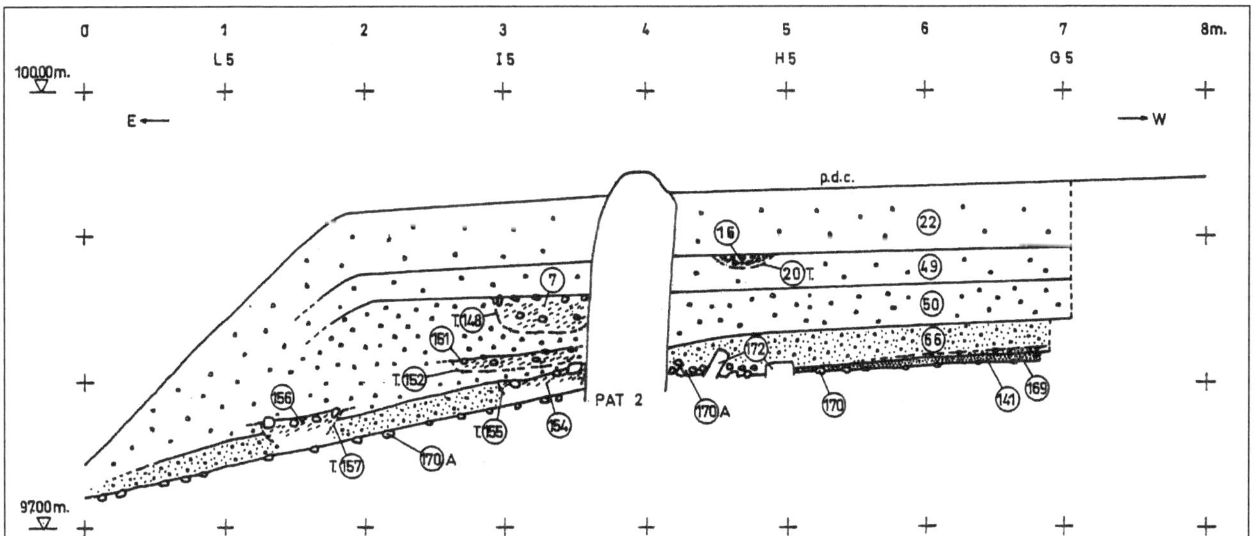

focolare	15	GX-23006	2120±140 BP	550-250	BC
focolare	7	GX-31247	2640±70 BP	980-750; 900-760	BC
focolare	151	GX-31249	2660±70 BP	1000-750	BC
focolare	154	GX-31246	2670±70 BP	1010-750;	BC

Fig. 12.9. Stratigraphy around the "Pat 2" with the fires (US 15, 7, 151, 154 e 156)

The last example is the sanctuary of Cemmo, originally discovered in 1909 as part of Valle Camonica's rock art. It is situated near the valley bottom in a depression that contained an ephemeral pool of water at the foot of a steep rock face. There was a contemporary settlement just to the north at Seradina. It was located on high ground overlooking the rivery.

Seradina has been investigated over 70 years, most recently by Anati (1972) and De Marinis (1988). It remained largely unexplored, until 2000, when work for the creation of the Massi di Cemmo National Archaeological Park began. During boring for the collection of palaeoenvironmental core samples, new steles were discovered. They had been uprooted and

Fig. 12.10. The Massi di Cemmo National Archaeological Park – excavation 2005.
Boundary wall before the Massi "Cemmo 1 e 2"

thrown into a hole during Christian destruction of the site. Excavations from 2000 to 2005 brought to light an extensive sanctuary with an imposing boundary wall, which enclosed the "Cemmo 1 and 2" rocks. Construction began in the Calcolithic and remained in use until the Early Bronze Age. It was subsequently reused in the Iron Age and Roman period until late Roman or Early Medieval times, when this pagan cult site was destroyed and the Pieve di S. Siro church built nearby (Poggiani Keller 2000). The main phases are summarized below as follows: The "Cemmo 1 and 2" rocks, blocks which had fallen from the nearby cliff face during a rockfall were engraved *in situ* during the mid-Copper Age (Anati 1967/1972) and completed towards the end of the period when the "Cemmo 3 and 4" steles were erected (De Marinis 1988 and 1994). Together with most of those recently unearthed stones, none of were in situ. The zone in front of the Copper Age rocks appears to be enclosed by three plough furrows (Poggiani Keller 2006), as yet seen only in a trench. This Subsequently, a boundary wall, 2.5 m wide at the base, was built (Fig. 12.10). This was semicircular in plan and followed the line of the three plough furrows that preceded it. The construction would appear to date to the Early Bronze Age, on the based on a leaf-headed pin and another with a rolled-up head. The base of the wall contains several large stele fragments reused as building materials. "Cemmo 17" had engravings of animals, anthropomorphic figures and a ploughing scene in which a man guides a plough pulled by oxen. This is similar to the representations of ploughing present on the "Cemmo 1 and 2" rocks. There is no evidence that the locality was used for the rest of the Bronze Age.

Renewed activity in the area is attested in the Iron Age, when the megalithic sanctuary was rebuilt. The height of the boundary wall was raised and lengthened, so as to enclose the southern area with a straight north-south portion which started from the "Cemmo 2" rock. Internally, the enclosure was levelled with gravel so as to form a new surface. At least one of the Calcolithic steles, the large "Cemmo 9" (Poggiani Keller-Ruggiero 2005, p. 44), was re-engraved on its sides with figures of ibexes with curved, ridged horns, similar to those on the Ibex Rock in Arcelle Neuve in the French Alps (Arcà *et al.* 1997). The latter is dated to the 2nd Iron Age (4th-3rd century BC). This monolith, made in the Copper Age and re-engraved in the Iron Age, remained upright within the wall until the late Roman or Early Medieval period, when it was pried out and slid into a large hole which had been dug for the purpose just in front of it.

Iron Age activity seemsto have been limited to mid to late Iron Age, based on pottery finds. It involved a series of transformations, such as the digging of a ditch which ran inside the perimeter wall and the creation of a circular area with hoe marks around the "Cemmo 1" rock. During the same period extensive work was conducted throughout the hollow, the southernmost portion of which was terraced (Poggiani Keller-Ruggiero 2005).

Fig. 12.11. Cemmo. The sanctuary during the Roman period

The sanctuary continued to function during the Roman period (Fig. 12.11). The boundary wall was furnished with a cobbled surface, involving the reuse of fragments of Calcolithic steles. Another platform and new steles were erected. The latter include "Cemmo 9" and the broken bases "Cemmo 14, 15 and 16" remain. This horizon also yielded a fragment of Roman low-relief sculpture ("Cemmo 12") portraying a duel. A road crossed the area at this time. Lastly, with the arrival of Christianity, use of this pagan cult and ceremonial site was terminated. The steles were knocked over and some were thrown into a large pit dug alongside the boundary wall. The most recent finds in the fill of this pit contained late-Roman potsherds. This last phase of activity, which marks the definitive abandonment of this megalithic cult site, may be dated to the late Roman or Early Medieval period.

FINAL CONSIDERATIONS

The systematic research launched throughout the territory by the *Soprintendenza per i Beni Archeologici della Lombardia* has provided reliable information concerning indisputable archaeological sites and demonstrated that the phenomenon of cult sites distinguished by engraved monoliths. They are restricted in Lombardy to the Oglio and Adda valleys. Many have not yet been investigated.

The ongoing excavations, of which we have provided three significant examples, are an important contribution to our understanding of the spatial and temporal complexity and articulation of megalithic sanctuaries. They show interrelations between the monuments' iconography and their complex symbolism. They also deepen our appreciation of the connections between the rock art found in the two valleys and the intense development that they underwent in the Copper and Iron Ages.

Regarding the chronology, the recent stratigraphic excavations, particularly those in Ossimo-Pat, indicate that the Lombard complexes started in the middle of the 4th millennium BC, i.e. the Italian Late Neolithic/early Copper Age. The sanctuaries were thus constructed at the end of the process of systematic and stable occupation of the piedmont valleys and Alps. This began during the Middle to Late Neolithic (4th millennium BC), when stable settlements were established on the valley floor. At present these are only known from Valcamonica.

The Calcolithic sanctuaries lasted for the entire Copper Ageand the Early Bronze Age. They were abandoned or in severe decline during the remainder of the Bronze Age, but experienced renewed activity in the Iron Age (1st millennium BC). In the case of Cemmo, they lasted until late Roman/Early Medieval times. However, there are exceptions, such as the small ceremonial site recently excavated in Ossimo-Anvòia (Fedele 2006). It was limited to the Copper Age.

During the 4th and 3rd millennium BC occurred what might be termed "*construction of the landscape*". It was brought about by deforestation through burning, the construction of terraces (Teglio-Caven) and the choice of scenic localities for the establishment of sanctuaries along the ways which led to summer pastures and areas of mineral resources, which then became reference points in the landscape.

The sanctuaries have some features in common. This includes the proximity to water and association with large rocks or boulders engraved during various (periods provided the local geomorphology allowed this).

The architectural progression is initiated by structures in earth and wood, followed by the use of stone, as is shown by in the excavations in Cemmo. There we first have the ploughed furrows, then the boundary wall. At Ossimo-Pat we first have pits and fixed posts, then aligned monoliths and platforms. Caven started with a pit below the platform.

Cult and ritual activities are indicated through fires and deposition of plant offerings in Pat and ritually ploughed furrows in the Cemmo foundation layers. Continuation of activity for several millennia, though with interruptions, occurs at several sites.

The monoliths' form and iconography varies between the valleys and between geographical zones. Steles are only found in Valtellina. In Valcamonica steles occur only in valley bottom sites, while boulder-menhirs and steles occur in higher elevations.

It is possible to discern hierarchies and roles amongst sites. For example, sites representing one or more extended communities and the monumental complexes have a more varied iconography and longer lifespan. They may be distinguished from those which were perhaps more limited in reference. Naturally, greater understanding can only come from comparisons between the stratigraphic data from different sites and the comparison of individual sequences and iconography. Therefore, research of the megalithic sanctuaries is part of a more wide-ranging policy pursued by the *Soprintendenza per i Beni Archeologici della Lombardia* which aims to develop the study of relations between these archaeological sites and rock art, using suitable field and recording methods and the rich heritage of Lombardy, which is of international importance.

(Translation by Jim Bishop)

References

ANATI, E., 1967, Arte preistorica in Valtellina. Sondrio.

ANATI, E., 1967/1972, I Massi di Cemmo. Capo di Ponte.

ANATI, E., 1990, L'altopiano di Ossimo-Borno nella preistoria: le statue-menhir – relazione preliminare. BCSP. Capo di Ponte. 25-26, p. 269-358.

ARCÀ, A.; GAMBARI, F.M.; MENNELLA, G., 1997, La roccia degli stambecchi: un'iscrizione latina reinterpreta incisioni dell'età del Ferro? Tracce. Online Rock Art Bulletin. 9, p. 30-31.

CASINI, S., (edited by) 1994, Le pietre degli dei. Menhir e stele dell'Età del Rame in Valcamonica e Valtellina. Bergamo.

DAL RI, L., *et al.* 2004, L'area megalitica dell'età del rame di Velturno-Località Tanzgasse (BZ). Aggiornamenti sullo stato delle ricerche. In Bianchin Citton, E., ed.- L'area funeraria e cultuale dell'età del Rame di Sovizzo nel contesto archeologico dell'Italia settentrionale. Vicenza. p. 123-174 (Quaderni di Archeologia Vicentina. 1. 2004).

DE MARINIS, R., 1988, Due nuovi frammenti istoriati da Cemmo (Capo di Ponte, Valcamonica). In Il Parco delle Incisioni rupestri di Grosio e la preistoria valtellinese. Atti I Convegno Archeologico Provinciale. Grosio 25-27 ottobre 1985. Sondrio, p. 117-150.

DE MARINIS, R.C., 1994, La datazione dello stile IIIA . In Casini, S. (1994), p. 69-87.

FEDELE, F., 2006, Asinino – Anvoia, il parco archeologico. Cerveno.

POGGIANI KELLER, R., (edited by) 1989, Valtellina e mondo alpino nella preistoria. Modena.

POGGIANI KELLER, R., 1999, Due siti megalitici in Valcamonica (Brescia- Italia): gli scavi in corso a Ossimo, località Pat e Passagròp. In Della Casa, PH. (ed.) -Atti Prehistoric alpine environment, society, and economy. Papers of the international colloquium PAESE '97. Zurich 1997. UPA 55. Bonn, p. 122-125.

POGGIANI KELLER, R., 2000, Il sito cultuale di Cemmo (Valcamonica): scoperta di nuove stele. Rivista di Scienze Preistoriche. Firenze. L 1999-2000, p. 229-259.

POGGIANI KELLER, R., 2002, Contesti di recente indagine nella Lombardia prealpina, tra tardo Neolitico e prima età del Rame. In Ferrari, A.; Visentini P. (eds.) – Il declino del mondo Neolitico. Ricerche in Italia centro-settentrionale fra aspetti peninsulari, occidentali e nord-alpini, Atti del convegno. Pordenone, p. 271-289. (Quaderni del Museo Archeologico del Friuli occidentale, 4, 2002).

POGGIANI KELLER, R. 2004b, Siti di culto megalitici e occupazione del territorio nell'età del Rame in Valtellina e Valcamonica. In Daudry D. –Implantations rurales et économie agro-pastorale dans les Alpes de la Préhistoire au Moyen Age. Actes Xe Colloque international sur les Alpes dans l'Antiquité. Cogne, Vallée d'Aoste 12-14 settembre 2003. Aoste, p. 143-160.

POGGIANI KELLER, R.; RUGGIERO, M.G., 2005, Parco Archeologico Nazionale dei Massi di Cemmo. In I Parchi d'Arte Rupestre di Capo di Ponte. Capo di Ponte, p. 33-50.

POGGIANI KELLER., R., 2006, Santuari megalitici nelle valli lombarde. In Preistoria dell'Italia settentrionale. Studi in ricordo di Bernardino Bagolini. Atti del Convegno. Udine settembre 2005. Udine, p. 245-268.

ANONYMOUS ANCESTORS? THE TILLEY/SHANKS HYPOTHESIS REVISITED

Karl-Göran SJÖGREN
Department of archaeology and ancient history, Göteborg university, Box 200, 405 30 Göteborg
Email: Kg.sjogren@archaeology.gu.se

***Abstract**: The purpose of this paper is to critically revaluate the dominant view of Scandinavian megalithic tombs as a form of ossuaries. The analysis is based on two recently excavated tombs in Falbygden, where the bones have been recorded in detail; the passage graves at Frälsegården and Landbogården. The analyses made so far suggest that the treatment of the dead in these tombs do not fit current models of mortuary practices in megalithic tombs. Instead of secondary burial of defleshed bones, primary burial seems to have common. Whole bodies were set in the chambers, and probably left intact for long periods. These would not have been anonymous parts of the collective of ancestors, but individual links in a genealogical network stretching over the border between life and death.*
***Key words**: Megalithic tombs, burial practices, ancestors, Falbygden, Sweden*

***Résumé**: Cette essaie propose une évaluation critique de la hypothèse dominante sur les tombes mégalithiques de Scandinavie, hypothèse que les voit comme une sorte d'ossuaire. L'analyse est basée sur deux tombes en la région de Falbygden, récemment fouillées; les tombes á couloir de Gökhem Frälsegården et de Gökhem Landbogården. Dans ces tombes, le traitement des morts ne s'adaptent pas facilement a les modèles des pratiques funéraires dans tombes mégalithiques couramment populaires. Au lieu de sépultures secondaires des os secs, les sépultures primaires parait très commun. Des corps complètes sont étés introduits dans les chambres, et probablement ils sont étés laissées intactes pour périodes longues. Ainsi, ils ont pas étés des parts anonymes d'une collectivité d'ancêtres, mais plutôt des chainons individuels d'une reseau généalogique qui dépasse la frontière entre la vie et la mort.*

The megalithic tombs in Sweden constitute a rather marginal phenomenon in relation to the European megalith tradition, both in spatial and in temporal terms. In spite of this, they have played a quite important role in the history of research, through the works of scholars like Oscar Montelius, Märta Strömberg and Christopher Tilley, among others.

For a long time now, the dominant view of burial practices in Scandinavian passage graves, and to some extent in dolmens, has been that of secondary burial and deposition of defleshed bones, using the chamber tombs as a kind of bone houses. I will refer to this as the "ossuary hypothesis".

The ossuary hypothesis was first introduced in Scandinavian archaeology by Bror-Emil Hildebrand, commenting on his excavations in the passage graves at Luttra Knaggården and Slöta Lockegården in 1863. Based on the apparent disorder of the bones in the chamber and on a number of ethnographic parallels, he suggested that only selected parts of defleshed skeletons had been placed in these chambers (Hildebrand 1864). This was in some contradiction to the statements of Carl Magnus von Düben, the anatomist who took part in the excavations. According to him, the disorder was not complete, but in many cases parts of bodies could be traced, such as legs, series of vertebrae etc.

In spite of this, Hildebrand's view became dominant, and was reinforced by the occurrence in some Danish tombs of collections of long bones or skulls in parts of the chambers. Only a few scholars expressed other views, notably Märta Strömberg (1971).

However, the ossuary hypothesis was given new life through the seminal paper by Christopher Tilley and Michael Shanks in the 1980s (Shanks & Tilley 1982). Now, the idea of secondary burial of dry bones was set in a completely new theoretical framework, and was used in a critique of empiricist theories of mortuary practice formulated by Binford, Saxe, Renfrew and others.

THE TILLEY/SHANKS HYPOTHESIS

Instead of directly mirroring social relations, Shanks and Tilley saw burial practices as ideological, whereby social contradictions could be denied or masked just as well as being demonstrated or emphasized. In the context of burials in megalithic tombs, they suggested the following points:

- The mortuary practice was one of secondary burials
- In this process, a main result was the dissolution of individuality through practices of dismemberment and redeposition of human bones
- Mortuary practices involved the creation of an anonymous collective of ancestors
- The burial practice served to emphasize a number of contrasts: articulated/disarticulated, male/female, adult/young, left/right
- Mortuary practices concealed real social relations. Based on anthropological models, these were seen as involving social contradictions, notably between sexes and between elders and younger males.
- In doing this, megalithic tombs functioned as vehicles for an ideology serving to mask inequality.

In later research, several authors have accepted and further expanded on these and similar ideas. For instance, Sarup type enclosures have been suggested to have been localities for primary deposition and defleshing of human bodies (Andersen 1997), and fragmentation has been viewed as a widespread ideological practice in the European Neolithic (Chapman 2000, Holten 2000).

In contrast to this anglo-saxon tradition, French archaeology has developed a distinct and quite different approach, based on a close reading of details in the positions of bones. In a number of well recorded cases, primary burial has been argued, but also various other practices such as rearrangement and cleaning out of chambers (Chambon 2003).

MEGALITHIC TOMBS IN SWEDEN

As noted above, the megalithic tombs in Sweden occur on the northern margin of this western European phenomenon. Useful surveys of the tombs have been published by Tilley (Tilley 1996, 1999). Three main types are usually distinguished: dolmens, passage graves and gallery graves. Today, about 455 dolmens and passage graves are known, but especially in the south a large number of tombs have been destroyed during the last two centuries. These tomb types were built in a rather short period ca. 3300-3000 BC cal, i.e. the transition between the early and the middle Neolithic periods, in the cultural setting of the Funnel Beaker tradition. Based on a large number of ^{14}C dates, the building of megalithic tombs seems to be simultaneous over a large area including northern Germany, Denmark, Sweden and even southern Norway (Persson & Sjögren 1995, 2001, Sjögren 2003). The about 1500 gallery graves, on the other hand, were built mainly in the late Neolithic. They will not be discussed here.

The Swedish tombs occur in two distinct types of landscape (Fig. 13.1). In Scania, Halland and Bohuslän, they are found close to the coast. Especially in Bohuslän, they are very close to the Neolithic shoreline and have been built in a rocky archipelago, in a strongly marine environment. In spite of these marine locations, the sea seems to have contributed very little to subsistence (Sjögren 2003, 2004a). Instead, terrestrial food, probably from domesticated plants and animals, dominated the diet.

Another and larger group of tombs is found in the inland area of Falbygden in Västergötland. Here, a spectacular concentration of at least 250 tombs coincides with one of the very few regions where bedrock consists of limestone and slate instead of primary rocks. This means among other things that conditions for the preservation of human bones are quite good, in contrast to many other regions.

The more systematic study of these monuments goes back to around 1860. In the period 1860-1900, a large number of chambers were excavated by scholars like Hildebrand, Montelius and Retzius. Later, Axel Bagge and Märta Strömberg made important contributions (Bagge & Kaelas 19950-52, Strömberg 1971). Their efforts were mainly concentrated on Scania in southern Sweden. In the last decades, new field work and studies have been made mainly in Falbygden (Persson & Sjögren 1995, 2001, Sjögren 2003, 2004b), and a series of interpretative papers have been published by Christopher Tilley (1984, 1996, 1999).

CARLSHÖGEN AND RAMSHÖG

The empirical basis of Tilleys and Shanks analysis was the bone material from five Neolithic tombs, the long barrows at Lanhill, Luckton and Fussell's Lodge in England and the passage graves Carlshögen and Ramshög in Scania, southern Sweden. Here, I will only comment on the two Swedish tombs. These had been excavated by Märta Strömberg in the 1960s (Strömberg 1971) and still constitute some of the best documented megalithic tombs in Scandinavia.

Basically, Tilley and Shanks concluded that the results supported the interpretation suggested above. According to them, the frequencies of different bone categories in these tombs could not be explained by differential preservation, but must be due to cultural practices. They found no evidence of articulated bodies, and concluded that whole bodies had never been introduced. Statistical analysis of different bone groups within the chambers led them to suggest that deliberate selection and rearrangement of body parts had taken place, at least for adult remains. Also, they suggested that left and right body parts had been treated differently, but no distinctions could be seen between males and females.

In fact, it must be pointed out that most of the bone material from Scandinavian megalithic tombs is far from ideal when it comes to discussing the treatment of human bodies. Many tombs were excavated before 1900, with rather crude excavation techniques and rudimentary documentation. Also, the goal of early excavations was often just to obtain samples of skulls or datable material, while the details of the masses of bone fragments were perceived as rather uninformative. Preservation is poor in many areas with acidic soils, the exception being some areas with limestone or chalk, such as Falbygden and parts of Scania in Sweden. Further, the bones are usually highly fragmented and have often been subject to secondary disturbances.

Thus, well preserved and well documented human bones from Scandinavian megalithic tombs are rather rare. This applies equally to both the Swedish and the Danish tombs. In cases where well preserved bones have been found, such as the Hulbjerg passage grave on Langeland (Bennike 1985), radiocarbon dating has shown that the bones are often quite late. At Hulbjerg, all the dates so far

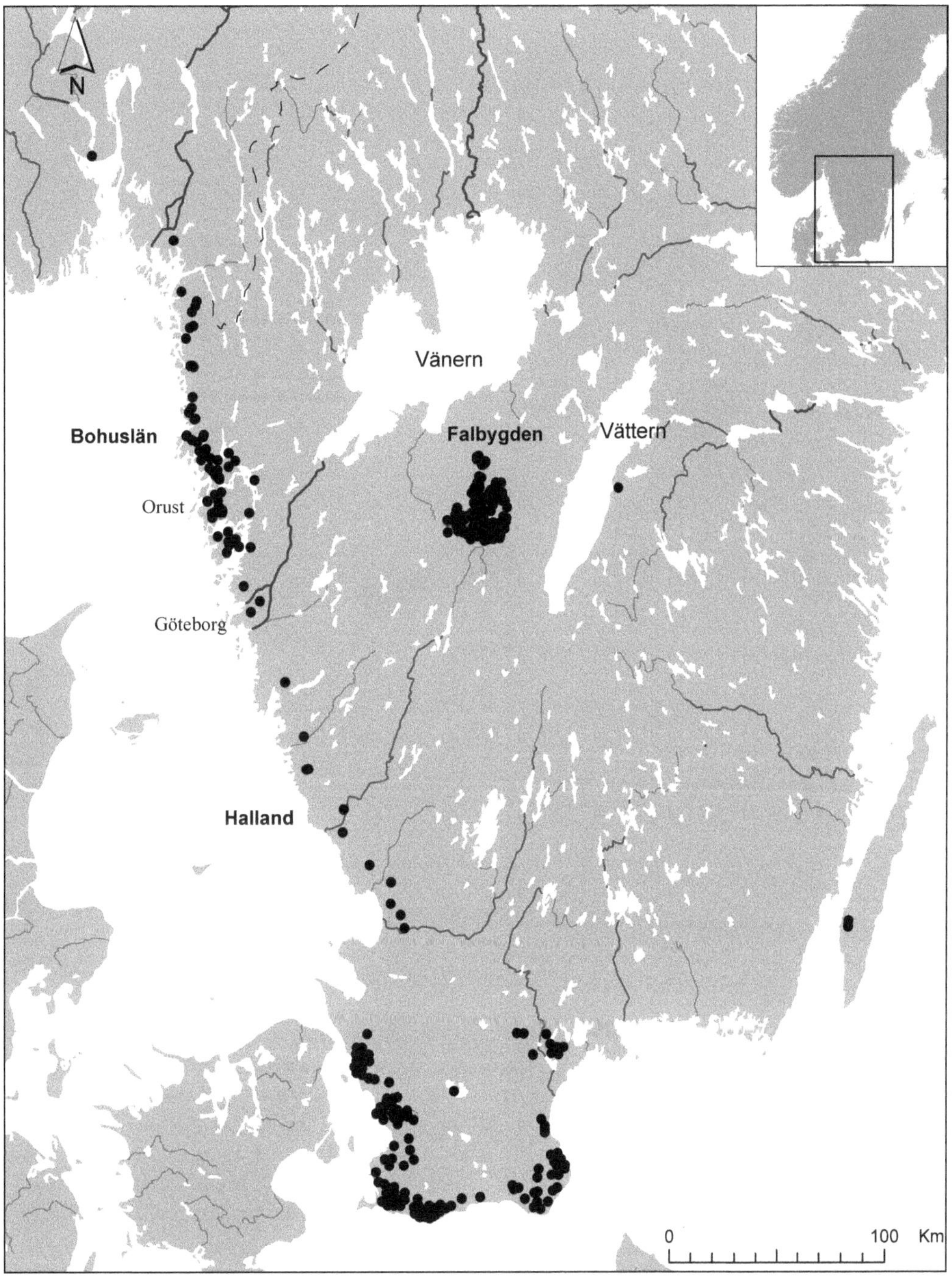

Fig. 13.1. Map of Swedish dolmens and passage graves

place the bones in the late Neolithic period, about 1000 years later than the erection of the tomb.

In spite of the thorough excavations at Ramshögen and Carlshögen, there are a number of problems with these materials. The bones are very heavily fragmented, and the chamber contents have been disturbed by earlier excavations (Bagge & Kaelas 1950, Strömberg 1971). Both tombs were excavated in 1875 by Kurk, and Ramshög was excavated again in 1930 by Hansen. Thus, the bones excavated at Ramshög by Strömberg are only an unknown part of the original deposit. At Carlshögen, the middle Neolithic layer seems to have been intact, but we still lack a thorough examination of possible differential bone degradation at this site. It can therefore be suspected that the taphonomic problems with these bones, particularly at Ramshög, are far greater than Tilley and Shanks suggest.

It is therefore of great interest that recent investigations in another area, Falbygden in Västergötland, western Sweden, have contributed new material allowing fresh insights into middle Neolithic burial practices. Here, I will primarily discuss one of these sites, the passage grave at Gökhem Frälsegården. Another passage grave, at Gökhem Landbogården, has also been excavated quite recently

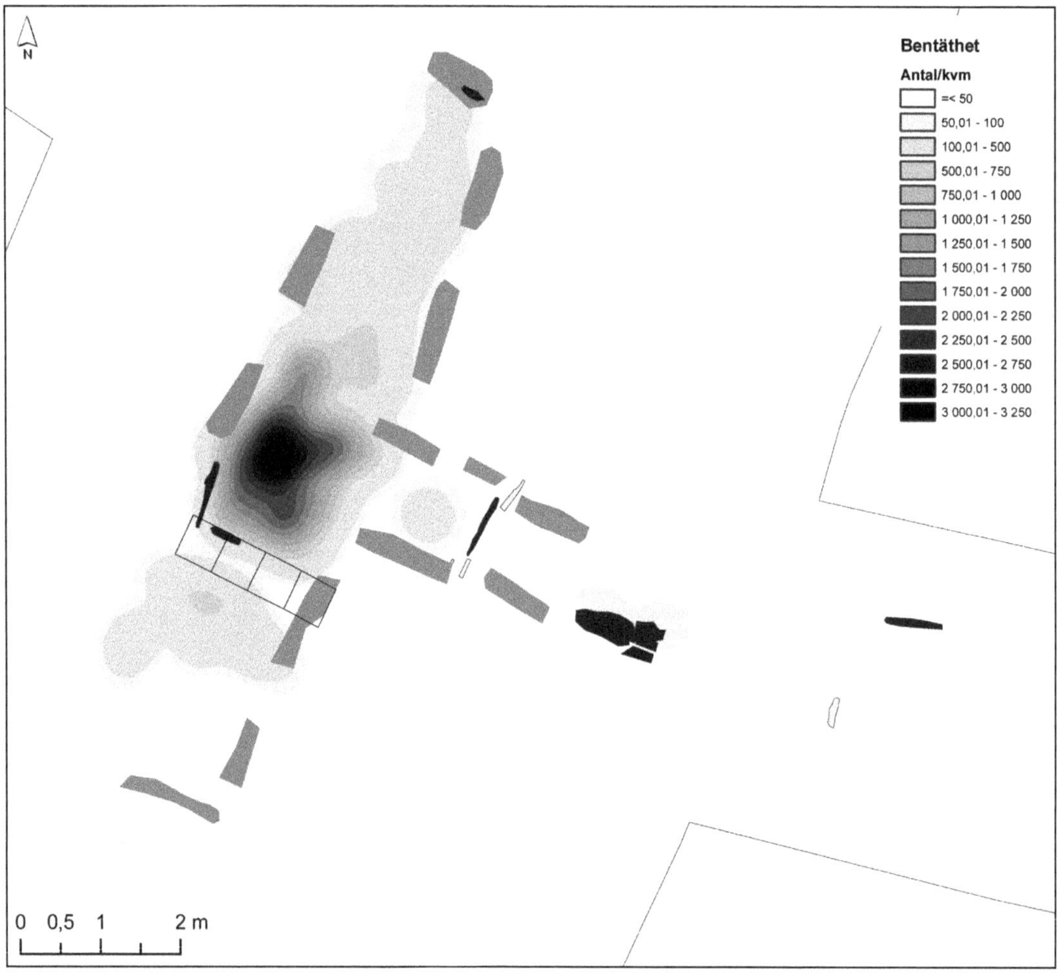

Fig. 13.2. Plan of the chamber with density of bones

(Bägerfeldt 1987, Persson & Sjögren 1995, 2001, Ahlström in press). In this grave, situated only two km from Frälsegården, a well preserved bone material with at least three articulated individuals was found.

THE PASSAGE GRAVE AT GÖKHEM FRÄLSEGÅRDEN

This tomb, situated in the limestone area of Falbygden, was excavated 1999-2001 (Axelsson & Sjögren 2001, Ahlström 2004, Sjögren in press). Most of the chamber stones had been removed ca. 1900, and the site had been ploughed over since. In spite of this destruction, the construction could be documented and a large bone material collected. The tomb was found to have been of rectangular form, ca. 9.1 x 8.1 m large, with a ca. 10 m long passage, and constructed of limestone slabs (Fig. 13.2). The chamber had been surrounded by a mound, about 30 m in diameter, now almost completely ploughed away.

Within the chamber, a massive deposit with about 9500 fragments of bone was found. This was excavated in detail. Osteological determinations have been performed by Torbjörn Ahlström (Ahlström 2004, in press). Most of the bones and other finds were measured individually with a total station, and recorded in a GIS database together with the osteological determinations. Even if parts of the bone layer have been ploughed away, this constitutes the most well-documented bone material to date from a Scandinavian megalithic tomb.

The bones were not evenly distributed but were concentrated in the central part, while the southern and northern ends had lower bone densities (Fig. 13.2). In the southern part this can be explained by heavy ploughing, but the northern part had been more protected and the lower amount of bones should therefore reflect the original depositions. The degree of fragmentation was also variable. The upper parts of the bone layer, as well as bones in the southern end, were more fragmented, while those in the bottom of the layer and to the north were surprisingly well preserved.

The osteological analysis indicates that at least 40 individuals have been deposited in the chamber (Ahlström in press). As this is a rather fragmented and partly destroyed material, this is most certainly an underestimation of the original number.

Fig. 13.3. Individual B, a 40-50 year old female

ARTICULATIONS AND PRESERVED INDIVIDUALS

Already during excavation, a number of articulations were noted. These comprised for instance stretches of vertebrae, sometimes connected to ribs, collections of hand and foot bones or pairs of lower leg or lower arm bones.

In the bottom of the bone layer, two almost complete skeletons were discovered (individuals A and B). In addition, 13 partial bodies have been identified so far, all but one in the central part of the chamber. The body position, where it can be determined, seems in all cases to be strongly contracted, and it has been suggested by Torbjörn Ahlström that they were originally tied or wrapped in skins. The presence of skins in the chamber may be indicated by the large number if pig phalanges found. Also, it seems that the bodies are oriented either along the chamber axis or perpendicular to it.

As an example, Individual B is shown in Fig. 13.3. This is the almost complete skeleton of a 40-50 years old female, lying on her back with the legs and arms in contracted positions. A bone sample was dated to 4315±40 bp uncal (Ua-20946). Strontium isotope analysis performed by Douglas Price, university of Wisconsin, on one of the teeth indicates that she was born outside the Falbygden area, probably somewhere in the surrounding gneiss regions (Sjögren & Price 2006). The skeleton was found near the bottom of the bone layer, but it is not one of the earliest burials in the chamber. This is indicated by the ^{14}C date, but also by a complete foot and lower leg found under this skeleton. A bone from this individual was dated to 4390±48 bp uncal (AAR-9543).

^{14}C DATES AND STRATIGRAPHY

So far, 14 radiocarbon dates have been performed on bones from the Gökhem Frälsegården grave. Apart from a late Neolithic date, they cluster in the period ca. 4200-4400 bp uncal, corresponding to about 3100-2900 cal BC. Since most of these datings were performed on articulated individuals, it is possible that the earliest burials are not among those that have been dated. All the same, the datings are in good agreement with dates from a number of other passage graves in the area and should indicate the main period of use of the chamber.

What is of special interest in this case is the striking correspondence between the dating sequence and the stratigraphic relations that may be seen between some of the identified individuals (Fig. 13.4). To my mind, this indicates that the position of these bodies is largely intact. Their relative positions have not been altered since the time they were placed in the chamber, or very shortly thereafter. This seems to be a strong argument against redepositon or manipulation going on, at least of these particular persons.

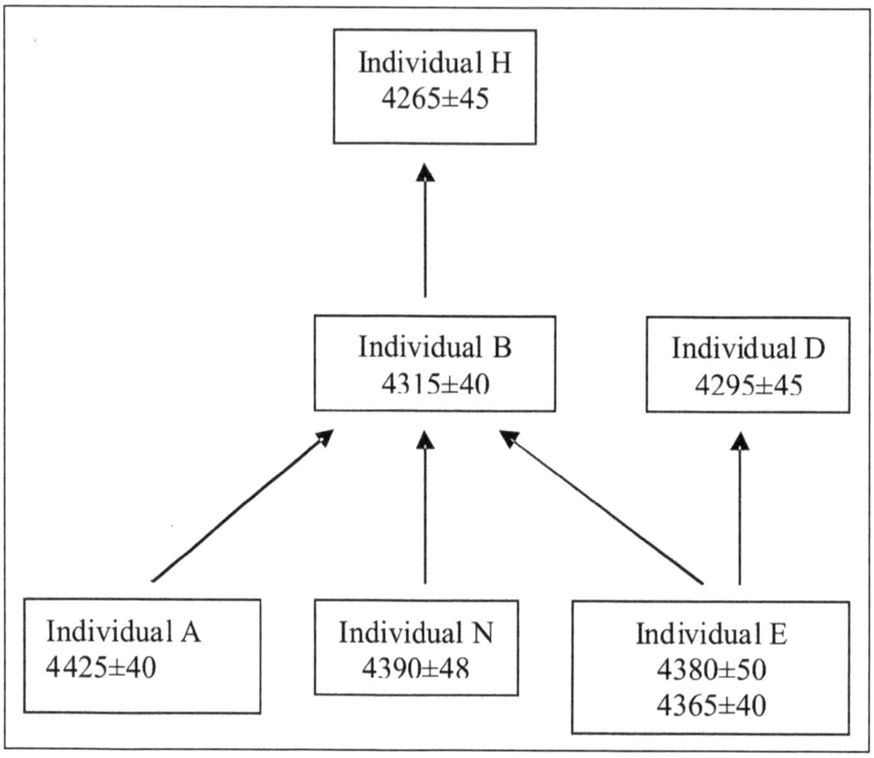

Fig. 13.4. ^{14}C and stratigraphy of individuals

REDEPOSITED BONES

The articulated bones are only part of the story, however. There are indeed examples of bones that strongly suggest redeposition. For instance, in the northernmost part of the chamber, two complete but isolated skulls of adult individuals were found lying close together. Another example is a shallow pit in the passage, near the chamber entrance. This pit contained a rather large number of small, fragmented bones. So far, none of these bones have been dated.

In the passage grave at Landbogården, a small, dense pack of bones was found in the passage (Bägerfeldt 1987). This contained bones from at least two individuals, an adult male and a child. The bones have been dated to 4415±55 bp uncal. (AAR-9991), i.e. contemporary with the main period of burial in Falbygden passage graves.

Thus, it is possible that some bones were subjected to an alternative treatment involving some form of rearrangement. However, it is not possible to say at which point in time the rearrangement took place. All we can say is that it involves some of the bones introduced early into the chamber.

In the case of Carlshögen, the disarticulated bones found in a tripartite pit under the chamber floor were dated to the end of the middle Neolithic TRB, and could represent a late form of burial practice (Strömberg 1971). At present, it is an open question whether such redepositions were also made earlier in the middle Neolithic.

SOME CONCLUSIONS

By way of conclusion, we can say that the ossuary hypothesis does not fit very well with the results from Gökhem Frälsegården and Landbogården. In these tombs, a number of complete bodies were introduced. Available ^{14}C datings do not support the idea that these were only late burials, instead they seem to cover most of the middle Neolithic TRB sequence.

Further, it seems that these bodies were left more or less undisturbed for long periods of time, and the arrangement of bodies found today may very well be a close match to the original positions.

As suggested by Torbjörn Ahlström (in press), the climatic conditions in megalith chambers would probably have been conducive to the formation of mortuary wax (adipocere), rather than the rotting away of soft parts. If this is true, buried bodies could very well have retained their form and their individuality for long periods, maybe several generations. This would have been further supported by the effect of clothing, binding, skin wrapping etc.

A common idea in much recent discussion of megalithic burial practices is that they served to emphasise the distinction between the flesh and the dry bones, by transforming bodies to collections of bones (Thomas 1999). Practices such as those in Frälsegården point to something very different. Here, it seems that the bodies introduced retained their form for a long time, and their individual traits as well as their specific histories could have been well known by the living, at least by some.

What mattered then, was not so much the bodily transformation of deceased members of the community, but to retain them as individuals, and probably to keep track of and maintain very specific genealogical links between certain people, some of which were living and some of which were dead. This could indeed have been a forceful tool for manipulation by genealogic and ritual specialists. It also suggests that ideology in this case would not have been functioning a mask for social realities, but rather to have a demonstrative function.

As mentioned above, there is some evidence of rearrangement of human bones also. Perhaps this indicates the existence of parallel treatments, or of changes of burial practices over time. Another problem is of course how to interpret the large number of bones that we at present can not link to individual bodies. Are these indications of earlier practices, of secondary burials, or of disturbed primary burials? Such questions are still unanswered.

In a recently started project, I will work more on these questions together with Torbjörn Ahlström (the project can be followed at http://hum.gu.se/institutioner/arkeologi/forskning/projekt/anonymous). We believe that the detailed recording of these bones gives us new possibilities to follow what has happened in the chamber, through the combined use of taphonomy, statistics, refitting and GIS.

References

AHLSTRÖM, Torbjörn, 2004, Grave or Ossuary? Osteological Finds from a Recently Excavated Passage Tomb in Falbygden. In Knutsson, H (ed): *Coast to coast – Arrival. Results and Reflections.* Coast to coast books no 10. Uppsala.

AHLSTRÖM, Torbjörn, in press, *Underjordiska dödsriken – humanosteologiska undersökningar av neolitiska kollektivgravar.* Manuscript for the Coast to coast project.

ANDERSEN, Niels H., 1997, *The Sarup Enclosures. The Funnel Beaker Culture of the Sarup site including two causewayed camps compared to the contemporary settlements in the area and other European enclosures.* Jutland Archaeological Society Publications XXXIII: 1. Århus.

BAGGE, Axel & KAELAS, Lili, 1950-52, *Die Funde aus Dolmen und Ganggräbern in Schonen, Schweden 1-2.* Kungliga Vitterhets- Historie. och Antikvitetsakademien. Stockholm.

BENNIKE, Pia, 1985, Stenalderbefolkningen på øerne syd for Fyn. En antropologisk redegörelse. Skaarup, J: *Yngre stenalder på øerne syd for Fyn*, pp 467-488. Meddelelser fra Langelands museum. Rudkøbing.

BÄGERFELDT, Lars, 1987, *Undersökningsrapport. Västergötland, Gökhems sn, Landbogården 11:1, Raä 17. Undersökning av en gånggrift 1987.* Ark. inst., Stockholms Universitet.

CHAMBON, Philippe, 2003, *Les morts dans les sépultures collectives néolithiques en France : du cadavre aux restes ultimes.* Supplément à "Gallia préhistoire", 35. Paris, CNRS.

CHAPMAN, John, 2000, *Fragmentation in archaeology: people, places, and broken objects in the prehistory of southeastern Europe.* London: Routledge.

HILDEBRAND, Bror-Emil, 1864, Berättelse om antiqvariska undersökningar i Vestergötland år 1863. *Antikvarisk Tidskrift för Sverige* I: 255-283.

HOLTEN, Lars, 2000, Death, Danger, Destruction and Unintended Megaliths: an Essay on Human Classification and its Material and Social Consequences in the Neolithic of South Scandinavia. Ritchie, A (ed): *Neolithic Orkney in its European Context.* McDonald institute Monographs. Oxbow Books, Oxford.

PERSSON, Per & Karl-Göran SJÖGREN, 1995, Radiocarbon and the chronology of Scandinavian megalithic graves. *Journal of European Archaeology* 3, pp 59-88.

PERSSON, Per & Karl-Göran SJÖGREN, 2001, *Falbygdens gånggrifter. Undersökningar 1985 till 1998.* Gotarc ser C nr 34. Institutionen för arkeologi, Göteborgs universitet.

SHANKS, Michael & TILLEY, Cristopher, 1982, Ideology, Symbolic Power and Ritual Communication: A Reinterpretation of Neolithic Mortuary Practices. Hodder, I. (red): *Symbolic and Structural Archaeology.* Cambridge.

SJÖGREN, Karl-Göran, 2003, *"Mångfalldige uhrminnes grafvar..." Megalitgravar och samhälle i Västsverige.* Gotarc ser B nr 27, Coast to coast-books nr 9. Dep. Of archaeology, Göteborg university.

SJÖGREN, Karl-Göran, 2004a, Megaliths, settlement and subsistence in Bohuslän, Sweden. Burenhult, G (red): *Stones and Bones. Proceedings of the Stones and Bones Conference in Sligo, Ireland, May 1-5, 2002*, pp 167-176. BAR Int Ser 1201.

SJÖGREN, Karl-Göran, 2004b, Megalithic tombs, ideology and society in western Sweden. Knutsson, H. (red): *Coast to coast – Arrival. Results and Reflections. Proceedings of the Final Coast to coast-conference 1-5 October 2002 in Falköping, Sweden.* Coast to coast-book no 10. Uppsala.

SJÖGREN, Karl-Göran, in prep, *Fragment av ordning. Undersökning av överplöjda megalitgravar vid Frälsegården, Gökhems socken, Västergötland, 1999-2001.* Gotarc Serie D nr 62, Länsstyrelsen i Västra Götalands län.

SJÖGREN, Karl-Göran & T. DOUGLAS PRICE, 2006, Mobilitet under neolitikum. Undersökningar av strontiumisotoper i människoben från Västsverige.

Glörstad, Skar & Skre (ed): *Forhistorien i historien. Festskrift till Einar Östmo på 60-årsdagen.* Kulturhistorisk museum, universitetet i Oslo, Skrifter nr 4.

STRÖMBERG, Märta, 1971, *Die Megalithgräber von Hagestad.* Acta Arch. Lund. Ser in 8 Nr 9. Lund/ Bonn.

THOMAS, Julian, 1999, *Understanding the Neolithic. A revised second edition of Rethinking the Neolithic.* Routledge, London & New York.

TILLEY, Christopher, 1984, Ideology and the legitimation of power in the Middle Neolithic of Southern Sweden. Miller, D & Tilley, C (ed): *Ideology, power and prehistory*, pp. 111-147. Cambridge.

TILLEY, Christopher, 1996, *An Ethnography of the Neolithic.* Cambridge university press, Cambridge.

TILLEY, Christopher, 1999, *The Dolmens and Passage graves of Sweden. An Introduction and Guide.* Institute of Archaeology, University College London.

TWO NEOLITHIC ENCLOSURES AT SORMÁS-TÖRÖK-FÖLDEK (SOUTHWEST-TRANSDANUBIA, HUNGARY) AND THEIR POSSIBLE GEOMETRICAL AND ASTRONOMICAL ROLE: A CASE STUDY

Judit P. BARNA
Balatoni Múzeum, H – 8360 Keszthely, Múzeum u. 2. Hungary
Email: pbarnajudit@yahoo.com

Emília PÁSZTOR
SEAC—European Society for Astronomy in Culture, H-7020 Dunafoldvar, Sohaz u. 4. Hungary
Email: pasztore@enternet.hu

Abstract: *The late Neolithic Lengyel culture site Sormás-Török-földek was found during a field survey preceding the M7 motorway construction project. In addition to the remains of a settlement considerable sections of two round-ditch systems (rondells) were unearthed during the excavation. They are dated to the very beginning of the cultural group, known as Sé horizon of the Lengyel culture. The calibrated radiocarbon date available for the site is 4800-4610 BC (calibrated). The results of the excavations enable us to assess the outline of the enclosures and their possible relationships to certain stations of the annual sun path.*
Key-words: *archaeoastronomy, enclosures, rondells, Neolithic societies, Lengyel culture*

INTRODUCTION

Round-ditch systems (enclosures or rondells) are monumental community structures built during the Central European Neolithic. The Hungarian Late Neolithic Lengyel-culture settlement of Sormás-Török-földek was discovered during a field survey preceding a motorway construction project (Fig. 14.1). Altogether 53.000 m^2 of the settlement, including considerable sections of two rondells, were excavated. The excavation was completed by the end of June, 2006.

Prior to the discovery of the two Neolithic enclosures there were no aerial photographs or magnetic surveys of the site. Nevertheless the results of the excavations yielded enough data to enable us to assess the outline of the rondells and their possible inter-relationships. This paper aims to discuss the rondells and their possible astronomical significance.

Geographical description of the site

Sormás is a small village in the southwestern part of Transdanubia (Figo. 14.1). The Lengyel site is situated on the plateau and the southern slope of a hill extending North-South at about 182 m above sea-level. The Mántai Stream borders this elevation in the east. The archaeological site of Sormás-Mántai dűlő (M710) is situated on the other bank of the stream. These two sites are very close to each other not only in a physical, but also in a chronological and cultural sense. As a result of the excavation the western and eastern boundaries of the Török-földek settlement can be stated with certainty; however, the N-S extension of the site still cannot be determined. As shown by the results of the excavation, the northern boundary of the settlement lies somewhere inside the area of the smaller, northern enclosure (Rondell I).

CULTURAL CONTEXT

Relative chronology of the site

The Late Neolithic-settlement of the Lengyel culture and the two rondells at Sormás-Török-földek are dated to the very beginning of the cultural group. This period is also known as the Sé horizon of the Lengyel culture, defined at the site of Sé in Vas county, Transdanubia.

The Sé horizon is characterized by pottery painted red and yellow, occasionally combined with incised designs. Mineral paints were applied after firing. Vessels were often painted on the inside as well as the outside. Typical pottery forms are S-profile cups and open-mouth bowls, sometimes with extremely thin walls. Bowls with low supports, pots decorated with knobs and sometimes by pinching with finger and nail impressions, and amphorae suspended by string. Typical finds include miniature vessels, lids with stylized zoomorphic knobs, and clay spoons. The characteristic Sé-type idols depict standing women.

The settlement is supposed to be long lasting and it may be presumed that it survived the initial phase of the culture. This means that the youngest features of the settlement may be dated to the beginning of the classical phase of the Lengyel culture. There are mainly the features in the area enclosed by the northern rondell. The houses remains have a northern orientation, quite unfavorable in the Carpathian Basin considering the prevailing winds. In spite of this, there is evidence that the tradition of orienting houses North-South goes back to the Early Neolithic (Bánffy 2004: 66-69).

Based on similarities of material culture, the following sites in Hungary may be considered at least partly—contemporary with the Lengyel settlement of Sormás-

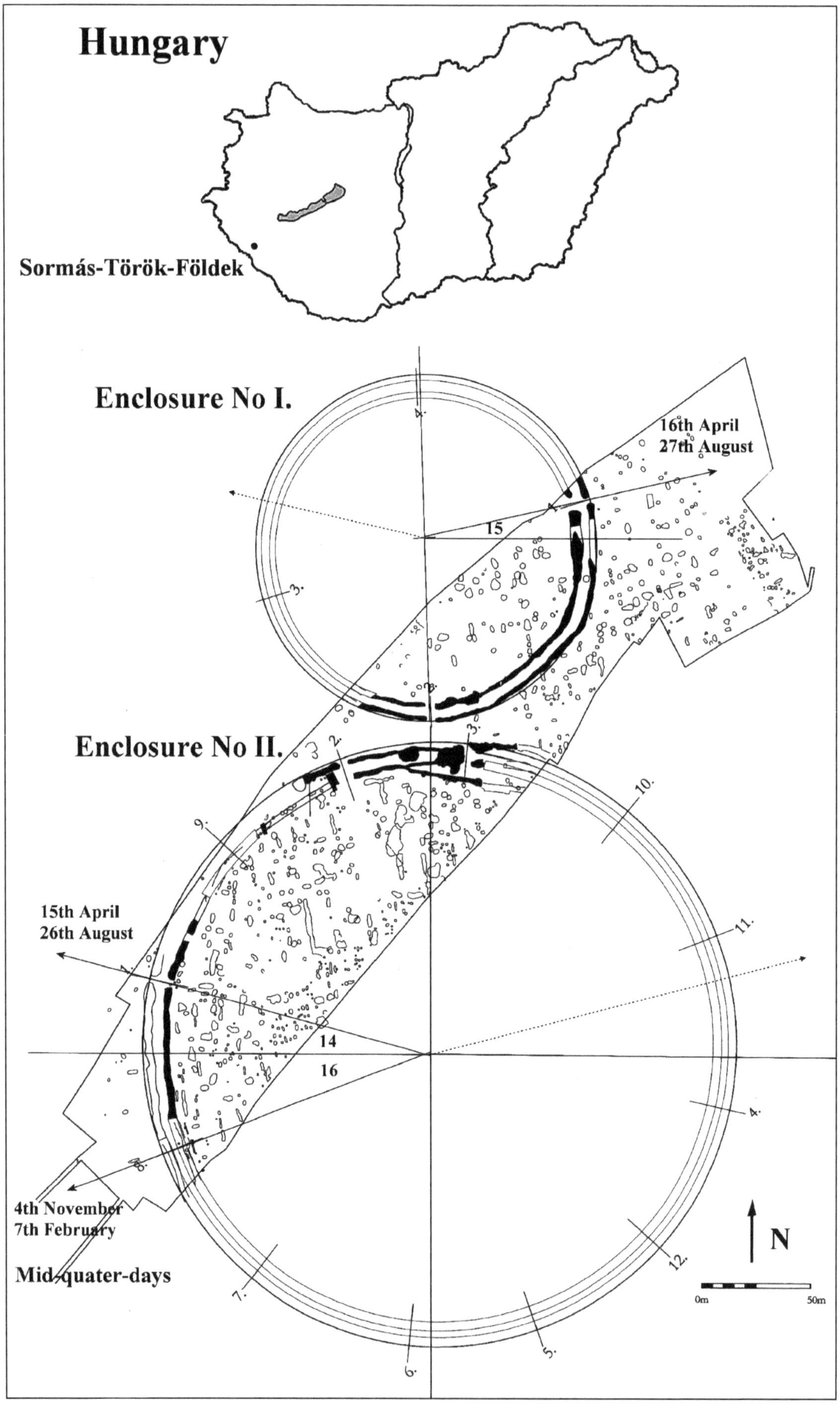

Fig. 14. 1. The double roundel system at Sormas-Török-földek, Hungary

Török-földek: the youngest features of Mántai-dűlő (Barna in press), the type-site of Sé (Kalicz 1983-84), Esztergályhorváti (Barna 1996); and Zalaszentbalázs (Bánffy 1996). In Austria the Wölbling-group (Ruttkay 1979), in Slovakia Lužianky (Novotný 1962) and the smaller enclosure of Svodín (Nemějcová-Pavúková 1995) may also be considered approximately contemporaneous.

Absolute chronology

The only radiocarbon date from this Early Lengyel site, measured at the Vienna Environmental Research Accelerator (VERA) via P. Stadler, calibrates to 4800-4610 BC with 95.4% probability (VERA-3538 5855 ± 35 bp). There are some other conventional radiocarbon data available from this time period, from Esztergályhorváti (Bronk Ramsey. *et al.* 1999), and calibrations of these are forthcoming (Barna in press).

DESCRIPTIONS OF THE NEOLITHIC RONDELLS

Both enclosures meet the formal requirements and criteria, formulated in the literature by experts of rondells (e.g., Petrasch 1991, Trnka 1991). The topographical position and an examination of the excavated material indicate that the two rondells are probably, at least partly, contemporary.

Rondell I, the northern enclosure

This double enclosure is round, even though the two ditches are not completely concentric. The divergence between the corresponding centers is minimal. The cross-sections of the ditches are V-shaped. A varied extent of erosion has resulted in very different and deceptive data considering the parameters of the ditches. The average width of the ditch varies between 1.65 and 2.40 m and its depth varies between 0.90 and 1.10 m. The diameter of the external ditch is 160 m and as for the internal one it measures 146 m. The excavation revealed two gates, but originally there may have been four or five. The orientations of the entrances are 75° East of North and 180° due South. No traces of a palisade could be discovered, presumably because of erosion. Both excavated causeways are made of soil.

Enclosure II, the southern enclosure

This is a very large double round or slightly oval enclosure. The cross-sections of the ditches are V-shaped and their average width varies between 1.30 and 2.25 m. Their average depth is one meter. The diameter of the external ditch is 276 m and for the internal it measures 260 m. In some places, lines of postholes or narrow foundation ditches following both sides of the internal ditch were found, suggesting possible palisades.

The excavation revealed three gates and a possible additional one; none of them are directed towards the cardinal points. Gate 1 is oriented 76° West of North, Gate 2 is 20° West of North, Gate 3 is 7° East of North and Gate 8 is 105° West of North. Two of the gates had earthen causeways, but a third had postholes, probably belonging to a wooden bridge. In one of the sections of the outer ditch two larger postholes had been cut into the sides of the ditch. Between these postholes there was a smaller foundation ditch, which crossed the main ditch. These features may be traces of a wooden bridge. This wooden bridge was located in exactly the location where a causeway would be expected. The reason for this feature is unknown. It may be assumed that there might have been more causeways.

In the neighboring section of the internal ditch the excavation revealed traces of a stronger wooden structure the function of which has not yet been determined. A section of the palisade was doubled right in front of the wooden bridge and the other, stronger wooden structure. The joint occurrence of these three features (namely the bridge, the fortification-like structure, and the duplicated palisade) suggests that this entrance played a distinguished role. In another entrances there were some postholes, which may have belonged to the wooden structure of the gate.

Obvious traces of several recutting episodes could be observed in the profiles of the ditch. Rondell II is also datable to the Early Lengyel culture, but it seems likely that there was an earlier ditch system for this enclosure perhaps dating back to the Sopot culture.

ORIGIN AND FUNCTION OF THE RONDELLS

Until now the question of the origin and function of these rondells has not been clarified. According to one interpretation, their origins are traced to the central part of the Danube Basin, because it has the highest concentration of rondells (Kuzma 1997: 50-51). However, the fact that the earliest Lengyel rondells in Transdanubia, such as Sé (Kalicz 1983-84: 276-277) and Sormás-Török-földek (Barna 2005: Fig. 1), already show the classical form contradicts this hypothesis. They are dated to the earliest (formative) phase of the culture. In terms of their form and structure the Neolithic rondells demonstrate the greatest similarity in Transdanubia (Western Hungary), SW Slovakia and Lower Austria. This is exactly the area that is associated with the territory of the genesis of the Lengyel culture (Zalai-Gaál 1990: 20).

The function of the rondells—likewise their origin—has not been fully addressed. Earlier most investigators set out 3 or 4 essential functions: defensive, economical, cultic, and social (Podborský 1976, 1988: 307). Of late, more and more studies have focused also on the possible astronomical function of the sites (Každová and Weber 1990, Neubauer and Trnka 2005: 9, Zotti 2005). Without going into a detailed analysis of these different interpretive models, we would offer two general observations. Of the above-mentioned functions assigned to the sites, none of them in isolation could be considered as the single, overriding motivation for the construction of the sites. Pros and cons can be listed in all cases. It is highly probable that several, or even all, of these diverse functions contributed to bringing about the structural features and overall design of these Neolithic rondells, i.e., synergistically. The sites served multiple purposes, simultaneously, being based cognitively on multiple and congruent conceptual supports.

One group of experts states that there is no evidence to support the astronomical interpretation; whereas others consider such approaches justified, especially when combined with social and cultic functions. According to their interpretive models, rondells could have served as observatories, calendar buildings, Sun-temples, monumental symbolic buildings, etc. Therefore, the structural designs of these sites would have been developed using knowledge of celestial phenomena such as periodical movements of the sun (Raczky *et al.* 2005: 204), the moon (Karlovský and Pavúk 2002) and the stars or planets (Gervautz and Neubauer 2005: 73).

Arguments in favor of an astronomically informed research model

The sun was an essential element in the life of sedentary agrarian societies. As such it must have played important ritual role in the Neolithic farming communities. On its yearly path, the sun rises along different locations on the horizon. These rising points stay within two bounds, the northernmost and southernmost sunrises, which are marked on the horizon by the summer and winter solstice sunrises. The geographical latitude determines the angle of this sector on the horizon. In the Carpathian Basin this angle is roughly ± 36° to the true East, and the sun's annual movement along the horizon is easily perceived as long as the viewer has a fixed horizon. In short, it is easy to observe changes in the location of the sun. That is why there is no difficulty in orienting monuments or graves toward its motion. Solar symbols on archaeological finds also demonstrate its importance in the life of a community.

Although the moon, according to both ethnographical and historical sources, also played an important role in all cultures, the orientation toward its movement—rising or setting—is more difficult because of its complex motion in the sky. The moon repeats its position in the sky every 18 years which means it takes the observer 18 years to see the moon at the same rising or setting point in the sky. In a society where the lifetime is not much longer than two or three such moon cycles and the literacy makes easier the remembrance, it is less likely that the moon was the target for such an orientation in the Neolithic Lengyel culture. While there are hardly any crescent representations on finds, it is difficult to distinguish the symbols for the full moon from solar ones.

The apparent motion of the stars is similar to that of the sun, apart from the fact that they do it at night. Circumpolar stars can be seen all year round, while others are visible only during certain seasons. Throughout the world, human imagination has created figures composed stars, constellations of stars and attached myths and legends to them.

The first known Greek description of the now classical constellations was made by Eudoxus of Cnidus around 370 BC, although his description of stars and constellations is assumed to date back at least a thousand years earlier. This ancient Greek system is assumed to have come together from multiple sources during several centuries or even millennia. The Greeks seem to have adopted most of the stellar constellations, among them the twelve zodiacal signs, not earlier than about 500 BC when astrology rapidly started to spread in the Classical World (Rogers 1998: 79-81). The Perseus group, however, has been shown to be of Greek origin and was placed in the sky between 1250 and 480 BC (Wilk 2000).

There are also some constellations, enormous serpents, bears, and giants, that were eventually integrated into the classical sky map (Rogers 1998: 80). These constellations may originat from other zones of prehistoric Europe, and they may date to much earlier times. The research project Hunting the European Sky Bears proposes that these creatures might have played roles in the pan-European Bear ceremonialism and were projected onto the sky as the spirit of animal guardians and the stations marking the ritual path of the shaman's and/or initiate's vision quests to the Upper and Lower World. Calculations based on the location of the zone of evasion on the classical map show that early Europeans were already becoming conscious of and interested in the starry sky between 4000 BC to 2000 BC (Frank *et al.* 2001: 17-22), although other evidence suggests that some of star figures could date back to much earlier astral traditions.

The star group of the bears with boots, is assumed by some to have been come into existence before 10.000 BC, being created in tandem with hunter-gatherer beliefs in bear ceremonialism. Those beliefs moved to North America when it was populated by people migrating across the Bering Strait. This would explain why in both Eurasia and North America we can identify primeval myths relating these circumpolar stars to hunting activities and sky bears (Gingerich 1984).

Naturally, by organizing stars into recognizably named groups they became available for different purposes. Their use for practical purposes such as establishing the season of the year and telling time at night. Fore example the stars of Ursa Major were used to keep track of time on a daily and monthly basis. In addition to taking bearings on land and at sea, they also played an important part in ritual life of the community as has been demonstrated even in the case of hunter-gatherer societies. However, the process whose first steps go far back into human history, was long and gradual. The creation of zodiacal constellations in Mesopotamia has been demonstrated to have taken several millennia according to the archaeological finds and written sources. Therefore, it is natural to suppose the same for the non–Mesopotamian constellations of the classical map as well. However, from prehistoric Europe there are no written sources dealing with this process as found in Mesopotamia or Egypt. Also, until now there are no prehistoric monuments or archaeological remains in Europe whose orientation in relation to specific constellations have been proven without any doubt, although in others parts of the globe, the existence of myths as ritual practices relating to star groups is very convincing.

The planets have their own motion so their apparent movement in the sky is very complex and not too easy to observe and remember. That is why they are not likely to be applied to orienting the rondells of the Lengyel culture in the Carpathian Basin. If a star group or a planet played an important role for a society so that they orientated their communal monuments toward them, one would expect similar practices for all such monuments of the archaeological culture. In addition one might expect decorative art to reflect these beliefs. This is not the case for the Lengyel culture. Therefore, we argue that there is little chance that celestial orientations form part of the conceptual design of the circular rondells in the Neolithic Lengyel culture. Earlier mainly the direction of the gates and the geometrical centre points of the enclosures were thought to be the bases of the astronomical investigations. Lately the palisades are seen as a so-called artificial horizon (Každová and Weber 1990: 166) and the particularity of the terrain (e.g., mountain peaks) are also taken into consideration.

GEOMETRICAL AND ARCHAEOASTRONOMICAL ANALYSIS

Setting out the cardinal directions was not a simple task in the Neolithic, when the magnetic compass was not available. Nonetheless, if a line is drawn across the supposed northern and excavated southern gates of the northern Enclosure I and extended south, it practically crosses the geometrical centre point of the bigger Enclosure II. Furthermore, the line deviates from centre of Enclosure II by only 3.65 m. Considering the 276 m diameter of Enclosure II, this difference merely 1.32% of its diameter and the deviation from the exact north-south orientation is only 1.6°. Since the topography did not determine this layout, the orientation seems to be deliberate. This suggesting that astronomical knowledge was used in its layout.

Given that the Gate 1 of Enclosure I deviates 15° North of East astronomical calculations indicate that the sun rose at this point on the 16th April and 27th of August around 4700 BC. Either of these days could mark the location or staking out of the gates. That these days were significant is supported by the orientation of Gate 1 in Enclosure II. It is oriented to the sun sets on the 15th of April and/or 28th of August. Since the same date is involved in both rondells we can assume common solar principles for raising such monuments in Lengyel culture. This is supported by the orientation of the excavated gate at the enclosure of Se, whose deviation is also 15° North of East (Kalicz 1983-84: 276-277).

The direction of the Gate 8 of Enclosure II offers a further interesting astronomical/calendar date. Here the sun sets on 4th of November and/or the 7th of February. The two days fall in time halfway between the autumn equinox and the winter solstice and between the winter solstice and the vernal equinox. They are called mid-quarter-days, because together with their two summer counterparts, they divide the seasonal year into four quarters. Based on accounts in early medieval Irish literature, it has been argued that the ancient pan-Celtic year was divided into the four seasonal mid-quarter-days of Samhain (November 1), Imbolc (February 1), Beltane (May 1), and Lughnasadh (August 1). It should be pointed out, that there has been no hard evidence for a similar division of the year earlier than the Middle Ages (Hutton 1996: 408-411).

The southern orientation of Gate 2 in Enclosure I also marks an important direction, which is easy to stake out since it is always the same every day. Thus the orientation marks the sun (and any other celestial body's) highest point in the sky on its daily path. The traditional belief is that the life-helping power of the sun is strongest at its zenith.

Another tantalizing aspect of the geometry of the site is suggested by the observation that the area Enclosure I is 20 096 m^2 (ca. 2 ha) and that of Enclosure II is 59.798 m^2 (ca. 6 ha). The proportions of the enclosed areas is 1:3.

CONCLUSIONS

In summary, this paper draws attention to the complex role of prehistoric architecture in the lives of ancient societies and provides new data for the interpretation of Neolithic rondells.

Based on the data from the Sormás-Török-földek double rondell, we cannot specify what the exact astronomical functions were. It is perhaps not even possible to justify that these rondells were designed with a specific kind of astronomical purpose in mind. Nevertheless, on the basis of the calculations discussed above, we cannot deny a likely connection between the geometry of the rondells and celestial phenomena. Furthermore, the orientations, dimensions and overall planning of the site point to the possible integration of astronomical and geometrical knowledge used in the architectural design.

In closing, it can be stated that members of prehistoric societies acquired a certain level of knowledge and understanding of the celestial landscape (Ruggles 1999). This knowledge must be sought in archaeological research. Thus, further study of the Sormás-Török-földek may shed light on the ritual and astronomical practices of Neolithic peoples in general and those of the Lengyel culture in particular.

References

BÁNFFY, E., 1996, Neolithic and Copper Age settlements at Hahót and Zalaszentbalázs (Zalaszentbalázs-Pusztatető, Hahót-Szartóri I-II), *Antaeus,* 22, p. 35-50.

BÁNFFY, E., 2004, *The 6th Millennium BC boundary in Western Transdanubia and its role in the Central European transition (The Szentgyörgyvölgy-Pityerdomb Settlement),* Varia Archaeologica Hungarica 15, Budapest.

BARNA, J.P., 1996, A lengyeli kultúra tömegsírja Esztergályhorvátiban. The common grave of the Lengyel Culture in Esztergályhorvátiban (County Zala), *Zalai Múzeum* 6, p. 149-160.

BARNA, J.P., 2005, Sormás-Török-földek településtörténeti áttekintése. A középső neolitikum. The history of a settlement at Sormás-Török-földek. Middle Neolithic, *Zalai Múzeum,* 14, p. 17–36.

BARNA, J.P., in press, A New Site of the Lengyel Culture in Sormás-Török-földek (County Zala, Southwestern Transdanubia), Krakow.

BRONK RAMSEY, C., PETTITT, P.B., HEDGES, R.E.M., & HODGINS, G.W.L., 1999, Radiocarbon dates from the Oxford AMS System: Date List 27. *Archeometry* 41, p. 197-206.

FRANK, M.R., & BENGOA, J.A., 2001, Hunting the European sky-bears: on the origin of the non-zodiacal constellation. In C. Ruggles, F. Prendergast, & T. Ray. (eds.), *Astronomy, Cosmology and Landscape,* Leicester: Ocarina Books, p. 15-44.

GERVAUTZ, M., & NEUBAUER, W., 2005, Sonne, Mond und Sterne. In F. Daim & W. Neubauer (eds.), *Zeitreise Heldenberg: Geheimnisvolle Kreisgräben—Niederösterreichische Landesaustellung 2005,* p. 73–74.

HUTTON, R., 1996, *The Pagan Religions of the British Isles.* Oxford & Cambridge: Blackwell.

KALICZ, N., 1983-84, Übersicht über den Forschungsstand der Entwicklung der Lengyel—Kultur und die älteste "Wehranlangen" in Ungarn, *Mitteilungen der Österreichischen Arbeitsgemeinschaft für Ur- und Frühgeschichte,* 33-34, p. 271–293.

KARLOVSKÝ, V. & PAVÚK, J., 2002, Astronomická orientácia rondelov lengyelskej kultúry. Astronomische Orientierung des Rondelss der Lengyel Kultur, *Otázky neolitu a eneolitu naših Krajín–2001,* Nitra, p. 113-127.

KAŽDOVÁ, E. & WEBER, Z., 1990, Architektur der Lengyel-Rondelle im mittleren Donauraum, *Jschr. Mitteldt. Vorgesch,* 73, p. 159-169.

KUZMA, I., 1997, Die Großen Kreise der ersten Bauern – Bildern der Jungsteinzeit in Zentraleuropa. In: J. Oexle (ed.), *Aus der Luft—Bilder unserer Geschichte: Luftbildarchäologie in Zentraleuropa,* Katalog zur Ausstellung, Dresden, p. 46–57.

NĚMEJCOVÁ-PAVÚKOVÁ, V., 1995, *Svodín I. Zwei Kreisgrabenanlagen der Lengyel-kultur,* Facultas Philosophica II, Studia Archaeologica et Medievalia Universitatis Comenianae Bratislavensis, Bratislava.

NEUBAUER, W. & TRNKA, G., 2005, Rätselhafte Monumente der Steinzeit. In F. Daim & W. Neubauer (eds.), *Zeitreise Heldenberg: Geheimnisvolle Kreisgräben—Niederösterreichische Landesaustellung 2005,* p. 3–9.

NOVOTNÝ, B., 1962, *Lužianska skupina a počiatky mal'ovanej keramiky na Slovensku,* Vydavatel'stva Slovenskej akadémie vied, Bratislava.

PETRASCH, J., 1991, Mittelneolithische Kreisgrabenanlagen in Mitteleuropa, *Bericht der R-G Kommission,* 71, p. 407–564.

PODBORSKÝ, V., 1976, Erkentnisse auf Grund der bisherigen Ausgrabungen in der Siedlung mit mährischer bemalter Keramik bei Těšetiče-Kyjovice, *Jschr. Mitteldt. Vorgesch* 60, p. 129–148.

PODBORSKÝ, V., 1988, *Těšetiče-Kyjovice 4. Rondel osady lidu s moravskou malovamou keramikou (Das Rondell der Niederlassung des Volkes mit Mährisch Bemalter Keramik),* Facultas Philosophica 277, Opera Universitatis Purkynianae Brunensis, Brno.

RACZKY, P., 2005, Zwischen Himmel und Erde—Polgár—Csőszhalom, eine Siedlung in Ostungarn. In F. Daim & W. Neubauer (eds.), *Zeitreise Heldenberg: Geheimnisvolle Kreisgräben—Niederösterreichische Landesaustellung 2005,* p. 203–209.

ROGERS, J.H., 1998, Origin of the ancient constellations: II. The Mediterranean traditions, *Journal of The British Astronomical Association* 108/2, p. 79-89.

RUGGLES, C.L.N., 1999, *Astronomy in Prehistoric Britain and Ireland,* New Haven & London: Yale University Press.

RUTTKAY, E., 1979, Ein Grubeninhalt der älteren bemalten Keramik aus Unterwölbling, p.B. St. Pölten, Niederösterreich, *Annalen Naturhistorischen Museums Wien* 82, p. 743-758.

GINGERICH, O., 1984, Astronomical Scrapbook. The Origin of the Zodiac, *Sky and Telescope* 67, p. 421-423.

TRNKA, G, 1991, *Studien zu mittelneolithischen Kreisgrabenanlagen (Mitteilungen der Prähistorischen Kommission der Österreichischen Akademie der Wissenschaften),* Verlag der Österreichischen Akademie der Wissenschaften:Wien.

WILK, S.R., 2000, *Medusa: Solving the Mystery of the Gorgon*, Oxford University Press:Oxford.

ZALAI-GAÁL, I. 1990, A neolitikus körárokrendszerek kutatása a Dél-Dunántúlon (Die Erforschung der neolithischen Kreisgrabenanlagen in SO-Transdanubien), *Archaeológiai Értesítõ* 117, p. 3-24.

ZOTTI, G, 2005, Kalendarbauten?—Zur astronomischen Ausrichtung der Kreisgrabenanlagen in Niederösterreich. In F. Daim & W. Neubauer (eds.), *Zeitreise Heldenberg: Geheimnisvolle Kreisgräben—Niederösterreichische Landesaustellung 2005*, p. 75–79.

HOUSES OF LIVING AND HOUSES OF DEAD IN THE NEOLITHIC AND COPPER AGE OF CENTRAL EUROPE

Jan TUREK

Abstract: *This paper is presenting an outline of the origin and development of burial mounds in Central Europe during the Neolithic and Eneolithic Periods. In the first part of the paper I am considering the possible interpretations for the origin of barrows in the context of dying Neolithic longhouses. The main purpose of the second part of the paper is to discuss the question on missing evidence of barrows of the late Eneolithic Corded Ware and Bell Beaker period in Central Europe. Variety of problems of demographic representation of cemeteries, burial customs and spatial structure of funerary areas are connected to the missing barrows. I emphasise the variability of late Eneolithic funerary monuments, including the discussion on burial chambers and circular ditches, yet another type of funerary construction without an earthed mound that may be described as houses of dead.*

One of symbolic roles of Neolithic long houses in central Europe might have been burial of ancestors. There is no hard evidence for the funerary function of long houses, however, it is commonly assumed (Bradley 2000). Already during their dwelling function some houses were possibly used for primary deposition of remains of ancestors. The burials were later in the time of abandonment of the house removed elsewhere or remained resting inside the building. This is the process of transformation from the house of living to the house of dead.

LIVING AND DYING IN THE NEOLITHIC PERIOD

Neolithic man created his own cultural space (cultural landscape) that he structured and adjusted to his needs. Such cultural space became property of whole community and individual families. A greater emphasis on demonstration of genealogy was also in line with such divisions of ownership. Perhaps for first time in human history occurred the need to demonstrate a link with preceding generations of their ancestors and to use their memory in order to re-confirm their right to use their land and to occupy their territory.

Perhaps this may be the main motive why the first farmers in the Near East initially did not create specialised funerary areas and they used to burry their dead within the habitation area, eventually directly underneath their dwellings. There is the evidence of extraction of ancestor's skulls from settlement graves, recreate their faces (e.i. Jericho, Palestine) using clay or plaster, or such as in the case of Çatal Hüyük in Anatolia to keep cleaned dried or mummified heads of their ancestors inside their houses in some kind of ancestral shrine corners. It is well possible that the similar pattern appeared to some extend also in the initial phases of the central European Neolithic and became one of many varieties of yet heterogeneous funerary customs. The evidence for Neolithic settlement burials and isolated human bones scattered within the habitation areas was analysed by J. Rulf (1996). The scatters of human remains surviving in the sunken features along the Neolithic longhouses are particularly the possible clue to the explanation of missing burials in some regions of Central Europe.

The re-examination of Linear Pottery Culture and Stroke Pottery Culture human burials found in burial contexts in Bohemia (Zápotocká 1999) is clear that the majority of population was buried in a different fashion that is leaving no traces that could be identified by current archaeological methods. One of such funerary practices may be burials on or above ground of the settlement or even in the interiors of Neolithic longhouses. There is also more frequent occurrence of child burials in the close proximity of some longhouses.

Richard Bradley (Bradley 2000) argues that certain part of Neolithic longhouses could possibly serve as a morgue or let's say a tomb compartment of the living house. This could be one of the explanations why the Neolithic houses are so long, even thought their probably accommodated just one family. Unfortunately there is no clear evidence for such funerary practices. However, some indirect clues offer a base for such assumptions.

An important discussion, concerning the symbolic function of Neolithic long houses, was introduced by Evžen Neustupný (1995, 208), who re-examined the interpretation of so-called construction pits along the long walls of houses (see Fig. 15.1). He is sceptical about the traditional interpretation of these features as pits for exploitation of clay for plastering of longhouse walls. Neustupný offered a wide range of arguments against the interpretation of such features as exploitation pits. Perhaps the most obvious argument is that these long pits were sunken both in loess as well as in sand and gravel subsoil. Loess is probably suitable material for plastering of walls, but considering the current knowledge on the Neolithic house for the same purpose could hardly be used gravel or sand.

Neustupný reached the conclusion that the ditches of irregular shape were of symbolically protective function and supposed protected a house against negative supernatural powers.

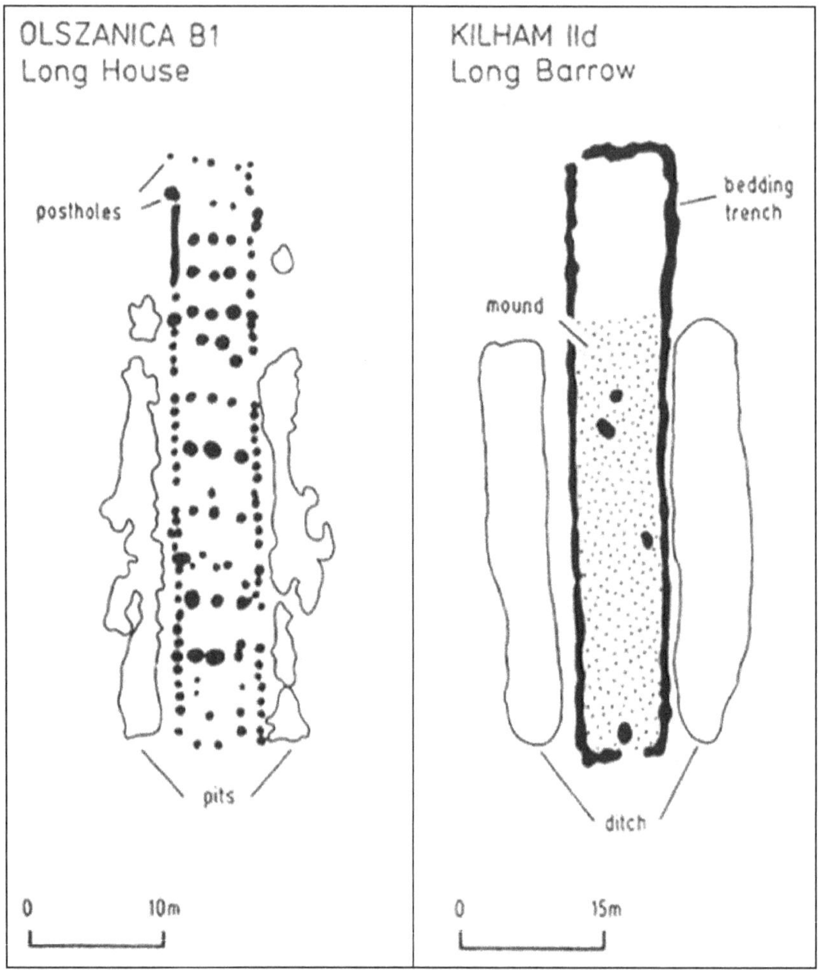

Fig. 15.1. The plan of the Linear Pottery Culture longhouse at Olszanica, Poland, compared with that of Kilham long barrow, England (after Bradley 1998, Fig. 13)

DYING HOUSES AND HOUSES OF DEAD

Both interpretations, the rationalistic one and the symbolic one, presume that these ditches were created during the construction and/or during the use of a house.

My view is, however, different. I argue that the ditches might have well been hollowed along the house even after its abandonment. Such act turned the deserted house into the house of dead or one may say a tomb. In this case the symbolically protective function of ditches may not be connected to the protection of ***interior space*** of the house of living, just the opposite they protected the ***outer surroundings*** of the house of dead against the negative influence of the ghosts of the dead dwelling inside the deserted building. Furthermore the soil dug out of the ditches might have been the base of a long mound piled up on top of the former house once it collapsed and this could be the origin of the idea to create burial mounds above funerary monuments. This hypothesis is obviously facing many problems and lack of clear evidence. Nevertheless, one has to bare in mind that already Vere Gordon Childe (1949) observed the link between the shape of the Late Neolithic houses in the Danubian region and the form Proto- and Early Eneolithic barrows within the same territory. It is very likely that the habit to built barrow funerary monuments of Proto-Eneolithic period has its roots in the form of late Neolithic long houses. Perhaps there was some kind of transition form of funerary monuments between long houses secondarily used as tombs and long barrows of Proto-and Early Eneolithic period. In this context it has to be considered that the later long barrows of north-western Europe and British Isles were also surrounded by long shallow ditches, as it was in the case of continental long houses (Bradley 1998; Bogucki 1988). It is therefore possible that the origin of the idea of burial mounds has its origin in the habit to pile up the mound over the ruins of deserted houses containing burials of ancestors. The fact that only some Neolithic long houses were accomplished with marginal ditches may suggest that only some of them were after their abandonment used for funerary purposes. To shed light on this problem it would be necessary to provide a systematic research of stratigraphical relations and postdepositional processes within postholes and other possible remains of long houses and long ditches and other pits in their proximity.

THE BRIEF OUTLINE OF THE DEVELOPMENT OF EARLY BARROWS IN BOHEMIA AND MORAVIA

Invisible long barrows of the Proto- and Early Eneolithic Period

Possible traces of burial mounds were possibly excavated within the later Neolithic Stroke pottery cremation cemetery in Prague – Bubeneč. When L. Horáková-Jansová (1934) in 1930s excavated remains of the cemetery, she recorded several stone structures of oval or oblong groundplan containing human cremations and numerous funerary offerings. These structures were not yet interpreted as remains of a burial mound and Stroke pottery Culture barrows are not known from the territory of its geographical spread, but it is well possible that they were in fact long barrows.

The first monuments of such character are known from the Proto-Eneolithic period. They are represented by two underground structures interpreted as long barrows from Březno (District Louny, North Bohemia, cf. Pleinerová 1980). Both monuments were outlined by shallow ditches orientated in east-west direction. The shorter structure was 24 meters long and it was of slightly trapezoid groundplan, the longer oblong barrow was 143,5 meters long (one end was however eroded by the watercourse of the nearby Ohře River). The long barrow was 4 meters wide and it was about one meter wider than the shorter structure. Few graves were found inside the building, which Ivana Pleinerová classified to be contemporary with the creation of the barrows. The burials respected the long axes of the barrow and the radiocarbon date (GrN 8803 – cal. 3890 BC) suggest that the burial from which the bone sample was extracted was inserted into the monument at the very end of the Proto-Eneolithic. There are, however, other sites in Bohemia that represent long barrows, such as Proto-Eneolithic structure at Klučov (Distr. Kolín), or Early Eneolithic Funnel Beaker Culture (TRB) possible barrow at Velké Žernoseky (Distr. Litoměřice, cf. Krištuf 2003).

Much better situation appears to be in Moravia, where there are several sites with long barow cemeteries still visibly preserved above ground in currently forested areas, such as Luděřov-Žlíbek, Křemela, Slatinky etc. (cf. Šmíd 1990). According to the evidence from archaeological excavations there is continuity of long barrows since the Early TRB Baalberge phase up to the Ohrozim horizon of Early Baden Culture.

It is probable that the burials covered by long barrows were amongst the common funerary practices during the Proto-Eneolithic Period in Central Europe and that this could be the archetype of later long barrows of the megalithic circle in the Western Europe (Cf. Neustupný 2001; here see Fig 1).

Invisible death in the Middle Eneolithic Period

The continuity in creation of barrows is seemingly interrupted during the Middle Eneolithic Period. The evidence of funerary activities seems to disappear from the archaeological record. The graves and barrows are "replaced" by enclosed hill-top sites. It is possible that the Middle Eneolithic fortifications in Bohemia and Moravia were structures of a symbolic character with some importance in rituals and cult. We presume some other activities such as production and exchange of stone axes might have been concentrated on these hill-top sites. Also the lack of evidence of burial rites in the Řivnáč, Cham and Jevišovice B period may be in connection with the symbolic function of fortified hill-top sites. Cremations or some other methods of disposing death (which do not leave any traces within the archaeological record) might have taken place on these hill-top sites.

Corded Ware and Bell Beaker barrows and the houses of dead

The trend of individual burials entirely dominated throughout the Late Eneolithic Period. Also the size and shape of barrows is designed to cover a single burial. Some further burials might have been later inserted into such single grave barrow. As I am going to argue the idea of houses of dead has probably survived the change from collective towards individual burials.

Perishable monuments

Burial rites of the late Eneolithic period in central Europe concerned on the symbolic demonstration of social status and representation of social categories. The funerary symbolism of Corded Ware and Bell Beaker Cultures is using similar expressions, such as positioning and orientation of inhumations and choice of significant gendered grave goods (Cf. Turek 2000; 2002; 2003 with further references). Another common phenomenon of the late Eneolithic burial customs was covering the grave cuts with burial mounds. The traces of prehistoric burial mounds however disappeared in most of the lowland deforested regions of central Europe due to the intense agricultural cultivation. This is very probably the reason why we cannot detect the Corded Ware and Bell Beaker burial mounds in the current countryside of Bohemia, Moravia and neighbouring regions. Another important destructive factor is erosion. The purely earthen burial mounds of the Corded Ware and Bell Beaker period were generally more affected by erosion then burial mounds of some other prehistoric periods (e.g. Tumuli Culture, Hallstatt D etc.), that were using more stone in their constructions. As we know from the subterranean parts of late Eneolithic graves the stone was only rarely used for construction of burial mounds. The sunken grave cuts contain very small amount of stones if any at all. This appears to be a great difference in comparison to the subsequent Únětice period. The Únětice graves, especially of the "classical" period are usually packed with stone

Fig. 15.2. A Bell Beaker female burial from Tišice District Mělník in Central Bohemia. Along the wall are visible traces of wooden lining (photograph by J. Turek)

(especially in the central Bohemia). However, it needs to be observed that the survival of Únětice barrows is very low too (e.g. Čejetičky-Choboty, District Mladá Boleslav, Plesl 1959).

Tracing the invisible barrows

The evidence of the late Eneolithic barrows is possible to divide into four categories: A – visible remains of barrows; B – negative traces of burial mounds within the spatial structure of a multi-period funerary area; C – An overlap of late Eneolithic and Early Bronze Age burials; D – traces of objects from a burial mound secondarily deposited within the fill of a grave cut.

The visible remains of Corded Ware barrows are very rare in Bohemia. Currently the only known cases come from Selibice and Toužetín (both District Louny) in north Bohemia (Moucha 2000). The forested areas of eastern Moravia are currently representing the only region of Czech Republic, where the Corded Ware and Bell Beaker barrows are still visible up to present day (e.g. Dřevohostice, Kostelec na Hané, Turovice etc.). Majority of east Moravian barrows were selectively excavated already in 19th and early 20th Century (Červinka 1911). Fortunately some of the original site records are of reasonable quality and it is generally possible to re-identify the plans of excavated graves, burial assemblages and the location of individual barrows within the cemetery (for the Corded Ware – Šebela 2000; for the Bell Beaker period is similar revision of data currently carried out by A. Matějíčková). The 19th/20th Century data from the Moravian barrow cemeteries suggest that the barrows were created using soil with minimum stone, that some barrows contained multiple burials and that there are traces of secondary insertion of later burials into the above ground mounds. There are many questions on the spatial and chronological development of such barrow cemeteries (including the questions of continuity in use, satellite burials, use of space between individual barrows) that would greatly contribute towards the modelling of the late Eneolithic cemeteries excavated in the eroded and ploughed landscapes (cf. Kruťová – Turek 2004). This would, however require a modern targeted revision excavation of such site.

The negative evidence of Corded Ware barrows may be traced in the spatial distribution of grave cuts within multi-period funerary sites. Such barrow negatives are visible on the ground plan as empty spots of roughly circular shape. The burial mound of a Corded Ware grave prevented the later graves from reaching the natural ground or perhaps it was respected by the successors even thousands years later. Similar pattern was recently

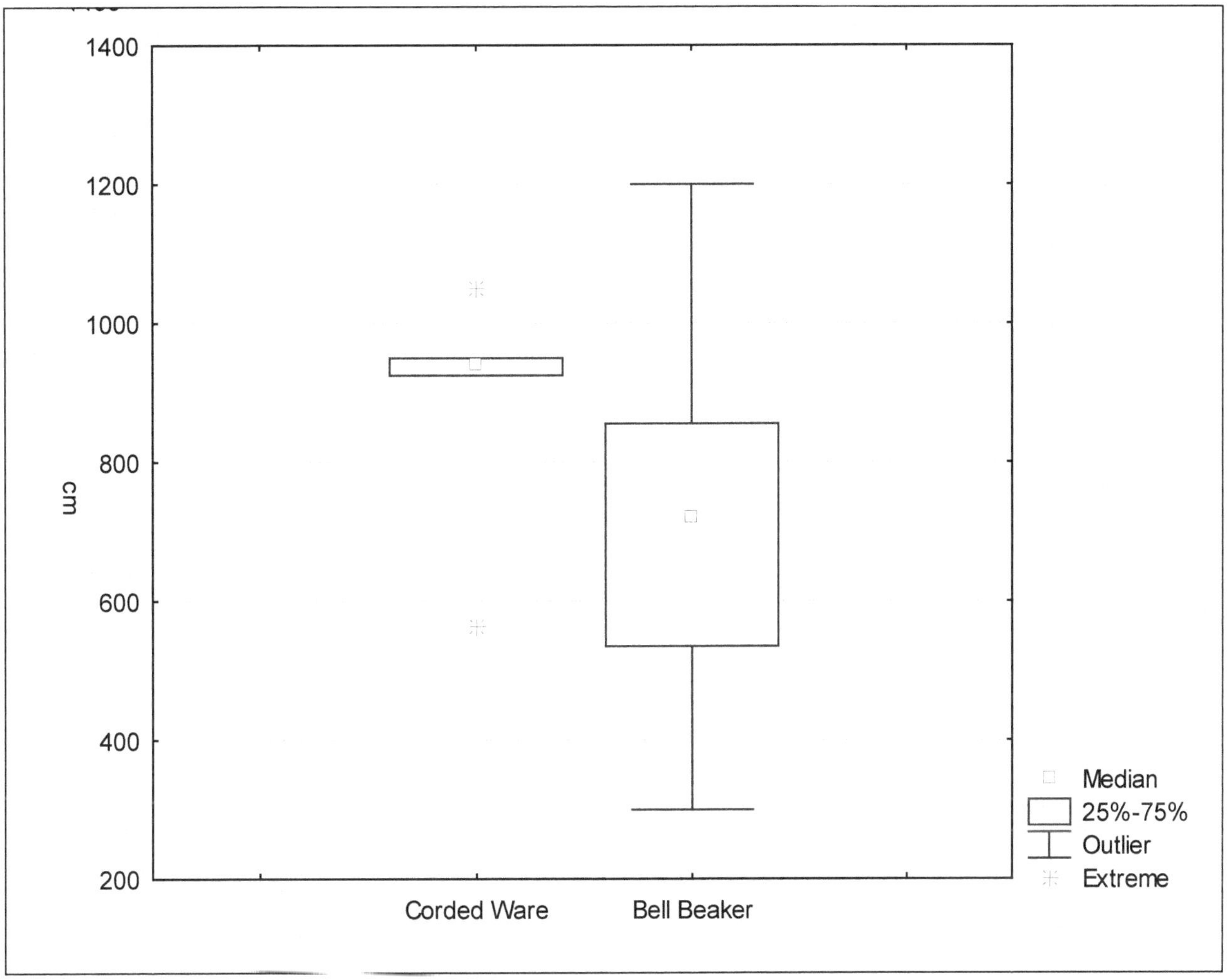

Fig. 15.3. Box-and-whisker plot of Corded Ware and Bell Beaker ditch diameters 200 (max. dimensions). Corded Ware Bell Beaker Median 25%, -75% Outlier Extreme

presented by Ladislav Šmejda (2001) based on the case of Corded Ware cemetery at Brandýsek, including the discussion of the spatial relationship of Late Eneolithic and Early Medieval cemetery and earlier hypothesis on existence of a wooden church.

Another indirect clue for reconstruction of barrows are fairly frequent observations of an overlap of the late Eneolithic and Early Bronze Age burials. Examples may be found at Prague-Kobylisy (Hájek 1968) for the Bell Beaker interference into an earlier Corded Ware grave or several cases of Early Bronze Age Únětice burials cutting into the Corded Ware graves (Březno – Pleinerová 2000, 201-204, obr. 1; Roztyly – Holodňák – Holodňáková 2002, 135-140, obr.1-2) or Únětice graves fitted into the ring ditches of Bell Beaker period at Dolní Věstonice III, graves 44 and 71, 73 (Dvořák *et al.* 1996, 17-18, Taf. 18-19). These examples are only the tip of an iceberg of frequently represented phenomenon of continuity in use of funerary areas and reuse of funerary monuments. It is more than obvious that the Corded Ware graves were visibly marked on ground so the successors might have reused the monument even several centuries later.

Last but not least there are traces of objects found within fills of some grave cuts that may be secondarily deposited coming from the original burial mound. The material for construction of barrows might have been gathered in the immediate vicinity of the current grave, perhaps also using earlier mounds. That could explain appearance of decorated bell beaker fragments in the fill of Early Bronze Age Únětice graves at Soběsuky (District Chomutov). These shards may well be parts of destroyed earlier burials that were inserted into the coat of burial mounds. The soil for piling up a burial mound could have been possibly carried on relatively far distance, perhaps from the habitation area (such movement could possibly be part of funerary ritual). This may explain the appearance of a fragment of an early Corded Ware settlement pottery inside of the later Corded Ware grave as it was recorded at Čachovice (District Chomutov, Neustupný – Smrž 1989).

Vanishing mounds – missing evidence

Considering the integrity and completeness of the late Eneolithic funerary sites in the ploughed landscape one

Tab. 15.1. Table summarising the basic characteristics of the Bell Beaker burial rites within some regions of the Eastern Province (after Turek 2002)

BURIALS IN BOHEMIA				
left side	right side	Cremation	other/unknown	total
126 (52%)	74 (30%)	21 (9%)	22 (9%)	242
BURIALS IN MORAVIA				
left side	right side	Cremation	other/unknown	total
90 (35%)	95 (37%)	56 (22%) [44 =17,9%]	16 (6%)	257 [245]
Burials from Šlapanice (Moravia)				
left side	right side	Cremation	other/unknown	total
12 (20%)	23 (38,3%)	9 (15%)	16 (26,7%)	60
BURIALS IN CENTRAL GERMANY				
left side	right side	Cremation	other/unknown	total
40 (57%)	19 (27%)	2 (3%)	9 (13%)	70
BURIALS IN SOUTHERN GERMANY				
left side	right side	Cremation	other/unknown	total
43 (35%)	36 (37%)	8 (22%)	5 (6%)	92

has to bear in mind that the subterranean part of a burial monument is usually less than half of the original tomb construction. As I suggested earlier, the amount of funerary data we are missing from eroded and ploughed away burial mounds is enormous. What could be missing? Later burials, votive offerings, traces of construction, reopening and possible extension and reuse of burial mounds, as well as, environmental data from levels buried within the mound.

In 2002 I have discussed the question of missing evidence of female burials in certain regions of central Europe during the Bell Beaker period (Turek 2002). The lack of female inhumations is characteristic for the Bohemian and central German group of Bell Beakers. The situation is however, different in Moravia and southern Germany, where both sexes are equally represented in common burial rites. (see Tab. 15.1.).

The lack of female burials in some regions must have been caused by an alternative method of burial that was used for certain number of deceased women. There are certainly many ways of disposing the body without leaving any traces retrievable by archaeological methods. In the case of Bell Beaker burial rites, it is important to note that secondary burials were often placed into the burial mounds above ground. Such practice is known from the regions where intact barrows survived (eastern Moravia, some sites in central Germany). The traces of prehistoric burial mounds however disappeared in most of the regions in central Europe due to the agricultural cultivation. These undiscovered burial mounds may be a key to the question on "missing" Bell Beaker women in Bohemia and central Germany.

Ring ditches and burial chambers, elite burials?

Within the Corded Ware and Bell Beaker cemeteries in Bohemia and Moravia appear tombs of a higher status. The common inhumations were usually inserted in a simple grave pit and perhaps covered by a simple burial mound. There are, however, also tombs with more elaborate construction of the burial chamber and sometimes with a ring ditch outlining the space around the grave cut.

Carefully selected grave goods that may be considered as prestigious were inserted into burial chambers, usually with wooden lining of walls (e.g. Tišice, see Fig. 15.2). Some of these burials were placed into a grave encircled by a ring ditch (e.g. Prosiměřice or Smolín in Moravia). In addition to this, human cremations were secondarily inserted into some of these wealthy graves or into the ring ditches.

Individuals buried in such wealthy graves are usually accompanied by decorated bell beakers traditionally classified as examples of early phase of the Beaker period. Some of these graves contain "mixed gender" assemblages containing both, artefacts considered to be specifically male, as well as female (for an example cf. Radovesice – graves 116/78 and 117/78, see Turek 2003, Fig. 5 and 6). It seems that specifically male artefacts appear sometimes in graves of women, however, it is rarely opposite. We have to bear in mind that not every item inserted into a burial context has to be indicative of social category of the buried person. Some funerary gifts may rather reflect the relations of mourners towards the deceased (cf. Brodie 1997, 300-301). Some grave goods perhaps reflected not only the social position of the

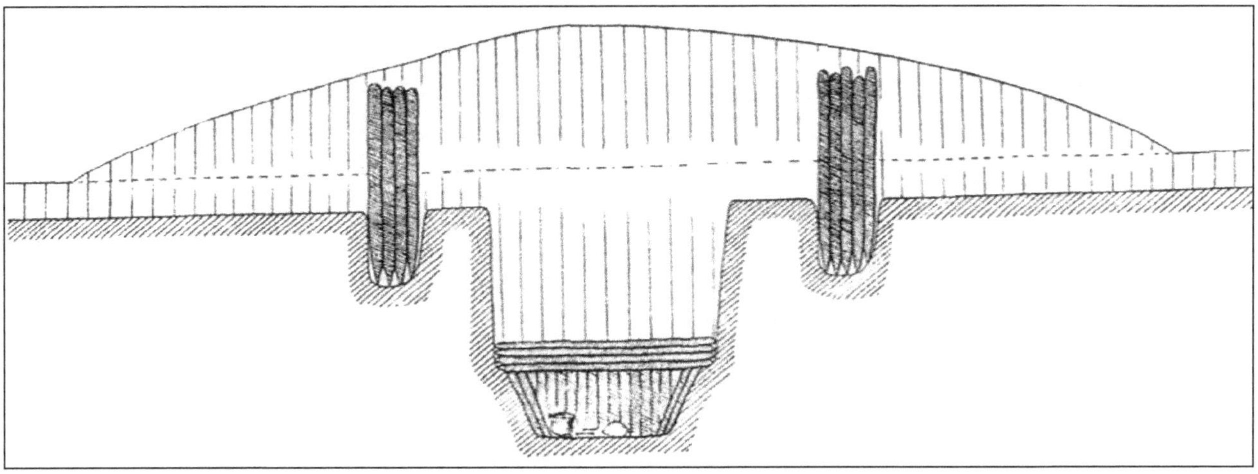

Fig. 15.4. An early reconstruction of the Bell Beaker tomb at Smolín (District Břeclav, south Moravia, after Novotný 1958, obr. 10)

person who died but also the rank status of the descendants and their shared social identity.

In the following paragraphs I am going to focus on formal characteristics of such elite tombs that are ring ditches and wood lined burial chambers.

Ring ditches

In Bohemia and Moravia ring ditches occurred in both Corded Ware and Bell Beaker periods. Their shape is roughly circular, with a grave pit in the centre. Diameters of these round ditches varies from 564 cm to 1050 cm in Corded Ware period and from 300 cm to 1200 cm in the Bell Beaker period. If we drop out the extremely small and large circle then the average Corded Ware ring ditch was about 9.4 m in diameter and average Bell Beaker ring was just over 7 m in diameter. Corded Ware ditches are larger and their most common size seems to be generally respected in northwest Bohemia, as well as, in Moravia. Petr Holodňák (2000) suggested earlier that the standard diameter of Corded Ware ditches is very near to 12 megalithic yards and he considers this phenomenon to be of some symbolic significance. The variability of the Bell Beaker ditches seems to be much greater (see the box-and-whisker plot of ditch diameters, Fig 15.3). It is, however, important to note that that the two extreme cases of bell Beaker ditches (Šlapanice 300 cm and Lhánice 1200 cm in diameter) were containing non-standard or currently invisible traces of burials and also the only example from Bohemia (Stehelčeves) was not considered due to inaccessibility of its data.

All currently known cases of Late Eneolithic ring ditches from Bohemia and Moravia are summarized in the following lists. The maximum diameters are listed for every site. The data were collected from original publications and articles summarising the finds of ring ditches (Měřínský – Stuchlík 1980, 373-376, obr. 5; Bálek *et al.* 1999, 16-19; Holodňák 2000, 88-89).

Corded Ware ring ditches in Bohemia

Hrdlovka grave C/89 – 564 cm; Radovesice 925 cm; Čachovice 938 cm; Chudeřín 940 cm; Strupčice 1050 cm.

Corded Ware ring ditches in Moravia

The only currently known site with evidence of a ring ditch comes from Holubice (950 cm, Čižmář 1985).

Bell Beaker ring ditches in Bohemia

Currently the only ring ditch was excavated at Stehelčeves (Knor 1966 mentions one ring ditch 12 meters in diameter).

Bell Beaker ring ditches in Moravia

Šlapanice 300 cm; Dolní Věstonice III grave 73 –500 cm; Maršovice-Jezeřany 520 cm; Smolín 550 cm; Bulhary 640 cm; Dolní Věstonice grave 44 –700 cm (see Fig. 15.5); Tvořihráz I ditch 3a/91– 740 m; Tvořihráz I ditch 2a/91–820 cm (see Fig. 15.6); Tvořihráz I ditch 1a/90–860 cm; Prosiměřice – iner ring 570 cm, outer ring 850 cm; Lechovice 900 cm; Lhánice 1200 cm.

Further ring ditches are known from Horní Bojanovice and Přísnotice (without relevant site record) and most recently from the cemetery at Hoštice (A. Matějíčková, personal communication).

In last two decades raised dramatically number of ring enclosures recorded as crop-marks by the aerial survey in Bohemia and Moravia (cf. Gojda 2004 with further references). Some of such sites were subsequently excavated and appeared to be of late Eneolithic date (Chudeřín, Holodňák 2000; Tvořihráz I, Bálek *et al.* 1999) others are of late Bronze Age or early Iron Age origin (Uhy, Sofaer – Turek 2004).

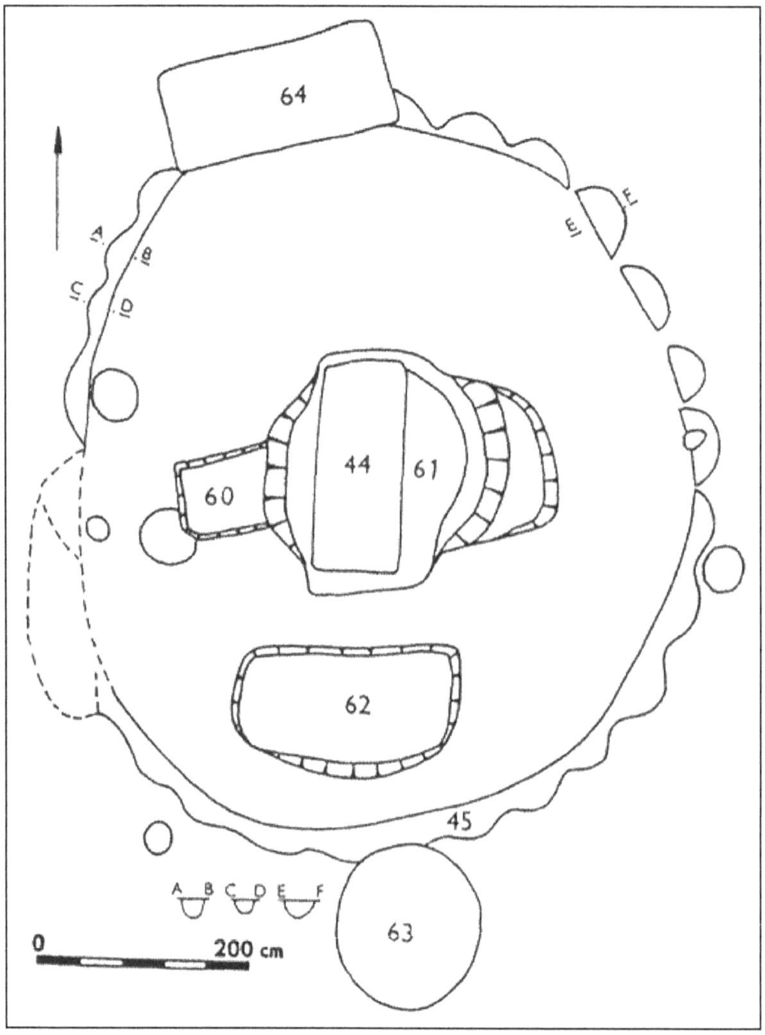

Fig. 15.5. A Bell Beaker grave with a ring ditch from Dolní Věstonice III. Traces of palisade made of halved tree trunks. (after Dvořák *et al.* 1996, Taf. 18)

Burial chambers

Almost every Bell Beaker grave encircled with a ring ditch had an internal construction of burial chamber of some kind. The grave pits of such chambers are of conical section with walls narrowing down towards the bottom of the grave. Traces wooden construction are usually visible as dark, ashy stripes along the walls and sometimes it is possible to distinguish remains of posts and postholes in corners of the chamber. However, there are cases of elite wealthy burials found in burial chambers without any traces of ring ditches (Radovesice, Tišice etc.). This may be also caused by a high degree of soil erosion or method of excavation techniques or simply by different construction of such burial monuments. The traces of internal construction of graves suggest that the chambers were lined with wood, perhaps in the fashion of a log cabin. It may be well possible that the "roof" of such tomb was elevated above the ground and created a visible monument as such. A burial "log cabin" was then accomplished with an enclosure created of tree trunks that might have been split, creating a timber circle.

Houses of dead

The earlier attempts of reconstruction of the graves with ring ditches usually involved a burial mound that was held and delimited by a wooden ring (cf. for example the reconstruction of the tomb from Smolín, Novotný 1958, here Fig. 4). Although, there are several observations suggesting that these monuments were not covered by a mound, or at least not by a mound that would fill entire inner area of the timber circle.

An important data for the re-consideration of this question may be found on south Moravian Bell Beaker sites at Dolní Věstonice (Dvořák *et al.* 1996) and Tvořihráz (Bálek *et al.* 1999). The Bell Beaker grave no. 44 at Dolní Věstonice was excavated within the ring ditch no. 45 (see Fig. 15.5). This ditch was sunken only 25 cm deep into the natural subsoil (measured from the stripped surface). The outline of the ditch was of a wavy shape and in the north-eastern part were clearly visible postholes in the shape of halved tree trunks (see Figure 15.5). One could imagine the construction of such monument to be similar

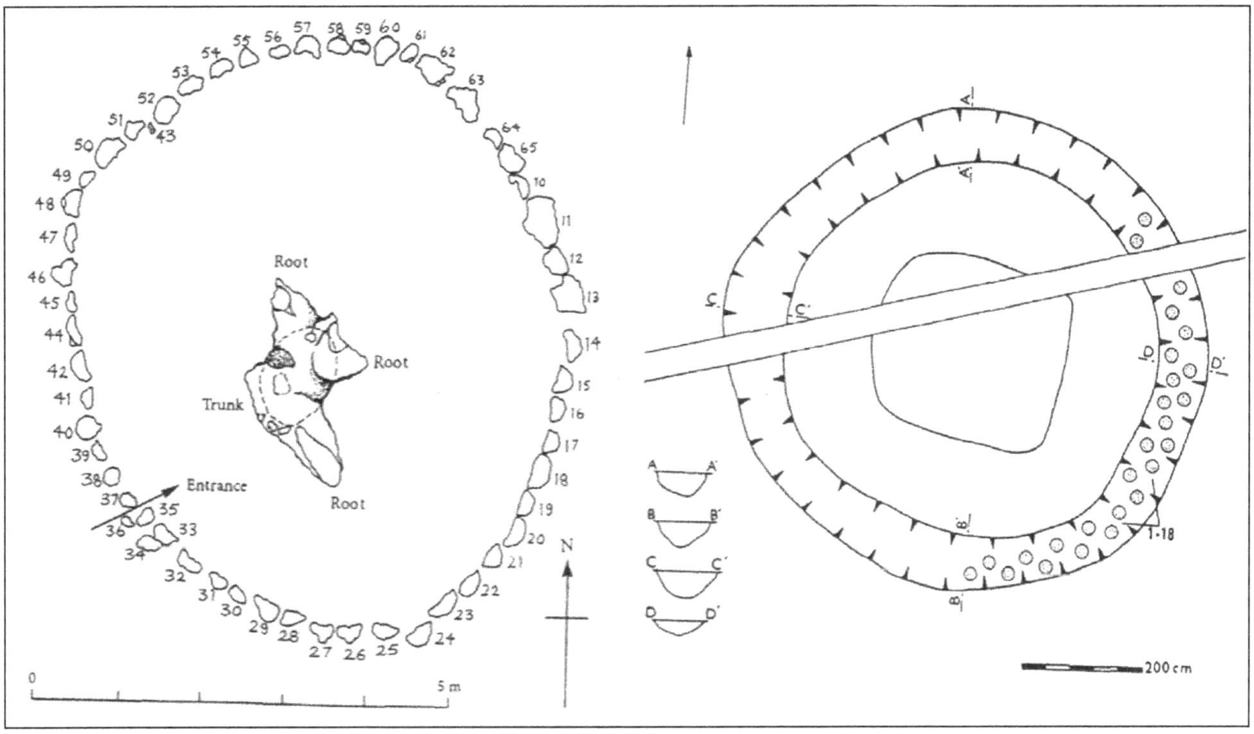

Fig. 15.6. Comparison of similar funerary features (left) Early Bronze Age funerary structure called Seahenge, Holm-next-the-Sea, Norfolk, England (after Pryor 2001, fig. 24) and (right) a multiple cremation burial 2/91 encircled by a ring ditch and pottery found inside the ditch. There were visible traces of 'zick-zack' small postholes in the bottom of the ditch (after Bálek *et al.* 1999, Tab. 5-6)

as recently discovered funerary timber circle at Holm-next the-Sea beach in Norfolk that is known as Seahenge (Pryor 2001, Turek 2000). The slightly oval shaped ring was created with 65 posts that were mainly split trunks of tree embedded into the ground (see Figure 15.6). At the south-western part of the ring there was an entrance into the internal area, where was a stump of an old oak embedded upside down into the ground. This central point is interpreted as the place where once rested human remains (body or cremated remains). Such monument was relatively easy to enter and the funerary events and/or subsequent ceremonies might have repeatedly taken place here. Also the monument from Dolní Věstonice was reused by three inhumations of the Únětice Culture. The repeated funerary ceremonies may also be presumed i the case of the grave 2/91 at Tvořihráz (see Fig. 15.6), where it was possible to identify cremations of at least five children (Langová 2004). Langová presumes that because the cremated bones of all five individuals were mixed together within three excavated deposits inside the burial chamber. Unlike Langová I do not consider the mixing of remains to be an evidence of a single funerary event and it may be well possible that burials were accumulated there over a period of time. The funerary construction in the terms of a log cabin or one may say "house of dead" would be ideal for such re-opening and continual use of the tomb.

The ring ditch of the grave 2/91 had several small post holes relatively sparsely distributed in a 'zick-zack' fashion over its bottom (see Figure 15.6). Another important discovery are 18 more or less complete pots, mainly decorated beakers, found in the fill of the ditch. Were they votive offerings inserted to the ditch during individual funerary events or repeatedly during some ceremonial memorial feasting?

CONCLUSION

This paper aimed to contribute towards the discussion on the origin of burial mounds in Central Europe, as well as, on interpretation of the late Eneolithic ring ditches, reconstruction of their function and form of the monuments inside them. In conclusion I would like to stress the need for creation of new models of some funerary monuments of the late Eneolithic period and revision of certain traditional views.

References

BÁLEK, M., DVOŘÁK, P., KOVÁRNÍK, J., MATĚJÍČKOVÁ, A., 1999, Pohřebiště kultury zvoncovitých pohárů v Tvořihrázi (okr. Znojmo) – Das Gräberfeld der Glockenbecherkultur in Tvořihráz (Bez. Znojmo), Pravěk Supplementum 4, Brno.

BOGUCKI, P., 1988, Forest Farmers and Stockherders. Early Agriculture and its Consequences in North-

Central Europe. New Studies in Archaeology, Cambridge UP.

BRADLEY, R., 1998, The Significance of Monuments, Routledge, London – New York.

BRADLEY, R., 2001, Orientations and origins: a symbolic dimensions to the long house in Neolithic Europe, Antiquity 75, 50-56.

BRODIE, N., 1997, New perspectives on the Bell beaker Culture. Oxford Journal of Archaeology 16, No. 3, 297–314.

ČERVINKA, I.L., 1911, O „zvoncovitých pohárech", časopis vlasteneckého spolku musejního v Olomouci, 28, 66-87, 109–125.

CHILDE, V.G., 1949, The origins of Neolithic culture in northern Europe, Antiquity 32, 129-135.

ČIŽMÁŘ, M., 1985, Hroby kultury se šňůrovou keramikou z Holubic a Tvarožné – Corded Ware Culture Graves from Holubice and Tvarožná, Archeologické rozhledy 37, 403–411.

DVOŘÁK, P., MATĚJÍČKOVÁ, A., PEŠKA, J., RAKOVSKÝ, I., 1996, Gräberfelder der Glockenbecherkultur in Mähren II (Bezirk Břeclav) Katalog der Funde, MAQ, Brno – Olomouc.

GOJDA, M. (ed.), 2004, Ancient landscape, Settlement dynamics and Non-destructive archaeology (Czech research project 1997–2002), Academia, Praha.

HÁJEK, L., 1968, Kultura zvoncovitých pohárů v Čechách – Die Glockenbecherkultur in Böhmen, Archeologické studijní materiály 5, Praha.

HOLODŇÁK, P., 2000, Hrob kultury se šňůrovou keramikou s kruhovým obvodovým příkopem z Chudeřína, okt. Louny – ein Grab mit Schnurkeramik mit kreisförmigen Umfanggraben aus Chudeřín, Kr. Louny, In: Petr Čech – Miroslav Dobeš (eds.): Sborník Miroslavu Buchvaldkovi, Most, 87–92.

HOLODŇÁK, P., HOLODŇÁKOVÁ, R., 2002, Superpozice hrobu KŠK s hroby kultury únětické v Roztylech, okr. Chomutov – eneolitická mohyla s dodatečnými pohřby starší doby bronzové – Die Superposition eines Grabes der Schnurkeramikkultur (SKK) mit Gräbern der Aunjetitzer Kultur aus der Sandgrube in Roztyly, Kr. Chomutov – ein äneolitisches Hügelgrab mit zusätzlichen Bestattungen aus der älteren Bronzezeit, In: Petr Čech – Zdeněk Smrž (eds.): Sborník Drahomíru Kouteckému, Most, 135–140.

HORÁKOVÁ-JANSOVÁ, L., 1934, Žárové hroby s vypíchanou keramikou v Praze-Bubenči, Zprávy Československého státního archeologického ústavu v Praze 1931, 4, 28-45, 68-72.

KNOR, A., 1966, Nécropole a Stehelčeves pres de Kladno (Boheme). In: Jan Filip (ed.): Investigations Archéologiques en Tchécoslovaquie. Etat actuel des recherches et leur organisation, Prague, 107–108.

KRUŤOVÁ, M., TUREK, J. 2004, Some spatial aspects of the ritual behavioural at the beginning of Bronze Age, In: Ladislav Šmejda – Jan Turek (eds.): Spatial Analysis of Funerary Areas, Plzeň, 48–56.

LANGOVÁ, J., 2004, Žárové hroby s vícenásobnými pohřby z Tvořihráze (Příspěvek k pohřebnímuritu kultury zvoncovitých pohárů na Moravě) – Brandgräber mit mehrmaligen Begräbnissen von Tvořihráz. Ein Beitrag zum Bestattungsritus der Glockenbecherkultur in Mähren, In: Vratislav Janák – Stanislav Stuchlík (eds.): Otázky neolitu a eneolitu našich zemí. Sborník referátů z 21. Pracovního setkání specialistů na výzkum neolitu a eneolitu Českých zemí a Slovenska, Hradec nad Moravicí, Opava, 117–126.

MĚŘÍNSKÝ, Z., STUCHLÍK, S., 1980, Hroby kultury se zvoncovitými poháry a středodunajské mohylové kultury v Bulharech, okr. Břeclav – The graves of the Bell Beaker and the Middle Danubian Tumulus cultures at Bulhary, Břeclav distr. Archeologické rozhledy 32, 368–379.

MOUCHA, V., 2000, K otázce eneolitických mohyl v Čechách – Zur Frage äneolithischer Hügelgräber in Böhmen, In: Petr Čech – Miroslav Dobeš (eds.): Sborník Miroslavu Buchvaldkovi, Most, 167–171.

NEUSTUPNÝ, E., 1995, The significance of facts, Journal of European Archaeology 3 (1), 189-212.

NEUSTUPNÝ, E., 2001, The Origin og Megalithic Architexture in Bohemia and Moravia, in: Biehl, P. F. – Bertemes, F. – Meller, H. (eds.): The Archaeology of Cult and Religion, Archaeolingua, Budapest 203-207.

NEUSTUPNÝ, E., – SMRŽ, Z. 1989, Čachovice – pohřebiště kultury se šňůrovou keramikou a zvoncovitých pohárů (Čachovice a Corded Ware and Bell Beaker cemetery. Památky archeologické 80, 282–383.

NOVOTNÝ, B., 1958, Hroby kultury zvoncovitých pohárů u Smolína na Moravě – Die Gräber der Glockenbecherkultur in Smolín (Mähren), Památky archeologické 49, 297-311.

PLESL, E., 1959, Nálezy únětické kultury na mohylníku v Mladé Boleslavi-Čejetičkách. Památky archeologické 50, 34–53.

PLEINEROVÁ, I., 1980, Kultovní objekty z pozdní doby kamenné v Březně u Loun, Památky archeologické 71, 10-60.

PLEINEROVÁ, I., 2000, Hrob kultury se šňůrovou keramikou v Březně u Loun – Ein Grab der Kultur mit Schnurkeramik in Březno bei Louny, In: Petr Čech – Miroslav Dobeš (eds.): Sborník Miroslavu Buchvaldkovi, Most, 201–204.

ŠEBELA, L., 2000, The Corded Ware Culture in Moravia and in the adjacent part of Silesia (Catalogue), Fontes Archaeologici Moravicae, Tomus XXIII, Brno.

ŠMÍD, M., 1990, Příspěvek k poznání eneolitických mohylových pohřebišť na střední Moravě, in: Pravěké a slovanské osídlení Moravy, Brno 44-65.

RULF, J., 1996, Problematika pohřbů na sídlištích v českomoravském pravěku, Študijné zvesti 32, 115-124.

PRYOR, F., 2001, Seahenge. A quest for Life and Death in Bronze Age Britain, Harper/Collins Publishers, London.

SOFAER, J., TUREK, J., 2004, The excavation of funerary area at Uhy (distr. Kladno). In: Martin Gojda (ed.): Ancient landscape, Settlement dynamics and Non-destructive archaeology (Czech research project 1997-2002), Academia, Praha, 286–305.

ŠMEJDA, L., 2001, Kostel nebo mohyla? Příspěvek ke studiu pohřebních areálů – Church or Tumulus? A contribution to the study of burial areas. Archeologické rozhledy 53, 499–514.

TUREK, J., 2000a, Being a Beaker child. The position of children in Late Eneolithic society. In: In Memoriam Jan Rulf, Památky archeologické – Supplementum 13, Praha, 422–436.

TUREK, J., 2000b, Seahenge – dřevěná svatyně na pobřeží v Norfolku, Archeologické rozhledy 52, 43–145.

TUREK, J., 2002, "Cherche la femme!" Archeologie ženského světa a chybějící doklady ženských pohřbů z období zvoncovitých pohárů v Čechách. "Cherche la femme!". The Archaeology of woman's world and the missing evidence of female burials in the Bell Beaker Period in Bohemia, in: Evžen Neustupný (ed): Archeologie nenalézaného, Plzeň – Praha, 217–240.

TUREK, J., 2004, Craft symbolism in the Bell Beaker burial customs. Resources, production and social structure at the end of Eneolithic period. In: Marie Besse & Jocelyne Desideri (eds): Graves and Funerary Rituals during the Late Neolithic and the Early Bronze Age in Europe (2700-2000 BC) Proceedings of the International Conference held at the Cantonal Archaeological Museum, Sion (Switzerland) October 4th –7th 2001. British Archaeological Reports (International Series) 1284, 147-156, BAR Publishing, Oxford

ZÁPOTOCKÁ, M., 1998, Bestattungsritus des bömischen Neolithikums (5500-4200 B.C.) Gräber und Gräberfelder der Kultur mit Linear-, Stichband- und Lengyelkeramik, Praha.

LA REGION DE TAGRERA (TASSILI-WAN-AHAGGAR, AHAGGAR, ALGERIE) – REPRESENTATIONS RUPESTRES ET MONUMENTS FUNERAIRES PROTOHISTORIQUES

Iddir AMARA
Chercheurs au Centre National de Recherche en Préhistoire, Anthropologie et Histoire, 3 avenue F.D. Roosevelt, Alger, Algérie

Abdelkader HEDDOUCHE
Chercheurs au Centre National de Recherche en Préhistoire, Anthropologie et Histoire, 3 avenue F.D. Roosevelt, Alger, Algérie

Smaïl IDDIR
Chercheurs au Centre National de Recherche en Préhistoire, Anthropologie et Histoire, 3 avenue F.D. Roosevelt, Alger, Algérie

The region of Tagrera (Tassili-wan-Ahaggar, Ahaggar, Algeria) – rock art and protohistoric funerary monuments

***Résumé**: Le site de Tagrera est situé dans le Tassili-wan-Ahaggar, au sud-est de la ville de Tamanrasset. Il est placé au nord – nord ouest du Tassili Ti-n-Meskour, entre I-n-Abeggui et Ti-n-Tezedjnet (carte NF-32 I-n-Azaoua au 1: 1.000.000 – coordonnées: 21°32'/21°33'N et 06°27'/06°28'E). Tagréra est le secteur le plus fréquenté avec Youf Eheket et Tahaggart par les touristes. Le site de Tagrera s'étend sur un vaste territoire et comprend trois petites stations: Tenensi, Girafe et Chambre. Les figures rupestres sont isolées les unes des autres. Les représentations se limitent à quelques figures bovines, d'autruches et de girafes. Le style et la technique laissent apparaître une tradition culturelle saharienne. Les figures sont réalisées dans de rares abris et sur des rochers en plein air. Les gravures et les rares peintures expriment la même chose, mais le rendu de l'image est plus réaliste à travers la peinture qu'à travers la gravure. Les figures sont attribuées à différentes phases culturelles. Les plus anciennes ont le trait piqueté que le processus de l'érosion rend peu visible et les plus récentes sont martelées ou incisées. Ces figures sont homogènes par leur style et leur technique. L'abondance de monuments funéraires et la rareté de l'art rupestre, pourraient supposer que le site de Tagrera constitue une sorte de région plutôt dédiée aux pratiques funéraires. L'art rupestre est rare et la plupart des gravures que nous avons relevées sont dérisoires, face aux fresques des autres sites. La majorité des figures est probablement post-néolithique. Les animaux représentés, comme les girafes, les bovins, les autruches, indiquent un milieu aride et ne correspondent pas aux animaux de traditions néolithiques. Seul les travaux en cours peuvent éclairer la tradition artistique de cette région saharienne bouleversée par les variations climatiques.*
***Mots-clés**: Thassili-wan-Ahaggar – Art Rupestre – Monument funéraire*

***Abstract**: The site of Tagrera is located in Tassili-wan-Ahaggar, in the southeast of the town of Tamanrasset. It is north-northwest of Tassili Ti-n-Meskour, between I-n-Abeggui and Ti-n-Tezedjnet (1: 1.000.000 map of I-n-Azaoua, Nf-32, at 21°32' /21°33' N and 06°27' /06°28' E). Tagréra, along with Youf Eheket and Tahaggart, is one of the sectors most visited by tourists. It encompasses a vast territory and includes three small stations: Tenensi, Girafe and Chambra. The rupestral figures at Tagrera are dispersed and isolated from each other. Representations in the rock art are limited to bovine figures, ostriches, and giraffes. The style and the technique of the rock art suggests a Saharan cultural tradition. The figures are executed in rare rockshelters and on open-air rock faces. Engravings and (more rarely) paintings express similar motifs, but images are rendered more realistically through painting rather than by engraving. The figures are ascribed to various cultural phases. The oldest were created using a process of dotted stretch, making them visible. The more recently produced ones were created by hammering or incising. The styles and creation techniques of these figures are homogeneous. The abundance of funerary monuments and the scarcity of rock art at Tagrera may indicate that the site constitutes a region dedicated to funerary practices. Rock art is rare, and the majority of engravings we observed are relatively simple, particularly when compared to the frescos present at other sites. The majority of figures at Tagrera were probably made after the Neolithic. The depicted Animals indicate an arid environment. They do not correspond to animals known from Neolithic traditions. This ongoing study seeks to clarify the Saharan-area artistic tradition that has been disrupted by climatic variations.*
***Keywords**: Tassili-wan-Ahaggar, rock art, funerary monument*

INTRODUCTION

L'Ahaggar comprend de nombreux sites archéologiques d'inégales importances; les régions des Tassilis-wan-Ahaggar, avec ses nombreux sites (Youf Eheket, Tagrera, Tahaggart, Imbroum, Ti-n-Edjeleh, Ti-n-Sersine) se trouvent en bordure sud du massif de l'Ahaggar. Ces sites, offrent différents aspects archéologiques. Les gisements de surfaces sont nombreux, tout comme les pièces lithiques qui datent du paléolithique ou du néolithique.

Le territoire de ce patrimoine archéologique est difficile à délimiter. Les mêmes figures ou les mêmes types de tumulus se retrouvent partout dans le Sahara central. La répartition régionale des monuments funéraires traduit une territorialité, donc des implantations particulières. Pour faciliter la recherche nous avons dû limiter notre terrain au seul site de Tagrera.

Le site de Tagrera "Tenensi, Girafe et Chambre" s'étend sur un vaste territoire. Les figures rupestres sont isolées les unes des autres. Les représentations se limitent à quelques figures bovines, nombreuses autruches et girafes. Le style et la technique laissent apparaître une tradition culturelle saharienne. Les figures sont réalisées dans de rares abris et sur des rochers de plein air. Les gravures et les rares peintures expriment la même chose, mais le rendu de l'image est plus réaliste à travers la peinture que la gravure. Les figures sont attribuées à différentes phases culturelles.

Des recherches récentes dans le cadre d'un projet de recherche sur les monuments protohistoriques de l'Ahaggar dans leur contexte chrono-culturel ont montré, outre les abris rupestres que nous avons aussi visiter et analyser, la présence de nombreuses constructions funéraires protohistoriques qui témoignent d'une occupation humaine de la région au cours de l'Holocène. Leur architecture et le mode d'inhumation permettent de connaître leurs coutumes funéraires et la distribution géographique ainsi que les éventuels rapports avec les représentations rupestres.

Sont représentés ici exclusivement les monuments funéraires ayant fait l'objet de fouilles archéologiques en janvier 2004 par l'équipe "Fonctionnement et évolution du peuplement de la fin des temps préhistoriques des régions sahariennes" du Centre national de Recherches Préhistoriques Anthropologiques et Historiques (CNRPAH) d'Alger. Une réflexion est également engagée sur les représentations rupestres.

C'est au nord – nord ouest du Tassili Ti-n-Meskour , entre I-n-Abeggui et Ti-n-Tezedjnet (carte NF-32 I-n-Azaoua au 1:1.000.000 – coordonnées: 21°32'/21°33'N et 06°27'/06°28'E) près du lieu dit "Tagrera chambre" que se trouve la nécropole de Tagrera où nous avons relevé plusieurs constructions funéraires.

ENVIRONNEMENT ARCHEOLOGIQUE DE TAGRERA

La région de Tagrera (Fig. 16.1) est une vaste étendue entaillée par de nombreux oueds. Près de ces rivières sèches se remarquent quelques figures rupestres et de nombreux monuments funéraires. Ces figurations et ces monuments n'ont fait l'objet d'aucune étude. Elles présentent différents types, styles et thèmes.

Le site peut être classé géographiquement en plusieurs zones:

- Le site de Tagrera dit "Girafe"
- Le site de Tagrera dit "Chambre" (lieu de la fouille)
- Le site de Tagrera dit "Tenensi"

L'environnement néolithique de Tagrera, présente quelques figures rupestres. Elles sont toutes gravées, mais nous avons remarqués quelques peintures, en mauvais état de conservation, dans le site de Tagrera "Tenensi". Ces figures correspondent à une simplification réaliste de l'environnement animal. Les quelques figures que nous avons relevées, coïncident avec la fin des temps Néolithiques et les autres s'inscrivent dans les temps postnéolithiques dit "libyco-berbère".

Les structures funéraires sont nombreuses. La platitude du relief permet de distinguer de loin la forme du monument funéraire. Les quelques sépultures fouillés indiquent l'intérêt porter aux morts. L'aménagement de la pierre donne des formes diverses dans la construction de multiples *tumulii.* C'est un indice culturel dans l'étude des populations anciennes de l'Ahaggar.

Les préhistoriques ont utilisé un support minéral pour transmettre des "messages" graphiques. Cet art rupestre correspond à une forme d'expression qui trouve sa définition dans un style commun à l'art saharien. Il est possible de le rapprocher du style Iheren Tahilahi (Muzzolini 1995) ou du Bovidien final du Tassili (Lhote 1970). Les phases successives présentent un art schématique. Il est ainsi défini du fait que l'artiste ne respecte pas les normes anatomiques du sujet figuré.

LES ARCHITECTURES FUNERAIRES

Nous avons relevé plusieurs constructions funéraires: 14 monuments simples, 4 monuments à antennes, 4 plates-formes, 2 monuments à cratère, 1 bazina et 6 monuments en croissant. Quatre de ces différents monuments ont fait l'objet de fouilles, en raison de leur architecture et leur localisation géographique: 2 monuments en croissant, 1 plate-forme et 1 monument à antennes.

Tout comme l'art rupestre, les monuments protohistoriques qu'ils soient funéraires ou cultuels sont très nombreux et variés dans l'Ahaggar. Leur étude est d'un grand intérêt pour la connaissance des pratiques et des rites funéraires des groupes culturels qui les ont édifiés.

La distribution géographique est de son côté un précieux indicateur de leurs territoires et susceptible de mieux nous renseigner sur les éventuels rapports ou liens entre les auteurs des peintures et gravures rupestres et les constructeurs des monuments funéraires. Cette relation a été, rappelons le, établie à Iwelen dans le massif de l'Aïr (Niger) entre un tumulus à cratère, un gisement archéologique et un site rupestre se rapportant à la période dite libyco-berbère.

Le programme de recherche en cours consacré aux monuments protohistoriques de l'Ahaggar dans leur contexte chrono-culturel est assez particulier puisqu'il couvre un vaste territoire et toute la période holocène. Le

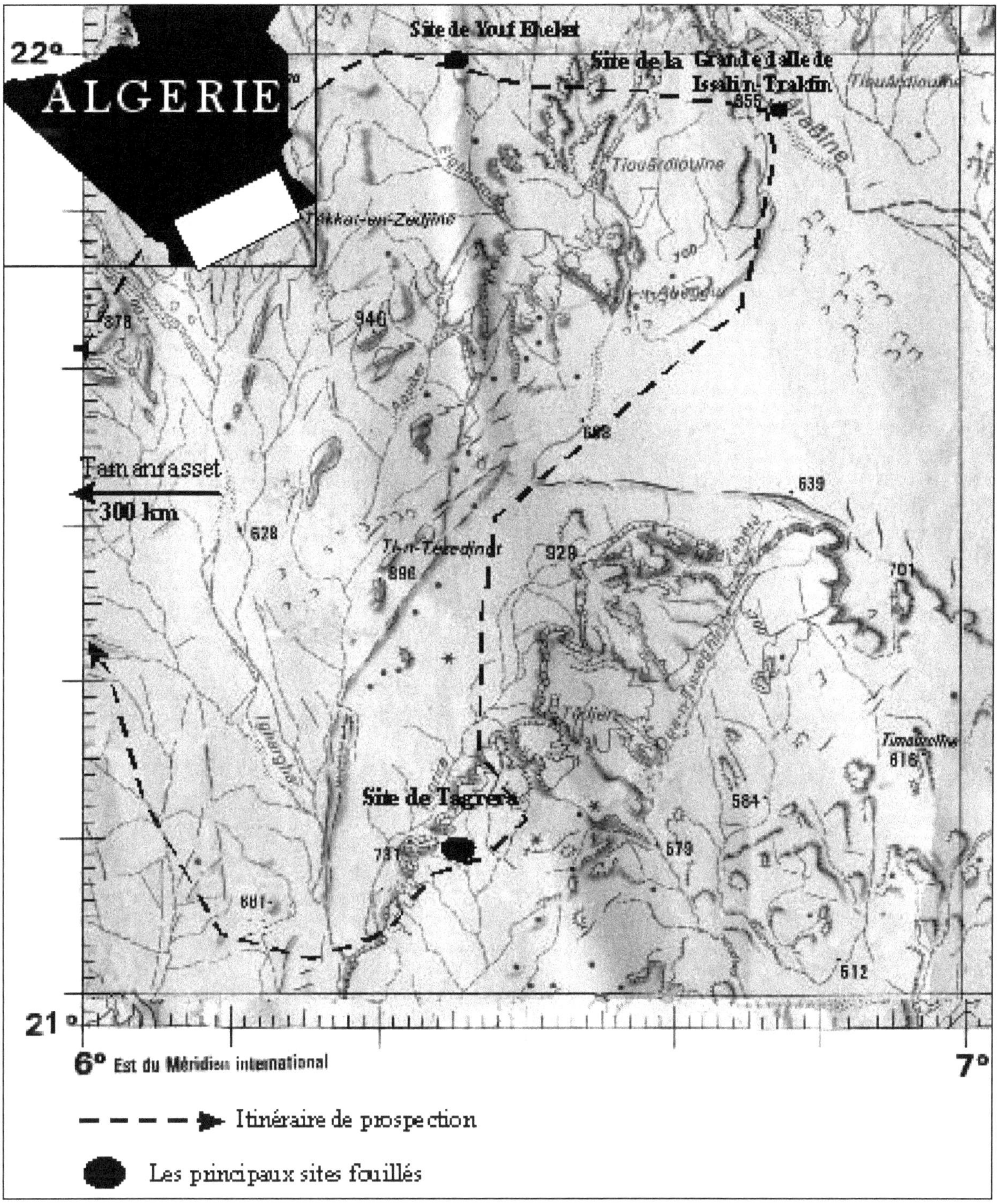

Fig. 16.1. Les principaux sites du Tassili Wan Ahaggar
(Feuille carte NF-32 I-N- Azaoua au 1:1.000.000. N: 22°00', E: 6°45')

recensement des architectures funéraires et cultuelles a permis la localisation de concentrations de monuments funéraires dont l'exploitation passait nécessairement par les fouilles archéologiques.

Dans le cas présent, nous présentons le site de Tagrera (Tassili-wan Ahaggar) où nous avons eu l'opportunité d'observer un site rupestre se rapportant à la période bovidienne dans un contexte de monuments funéraires du post-Néolithique (*tumulus* à cratère, bazinas, monuments à antennes).

Nous n'avons pas effectué le décompte exact de toutes les constructions funéraires du secteur mais elles semblent plus fréquentes à proximité du site rupestre signalé où elles sont regroupées. Plusieurs types de monuments funéraires sont recensés et certaines de ces architectures ont fait l'objet de fouilles.

LES MONUMENTS FUNERAIRES FOUILLES

Le monument à antennes

Les monuments à antennes sont des structures bordées par deux bras formant une sorte de "V" d'où parfois leur dénomination sous le label monuments à deux antennes en "V". Ils sont anciennement connus et se distinguent par plusieurs variantes au niveau de la partie centrale et leurs bras ne sont pas automatiquement parallèles.

Cette architecture qui occupe un vaste territoire semble cependant être absente à ce jour au sud des limites 20°53'N et 6°08'E d'où l'intérêt de telles constructions dans la région de Tagrera.

Nous ne connaissons pas tous les monuments à antennes fouillés à ce jour excepté ceux relevés ou fouillés par L. Voinot (1908) et M. Reygassse (1950). Un monument de ce type a été récemment fouillé par nous-mêmes près de Hirafok dans la région naturelle de l'Aghéchoum (mission de A. Heddouche et S. Iddir 2003).

Le monument à antennes que nous présentons ici est de petite dimension. La partie centrale circulaire est dallée et a un diamètre de 2.80 m NS et 3.30 m EO, sa hauteur est de 0.75 m. Ses antennes orientées NE (50°) et SE (150°) mesurent 6.35 m pour l'une et 6.30 m pour l'autre se distinguent par des pierres levées plantées aux deux extrémités.

Le dégagement de la partie centrale a permis de reconnaître un dépôt de tessons de poterie lisse dans un endroit qui s'avèrera être par la suite l'emplacement de la tête du défunt ainsi que la présence de dalles plates importantes (comme à Hirafok) qui indiqueraient le lieu d'inhumation.

Après le dégagement des premières dalles plates, apparaissent deux grandes et épaisses dalles de même aspect. La première à 0.25 m de profondeur (0.80 m x 0.87 m, épaisseur 0.13 m), la deuxième lui faisait immédiatement suite à 0.25 m de profondeur (1.10 m x 0.70 m, épaisseur 0.13 m).

Cet ensemble recouvre à 0.50 m de profondeur une fosse mesurant 1.10 m x 0.70 m qui renferme un squelette dans un bon état de conservation puisque la quasi-totalité de ses parties peuvent être étudiées en laboratoire. Le corps reposait en décubitus latéral droit fléchi, orienté selon un axe Nord/Sud et la face dirigée vers l'Est. Selon les premières observations, il s'agit d'un adulte probablement de sexe masculin. Aucune datation ne permet actuellement de situer ces constructions.

Le monument en croissant

Ces monuments qui se rencontrent surtout au sud du 22° N sont assez nombreux à Tagrera où l'on rencontre plusieurs constructions de ce type. Les travaux effectués dans le Niger septentrional et nos différentes reconnaissances archéologiques montent que dans la plupart des cas leurs bras sont ouverts vers l'Est mais certains ont leurs cornes orientées vers l'Ouest et seraient des sépultures de femmes. Deux monuments appartenant à cette famille aux bras ouverts vers l'Est et vers l'Ouest ont fait l'objet de fouilles.

Le premier monument est une construction orientée vers l'Ouest. Elle présente des bras assez longs (23.20 m et 24.90 m) et une partie centrale "renflée" mesurant 9.40 m Nord/Sud et 4 m Est/Ouest pour une hauteur de 1 m.

En dégageant la partie centrale, nous atteignons une fosse de 1.10 m x 0.70 m à 1.90 m de profondeur où reposait le squelette d'un adulte (fémur 0.55 m) en décubitus latéral droit fléchi, selon un axe Nord/Sud, la tête à 170°. L'analyse en laboratoire des parties essentielles du squelette permettrait de préciser son sexe et de vérifier l'hypothèse selon laquelle les tumulus en croissant orientés vers l'Ouest seraient destinés aux femmes (fouilles de F. Paris 1992, Niger septentrional).

Le deuxième monument aux cornes ouvertes vers l'Est se distingue par une concentration de pierres au milieu de sa partie centrale. Il mesure 10 m de diamètre Nord/Sud, 6 m Est/Ouest pour une hauteur de 1.90 m; les bras sont plus longs (26.20 m et 34 m) par rapport aux bras du monument précédemment décrit.

L'inhumation, contrairement aux monuments de la même famille précédemment fouillés à Youf Eheket (Amara *et al.* 2004) n'a pas été pratiquée à la base du tumulus mais au sommet (observation à vérifier ultérieurement) puisque le corps d'un individu probablement adulte (fémur 0.43 m) reposait dans une cuvette soigneusement aménagée, à 0.80 m de profondeur en décubitus latéral droit fléchi, selon un axe Nord/Sud, tête à 280°.

LES DATATIONS OBTENUES AU NIGER PERMETTENT DE SITUER CES MONUMENTS ENTRE 3300 ET 1900 AV. J.-C.

Le monument type "La plate – forme"

Les plates-formes se rencontrent un peu partout au Sahara, du Fezzan en Libye à l'Aïr au Niger où elles apparaissent vers 3800 av. J.-C et perdurent jusqu'à 1200 av. J.-C.

Cette architecture, très fréquente dans plusieurs régions de l'Ahaggar se rencontre surtout dans les pourtours de l'Amadror et la Tourha mais ne constitue pas de véritables nécropoles.

Les plates-formes relevées dans la région de Tagrera sont de type circulaire. La plate- forme est généralement délimitée par une ceinture de pierres dressées qui dépasse peu le sol (0.20 m à 0.50 m) d'où sa dénomination par certains auteurs sous le label "monument en corbeille".

La construction fouillée est située dans le même périmètre que les deux tumulus en croissant étudiés où on dénombre également un petit monument à antennes et un monument à cratère. Il s'agit d'une structure de petite dimension qui mesure 5.80 m de diamètre Est/Ouest pour 5.60 m Nord/Sud; sa hauteur est de 0.45 m. Elle porte dans sa partie centrale, des dalles de dimensions moyennes qui recouvrent une fosse de 1.40 m x 0.80 m creusée à 1 m de profondeur dans laquelle repose un individu en décubitus latéral droit fléchi selon un axe Sud/Ouest (la tête) – Nord/Ouest (les pieds), et la tête est à 90° Est. Le squelette est dans un assez bon état de conservation permettant de faire les analyses nécessaires sur le terrain et au laboratoire.

L'ICONOGRAPHIE

La région de Tagrera est l'une des zones d'art rupestre du Sahara les plus pauvres. Les figures sont homogènes, tant par le milieu que par la tradition de son art rupestre. Les parois rocheuses sont très érodées et certaines sont ensablées (nous avons dégagé quelques figures de girafes). La nature de la roche et le climat ne permettent pas une bonne conservation des figures. Ce fait et les espèces animales représentées illustrent les conditions climatiques de l'époque et la réponse que l'homme y a apportée.

Le site présente de fortes similitudes avec les gravures bovidiennes et libyco-berbères de l'art rupestre saharien. Une situation qui n'est pas propre à ce site. Du côté nigérien et malien (frontières actuelles) existent d'autres sites de nature similaire. Cet art appartient également à un milieu désertique et présentent une parenté évidente avec les figures de la tradition bovidienne. Les figures animales sont fortement patinées et profondément gravés selon la tradition saharienne. La taille de ces figures et leur technique de réalisation indique le même type de parenté culturelle.

Le site de Tagrera "Chambre" se trouve dans un milieu aride, les quelques grès qui émergent des dunes de sable portent quelques rares figures et illustrent les conditions environnementales à l'époque de leur origine. Les nombreux abris sous-roche ne sont pas tous exploités par les préhistoriques. Le seul qui porte les traces d'occupation est celui de Tagrera "Tenensi".

Tagrera "Tenensi, Girafe et Chambre" présente un mélange de gravures du Néolithique récent (bovidien final) et plus tardivement des dessins généralement piquetés des périodes tardives (caballin et camelin). L'absence de certaines espèces (présente sur la dalle de Ti-n-Tarabin comme l'hippopotame, le rhinocéros, le félin), peu s'expliquer par l'âge récent des figures et les limites de la distribution géographique de ces espèces. C'est aussi le cas des autres espèces liées à l'eau comme le bovin (aurochs: *Bos primigenius*, le bubal: *Syncerus antiquus*). Par contre les espèces habituées à l'aridité comme la girafe et l'autruche se retrouvent en grand nombre.

Etant donné la grande surface du site, elle mérite une prospection fine pour permettre à l'art de cette région d'être connue et que l'on prenne en considération les données archéologiques des sites les plus prometteurs. La datation absolue devrait être une composante obligée de cette recherche.

Il ne fait aucun doute que le site de Tagrera constitue une sorte de région initiée plutôt aux pratiques funéraires. L'art rupestre n'est qu'accessoire et la plus part des gravures que nous avons relevées sont insignifiantes et dont la majorité est probablement post- néolithique. Quoi qu'il en soit, les animaux représentés, c'est à dire les girafes, les bovins, les autruches, indiquent un milieu aride et ne correspondent pas aux animaux des traditions du Néolithique ancien. Seul les travaux en cours peuvent éclairer la tradition artistique de cette région, influencée par les conditions climatiques qui bouleversaient le climat général du Sahara.

Dans cet espace vaste et aride de Tagrera, les sites rupestres et d'habitats préhistoriques se situent souvent à la proximité de monuments funéraires. Ce que F. Paris (1992), dans ses travaux dans l'Aïr, a réussi à mettre en relation un site rupestre avec une construction funéraire. Il s'agit de quelques objets métalliques découverts dans le site d'Iwalen. Les mêmes constructions funéraires sont présentes sur le site de Tagrera.

F. Paris (1992) donne quelques datations suites aux travaux effectués au Nord du Niger.[1] Youf Eheket offre le même environnement archéologique. Sur ce site, nous avons procédé à la fouille de quelques types. Nous pouvons tenter de relier certaines constructions funéraires à des formes d'art rupestre. Dans ce cas il s'agit bien du type "Tumulus à cratère" et du type "Bazina" datés du IIe millénaire av. J.-C et les figures "Libyco-berbères".

Si on compare notre site avec Iwelen, fouillé et étudié par F. Paris, nous arriverons peut – être à avoir les mêmes indices. Les plates-formes et les tumulus en croissant seront datés du néolithique et sont généralement antérieurs à 1900 BC. Cette date marque la phase post-néolithique qui voit l'apparition des tumulus à cratère. Cette phase correspond à la période caballine. Le rapprochement est fait sur la base d'une comparaison de pointes métalliques découvertes dans ces sépultures. Leur forme se rapproche de celle des pointes de lances des guerriers libyco-berbères.

Ces figures peuvent nous renseigner sur le vécu de l'homme. Elles suivent l'évolution que subit l'homme tout au long de l'Holocène. Durant la protohistoire, la

[1]. Tous ces types datés se retrouvent dans le Tassili-wan-Ahaggar. Le "Tumulus à couloir" est apparu vers le Ve millénaire. La "Plate-forme", le "Tumulus en croissant", le "Tumulus simple" apparaissent vers le IVe millénaire.

métallurgie est l'un des éléments les plus innovateur pour la compréhension de ces sociétés anciennes. Cette nouvelle technologie est présente à travers les figurations d'armes (principalement des lances, des javelots et des boucliers ronds).

Ces objets, prédilection de l'homme de cette période est présent sur l'ensemble du territoire nord africain et principalement dans cette région du sud-est de l'Ahaggar. La technologie métallurgique coïncide avec l'arrivée du cheval, du dromadaire et des premiers caractères alphabétiques dans la vie de ces hommes.

Le "libyco-berbère", à travers le cheval et le dromadaire par la suite, découvre un nouveau moyen de locomotion facilitant la mobilité et surtout la maîtrise de l'immensité de l'espace saharien. Ces innovations interviennent dans un environnement encore fidèle aux traditions néolithiques, qui se sont maintenu encore longtemps.

CONCLUSION

L'essentiel de l'art rupestre de Tagrera appartient à la période dite Libyco – berbère. Quelques rares représentations appartiennent au bovidien tardif. Les monuments funéraires offrent une grande variété de type se rapportant à différents âges. Les monuments funéraires et les figurations découverts dans la région de Tagrera présentent des traces anciennes d'occupations de ces régions.

Les figures, représentées sur divers sites, sont attribuées à différentes phases culturelles. Le travail effectué sur les figurations apporte des précisions sur l'ensemble de la région de l'Ahaggar. Il permet de comprendre les différents graphismes pour ces cultures préhistorique et protohistorique. Le site de Tagrera a livré un ensemble de figures homogènes par le style et la technique. Les figures sont pour leur majorité piquetées.

Nous avons fouillés quelques monuments funéraires et nous observé l'état de conservation des restes osseux. Les échantillons ramassés peuvent permettra d'effectuer des datations radiométriques pour établir une chronologie. Il permet également de faire les premières observations anthroplogiques et de poursuivre les études spécialisées d'anthropologie physique pour identifier les groupes paléanthropologiques.

Les observations faites montrent que la recherche est prometteuse dans la relation art rupestre-monuments funéraires. Les constructions funéraires de type tumulus à cratère et bazina semblent être en rapport avec les figures "libyco-berbères". La relation entre l'art rupestre et les sépultures protohistoriques passent impérativement par la fouille.

Le programme de recherche que c'est tracé notre centre de recherche sur la fin des temps préhistoriques dans l'Ahaggar apportera plus de précisions sur le "Fonctionnement et évolution du peuplement de la fin des temps préhistoriques des régions sahariennes".

References

AMARA, I., HEDDOUCHE, A. & IDDIR, S., 2004, Le site de Youf Eheket: art rupestre et monuments funéraires, *XXI*[e] *Symposium de Valcamonica*, Italie.

LHOTE, H., 1970, Gravures rupestres de Ti-n-Terirt, Iharir, Ahararar Mellen, Amsedenet et In Tebourbouga (Tassili-n-Ajjer, Sahara central), *L.A.P.E.*, t. XVIII, p. 185-234.

PARIS, F., 1992, *Les sépultures du Sahara nigérien du néolithique à l'islamisation. Coutumes funéraires, chronologie, civilisations*, Thèse de Doctorat nouveau régime de l'Université de Paris I-Panthéon-Sorbonne, Paris.

MUZZOLINI, A., 1995, *Les images rupestres du Sahara*, édité par l'auteur, Toulouse, 448 p.

REYGASSE, M., 1950, A propos des monuments garamantiques. Monuments funéraires préislamiques de l'Afrique du Nord, *Publ. Gouv. Gén. de l'Algérie, Services des Antiquités.*

VOINOT, L., 1908, Notes pour servir à l'Ethnographie ancienne du Sahara, *Bull. Soc. Géogr. et Archéol. D'Oran*, XVIII, 4, pp. 325-368.

STRUCTURED DEPOSITION AND DITCHED ENCLOSURES IN THE LATE PREHISTORY OF SOUTHERN IBERIA (IV-III MILLENNIA BC)

Víctor JIMÉNEZ JÁIMEZ
Área de Prehistoria, Facultad de Filosofía y Letras, Universidad de Málaga,
Campus de Teatinos s/n, 29071, Málaga, Spain
Email: vjjaimez@uma.es

José Enrique MÁRQUEZ ROMERO
Área de Prehistoria, Facultad de Filosofía y Letras, Universidad de Málaga,
Campus de Teatinos s/n, 29071, Málaga, Spain
Email: jemarquez@uma.es

***Abstract**: The existence of structured depositions in pits and ditches during Late Prehistory has been lately recognized in the South of Iberian Peninsula. Instead, classical thesis have stressed for decades a kind of relationship between the archaeological data and hypothetical farmer villages in IV-III millennia BC. In our opinion, the classical statements about Iberian ditched enclosures rest on several preconceptions and common places about formation processes of the archaeological record at the aforementioned sites; in fact, instead of clear and well-formulated theses, most advocates use implicit or hastily formulated categories. In this article we will try to make explicit some of the inexplicit principles frequently applied to the problem of formation processes at Southern Iberian ditched enclosures. In order to achieve this, we will employ three parameters as analytical tools: depositional cause/agent, type of deposition (primary or secondary) and degree of post-depositional damage. After examining the traditional/current theses from this standpoint, we will present our own interpretative proposal, which will also be expressed in the same terms.*
***Key words**: Late Prehistory, Ditched enclosures, Formation processes*

Deposición estructurada y recintos de fosos en la Prehistoria Reciente del sur de la Península Ibérica (IV-III milenios AC)

***Resumen**: La existencia de deposiciones estructuradas en pozos y zanjas durante la Prehistoria Reciente ha sido tardíamente advertida en el sur de la Península Ibérica. En su lugar, las tesis clásicas han insistido durante décadas en relacionar esta fenomenología arqueológica con las propias de hipotéticos poblados campesinos del IV-III milenio a. C. Estamos convencidos de que en la interpretación clásica subyacen ideas preconcebidas y lugares comunes sobre la formación del registro arqueológico de estos yacimientos que no han sido discutidas en profundidad. Sobre este particular trata este artículo. Aunque más que asumir o criticar tesis explícitamente formuladas, lo que haremos será intentar explicitar cómo han pensado y piensan muchos de los investigadores dedicados al estudio de este fenómeno. Para ello emplearemos como herramientas analíticas tres parámetros: causa y agente deposicional, tipo de deposición (primaria o secundaria) e incidencia de los procesos postdeposicionales. Una vez analizadas las tesis tradicionales bajo esta óptica, efectuaremos nuestra propia propuesta interpretativa y la someteremos a los mismos principios analíticos.*
***Palabras-clave**: Prehistoria reciente – Recintos con fosa – Procesos de formación*

INTRODUCTION

Southern Spain in general and Andalusia in particular, has gone through a belated industrialization process from the late seventies of the twentieth century to the present, basically in the fields of tourism and urban development. As a consequence of this, a lot of archaeological sites were discovered at the building sites. The most intriguing sites were arguably those composed exclusively of underground features, little known until then, since they could hardly be found through traditional (surface) archaeological methods. The underground features had a wide variety of shapes and sizes, but most of them were either V-shaped ditches or bell-shaped pits. Their archaeological fills were, at the very least, unusual: potsherds, prismatic blades and other flint tools, flint knapping waste, broken quern stones, animal and human remains (complete or incomplete), etc. Some examples of these sites include Valencina de la Concepción (Ruiz Mata 1983, Fernández & Oliva 1985, 1986), Papa Uvas (Martín De La Cruz 1985, 1986), La Pijotilla (Hurtado 1991), Polideportivo de Martos (Lizcano *et al.* 1991-1992), Marroquíes Bajos (Zafra *et al.* 1999) and Porto Torrão (Valera & Filipe 2004).

Since then, almost all these sites, dating from Late Neolithic and Early Copper Age (IV millennium and first half of the III millennium BC), have been interpreted as large settlements. On one hand, the ditches are considered to set the boundaries of a delimited residential area, either with a defensive function or as part of an ancient drain system. Whatever the primary function attributed to the ditches, it is assumed that at the end of their use-lives they were filled with "rubbish" from the settlement. On the other hand, the rest of the underground structures –bell-shaped pits- are interpreted either as grain storage pits (silos) or as the underground half of some kind of semi-subterranean hut.

Nowadays, this set of ideas continues to be the most common view on this issue, not only in Southern Iberia, but in other regions of Spain and Portugal, even after being criticized at the beginning of the twenty-first century (Márquez 2001, 2002, 2003, 2004, 2006a, 2006b, Márquez & Fernández 2002, Jiménez, n.d., Jiménez & Márquez n.d.). First and foremost, if we address the issue of Neolithic-Copper Age ditched sites in the Iberian Peninsula from a non-local perspective, we will realize that the same subject has been discussed for decades in other European regions regarding very similar and contemporary sites. The best example may be Great Britain, where, since the 1960's, the perception of Neolithic ditched enclosures as permanent settlements has been questioned, the obvious inefficiency of these ditches as defensive systems has been pointed out, and the interpretation of the pits as "storage pits" or "dwelling pits" has been dismissed (see for example Smith 1966, Drewett 1977, Pryor 1988; Edmonds 1999, Thomas 1999). In our opinion, with the exception of few characteristics that probably depend on the local context, **Iberian ditched enclosures** –as we will call them- are not essentially different from European ditched enclosures. In addition, the classical statements about Iberian ditched enclosures rest on several preconceptions and common places about formation processes of the archaeological record at the aforementioned sites; in fact, instead of clear and well-formulated theses, most advocates use implicit or hastily formulated categories.

In this article we will try to make explicit some of the inexplicit principles frequently applied to the problem of formation processes at Southern Iberian ditched enclosures. In order to achieve this, we will employ three parameters as analytical tools: depositional cause/agent, type of deposition (primary or secondary) and degree of post-depositional damage. After examining the traditional/current theses from this standpoint, we will present our own interpretative proposal, which will also be expressed in the same terms. Throughout the process, we will see that some of the most frequently used theoretical categories in the study of Iberian ditched enclosures are, in our opinion, inappropriate and misleading. As a result, it will be necessary to introduce a new concept into the discussion, ignored by other researchers so far: "structured deposition". First of all, we must define in a precise way our analytical parameters.

THEORETICAL FRAMEWORK (I): PRIMARY AND SECONDARY DEPOSITION

The analytical tools to be used in this paper come from a rich and complex theoretical model that Patrik (1985) named "Physical model of the archaeological record", to which most processual archaeologists are committed. According to this scientific model, the archaeological record consists of physical objects and features that are static effects of past causes. The recording connection between the record and what it records is a strict causal connection.

We will not discuss the physical model. Nevertheless, we will describe one of the attempts to rethink such a model, i.e. M. Schiffer's "Behavioral Archaeology" (Schiffer 1972, 1976, 1987, Lamotta & Schiffer 2001). Unlike other versions of the physical model, Schiffer's model advocates that the archaeological record is not exactly a fossil record. On the contrary, he argues that archaeological remains are "*a distorted reflection of a past behavioral system*" (1976: 12). The relations between the static effects of the present and their causes in the past, that is, the cultural and non-cultural processes responsible for such distortions, are regular and can be formulated as universal behavioural statements. In order to "read" the archaeological record, archaeologists have to identify the distortions. Hence, it is necessary to distinguish between the *systemic context* and the *archaeological context* (Schiffer 1972). The systemic context is the ongoing behavioural system which once contained the material remains of the archaeological record. The archaeological context is the set of materials which have passed through a cultural system, and which are now the objects of investigation of archaeologists. The transition of an object from the systemic context to the archaeological context –which begins with discard- is not a direct one: there are numerous depositional and post-depositional processes (Schiffer 1987).

Concerning the definition of the analytical parameters to be used in this article, we think the concepts of depositional cause/agent and post-depositional disturbance are simple and sufficiently known. We will not, therefore, discuss them in depth. There is one aspect which should be clarified, though. Schiffer considers basically two types of depositional and post-depositional agents: natural and human. Human agents, specially, can act in complex situations, and we can wonder whether or not depositions and post-depositional disturbances were intentional and, in that case, which were the reasons behind that behaviour. The type of deposition, on the other hand, will be the main topic of the following lines. In general terms, and in order to simplify, the way the discard process is carried out lets us distinguish two different types of deposition: primary and secondary.

Primary Deposition (Lamotta & Schiffer 1999: 21). This is the process through which objects enter the archaeological record at their spaces of use and/or consumption within the site. Therefore, the items deposited at their area(s) of use and/or consumption are named *primary refuse*. Primary deposition processes provide the archaeologists with a lot of information about the systemic context, given the direct relationship between activities carried out in the past in a particular space and attributes of the archaeological record at the same spot. If each and every archaeological context were composed by primary refuse, it would be relatively easy to infer the function or even the meaning of most artefacts, structures and sites. But therein lies the problem. Since the seventies of the last century, it is generally admitted that primary deposition is rare and scarce, as many ethnoarchaeological surveys have shown (e.g. Murray 1980, Hayden & Cannon 1983, Stevenson 1985, Deal 1985, Tani 1995). Huts and other activity areas are mostly cleaned up periodically, since refuse hinders the execution of new activities and may even be dangerous for human beings. Cleaning and maintenance tasks are almost inevitable when a site is occupied for long periods (Schiffer 1987).

Secondary Deposition (Lamotta & Schiffer 1999: 21). When actions to remove waste from human activity areas are executed -in order to clear them and make them suitable for new tasks-, it is necessary to place that refuse in another space. So, right after cleaning and maintenance, secondary deposition takes place. The human activity by-products which go through this process are known as *secondary refuse*, and are defined as the items deposited anywhere other than their location(s) of use and/or consumption (Schiffer 1987).

Unlike other theoretical models about site formation processes –especially other versions of the physical model-, Schiffer's theoretical framework does not take the archaeological deposit, a specific structure or the whole site as unit of analysis. On the contrary, the above-mentioned categories concern only the objects made, used and discarded by past cultural systems (Kligmann 1998). Thus, the adjectives *primary* and *secondary*, in this text, will be employed only to describe the artefacts and/or ecofacts deposited at a particular space. In other words, in this paper we will not use these terms regarding the hypothetical "primary" or "secondary" function of the underground features that compose ditched enclosures, an eventuality that will be referred to as the "reuse" of the feature.

CURRENT THOUGHTS ON IBERIAN DITCHED ENCLOSURES FORMATION PROCESSES

Today, most Iberian Prehistorians consider ditched enclosures as the oldest evidence for permanent settlements, some of them even proto-urban centres, inhabited by sedentary and peasant communities (a more detailed historiographical review with all the bibliographical references can be found in Márquez 2006b). This thesis required the reconciliation of an idealised image of the Neolithic farmer with an inadequate archaeological record. This was achieved through a series of preconceptions: a) that the sites are fortified settlements with defensive ditch systems, b) that the absence of domestic surface structures is due to the subterranean or semi-subterranean nature of the huts, c) that the absence of any evidence of post-holes or any other architectural elements in the above-mentioned semi-subterranean features is the outcome of post-depositional processes leading to their destruction, d) that the proliferation of what are seen as grain storage silos reflects consolidated farming communities, e) that many of the underground structures were reused as refuse pits once their initial function had been lost, and finally, f) that the presence of human remains (complete and incomplete, articulated and disarticulated) is a sign of social inequality, since it shows an asymmetric funerary treatment: the unprivileged part of the population is buried in rubbish pits or former storage pits, whilst the privileged one "enjoys" the classic megalithic funerary ritual.

Therefore, formation processes of the archaeological record at these sites have always been explained at the light of the theory about the sedentary and peasant character of Neolithic and Copper Age populations. This, however, have not resulted in a corpus of explicitly formulated and empirically tested hypothesis, but in a set of implicit, ambiguous and deceptive preconceptions. We have attempted to arrange them employing the above-mentioned analytical tools, so we could isolate some sort of "thesis": "dwelling-pits thesis", "storage pits/refuse pits thesis" and "Siret thesis". None of them is exclusive of a researcher or a site; in fact, most times all of them are combined to provide explanations for the same site or within the same paper.

"Dwelling-pits thesis"

Some of the pits found at ditched enclosures –those with a less unsuitable size and/or shape- are interpreted as the underground half of semi-subterranean huts. Such pithouses or dwelling-pits are thought to be slowly filled with refuse from everyday activities executed inside the pit, generating so-called "cultural layers" or "occupation deposits". Therefore, several occupation phases can be identified in each of them and the stratigraphic method is believed to be a convenient tool to address these issues. This type of deposition could be labelled as *primary deposition*, because the items deposited are considered to be primary refuse. The depositional agent would be human, being the cause of deposition the lack of cleansing activities. There would be major post-depositional alterations at post-abandonment stage, since all the surface evidences regarding the aboveground half of the dwelling-pits, and the so-called settlement as a whole, would be completely destroyed.

"Storage pits/refuse pits thesis"

Generally speaking, this is the most common interpretation when the feature is too small to be labelled as a "dwelling pit" –the majority of pits, indeed. This category includes all the proposals that advocate a hypothetical initial function of a particular pit (basically storage), followed by the reuse of the structure as a refuse pit. In other words, at the end of the use-life of the so-called grain storage pit, it would be filled with "rubbish", that is, an unstructured, chaotic and randomly assembled set of secondary refuse. The same can be said about the ditches, which originally would be a part of a defensive/drain system and later would be filled with rubbish. Hence, deposition would be *secondary*, since the artefacts and ecofacts which compose the assemblages – interpreted as rubbish- were not allegedly used inside the pit, but in another area, being later removed from there and deposited in the pit. The depositional agent is human, and the cause of deposition is the human necessity of dealing with the by-products generated at activity areas, that is to say, waste management. After abandonment, post-depositional processes would be very intense and destructive, because, aside from the pits themselves, there is nothing left from the settlement.

"Siret Thesis"

We named this thesis after L. Siret, the first researcher who expressed these ideas in the nineteenth century (Siret (1893) 2001), but many other scholars assumed them throughout the following century. The starting point is a vast settlement with several surface habitation units and a number of functionally diverse underground structures. At post-abandonment stage, a powerful erosive process would highly damage all the aboveground structures, displacing their remains and the occupation deposits previously formed into the underground features. Thus, pits and ditches would be slowly filled with deposits from the former settlement. Since most items were not supposedly used inside the pits and the ditches, we must consider them secondary refuse and, therefore, their deposition would be, again, *secondary*. The main difference between this thesis and the earlier ones is the agent/cause of deposition. Unlike them, "Siret thesis" states that the agent of deposition is natural, namely major post-depositional displacement. In short, it would be a random, non-human, secondary deposition, caused by extremely severe erosive processes.

THEORETICAL FRAMEWORK (II): STRUCTURED DEPOSITION

Ongoing thoughts on this topic, especially "storage pits/refuse pits" thesis, rest on several pre-understandings and preconceptions which need to be clarified before presenting our own view on the matter. One of their flaws is the notion of "rubbish", which has some deceptive connotations. Items labelled "rubbish" are thought to be damaged, broken or useless. The deposition of rubbish is seen as random, guided only by physical hygienic criteria. At a methodological level, it is misleading in the sense that we might erroneously pay less attention to spatial relationships between objects found in the features in the course of the archaeological excavation. Why should we be absolutely rigorous if we believe that its deposition was hasty, haphazard and careless? Further, at an interpretative level, the concept of rubbish might lead us to make quantitative inferences, apparently "objective". That is because rubbish is supposed to be a reliable reflection of past economic strategies, a by-product of human economic activities -purely economic, in the modern sense of the word. To address this issue through an alternative approach, in this section we will make a brief reference to another scientific model of the archaeological record, which stems from post-processual archaeologies: the textual model (Patrik 1985).

The textual model sees the archaeological record as a structured whole. Based on the ideas of P. Bourdieu and A. Giddens, it is argued that every human activity is symbolically structured, i.e. reproduces social rules and conventionalisms which Bourdieu called *habitus* (Bourdieu 1977, 1990, Giddens 1984). From that standpoint, activities related to refuse management are structured following cultural patterns, as well. Thus, the way waste is classified, the area where deposition takes place, the objects chosen for deposition, even the way they are deposited, cannot contradict the beliefs and attitudes of the community. As a matter of fact, they must interact with each other (Moore 1982: 76, Hodder 1982: 62-63, 1987). When it comes to waste management, nothing is random or careless; everything must be in its place. We, as archaeologists, should not take anything for granted regarding this issue.

The *habitus* is not a set of universal principles. It depends on the cultural context, so every cultural group has its own standards of value, its own patterns of behaviour. To a certain extent, as regards the archaeological record, there is no direct, universal, purely physical relation between cause and effect. The concept of "rubbish", like many others, is not universal, but culturally specific. It does not exist as a separate category in a lot of well-known "primitive" societies. In non-industrial communities, not every discarded object is automatically classified as "rubbish". Human activity by-products can be classified according to numerous criteria, often very different from ours, and it is possible that none of the categories thought are completely equivalent to our notion of "rubbish" (Moore 1982: 76). As J. Chapman wrote, "*archaeology is not about rubbish as much as about deposition*" (2000: 63). If the modern concept of rubbish is not appropriate for defining past refuse, then the samples under study may not be representative of past economic strategies, at least in quantitative terms. So, the textual model implies believing, for instance, that "*it is easier to study the concerns of symbolic and structural analysis*", that is, the prejudices, pre-understandings, beliefs, attitudes, cosmologies, etc., of a given human community, "*than the reconstruction of economy, exchange and agricultural systems from assemblages of animal bone and pottery*" (Hill 1995: 96).

Structured deposition, a notion which will be of extraordinary importance later in this article, stems from the textual model of the archaeological record. The term was coined by C. Richards and J. Thomas (1984) to describe several British Neolithic archaeological deposits apparently not formed in a conventional way – *conventional* by textual model standards, that is, as a result of the unconscious reproduction of cultural rules governing human refuse management. The deposits under consideration showed obvious patterns and regularities in the way in which some kinds of objects related to each other and in their spatial distribution. Thus, there were seemingly not random associations and dissociations between objects: on one hand, certain types of objects were always found together and/or associated; on the other hand, disassociations and mutually exclusive depositions of artefacts were usual. In that seminal paper, it was shown that the unconventional structures of the assemblages were not the outcome of natural formation processes. Rather, the artefacts and ecofacts contained within such deposits seemed to have been placed deliberately, on purpose, in a conscious manner. In addition, "*when the material was deposited, it was done in a particular manner, obeying certain rules which were important to the actors involved*" (Richards & Thomas 1984: 215). The connection of such deposits to "ritual" practices seemed straightforward. In the following years, deposits with similar formative processes were discovered in other sites (many of them European Ditched Enclosures) regions and phases of European Prehistory, so it is plausible that a whole tradition of structured deposition took place throughout European Late Prehistory (Levy 1982, Hill 1995, Bradley 1998, Chapman 2000, Pollard 2001, Pollard & Ruggles 2001, among others).

But the fact is that every deposition is structured, according to the textual model of the archaeological record. Why "structured depositions" should be different? Actually, they are not, this is just a matter of scale (Richards & Thomas 1984: 215). When it comes down to it, the only arguable difference between these depositional practices, called "structured", and the rest, is the degree of structure, i.e. the associations and dissociations between objects are clearer, more perceivable, more evident to the archaeologists. This is the reason why many prefer to use the expression "highly structured" with regard to these depositions. Whether or not they are the consequence of a more rigorous, explicit or conscious way of obeying the cultural rules of deposition is the subject of an ongoing discussion, as it is their possible "ritual" nature. In fact, attitudes, beliefs and principles like taboo or purity, which can themselves lead to repetitive or formalised behaviour, are also relevant in everyday activities (see for example Richard & Thomas 1984, Hill 1995: 95-101, Brück 1999).

The concept of (highly) structured deposition, as defined in this section, gives us some valuable information about a crucial aspect of the processes that led to the formation of such deposits. Since the alluded regularities are considered evidence of how human attitudes affects depositional processes, the fact that we are able to perceive them today is only possible because these assemblages are little distorted by post-depositional processes: "*finding 'structure' in archaeological deposits is primarily telling us something about how well that material has been preserved; how soon it entered a feature that protected it from further attrition and displacement*" (Hill 1995: 96); "*deliberate, structured deposition, often in pits, is an important social practice, leading to the incorporation of large quantities of material in contexts favouring excellent preservation*" (Chapman 2000: 61).

ALTERNATIVE PROPOSAL: HUMAN ACTION

With that in mind, we honestly believe that the traditional views on formation processes at Iberian ditched enclosures have some flaws, not necessarily regarding their internal coherence, but rather their correspondence with the available data. On one hand, it seems to us that they fail to interpret certain properties of the archaeological record. On the other hand, they are grounded in what we consider undemonstrated destructive post-depositional processes.

Unexpected attributes of the archaeological record

Throughout the decades, Iberian scholars have witnessed certain features of the archaeological record at ditched enclosures which could be called 'odd', unexpected or anomalous, especially from the "dwelling-pits" perspective. Their reaction has been either to ignore the lack of agreement between theory and data or to belittle it, unsuccessfully trying to integrate them into their models. Three odd characteristics are:

Asymmetrical distribution ("invisibility") of archaeological deposits. Whilst there is a massive presence of archaeological material inside the underground structures, there is an unexpected scarcity of cultural material outside the same features and at the spaces between them. Thus, although the total amount of items (animal and human bones, sherds, lithics, etc.) recorded in every enclosure is most of the times huge, it is almost impossible to find what we usually call "occupation deposits" outside the structures, i.e. cultural material spread over the former surface of the site. Actually, we do not know any clear case of surface occupation deposit dating from Late Neolithic-Early Copper Age at Southern Iberian ditched enclosures; the great majority of data from IV and first half of the III millennia BC at these sites comes from pit and ditch fills. There seem to be no contemporary surface occupation deposits. To our knowledge, when a surface deposit is recorded in excavation reports, it always dates from a later stage in the biography of the place –Bell Beaker period, Bronze Age, Roman period, etc. This is totally anomalous, unusual, abnormal. Iberian archaeologists never observe anything like that when they excavate other types of sites or when they study later occupations at ditched enclosures sites. So far, this quantitative asymmetry between what is present and what is absent, despite being mentioned multiple times in archaeological reports, has surprisingly never been considered to be an exclusive characteristic of ditched enclosures. We think that the absence of above-ground archaeological evidence is a sole feature of Late Neolithic-Early Copper Age Iberian ditched enclosures. And this is probably true for every or almost every ditched enclosure site, not just one or two particular cases. This statement is supported by the fact that it is extremely difficult to find Southern Iberian ditched enclosures through conventional (surface) archaeological prospection, unless there are later occupations at the site with their own surface material remains.

Signs of secondary deposition and deliberate filling. The currently known data strongly suggests that the process through which many of the underground structures were filled was relatively rapid, either in one or in several steps. But, more importantly, the evidence seems to point towards pit and ditch fills being the outcome of deliberate human actions. Sometimes, it seems that whoever did it had the intention of filling them completely in order to make them "invisible" from the outside. This is valid for the ditches and the structures interpreted as refuse pits, but, amazingly, also for the so-called semi-subterranean huts (Jiménez, n.d., Jiménez & Márquez n.d.). Instead of what we should expect from a slow, unintentional primary deposition, many archaeological deposits from pit fills are barely horizontal or simply nothing horizontal at all, have anomalous shapes (e.g. conical), have high densities of finds and/or contain just one kind of cultural material (only shells, only potsherds, etc.). Secondary deposition, then, seems much more likely.

Highly structured deposition. Finally, pit and ditch fills contain non-random associations and dissociations between objects such as human and animal remains (complete or not), potsherds, etc. This has been seen so far as occasional anomalies in a general context of waste management primarily governed by functional and practical requirements (in the modern sense), being such "odd" deposits attributed to the intervention of "religious" factors, or simply as a reflection of social inequality. Instead, based on that evidence, we honestly believe that the archaeological deposits under consideration in this paper should be labelled "highly structured deposits", produced by highly structured depositional practices (Márquez 2001, 2004, 2006a). If this is true, then: a) human action played an essential role in formation processes at ditched enclosures sites; b) the modern concept of rubbish is not appropriate at all in this context; c) the sites are well preserved in terms of post-depositional disturbances.

Need for severe post-depositional damage

When linked with Iberian ditched enclosures, post-depositional processes have become the easiest solution if the archaeological evidence possesses unexpected or unfriendly attributes as regards the starting theory. Hence, it is hardly surprising that all the current theses on the matter essentially need to believe in the occurrence of major post-depositional alterations in order to achieve internal coherence and correspondence with the data. The idea of damaging erosive processes affecting ditched enclosures is then assumed without further research. The problem, in our view, is that archaeological data does not support these speculations: Which is/are the post-depositional agent(s)? How did it happen? What are the implications of this? And finally, since "erosion" usually implies transport and deposition in another area, where are the missing cultural materials?

When it comes to post-depositional processes at these sites, we do not mean that they are nonexistent. In fact, we acknowledge that a lot of pits and ditches have been partially or completely destroyed at the building sites where they were found. But we think that the recurrent references to undemonstrated post-depositional disturbances in this context have become a prejudice and a common place. Otherwise, the absolute absence of data concerning the hypothetical above-ground half of the so-called dwelling-pits, for instance, would not have been underestimated, and it has: it has been suggested multiple times that some kind of erosive processes would have removed any traces of post-holes or basements, but too many pits are known in Southern Iberia (hundreds or even thousands) to accept the general character of such statement. Moreover, when one of these places has been occupied in later periods –Middle or Late Copper Age, for example- the post-holes, house basements and other remains from that occupations show no signs of abnormally severe post-depositional damage (e.g. Valencina de la Concepción, Marroquíes Bajos, etc.). Lastly, the structured deposits found inside pits and ditches, which by definition possess a good state of preservation, make us think that post-depositional perturbations in many cases were not as intense as thought. In short, we believe that the structures under study constitute almost "sealed" archaeological contexts, in the sense that they rarely let their contents leave and spread over the surface of the site.

As the reader may have figured out, we are not satisfied at all with the current ideas on formation processes at Southern Iberian ditched enclosures. Therefore, it is time for us to express our views on the subject and propose an alternative approach that we think is not only coherent with itself, but has better correspondence with the available data.

Earlier in this text, we have mentioned some reasons for not to conceive formation processes at ditched enclosures as essentially determined by chance and post-depositional processes: the anomalous or "unnatural" *invisibility* of the archaeological record; the evidence of secondary, deliberate deposition; the likely presence of (highly) structured deposits. In short, we believe that the ultimate cause of this is not erosion or any other post-depositional process. More importantly, those attributes of the archaeological record lead us to think that depositional processes are the key to understand the issue. Thus, the primary factor affecting the formation of these sites seems to be human action, namely meaningful practices or events of material culture abandonment performed under culturally specific rules of object abandonment and deposition, which determined what items were deposited, where and how. Therefore, whatever the activities executed inside the enclosed space, it seems plausible that most of the objects involved in them, at the end of their lifecycle, left the systemic context and entered the archaeological context (*sensu* Schiffer 1972) according to certain rules. The two most archaeologically visible consequences of this are a) the intentional removal of nearly all the waste which otherwise would have been left on the surface of the site and would have eventually formed "occupation deposits"; b) the deliberate deposition of high quantities and densities of cultural material underground. That could mean that during the occupation of the site no surface "occupation layers" were allowed to form. Or that could mean that at the time of abandonment, cleaning activities were carried out to remove the refuse accumulated on the surface of the site and a considerable portion of it was deposited underground.

If this is true, ditch and pit fills would be predominantly composed of secondary refuse, that is, objects not deposited in their areas of use/consumption. It would be, therefore, **secondary deposition by human agents**. Some deposits, however, contain certain objects *not used* outside the features: complete and articulated human and animal bone groups, which could be interpreted as some kind of "ritual" burials, were deposited in what could be viewed as their "space of use", although at this point Schiffer's categories become ambiguous and ineffective because of the misleading nature of the verb "to use" in these cases. In addition, the notion of rubbish would be, again, deceptive and useless. Anyway, from this perspective, we should consider a general **good state of preservation** of the archaeological record at ditched enclosures regarding post-depositional processes. Having said that, we do not mean that erosive deposits are totally absent in pit and ditch fills. Actually, depositional processes remain quite unknown. Nowadays, we do not know, for example, if the process of filling takes place in one step or as a sequence of acts, and how long the whole process takes. We do not know either if the deliberate filling is performed during the occupation phase or at abandonment stage. Hence, further research is much needed according to the guidelines presented in this article.

References

BOURDIEU, P., 1977, Outline of a Theory of Practice, Cambridge University Press.

BOURDIEU, P., 1990, The logic of practice, Polity Press.

BRADLEY, R., 1998, The passage of Arms: an archaeological analysis of prehistoric hoards and votive deposits, Cambridge University Press.

BRÜCK, J., 1999, Ritual and rationality: some problems of interpretation in European Archaeology, European Journal of Archaeology 2/3, p. 313-344.

CHAPMAN, J., 2000, Pit-digging and Structured Deposition in the Neolithic and Copper Age, Proceedings of the Prehistoric Society 66, p. 61-87.

DREWETT, P., 1977, The excavation of a Neolithic Causewayed Enclosure on Offham Hill, East Sussex, 1976, Proceedings of the Prehistoric Society 43, p. 201-241.

EDMONS, M., 1999, Ancestral Geographies of the Neolithic. Landscape, monuments and memory, Routledge.

FERNÁNDEZ, J. & OLIVA, D., 1985, Excavaciones en el yacimiento Calcolítico de Valencina de la Concepción (Sevilla). El corte C La Perrera, Noticiario Arqueológico Hispánico 25, p. 7-131.

FERNÁNDEZ, J. & OLIVA, D., 1986, Valencina de la Concepción. Excavaciones de urgencia, Revista de Arqueología 58, p. 19-33.

GIDDENS, A., 1984, The constitution of society: outline of a theory of structuration, Polity Press.

HAYDEN, B., & CANNON, A., 1983, Where the garbage goes: refuse disposal in the Maya highlands, Journal of Anthropological Archaeology 2, p. 117-163.

HILL, J.D., 1995, Ritual and Rubbish in the Iron Age of Wessex. A study on the formation of a specific archaeological record. B.A.R British Series 242. Oxford.

HODDER, I., 1982, The present past: an introduction to anthropology for archaeologists. Pica Press.

HODDER, I., 1987, The meaning of discard: ash and domestic space in Baringo, Kenya. In Kent, S. (ed.), Method and theory for activity area research: an ethnoarchaeological approach, p. 424-448. Columbia University Press.

HURTADO, V., 1991, Informe de las excavaciones de urgencia en la Pijotilla. Campaña de 1990, In I Jornadas Prehistoria Arqueología Extremadura (1986-1990). Extremadura Arqueológica II, p. 45-67.

JIMÉNEZ, V., n.d., La Premisa Pompeya y las 'Casas semisubterráneas' del sur de la Península Ibérica (IV-III milenios AC.), Mainake.

JIMÉNEZ, V., & MÁRQUEZ, J.E., n.d., 'Aquí no hay quien viva'. Sobre la existencia de casas-pozo en Andalucía durante el IV y III milenios AC, Spal.

KLIGMANN, D., 1998, Procesos de formación del registro arqueológico: una propuesta alternativa a los modelos clásicos, Actas y memorias del XI Congreso Nacional de Arqueología Argentina (8ª parte), Revista del Museo de Historia Natural de San Rafael (Mendoza), XX (1/4).

LAMOTTA, V.M. & SCHIFFER, M.B., 1999, Formation Processes of House Floor Assemblages. In Allison, P. M.(ed.): The Archaeology of Household Activities, Routledge, p. 19-29.

LAMOTTA, V.M. & SCHIFFER, M.B., 2001, Behavioral Archaeology: Toward a New Synthesis. In Hodder, I. (ed.), Archaeological Theory Today, p. 14-64, Cambridge.

LIZCANO, R., CÁMARA, J.A., RIQUELME, J.A., CAÑABATE, Mª.L., SÁNCHEZ, A. & AFONSO, J.A., 1991-92, El polideportivo de Martos. Producción económica y símbolo de cohesión en un asentamiento del Neolítico final en las campiñas del Alto Guadalquivir, Cuadernos de Prehistoria de Granada 16-17, p. 5-101.

LEVY, J., 1982, Social and Religious Organization in Bronze Age Denmark – An Analysis of Ritual Hoard Finds. B.A.R. International Series 124. Oxford.

MÁRQUEZ, J.E., 2001, De los campos de silos a los agujeros negros: Sobre pozos, depósitos y zanjas en la Prehistoria Reciente del Sur de la Península Ibérica, Spal Revista de Prehistoria y Arqueología 10, p. 207-220.

MÁRQUEZ, J.E., 2002, Megalitismo, agricultura y complejidad social: algunas consideraciones, Baetica. 24, p. 193-222.

MÁRQUEZ, J.E., 2003, Recintos Prehistóricos Atrincherados (RPA) en Andalucía (España): Una propuesta interpretativa. In Jorge, S.O. (coord): Recintos murados da Pré-história recente, p. 269-284.

MÁRQUEZ, J.E., 2004, Muerte ubícua: sobre deposiciones de esqueletos humanos en zanjas y pozos en la prehistoria reciente de Andalucía, Mainake XXVI, p. 115 -138.

MÁRQUEZ, J.E., 2006a, Sobre los depósitos estructurados de animales en yacimientos de fosos del sur de la Península Ibérica. In Weiss-Krejci, E. (coord.): Animais na Pré-história e Arqueologia da Península Ibérica, actas do IV Congresso de arqueología peninsular, p. 15-25.

MÁRQUEZ, J.E., 2006b, Neolithic and Copper Age ditched enclosures and social inequality in the Iberian south (IV-III millennia cal BC). In Díaz-del-Río, P. & García Sanjuán, L. (eds.), Social Inequality in Iberian Late Prehistory, B.A.R. International Series XXX.

MÁRQUEZ, J.E. & FERNÁNDEZ, J., 2002, Viejos depósitos, nuevas interpretaciones: estructura 2 del yacimiento prehistórico de los Villares de Algane (Coín, Málaga), Mainake XXI-XXII, p. 301-333.

MARTÍN DE LA CRUZ, J.C., 1985, Papa Uvas I. Aljaraque, Huelva Campañas de 1976 a 1979, Excavaciones Arqueológicas en España 136, Madrid.

MARTÍN DE LA CRUZ, J.C., 1986, Papa Uvas II. Aljaraque, Huelva Campañas de 1981 a 1983, Excavaciones Arqueológicas en España 149, Madrid.

MOORE, H., 1982, The interpretation of spatial patterning in settlement residues. In Hodder (ed.), Symbolic and structural archaeology, p. 74-79, Cambridge University Press.

MURRAY, P., 1980, Discard location: the ethnographic data, American Antiquity, 45, p. 490-502.

PATRIK, L., 1985, Is there an archaeological record?, Advances in Archaeological Method and Theory 8, p. 27-62.

POLLARD, J., 2001, The aesthetics of depositional practice, World Archaeology, 33/2, p. 315-333.

POLLARD, J. & RUGGLES, C., 2001, Shifting Perceptions: spatial order, cosmology, and patterns of deposition at Stonehenge, Cambridge Archaeological Journal 11/1, p. 69-90.

PRYOR, F., 1988, Etton, near Maxey, Cambridgeshire: A causewayed enclosure on the fen-edge. In Burgess, C., Topping, P., Mordant, C., & Maddison, M. (eds.), Enclosures and defences in the Neolithic of Western Europe, B.A.R. International Series 403 (II), p. 107-126.

RICHARDS, C., THOMAS, J., 1984, Ritual activity and structured deposition in later Neolithic Wessex. In Bradley, R. & Gardiner, J. (eds.), Neolithic studies, B.A.R. British Series 133, p. 189– 218.

RUIZ MATA, D., 1983, El yacimiento de la Edad del Bronce de Valencina de la Concepción (Sevilla) en el marco cultural del Bajo Guadalquivir. In Actas I Congreso de Historia de Andalucía, p. 183-208.

SCHIFFER, M., 1972, Archaeological context & Systemic context, American Antiquity 37/2, p. 156-165.

SCHIFFER, M., 1976, Behavioral Archaeology, Academic Press.

SCHIFFER, M., 1987, Formation Processes of the Archaeological Record, University of New Mexico Press.

SMITH, I., 1966, Windmill Hill and its implications, Palaeohistoria XII, p. 469-481.

SIRET, L., 2001, España prehistórica. Junta de Andalucía (=L'Espagne Prehistorique 1893).

STEVENSON, M., 1985, The formation of artifact assemblages at workshop/habitation sites: models from Peace Point in northern Alberta, American Antiquity 50/1, p. 63-81.

TANI, M., 1995, Beyond the identification of formation processes: behavioral inference based on traces left by cultural formation processes, Journal of Archaeological Method and Theory 2/3, p. 231-252.

THOMAS, J., 1999, Understanding the Neolithic. Routledge.

VALERA, A.C. & FILIPE, I., 2004, O povoado do Porto Torrão (Ferreira do Alentejo), ERA-Arqueologia 6, p. 28-61.

ZAFRA, N., HORNOS, F., & CASTRO. M., 1999, Una macro-aldea en el origen del modo de vida campesino: Marroquíes Bajos (Jaén) c. 2500-2000 cal. ANE, Trabajos de Prehistoria 56/1, p. 77-102.

www.ingramcontent.com/pod-product-compliance
Lightning Source LLC
LaVergne TN
LVHW071214210926
848482LV00015B/812